**BRITISH
ELECTORAL
FACTS
1885-1975**

Other Books in this Series Compiled and Edited by F.W.S. Craig

British Parliamentary Election Results 1832—1885 (in preparation)
British Parliamentary Election Results 1885—1918
British Parliamentary Election Results 1918—1949
British Parliamentary Election Results 1950—1970
Boundaries of Parliamentary Constituencies 1885—1972
The Minor Parties at British Parliamentary Elections 1885—1974
The Parliaments of England from 1715—1847 (Second Edition)
British General Election Manifestos 1900—1974 (Second Edition)
The Most Gracious Speeches to Parliament 1900—1974

BRITISH
ELECTORAL
FACTS
1885-1975

COMPILED & EDITED BY
F.W.S. CRAIG

M

First published in 1968 under the title
British Parliamentary Election Statistics

Second edition 1971

Third edition under the present title 1976

ISBN: 0 333 21624 5 (Limp Edn)
ISBN: 0 333 19734 8 (Cased Edn)

THE MACMILLAN PRESS LTD
London and Basingstoke
Associated companies in
New York, Dublin, Melbourne,
Johannesburg and Madras

Typeset by
LITHOSET
Chichester

Printed in Great Britain by
Butler and Tanner Ltd
Frome and London

For PHYLLIS, SUSAN, CHRISTINE and ANNE

CONTENTS

PREFACE

Since this book first appeared in 1968 under the title *British Parliamentary Election Statistics* it has undergone a number of important changes in design and content. The second edition, published in 1971, incorporated a new typographical layout which improved readability and this edition, re-titled *British Electoral Facts,* extends the period covered back to 1885 (previously it was 1918) and includes a number of new tables.

The book still maintains the original aim of providing an accurate and definitive reference source to British parliamentary election statistics and makes no claim to be a study of voting behaviour. It does however bring together all the basic facts and figures ever likely to be required by the psephologist, journalist or politician.

I could not have compiled this book without the co-operation of numerous individuals, government departments, political parties, libraries, etc. and I would like to express my sincere thanks to all those who have contributed in one way or another to my research work. A new feature of this edition is an index and I am grateful to Jennifer Tanfield for suggesting that an index would be useful and undertaking the work involved.

Although the very greatest care has been taken to ensure accuracy, it would be unrealistic to expect that no errors, arithmetical or typographical, have slipped through and I hope that readers will let me know of any they may detect.

I shall always be delighted to receive constructive criticisms and suggestions which will improve future editions of this reference book.

F.W.S. CRAIG

Parliamentary Research Services
18 Lincoln Green
Chichester
West Sussex

June 1976

INTRODUCTORY NOTES

COALITION CANDIDATES 1918-1922 In the majority of tables, official Coalition candidates are not distinguished from other candidates of the same party. The only exception is in respect of the five Coalition Labour candidates at the General Election of 1918 who could not be classed with other Labour candidates as they were not endorsed by the Labour Party. The Coalition prefix has only been used for official candidates of the Coalition, *i.e.* those who received the 'coupon', a letter signed by Lloyd George and Bonar Law which was sent to approved nominees.

CO-OPERATIVE PARTY From the General Election of 1922, all Co-operative Party candidates have been endorsed by the Labour Party and sought election as 'Labour and Co-operative'. No distinction is made in the tables between these joint candidates and other Labour candidates.

ELECTORATE As a result of the Representation of the People Act, 1969, the franchise was extended to persons reaching 18 years of age by polling day in a parliamentary or local government election. Those becoming 18 during the period covered by the annual Electoral Register now have the date on which they attain their 18th birthday inserted in the Register and they can vote from that date.

This change in the registration procedure meant that it was no longer possible to know the exact electorate in a constituency on a particular date without asking Electoral Registration Officers to go through each register and deduct the number of post-election "dated names" from the total electorate. This was a laborious task which caused delays in the obtaining of electorate figures and frequently resulted in Electoral Registration Officers providing estimated rather than exact figures.

In 1974, Parliamentary Research Services initiated discussions with the Office of Population Censuses and Surveys, the Home Office, the Press Association, the British Broadcasting Corporation, Independent Television News and a number of interested academics in an attempt to find an acceptable formula for calculating electorates on a particular date. As a result the following formula was used by the media in calculating the electorate in October 1974 and will be used for future elections:

Total number of "dated names" on the Register multiplied by the fraction

Number of days from February 17 to Polling Day (both dates inclusive)

----

364 (or 365 in a Leap Year)

The following is an example of the calculation:-

Electorate at 16 February	64,162
Number of "dated names"	757
Total	64,919

Using the Electorate Calculator on page 169 and assuming polling day was October 10 the formula would be:

$$757 \times \frac{236}{364} \ (0.648351) = 490.801707 \ \text{(truncate)}$$

The estimated electorate at October 10 would be:

$$64,162 + 490 = 64,652$$

The figures for electorate given in this book for the two General Elections of 1974 and all subsequent by-elections have been calcuated using the above formula.

GAINS AND LOSSES When compiling the tables of gains and losses, a gain or loss has been recorded on the basis of the incumbent's party allegiance at the time of the Dissolution or by-election. This means that where an M.P. changed from one party to another or became an Independent during a Parliament and did not resign immediately, his seat was from then on considered to be held by his new party. A detailed list of changes of party allegiance since 1900 will be found in *British Political Facts*, 4th edition, by David Butler and Anne Sloman, pp. 190-194.

INDEPENDENT LABOUR PARTY From 1900 until August 1932, the Independent Labour Party (ILP) was affiliated to the Labour Party and as their candidates normally received endorsement they are treated as official Labour candidates in the tables. There were however four by-elections where ILP candidates went forward without Labour Party endorsement and they have therefore been classed as ILP and not Labour candidates. For details of the twenty-four members of the ILP who were refused endorsement at the General Election of 1931 see table 1.14, footnote[3].

INDEPENDENTS AND MINOR PARTIES The columns headed 'Others' include all Indpendents and candidates of minor parties and organisations.

For a detailed analysis of the electoral activity of the minor parties see *Minor Parties at British Parliamentary Elections 1885-1974*, compiled and edited by F.W.S. Craig.

LIBERALS AND NATIONAL LIBERALS 1922-1923 In the majority of tables, no distinction is made between (Asquith) Liberal and (Lloyd George) National Liberal candidates. The two groups merged in November 1923 to fight the forthcoming General Election as a united party.

NATIONAL LIBERAL AND CONSERVATIVE CANDIDATES In the majority of tables, no distinction is made between joint National Liberal and Conservative candidates and other Conservative candidates. In May 1947, recommendations were issued by Lord Woolton, on behalf of the Conservative Party, and Lord Teviot, on behalf of the National Liberal Organization, which advocated that the two parties should come together in constituencies and form combined associations under a mutually agreed title. Immediately following the 1950 election, a Liberal-Unionist Group was formed in the House of Commons by those M.P.s elected under the auspices of joint local associations. Owing to local circumstances and preferences, the actual 'labels' used by candidates varied from one constituency to another but for the sake of

uniformity the designation National Liberal and Conservative (NL & C) has been used throughout this book.
In May 1968 the National Liberal Council decided to disband.

NORTHERN IRELAND Until the General Election of 1974 (February) no distinction has been made between candidates of the Ulster Unionist Council and Conservative Party candidates in Great Britain nor between candidates of the Northern Ireland Labour Party (provided they received endorsement by the Labour Party in London) and Labour Party candidates in Great Britain.
From the General Election of 1974 (February) onwards, candidates of the Ulster Unionist Council and of the Northern Ireland Labour Party have been classed as 'Others' in all the tables. This reflects the changed political situation in Ulster which now makes it unrealistic to continue the former method of classification.

PERCENTAGES All percentages have been rounded to one decimal place. If necessary the largest percentage has been adjusted to provide an exact total of 100.0%.

SOURCES Unless otherwise stated, all statistics have been compiled from *British Parliamentary Election Results 1885-1918*, *British Parliamentary Election Results 1918-1949* and *British Parliamentary Election Results 1950-1970*, compiled and edited by F.W.S. Craig. The number of votes cast for candidates at General Elections have been taken, except in 1918, from the *Returns of Election Expenses* compiled by the Home Office. For 1918 when no *Return of Election Expenses* was published, figures of voting have been extracted from *Debrett's House of Commons and Judicial Bench* (1922 edition). The publishers of *Debrett* claimed that all figures were submitted to Returning Officers for verification and revision and it was felt that this publication was an acceptable substitute for an Official Return. In both *Debrett* and the *Returns of Election Expenses* some obvious errors were noticed and have been corrected.
By-election figures have in most cases been taken from *The Times* and revised where necessary by extensive checking against other sources.

SPEAKER OF THE HOUSE OF COMMONS The Speaker of the House of Commons takes no active part in an election campaign and since 1950 (when the Speaker requested that he be given no party 'label') has sought re-election as 'The Speaker' and not as a party candidate. It would however be unrealistic for statistical purposes to include votes cast for the Speaker among 'Others' as clearly the majority of electors voting for him do so on a political basis. Therefore, throughout the tables the Speaker has been regarded as a candidate of the party he represented before his appointment.

SWING This is calculated as the average of the Conservative % gain and the Labour % loss between elections. Percentage is defined as the "percentage of the total votes cast" and not only of the votes cast for Conservative and Labour candidates (known as the "two-party swing").

TWO-MEMBER SEATS Percentage figures of votes cast and turnout have been adjusted to allow for the two-member seats which existed prior to 1950. In calculating the percentage of votes, each vote in a two-member seat has been counted as half a vote. In calculating turnout, the total of electors voting has been used and in a few cases where this figure was not available an estimate has been made based on previous results.

UNIVERSITY SEATS From 1918 in the university constituencies returning more than one member, General Elections were conducted by Proportional Representation (single transferable vote). In compiling the tables, figures of first preference votes have been used.

WALES The term 'Wales' includes Monmouthshire.

ABBREVIATIONS

PARTIES

AP	Anti-Partitionist (candidate of the Anti-Partition of Ireland League of Great Britain)
APNI	Alliance Party of Northern Ireland
BEP	British Empire Party
BLP	Belfast Labour Party (subsequently became Northern Ireland Labour Party)
BM	British Movement
BNP	British National Party
BSP	British Socialist Party
C	Conservative (or Unionist) Party
CFMPB	Campaign for a More Prosperous Britain
Co	Coalition
Com	Communist Party of Great Britain
Const	Constitutionalist
Co-op	Co-operative Party
CP	Christian Pacifist
CPE	Communist Party of England (Marxist-Leninist)
Crf	Crofter
CW	Common Wealth Movement
CW Land P	Commonwealth Land Party
CWLP	Commonwealth Labour Party (Northern Ireland)
Dem Lab	Democratic Labour
Dem P	Democratic Party (1942-45)
DP	Democratic Party (1969-71)
DUP	Democratic Unionist Party (formerly Protestant Unionist Party)
FP	Fellowship Party
HLL	Highland Land League
ICRA	Irish Civil Rights Association
IDA	Independent Democratic Alliance
ILP	Independent Labour Party
IMG	International Marxist Group
Ind	Independent (indicates an unofficial candidate when placed before a party abbreviation)
INDEC	Independent Nuclear Disarmament Election Committee
Irish LP	Labour Party (Dublin)
L	Liberal Party
Lab	Labour Party
L/Lab or L-Lab	Liberal-Labour
Loyalist	Independent Loyalist (candidate of the League of Empire Loyalists)
LPP	Liverpool Protestant Party
LU	Liberal Unionist Party
MGC	Mudiad Gweriniaethol Cymru (Welsh Republican Movement)
MK	Mebyon Kernow (Sons of Cornwall) — Cornish Nationalist Movement
N	Irish Nationalist/Anti-Partitionist
Nat	National
Nat DP	National Democratic Party (Northern Ireland)
Nat P	National Party (1917-21)
N Dem P	National Democratic Party
NDP	National Democratic and Labour Party
NF	National Front
NFDSS	National Federation of Discharged and Demobilized Sailors and Soldiers
NI Ind Lab	Independent Labour Party (Northern Ireland)

NI Lab	Northern Ireland Labour Party
NIP	National Independence Party
NL	National Liberal (candidate of Lloyd George's National Liberal Council, 1922-23 or of the National Liberal Organization (Liberal National Organization, 1931-48), 1931-68)
N Lab	National Labour Organization
NL & C	National Liberal and Conservative (joint candidate of the Conservative Party and the National Liberal Organization)
NLP	National Labour Party
NP	New Party
NPP	National Prohibition Party
NSP	National Socialist Party
Pat P	Patriotic Party
PC	Plaid Cymru (pronounced *Plide Cumree*) — Welsh (Nationalist) Party
People	People Movement
Prog	Progressive
Prot U	Protestant Unionist Party (subsequently Democratic Unionist Party)
RA	Radical Alliance
Rep	Irish Republican
Rep LP	Republican Labour Party
SCPGB	Social Credit Party of Great Britain
SD	Social Democrat (candidate of the Campaign for Social Democracy)
SDF	Social Democratic Federation (subsequently Social Democratic Party)
SDLP	Social Democratic and Labour Party
SDP	Social Democratic Party (formerly Social Democratic Federation)
SF	Sinn Fein (pronounced *Shin Fane*) — Irish Republican Organization
SLP	Socialist Labour Party
SLRL	Scottish Land Restoration League
SNP	Scottish National Party
SPGB	Socialist Party of Great Britain
SPLP	Scottish (Parliamentary) Labour Party
SPP	Scottish Prohibition Party
SSF	Scottish Socialist Federation
SUTCLP	Scottish United Trades Councils Labour Party
SWRC	Scottish Workers Representation Committee
UDP	United Democratic Party
UM	Union Movement
Unity	Opposition Unity (candidate in Northern Ireland opposed to the Government and sponsored by various organisations)
UPNI	Unionist Party of Northern Ireland
UU	Ulster Unionist (candidate of the Ulster Unionist Council)
UUUC	United Ulster Unionist Coalition
VNP	Vectis (Isle of Wight) Nationalist Party
VUPP	Vanguard Unionist Progressive Party
WP	Women's Party
WRP	Workers Revolutionary Party

MISCELLANEOUS

Bt.	Baronet
Dr.	Doctor
G.B.	Great Britain
H.M.	His/Her Majesty
Hon.	Honourable
M.Ps.	Members of Parliament
Rev.	Reverend
Rt. Hon.	Right Honourable (Member of the Privy Council)
U.K.	United Kingdom

Table 1.01 GENERAL ELECTION 1885

	Total votes	% share of total votes†	Candidates	M.P.s. Elected	Unopposed Returns
ENGLAND					
C	1,675,757	47.5	440	213	1
L	1,809,665	51.4	452	238	4
N	3,489	0.1	2	1	0
Others	40,990	1.0	26	4	0
Total	**3,529,901**	**100.0**	**920**	**456**	**5**
WALES					
C	79,690	38.9	29	4	0
L	119,231	58.3	34	29	4
Others	5,766	2.8	2	1	0
Total	**204,687**	**100.0**	**65**	**34**	**4**
SCOTLAND					
C	151,137	34.3	55	8	0
L	238,627	53.3	70	51	5
Others	57,124	12.4	32	11	0
Total	**446,888**	**100.0**	**157**	**70**	**5**
IRELAND					
C	111,503	24.8	70	16	2
L	30,022	6.8	14	0	0
N	307,119	67.8	92	85	19
Others	2,822	0.6	10	0	0
Total	**451,466**	**100.0**	**186**	**101**	**21**
UNIVERSITIES					
C	2,840	53.7	8	8	7
L	2,453	46.3	2	1	1
Total	**5,293**	**100.0**	**10**	**9**	**8**
UNITED KINGDOM					
C	2,020,927	43.5	602	249	10
L	2,199,998	47.4	572	319	14
N	310,608	6.9	94	86	19
Others	106,702	2.2	70[1]	16[2]	0
Total	**4,638,235**	**100.0**	**1,338**	**670**	**43**

[1] Including 5 SLRL, 3 SDF

[2] Namely: W. Abraham (Glamorganshire, Rhondda—Ind L/Lab); Sir R. Anstruther, Bt. (St. Andrews Burghs—Ind L); J.M. Cameron (Wick Burghs—Ind L); Sir G. Campbell (Kirkcaldy Burghs—Ind L); Dr. G.B. Clark (Caithness—Ind L/Crf); C.A.V. Conybeare (Cornwall, Camborne—Ind L); J. Cowen (Newcastle upon Tyne—Ind L); Hon. W.J.W. Fitzwilliam (Peterborough—Ind L); G. Fraser-Mackintosh (Inverness-shire—Ind L/Crf); Rt. Hon. G.J. Goschen (Edinburgh, East—Ind L); Sir G. Harrison (Edinburgh, South—Ind L); Dr. R. Macdonald (Ross and Cromarty—Ind L/Crf); D.H. Macfarlane (Argyll—Ind L/Crf); C.S. Parker (Perth—Ind L); Sir E.W. Watkin, Bt. (Hythe—Ind L); J. Wilson (Edinburgh, Central—Ind L).

†Adjusted to allow for two-member seats. See Introductory Notes.

Table 1.02 **GENERAL ELECTION 1886**

	Total votes	% share of total votes†	Candidates	M.P.s. Elected	Unopposed Returns
ENGLAND					
C & LU	1,193,289	52.6	432	333	105
L	1,087,065	47.2	347	122	23
N	2,911	0.1	1	1	0
Others	1,791	0.1	3	0	0
Total	2,285,056	100.0	783	456	128
WALES					
C & LU	60,048	46.1	24	8	2
L	70,289	53.9	32	26	10
Total	130,337	100.0	56	34	12
SCOTLAND					
C & LU	164,314	46.4	63	27	2
L	193,801	53.6	68	43	7
Total	358,115	100.0	131	70	9
IRELAND					
C & LU	98,201	50.3	35	16	3
L	1,910	1.0	1	0	0
N	94,883	48.7	97	85	66
Total	194,994	100.0	133	101	69
UNIVERSITIES					
C & LU	5,034	84.7	9	9	6
L	516	13.8	1	0	0
N	111	1.5	2	0	0
Total	5,661	100.0	12	9	6
UNITED KINGDOM					
C & LU	1,520,886	51.4	563	393[1]	118
L	1,353,581	45.0	449	191	40
N	97,905	3.5	100	86	66
Others	1,791	0.1	3	0	0
Total	2,974,163	100.0	1,115	670	224

[1] Including approximately 77 Liberal Unionists.

†Adjusted to allow for two-member seats. See Introductory Notes.

Table 1.03 GENERAL ELECTION 1892

	Total votes	% share of total votes†	Candidates	M.P.s. Elected	Unopposed Returns
ENGLAND					
C & LU	1,788,108	51.1	441	261	22
L	1,685,283	48.0	426	190	9
N	2,537	0.1	1	1	0
Others	29,891	0.8	18	4	1
Total	3,505,819	100.0	886	456	32
WALES					
C & LU	78,038	37.2	29	3	0
L	141,465	62.8	34	31	4
Total	219,503	100.0	63	34	4
SCOTLAND					
C & LU	209,944	44.4	68	20	0
L	256,944	53.9	70	50	0
Others	8,242	1.7	11	0	0
Total	475,130	100.0	149	70	0
IRELAND					
C & LU	79,263	20.6	59	21	11
L	4,327	1.1	2	0	0
N	308,972	78.1	133	80	9
Others	611	0.2	1	0	0
Total	393,173	100.0	195	101	20
UNIVERSITIES					
C & LU	3,797	80.9	9	9	7
Others	897	19.1	1	0	0
Total	4,694	100.0	10	9	7
UNITED KINGDOM					
C & LU	2,159,150	47.0	606	314[1]	40
L	2,088,019	45.1	532	271	13
N	311,509	7.0	134	81[2]	9
Others	39,641	0.9	31[3]	4[4]	1
Total	4,598,319	100.0	1,303	670	63

[1] Including approximately 46 Liberal Unionists.

[2] Including 9 'Parnellites'.

[3] Including 3 SPLP, 3 SUTCLP, 2 SDF, 1 joint SSF and SUTCLP.

[4] Namely: J.W. Burns (Battersea and Clapham, Battersea—Ind Lab); J.K. Hardie (West Ham, South—Ind Lab); Sir E.W. Watkin, Bt. (Hythe—Ind L); J.H. Wilson (Middlesbrough—Ind Lab).

†Adjusted to allow for two-member seats. See Introductory Notes.

Table 1.04 **GENERAL ELECTION 1895**

	Total votes	% share of total votes†	Candidates	M.P.s. Elected	Unopposed Returns
ENGLAND					
C & LU	1,521,938	51.9	442	343	106
L	1,369,598	46.7	342	112	8
ILP	40,056	1.1	21	0	0
N	2,089	0.1	1	1	0
Others	5,675	0.2	9	0	0
Total	2,939,356	100.0	815	456	114
WALES					
C & LU	103,802	42.2	31	9	0
L	144,216	56.8	34	25	2
Others	2,677	1.0	2	0	0
Total	250,695	100.0	67	34	2
SCOTLAND					
C & LU	214,403	47.4	68	31	4
L	236,446	51.7	66	39	1
ILP	4,269	0.8	7	0	0
Others	608	0.1	1	0	0
Total	455,726	100.0	142	70	5
IRELAND					
C & LU	54,629	26.0	38	19	13
L	15,006	7.1	5	1	0
N	150,870	66.9	104	81	46
Total	220,505	100.0	147	101	59
UNIVERSITIES					
C & LU	—	—	9	9	9
Total	—	—	9	9	9
UNITED KINGDOM					
C & LU	1,894,772	49.1	588	411[1]	132
L	1,765,266	45.7	447	177	11
ILP	44,325	1.0	28	0	0
N	152,959	4.0	105	82[2]	46
Others	8,960	0.2	12[3]	0	0
Total	3,866,282	100.0	1,180	670	189

[1] Including approximately 71 Liberal Unionists.

[2] Including 12 'Parnellites'.

[3] Including 4 SDF.

†Adjusted to allow for two-member seats. See Introductory Notes.

Table 1.05 **GENERAL ELECTION 1900**

	Total votes·	% share of total votest	Candidates	M.P.s. Elected	Unopposed Returns
ENGLAND					
C & LU	1,421,195	52.4	441	332	139
L	1,218,525	45.6	302	121	12
Lab	53,100	1.4	13	1	0
N	2,044	0.1	1	1	0
Others	13,628	0.5	6	1	0
Total	**2,708,492**	**100.0**	**763**	**456**	**151**
WALES					
C & LU	63,932	37.6	21	6	1
L	105,837	58.5	33	27	10
Lab	9,598	3.9	2	1	0
Total	**179,367**	**100.0**	**56**	**34**	**11**
SCOTLAND					
C & LU	237,217	49.0	70	36	3
L	245,092	50.2	66	34	0
Others	3,921	0.8	3	0	0
Total	**486,230**	**100.0**	**139**	**70**	**3**
IRELAND					
C & LU	45,614	32.2	28	19	11
L	2,869	2.0	1	1	0
N	89,011	57.4	100	81	58
Others	11,899	8.4	6	0	0
Total	**149,393**	**100.0**	**135**	**101**	**69**
UNIVERSITIES					
C & LU	—	—	9	9	9
Total	**—**	**—**	**9**	**9**	**9**
UNITED KINGDOM					
C & LU	1,767,958	50.3	569	402[1]	163
L	1,572,323	45.0	402	183	22
Lab	62,698	1.3	15	2	0
N	91,055	2.6	101	82[2]	58
Others	29,448	0.8	15[3]	1[4]	0
Total	**3,523,482**	**100.0**	**1,102**	**670**	**243**

[1] Including approximately 68 Liberal Unionists.

[2] Including 5 Independents.

[3] Including 1 SWRC.

[4] Namely: Sir J. Austin, Bt. (Yorkshire, Osgoldcross—Ind L).

†Adjusted to allow for two-member seats. See Introductory Notes.

Table 1.06 GENERAL ELECTION 1906

	Total votes	% share of total votes†	Candidates	M.P.s. Elected	Unopposed Returns
ENGLAND					
C & LU	2,050,800	44.3	435	122	3
L	2,255,358	49.0	421	306	14
Lab	288,285	5.3	43	26	0
N	2,808	0.1	1	1	0
Others	60,358	1.3	28	1	0
Total	**4,657,609**	**100.0**	**928**	**456**	**17**
WALES					
C & LU	65,949	33.8	20	0	0
L	128,461	60.2	34	32	12
Lab	11,865	3.5	2	1	0
Others	4,841	2.5	1	1	0
Total	**211,116**	**100.0**	**57**	**34**	**12**
SCOTLAND					
C & LU	225,802	38.2	69	10	0
L	336,400	56.4	70	58	1
Lab	16,897	2.3	4	2	0
Others	17,815	3.1	8	0	0
Total	**596,914**	**100.0**	**151**	**70**	**1**
IRELAND					
C & LU	63,218	47.0	23	15	6
L	26,572	19.7	9	3	0
Lab	4,616	3.4	1	0	0
N	32,223	23.9	86	82	74
Others	8,052	6.0	4	1	0
Total	**134,681**	**100.0**	**123**	**101**	**80**
UNIVERSITIES					
C & LU	16,302	60.6	9	9	4
L	4,266	19.4	2	0	0
Others	5,203	20.0	3	0	0
Total	**25,771**	**100.0**	**14**	**9**	**4**
UNITED KINGDOM					
C & LU	2,422,071	43.4	556	156[1]	13
L	2,751,057	49.4	536	399[2]	27
Lab	321,663	4.8	50	29	0
N	35,031	0.7	87	83	74
Others	96,269	1.7	44[3]	3[4]	0
Total	**5,626,091**	**100.0**	**1,273**	**670**	**114**

[1] Including approximately 25 Liberal Unionists.

[2] Including 7 'Russellite' candidates in Ireland.

[3] Including 8 SDF, 5 SWRC.

[4] Namely: T.H. Sloan (Belfast, South—Ind C); J.W. Taylor (Durham, Chester-le-Street—Ind Lab); J. Williams (Glamorganshire, Gower—Ind L/Lab). Taylor's candidature had for technical reasons not been endorsed by the Labour Representation Committee but he joined the Parliamentary Labour Party upon election.

†Adjusted to allow for two-member seats. See Introductory Notes.

Table 1.07 GENERAL ELECTION 1910 (January)

	Total votes	% share of total votes†	Candidates	M.P.s. Elected	Unopposed Returns
ENGLAND					
C & LU	2,645,914	49.3	453	233	5
L	2,291,062	43.0	405	188	1
Lab	403,358	6.9	62	33	0
N	2,943	0.1	1	1	0
Others	44,768	0.7	19	1	0
Total	**5,388,045**	**100.0**	**940**	**456**	**6**
WALES					
C & LU	116,769	31.9	33	2	0
L	195,288	52.3	29	27	0
Lab	60,496	14.9	5	5	0
Others	5,090	0.9	2	0	0
Total	**377,643**	**100.0**	**69**	**34**	**0**
SCOTLAND					
C & LU	260,033	39.6	70	9	0
L	354,847	54.2	68	58	0
Lab	37,852	5.1	10	2	0
Others	7,710	1.1	4	1	0
Total	**660,442**	**100.0**	**152**	**70**	**0**
IRELAND					
C & LU	68,982	32.7	29	19	8
L	20,339	9.6	7	1	0
Lab	3,951	1.9	1	0	0
N	123,704	54.1	104	81	55
Others	3,553	1.7	1	0	0
Total	**220,529**	**100.0**	**142**	**101**	**63**
UNIVERSITIES					
C & LU	12,709	61.3	9	9	6
L	4,621	22.3	2	0	0
Others	3,411	16.4	1	0	0
Total	**20,741**	**100.0**	**12**	**9**	**6**
UNITED KINGDOM					
C & LU	3,104,407	46.8	594	272[1]	19
L	2,866,157	43.5	511	274	1
Lab	505,657	7.0	78	40	0
N	126,647	1.9	105	82[2]	55
Others	64,532	0.8	27[3]	2[4]	0
Total	**6,667,400**	**100.0**	**1,315**	**670**	**75**

[1] Including approximately 32 Liberal Unionists.

[2] Including 11 Independents.

[3] Including 9 SDP, 1 SPP.

[4] Namely: A.C. Corbett (Glasgow, Tradeston—Ind L); S. Storey (Sunderland—Ind C).

†Adjusted to allow for two-member seats. See Introductory Notes.

Table 1.08 GENERAL ELECTION 1910 (December)

	Total votes	% share of total vote†	Candidates	M.P.s. Elected	Unopposed Returns
ENGLAND					
C & LU	2,035,297	48.8	436	234	54
L	1,849,098	44.4	362	186	14
Lab	300,142	6.4	44	34	2
N	2,458	0.1	1	1	0
Others	11,630	0.3	8	1	0
Total	4,198,625	100.0	851	456	70
WALES					
C & LU	81,100	33.8	20	3	0
L	117,533	47.9	30	26	10
Lab	47,027	17.8	7	5	1
Others	1,176	0.5	1	0	0
Total	246,836	100.0	58	34	11
SCOTLAND					
C & LU	244,785	42.6	57	9	1
L	306,378	53.6	67	58	11
Lab	24,633	3.6	5	3	0
Others	1,947	0.2	3	0	0
Total	577,743	100.0	132	70	12
IRELAND					
C & LU	56,408	28.6	26	17	9
L	19,003	9.6	7	1	0
N	129,262	60.3	105	83	53
Others	2,925	1.5	2	0	0
Total	207,598	100.0	140	101	62
UNIVERSITIES					
C & LU	2,579	58.1	9	9	8
L	1,857	41.9	1	0	0
Total	4,436	100.0	10	9	8
UNITED KINGDOM					
C & LU	2,420,169	46.6	548	272[1]	72
L	2,293,869	44.2	467	271	35
Lab	371,802	6.4	56	42	3
N	131,720	2.5	106	84[2]	53
Others	17,678	0.3	14[3]	1[4]	0
Total	5,235,238	100.0	1,191	670	163

[1] Including approximately 36 Liberal Unionists.

[2] Including 10 Independents.

[3] Including 2 SDP, 1 SPP.

[4] Namely: F. Bennett-Goldney (Canterbury—Ind C).

†Adjusted to allow for two-member seats. See Introductory Notes.

Table 1.09   GENERAL ELECTION 1918

	Total votes	% share of total votes†	Candidates	M.P.s Elected	Unopposed Returns
ENGLAND					
Co C	3,097,350	38.9	318	295	40
Co L	962,871	11.6	95	82	12
Co Lab	39,715	0.3	4	3	1
Co NDP	121,673	1.6	15	8	0
Co Ind	9,274	0.1	1	1	0
(Total Co)	(4,230,883)	(52.5)	(433)	(389)	(53)
C	317,281	3.7	34	20	0
L	1,172,700	14.7	232	25	2
Lab	1,811,739	22.6	291	42	6
Co-op	37,944	0.5	7	1	0
N	8,225	0.1	2	1	1
Nat P	94,389	1.2	26	2	0
NDP	20,200	0.2	7	0	0
NFDSS	12,329	0.1	5	0	0
Others	345,188	4.4	114	5	1
Total	**8,050,878**	**100.0**	**1,151**	**485**	**63**
WALES					
Co C	20,328	3.9	2	1	0
Co L	207,377	39.2	19	17	4
Co NDP	22,824	4.3	1	1	0
(Total Co)	(250,529)	(47.4)	(22)	(19)	(4)
C	39,264	7.4	6	3	0
L	51,382	9.7	10	3	2
Lab	163,055	30.8	25	9	5
Others	24,804	4.7	8	1	0
Total	**529,034**	**100.0**	**71**	**35**	**11**
SCOTLAND					
Co C	336,530	30.8	34	28	1
Co L	221,145	19.1	28	25	7
Co Lab	14,247	1.3	1	1	0
Co NDP	12,337	1.1	2	0	0
(Total Co)	(584,259)	(52.3)	(65)	(54)	(8)
C	21,939	2.0	3	2	0
L	163,960	15.0	33	8	0
Lab	265,744	22.9	39	6	0
Co-op	19,841	1.8	3	0	0
NDP	4,297	0.4	1	0	0
Others	66,671	5.6	21	1	0
Total	**1,126,711**	**100.0**	**165**	**71**	**8**
IRELAND					
C	289,213	28.4	36	23	0
N	228,902	22.0	56	6	0
SF	495,345	47.0	100	72	25
Others	25,765	2.6	12	0	0
Total	**1,039,225**	**100.0**	**204**	**101**	**25**
UNIVERSITIES					
Co C	18,530	45.2	8	8	0
Co L	5,197	12.7	3	3	0
(Total Co)	(23,727)	(57.9)	(11)	(11)	0
C	3,757	9.2	4	2	0
L	742	1.8	1	0	0
Lab	5,239	12.8	6	0	0
N	1,070	2.6	2	0	0
SF	1,762	4.3	2	1	0
Others	4,673	11.4	6	1	0
Total	**40,970**	**100.0**	**32**	**15**	**0**

GENERAL ELECTION 1918 (Cont.)

	Total votes	% share of total votes†	Candidates	M.P.s Elected	Unopposed Returns
UNITED KINGDOM					
Co C	3,472,738	32.5	362	332	41
Co L	1,396,590	12.6	145[1]	127	23
Co Lab	53,962	0.4	5[2]	4	1
Co Ind	9,274	0.1	1	1	0
Co NDP	156,834	1.5	18	9	0
(Total Co)	(5,089,398)	(47.1)	(531)	(473)	(65)
C	671,454	6.1	83[3]	50[4]	0
L	1,388,784	13.0	276	36[5]	4
Lab	2,245,777	20.8	361	57	11
Co-op	57,785	0.6	10	1[6]	0
N	238,197	2.2	60	7	1
Nat P	94,389	0.9	26	2	0
NDP	24,497	0.2	8	0	0
NFDSS	12,329	0.1	5	0	0
SF	497,107	4.6	102	73[7]	25
Others	467,101	4.4	161[8]	8[9]	1
Total	**10,786,818**	**100.0**	**1,623**[10]	**707**	**107**

[1] Excluding 14 candidates who received the 'coupon' (the endorsement given to officially approved candidates) but repudiated it.

[2] Of the five Coalition Labour candidates, only two were official and received the 'coupon'. They were J.R. Bell (Kingston-upon-Hull, South-West) and J. Parker (Staffordshire, Cannock). They were however incorrectly designated in the official list of Coalition candidates as National Democratic Party and Liberal respectively.

[3] The majority of Conservative candidates supported the Coalition although not all received the 'coupon'. There were also numerous other candidates, among them members of the National Party and National Democratic Party and at least half the Independents, who were certainly not opposed to the Coalition and the figures of votes polled by the official Coalition candidates must underestimate very considerably the number of electors who supported the Coalition.

[4] Including three members of the Ulster Unionist Labour Association who were elected for Belfast constituencies and ran under the title 'Labour-Unionist'.

[5] This is in fact an overestimate of the number of non-Coalition Liberals as nine who had not received the 'coupon' accepted the Coalition Whip upon election. They were: Sir F.D. Blake, Bt. (Northumberland, Berwick-upon-Tweed); G.P. Collins (Greenock); Hon. W.H. Cozens-Hardy (Norfolk, Southern); J. Gardiner (Perthshire and Kinross-shire, Kinross and Western); S.G. Howard (Suffolk, Sudbury); Rt. Hon. G. Lambert (Devon, South Molton); J.T.T. Rees (Devon, Barnstaple); Sir W.H. Seager (Cardiff, East); E.H. Young (Norwich).

A few other Liberals were, with reservations, general supporters of the Coalition and the number of anti-Coalition Liberals (commonly called 'Free' or 'Asquithian' Liberals) who were prepared to follow Asquith's leadership was estimated by *The Times* in January 1919, to be about fourteen members who could be relied upon to consistently oppose the Coalition Government. The other non-Coalition Liberals at first adopted an independent attitude but as opposition to the Coalition grew, they tended to drift into the Asquith group.

[6] Joined the Parliamentary Labour Party upon election.

[7] The actual number was 69 as four Sinn Fein candidates were returned for two constituencies. They were: E. de Valera (Clare, East and Mayo, East); A. Griffith (Cavan, East and Tyrone, North-West); J.E. MacNeill (Londonderry, and National University); W.L.J. Mellows (Galway, East, and Meath, North). The Sinn Fein members did not take their seat in the House of Commons.

[8] Including 4 HLL, 3 NSP, 3 SLP, 3 BSP, 1 SPP, 1 WP.

[9] Namely: R.H. Barker (Yorkshire, Sowerby); N.P. Billing (Hertfordshire, Hertford); H.W. Bottomley (Hackney, South); J.J. Jones (West Ham, Silvertown—NSP); F.H. Rose (Aberdeen, North—Ind Lab); Sir O. Thomas (Anglesey—Ind Lab); J.C. Wedgwood (Newcastle-under Lyme—Ind L); Sir R.H. Woods (Dublin University—Ind C).

Jones, Rose and Sir O. Thomas joined the Labour Party immediately after being elected. Wedgwood joined the Labour Party in August 1919. Sir O. Thomas resigned from the Labour Party in July 1919. Sir R.H. Woods accepted the Conservative Whip upon election.

[10] The number of persons seeking election was 1,611 owing to the fact that in Ireland nine candidates contested two constituencies each and one contested four constituencies.

† Adjusted to allow for two-member seats. See Introductory Notes.

Table 1.10 GENERAL ELECTION 1922

	Total votes	% share of total vote†	Candidates	M.P.s Elected	Unopposed Returns
ENGLAND					
C	4,809,797	41.5	406	307	29
L	2,260,423	19.6	270	44	3
NL	950,515	7.6	98	31	2
Lab	3,370,430	28.8	340	95	2
Com	9,693	0.1	2	0	0
N	12,614	0.1	2	1	1
Others	282,958	2.3	38	7	0
Total	**11,696,430**	**100.0**	**1,156**	**485**	**37**
WALES					
C	190,919	21.4	19	6	1
L	74,996	8.4	11	2	1
NL	230,961	25.8	19	8	1
Lab	363,568	40.8	28	18	1
Others	32,256	3.6	3	1	0
Total	**892,700**	**100.0**	**80**	**35**	**4**
SCOTLAND					
C	379,396	25.1	36	13	0
L	328,649	21.5	48	15	1
NL	288,529	17.7	33	12	1
Lab	501,254	32.2	43	29	1
Com	23,944	1.4	3	1	0
Others	47,589	2.1	5	1	0
Total	**1,569,361**	**100.0**	**168**	**71**	**3**
NORTHERN IRELAND					
C	107,972	55.9	12	10	9
N	90,053	36.2	2	2	0
Others	9,861	7.9	1	0	0
Total	**207,886**	**100.0**	**15**	**12**	**9**
UNIVERSITIES					
C	14,214	54.8	9	8	3
L	4,075	15.7	4	1	1
NL	1,312	5.0	2	2	0
Lab	2,097	8.1	3	0	0
Others	4,255	16.4	4	1	0
Total	**25,953**	**100.0**	**22**	**12**	**4**

GENERAL ELECTION 1922 (Cont.)

	Total votes	% share of total votes†	Candidates	M.P.s Elected	Unopposed Returns
UNITED KINGDOM					
C	5,502,298	38.5	482	344	42
L	2,668,143	18.9	333	62[1]	6
NL	1,471,317	9.9	152	53[1]	4
Lab	4,237,349	29.7	414	142	4
Com	33,637	0.2	5[2]	1	0
N	102,667	0.4	4	3	1
Others	376,919	2.4	51[3]	10[4]	0
Total	**14,392,330**	**100.0**	**1,441**	**615**	**57**

[1] Two National Liberals, T.M. Guthrie (Moray and Nairnshire) and J. Hinds (Carmarthenshire, Carmarthen) accepted the Liberal Whip upon election bringing that party's strength up to 64 members.

[2] For details of Communists who secured endorsement as official Labour candidates see Table 7.07.

[3] Including 1 SPP.

[4] Namely: H.T.A. Becker (Richmond—Ind C); J.R.M. Butler (Cambridge University—Ind L); J.M.M. Erskine (Westminster, St. George's—Ind C); G.R. Hall Caine (Dorset, Eastern—Ind C); A. Hopkinson (Lancashire, Mossley); G.W.S. Jarrett (Kent, Dartford—Const); O.E. Mosley (Middlesex, Harrow); Rt. Hon. G.H. Roberts (Norwich); E. Scrymgeour (Dundee—SPP); Sir O. Thomas (Anglesey—Ind Lab). Becker, Erskine, Hall Caine and Roberts were subsequently granted the Conservative Whip.

†Adjusted to allow for two-member seats. See Introductory Notes.

Table 1.11 GENERAL ELECTION 1923

	Total votes	% share of total votes†	Candidates	M.P.s Elected	Unopposed Returns
ENGLAND					
C	4,732,176	39.8	444	221	24
L	3,572,335	29.9	362	123	3
Lab	3,549,888	29.7	350	138	1
N	10,322	0.1	2	1	1
Others	62,364	0.5	8	2	0
Total	**11,927,085**	**100.0**	**1,166**	**485**	**29**
WALES					
C	178,113	21.1	19	4	0
L	299,314	35.4	31	11	3
Lab	355,172	42.0	27	19	2
Others	12,469	1.5	1	1	0
Total	**845,068**	**100.0**	**78**	**35**	**5**
SCOTLAND					
C	468,526	31.6	52	14	0
L	422,995	28.4	59	22	4
Lab	532,450	35.9	48	34	0
Com	39,448	2.4	4	0	0
Others	37,908	1.7	4	1	0
Total	**1,501,327**	**100.0**	**167**	**71**	**4**
NORTHERN IRELAND					
C	117,161	49.4	12	10	8
N	87,671	27.3	2	2	0
Others	37,426	23.3	2	0	0
Total	**242,258**	**100.0**	**16**	**12**	**8**
UNIVERSITIES					
C	18,565	58.1	9	9	3
L	6,837	21.4	5	2	1
Lab	2,270	7.1	2	0	0
Others	4,285	13.4	3	1	0
Total	**31,957**	**100.0**	**19**	**12**	**4**
UNITED KINGDOM					
C	5,514,541	38.0	536	258	35
L	4,301,481	29.7	457	158	11
Lab	4,439,780	30.7	427	191	3
Com	39,448	0.2	4[1]	0	0
N	97,993	0.4	4	3	1
Others	154,452	1.0	18[2]	5[3]	0
Total	**14,547,695**	**100.0**	**1,446**	**615**	**50**

[1] For details of Communists who secured endorsement as official Labour candidates see Table 7.07.

[2] Including 1 BLP, 1 SPP.

[3] Namely: G.M.L. Davies (University of Wales—CP); A. Hopkinson (Lancashire, Mossley); R.H. Morris (Cardiganshire—Ind L);
O.E. Mosley (Middlesex, Harrow); E. Scrymgeour (Dundee—SPP).
Davies and Mosley joined the Labour Party shortly after the election and Morris was granted the Liberal Whip.

†Adjusted to allow for two-member seats. See Introductory Notes.

Table 1.12 GENERAL ELECTION 1924

	Total votes	% share of total votes†	Candidates	M.P.s Elected	Unopposed Returns
ENGLAND					
C	6,460,266	47.6	440	347	13
L	2,388,429	17.6	280	19	2
Lab	4,467,236	32.9	414	109	2
Com	39,416	0.3	6	1	0
Const	185,075	1.4	12	7	0
N	–	–	1	1	1
Others	21,136	0.2	6	1	0
Total	**13,561,558**	**100.0**	**1,159**	**485**	**18**
WALES					
C	224,014	28.4	17	9	0
L	244,828	31.0	21	10	1
Lab	320,397	40.6	33	16	7
Total	**789,239**	**100.0**	**71**	**35**	**8**
SCOTLAND					
C	688,299	40.8	56	36	0
L	286,540	16.5	34	8	3
Lab	697,146	41.1	63	26	0
Com	15,930	0.7	2	0	0
Others	29,193	0.9	1	1	0
Total	**1,717,108**	**100.0**	**156**	**71**	**3**
NORTHERN IRELAND					
C	451,278	83.8	12	12	2
SF	46,457	9.9	8	0	0
Others	21,639	6.3	2	0	0
Total	**519,374**	**100.0**	**22**	**12**	**2**
UNIVERSITIES					
C	30,666	57.9	9	8	1
L	8,940	16.9	4	3	0
Lab	4,308	8.1	4	0	0
Others	9,086	17.1	3	1	0
Total	**53,000**	**100.0**	**20**	**12**	**1**
UNITED KINGDOM					
C	7,854,523	46.8	534	412	16
L	2,928,737	17.8	339	40[1]	6
Lab	5,489,087	33.3	514	151	9
Com	55,346	0.3	8	1	0
Const	185,075	1.2	12[2]	7	0
N	–	–	1	1	1
SF	46,457	0.2	8	0	0
Others	81,054	0.4	12[3]	3[4]	0
Total	**16,640,279**	**100.0**	**1,428**	**615**	**32**

[1] Including Rt. Hon. F.E. Guest (Bristol, North) whose name was originally given in the list of Constitutionalist candidates. In the final list his name was omitted and although supported officially by the local Conservative Association he ran as a Liberal.

[2] Of the twelve who ran as Constitutionalists, six [Rt. Hon. W.L.S. Churchill (Essex, Epping); J.E. Davis (Durham, Consett); Rt. Hon. Sir H. Greenwood, Bt. (Walthamstow, East); C.E. Loseby (Nottingham, West); A.H. Moreing (Cornwall, Camborne); J.L. Sturrock (Tottenham, North)] were ex-Liberals, most of whom subsequently joined the Conservative Party.

The other six candidates [W. Allen (Stoke-on-Trent, Burslem); J.H. Edwards (Accrington); A. England (Lancashire, Heywood and Radcliffe); H.C. Hogbin (Battersea, North); Sir T. Robinson (Lancashire, Stretford); J. Ward (Stoke-on-Trent, Stoke)] were Liberals and their names appear to have been included in the official list of Liberal candidates.

Those elected were: (Conservatives)—Churchill, Sir H. Greenwood, Bt. and Moreing. (Liberals)—Edwards, England, Sir T. Robinson and Ward.

[3] Including 1 NI Lab, 1 SPP.

[4] Namely: Dr. E.G.G. Graham-Little (London University); A. Hopkinson (Lancashire, Mossley); E. Scrymgeour (Dundee—SPP).

† Adjusted to allow for two-member seats. See Introductory Notes.

Table 1.13 GENERAL ELECTION 1929

	Total votes	% share of total votes†	Candidates	M.P.s Elected	Unopposed Returns
ENGLAND					
C	7,177,551	38.8	469	221	2
L	4,340,703	23.6	422	35	0
Lab	6,850,738	36.9	467	226	0
Com	15,377	0.1	12	0	0
N	–	–	1	1	1
Others	117,876	0.6	17	2	0
Total	**18,502,245**	**100.0**	**1,388**	**485**	**3**
WALES					
C	289,695	22.0	35	1	0
L	440,911	33.5	34	9	0
Lab	577,554	43.9	33	25	0
Com	8,143	0.6	3	0	0
PC	609	0.0	1	0	0
Total	**1,316,912**	**100.0**	**106**	**35**	**0**
SCOTLAND					
C	792,063	35.9	65	20	0
L	407,081	18.1	45	13	0
Lab	937,300	42.4	66	36	0
Com	27,114	1.1	10	0	0
SNP	3,313	0.1	2	0	0
Others	76,070	2.4	4	2	0
Total	**2,242,941**	**100.0**	**192**	**71**	**0**
NORTHERN IRELAND					
C	354,657	68.0	10	10	1
L	100,103	16.8	6	0	0
N	24,177	6.6	3	2	2
Others	31,116	8.6	3	0	0
Total	**510,053**	**100.0**	**22**	**12**	**3**
UNIVERSITIES					
C	42,259	55.4	11	8	1
L	19,940	26.2	6	2	0
Lab	4,825	6.3	3	0	0
Others	9,200	12.1	2	2	0
Total	**76,224**	**100.0**	**22**	**12**	**1**
UNITED KINGDOM					
C	8,656,225	38.1	590	260	4
L	5,308,738	23.6	513	59[1]	0
Lab	8,370,417	37.1	569	287	0
Com	50,634	0.2	25	0	0
N	24,177	0.1	4	3	3
PC	609	0.0	1	0	0
SNP	3,313	0.0	2	0	0
Others	234,262	0.9	26[2]	6[3]	0
Total	**22,648,375**	**100.0**	**1,730**	**615**	**7**

[1] Including Sir W.A. Jowitt (Preston) who joined the Labour Party one week after the election.

[2] Including 1 SPP.

[3] Namely: Dr. E.G.G. Graham-Little (London University); N. Maclean (Glasgow, Govan–Ind Lab); Sir R.H.S.D.L. Newman, Bt. (Exeter); Miss E.F. Rathbone (Combined English Universities); Sir T. Robinson (Lancashire, Stretford); E. Scrymgeour (Dundee–SPP). Maclean was re-admitted into the Parliamentary Labour Party in February 1930.

†Adjusted to allow for two-member seats. See Introductory Notes.

Table 1.14 GENERAL ELECTION 1931

	Total votes	% share of total votes†	Candidates	M.P.s Elected	Unopposed Returns
ENGLAND					
C	10,453,349	57.8	427	398	31
L	1,007,510	5.8	85	19	1
Nat	100,193	0.6	4	4	0
NL	632,155	3.4	28	23	3
N Lab	292,688	1.5	17	11	0
(Total Nat)	(12,485,895)	(69.1)	(561)	(455)	(35)
Ind L	31,989	0.2	2	0	0
Lab	5,464,425	30.2	428	29	2
Com	21,452	0.1	15	0	0
NP	20,721	0.1	16	0	0
Others	58,552	0.3	10	1	0
Total	**18,083,034**	**100.0**	**1,032**	**485**	**37**
WALES					
C	240,861	22.1	14	6	0
L	157,472	14.5	10	4	0
NL	75,717	7.0	5	4	2
N Lab	24,120	2.2	1	1	0
(Total Nat)	(498,170)	(45.8)	(30)	(15)	(2)
Ind L	71,539	6.6	4	4	0
Lab	479,547	44.1	30	16	4
Com	17,754	1.6	3	0	0
NP	11,300	1.0	2	0	0
PC	1,136	0.1	1	0	0
Others	9,100	0.8	2	0	0
Total	**1,088,546**	**100.0**	**72**	**35**	**6**
SCOTLAND					
C	1,056,768	49.5	56	48	3
L	205,384	8.6	14	7	3
NL	101,430	4.8	8	8	2
N Lab	21,803	1.0	1	1	0
(Total Nat)	(1,385,385)	(63.9)	(79)	(64)	(8)
Lab	696,248	32.6	57	7	0
Com	35,618	1.5	8	0	0
NP	3,895	0.2	5	0	0
SNP	20,954	1.0	5	0	0
Others	32,229	0.8	1	0	0
Total	**2,174,329**	**100.0**	**155**	**71**	**8**
NORTHERN IRELAND					
C	149,566	56.1	12	10	8
(Total Nat)	(149,566)	(56.1)	(12)	(10)	(8)
Lab	9,410	5.0	1	0	0
N	123,053	38.9	3	2	0
Total	**282,029**	**100.0**	**16**	**12**	**8**
UNIVERSITIES					
C	5,381	18.9	9	8	7
L	2,229	7.9	2	2	1
N Lab	2,759	9.7	1	0	0
(Total Nat)	(10,369)	(36.5)	(12)	(10)	(8)
NP	461	1.6	1	0	0
PC	914	3.2	1	0	0
Others	16,691	58.7	3	2	0
Total	**28,435**	**100.0**	**17**	**12**	**8**

GENERAL ELECTION 1931 (Cont.)

	Total votes	% share of total votes†	Candidates	M.P.s Elected	Unopposed Returns
UNITED KINGDOM					
C	11,905,925	55.0	518	470	49
L	1,372,595	6.5	111	32	5
Nat	100,193	0.5	4	4	0
NL	809,302	3.7	41[1]	35	7
N Lab	341,370	1.5	20	13	0
(Total Nat)	(14,529,385)	(67.2)	(694)	(554)	(61)
Ind L	103,528	0.5	6[2]	4	0
Lab	6,649,630	30.8	516[3]	52[4]	6[5]
Com	74,824	0.3	26	0	0
N	123,053	0.4	3	2	0
NP	36,377	0.2	24	0	0
PC	2,050	0.0	2	0	0
SNP	20,954	0.1	5	0	0
Others	116,572	0.5	16[6]	3[7]	0
Total	**21,656,373**	**100.0**	**1,292**	**615**	**67**

[1] Although standing as National Liberals and using a separate election organisation, the National Liberal candidates had their names included in the official list of Liberal Party candidates and those elected were claimed by the Liberal Party as their members. It appears that it was not until after the Liberal Party finally withdrew its support from the National Government in September 1932, that the party finally accepted that National Liberals could no longer be classed with Liberals who had stood without the National prefix.

[2] Of the Liberal candidates opposed to the National Government, the four who secured election (the Lloyd George family group) took their seats on the Opposition Benches in the House of Commons and were subsequently joined by the other Liberal M.P.s who decided to cross the floor and go into opposition when the new Parliamentary Session opened on November 21, 1933. The Rt. Hon. D. Lloyd George never again sat on the Liberal Benches from the time of the 1931 election until his elevation to the Peerage in 1945. He always occupied the corner seat on the Opposition (Labour) Front Bench.

[3] Including 25 candidates who did not receive official endorsement. Of this number, 24 were members of the ILP (including 19 official ILP nominees, the remaining 5 although members of the ILP were the nominees of trade unions and Constituency Labour Parties) and refused to sign a form accepting the Standing Orders of the Parliamentary Labour Party, a condition of endorsement which was introduced just prior to the election. The remaining case of a candidate not receiving endorsement was at Glasgow, Hillhead where the candidate, although adopted by the Constituency Labour Party, was refused endorsement on the grounds that neither local finance or organisation warranted the adoption of a candidate. The total votes polled by the 25 non-endorsed candidates were 324,893.

[4] Including six unendorsed members: G. Buchanan (Glasgow, Gorbals); D. Kirkwood (Dumbarton Burghs); J. McGovern (Glasgow, Shettleston); J. Maxton (Glasgow, Bridgeton); R.C. Wallhead (Merthyr Tydfil, Merthyr); Rt. Hon. J.C. Wedgwood (Newcastle-under-Lyme).
McGovern, Maxton and Wallhead formed an ILP Parliamentary Group and were joined by Buchanan and Kirkwood. Wedgwood remained an Independent.
Subsequently Kirkwood, Wallhead and Wedgwood re-entered the Parliamentary Labour Party.

[5] Including 1 unendorsed.

[6] Including 2 CW Land P, 1 LPP, 1 SPP.

[7] Namely: Sir E.G.G. Graham-Little (London University—Nat Ind); A. Hopkinson (Lancashire, Mossley—Nat Ind); Miss E.F. Rathbone (Combined English Universities).

†Adjusted to allow for two-member seats. See Introductory Notes.

Table 1.15 GENERAL ELECTION 1935

	Total votes	% share of total votes†	Candidates	M.P.s Elected	Unopposed Returns
ENGLAND					
C	8,997,348	49.4	423	329	14
Nat	13,250	0.1	1	0	0
NL	673,597	3.4	31	22	2
N Lab	303,742	1.6	18	6	0
(Total Nat)	(9,987,937)	(54.5)	(473)	(357)	(16)
L	1,108,971	6.3	132	11	0
Lab	7,054,050	38.5	452	116	3
ILP	18,681	0.1	5	0	0
Others	103,396	0.6	16	1	0
Total	**18,273,035**	**100.0**	**1,078**	**485**	**i9**
WALES					
C	204,099	23.4	14	6	0
Nat	35,318	4.1	2	1	0
NL	36,156	4.2	3	3	1
N Lab	16,954	1.9	1	1	0
(Total Nat)	(292,527)	(33.6)	(20)	(11)	(1)
L	157,091	18.0	12	6	0
Lab	395,830	45.4	33	18	10
Com	13,655	1.6	1	0	0
ILP	9,640	1.1	1	0	0
PC	2,534	0.3	1	0	0
Total	**871,277**	**100.0**	**68**	**35**	**11**
SCOTLAND					
C	962,595	42.0	58	35	1
Nat	4,621	0.2	1	0	0
NL	149,072	6.7	9	7	0
N Lab	19,115	0.9	1	1	0
(Total Nat)	(1,135,403)	(49.8)	(69)	(43)	(1)
L	174,235	6.7	16	3	0
Lab	863,789	36.8	63	20	0
Com	13,462	0.6	1	1	0
ILP	111,256	5.0	11	4	0
SNP	25,652	1.1	7	0	0
Total	**2,323,797**	**100.0**	**167**	**71**	**1**
NORTHERN IRELAND					
C	292,840	64.9	12	10	6
(Total Nat)	(292,840)	(64.9)	(12)	(10)	(6)
N	101,494	18.3	2	2	0
Rep	56,833	16.8	3	0	0
Total	**451,167**	**100.0**	**17**	**12**	**6**
UNIVERSITIES					
C	39,418	50.7	8	7	2
NL	7,529	9.7	1	1	0
(Total Nat)	(46,947)	(60.4)	(9)	(8)	(2)
L	2,796	3.6	1	1	0
Lab	11,822	15.2	4	0	0
SNP	3,865	4.9	1	0	0
Others	12,348	15.9	3	3	1
Total	**77,778**	**100.0**	**18**	**12**	**3**

GENERAL ELECTION 1935 (Cont.)

	Total votes	% share of total votes†	Candidates	M.P.s Elected	Unopposed Returns
UNITED KINGDOM					
C	10,496,300	47.8	515	387	23
Nat	53,189	0.3	4	1	0
NL	866,354	3.7	44	33	3
N Lab	339,811	1.5	20	8	0
(Total Nat)	(11,755,654)	(53.3)	(583)	(429)	(26)
L	1,443,093	6.7	161	21[1]	0
Lab	8,325,491	38.0	552	154	13
Com	27,117	0.1	2	1	0
ILP	139,577	0.6	17	4	0
N	101,494	0.3	2	2	0
PC	2,534	0.0	1	0	0
Rep	56,833	0.2	3	0	0
SNP	29,517	0.2	8	0	0
Others	115,744	0.6	19[2]	4[3]	1
Total	**21,997,054**	**100.0**	**1,348**	**615**	**40**

[1] Including R.H. Bernays (Bristol, North) and the Hon. J.P. Maclay (Paisley) who although elected as Liberals without prefix, supported the National Government. Bernays accepted the National Liberal Whip in October 1936.

[2] Including 1 LPP, 1 SCPGB.

[3] Namely: Sir E.G.G. Graham-Little (London University—Nat Ind); A.P. Herbert (Oxford University); A. Hopkinson (Lancashire, Mossley—Nat Ind); Miss E.F. Rathbone (Combined English Universities).

†Adjusted to allow for two-member seats. See Introductory Notes.

Table 1.16 GENERAL ELECTION 1945

	Total votes	% share of total votes†	Candidates	M.P.s Elected	Unopposed Returns
ENGLAND					
C	7,575,577	37.0	461	159	0
Nat	105,862	0.5	8	1	0
NL	587,752	2.7	38	7	0
(Total Nat)	(8,269,191)	(40.2)	(507)	(167)	(0)
L	1,913,917	9.4	265	5	0
Lab	9,972,519	48.5	494	331	1
Com	53,754	0.3	15	1	0
CW	106,403	0.5	21	1	0
ILP	6,044	0.0	2	0	0
Others	217,192	1.1	59	5	0
Total	20,539,020	100.0	1,363	510	1
WALES					
C	241,380	18.1	21	3	0
Nat	11,306	0.9	1	0	0
NL	64,043	4.8	5	1	0
(Total Nat)	(316,729)	(23.8)	(27)	(4)	(0)
L	198,553	14.9	17	6	0
Lab	779,184	58.5	34	25	1
Com	15,761	1.2	1	0	0
PC	14,321	1.1	6	0	0
Others	6,123	0.5	2	0	0
Total	1,330,671	100.0	87	35	1
SCOTLAND					
C	878,206	37.4	62	24	0
NL	85,937	3.7	6	3	0
(Total Nat)	(964,143)	(41.1)	(68)	(27)	(0)
L	132,849	5.0	22	0	0
Lab	1,144,310	47.6	68	37	0
Com	33,265	1.4	5	1	0
CW	4,231	0.2	2	0	0
ILP	40,725	1.8	3	3	0
SNP	30,595	1.2	8	0	0
Others	39,774	1.7	8	3	0
Total	2,389,892	100.0	184	71	0
NORTHERN IRELAND					
C	392,450	53.7	12	8	1
(Total Nat)	(392,450)	(53.7)	(12)	(8)	(1)
Lab	65,459	11.4	5	0	0
N	148,078	18.8	3	2	0
Others	113,778	16.1	4	2	0
Total	719,765	100.0	24	12	1
UNIVERSITIES					
C	13,486	11.7	3	3	0
Nat	16,011	13.8	1	1	0
(Total Nat)	(29,497)	(25.5)	(4)	(4)	(0)
L	7,111	6.1	2	1	0
Lab	6,274	5.4	2	0	0
PC	1,696	1.5	1	0	0
Others	71,269	61.5	16	7	0
Total	115,847	100.0	25	12	0

GENERAL ELECTION 1945 (Cont.)

	Total votes	% share of total votes†	Candidates	M.P.s Elected	Unopposed Returns
UNITED KINGDOM					
C	9,101,099	36.2	559	197	1
Nat	133,179	0.5	10	2	0
NL	737,732	2.9	49	11	0
(Total Nat)	(9,972,010)	(39.6)	(618)	(210)	(1)
L	2,252,430	9.0	306	12[1]	0
Lab	11,967,746	48.0	603	393	2
Com	102,780	0.4	21	2	0
CW	110,634	0.5	23	1	0
ILP	46,769	0.2	5	3	0
N	148,078	0.4	3	2	0
PC	16,017	0.1	7	0	0
SNP	30,595	0.1	8	0	0
Others	448,136	1.7	89[2]	17[3]	0
Total	**25,095,195**	**100.0**	**1,683**	**640**	**3**

[1] Including G. Lloyd George (Pembrokeshire) who had accepted office in the National (Caretaker) Government and supported Churchill.

[2] Including 5 Dem P, 1 CWLP, 1 LPP, 1 SPGB.

[3] Namely: C.V.O. Bartlett (Somerset, Bridgwater—Ind Prog); J. Beattie (Belfast, West—Ind Lab); Sir J. Boyd Orr (Combined Scottish Universities); W.J. Brown (Warwickshire, Rugby); Sir E.G.G. Graham-Little (London University—Nat Ind); H.W. Harris (Cambridge University); A.P. Herbert (Oxford University); W.D. Kendall (Lincolnshire, Grantham); K.M. Lindsay (Combined English Universities); D.L. Lipson (Cheltenham—Nat Ind); Rev. Dr. J. Little (Down—Ind C); Sir M. Macdonald (Inverness-shire and Ross and Cromarty, Inverness—Ind L); J.H. Mackie (Galloway—Ind C); J. MacLeod (Inverness-shire and Ross and Cromarty, Ross and Cromarty—Ind L); D.N. Pritt (Hammersmith, North—Ind Lab); Miss E.F. Rathbone (Combined English Universities); Rt. Hon. Sir J.A. Salter (Oxford University).

Mackie was granted the Conservative Whip in March 1948 and Beattie joined the Irish Labour Party in 1949. Sir M. Macdonald and MacLeod aligned themselves with the National Liberal Party in the House of Commons.

†Adjusted to allow for two-member seats. See Introductory Notes.

Table 1.17 GENERAL ELECTION 1950

	Total votes	% share of total votes	Candidates	M.P.s Elected	Unopposed Returns
ENGLAND					
C	9,820,068	41.0	466	243	0
NL & C	679,324	2.8	38	10	0
(Total C)	(10,499,392)	(43.8)	(504)	(253)	(0)
L	2,248,127	9.4	413	2	0
Lab	11,050,966	46.2	505	251	0
Com	55,158	0.2	80	0	0
Others	100,805	0.4	26	0	0
Total	23,954,448	100.0	1,528	506	0
WALES					
C	320,750	21.0	29	3	0
NL & C	97,918	6.4	6	1	0
(Total C)	(418,668)	(27.4)	(35)	(4)	(0)
L	193,090	12.6	21	5	0
Lab	887,984	58.1	36	27	0
Com	9,048	0.6	4	0	0
PC	17,580	1.2	7	0	0
Others	2,184	0.1	2	0	0
Total	1,528,554	100.0	105	36	0
SCOTLAND					
C	1,013,909	37.2	57	26	0
NL & C	208,101	7.6	11	5	0
(Total C)	(1,222,010)	(44.8)	(68)	(31)	(0)
L	180,270	6.6	41	2	0
Lab	1,259,410	46.2	71	37	0
Com	27,559	1.0	16	0	0
SNP	9,708	0.4	3	0	0
Others	27,727	1.0	13	1	0
Total	2,726,684	100.0	212	71	0
NORTHERN IRELAND					
C	352,334	62.7	12	10	2
Lab	67,816	12.1	5	0	0
N	65,211	11.6	2	2	0
SF	23,362	4.2	2	0	0
Others	52,715	9.4	2	0	0
Total	561,438	100.0	23	12	2
UNITED KINGDOM					
C	11,507,061	40.1	564	282	2
NL & C	985,343	3.4	55	16	0
(Total C)	(12,492,404)	(43.5)	(619)	(298)	(2)
L	2,621,487	9.1	475	9	0
Lab	13,266,176	46.1	617	315	0
Com	91,765	0.3	100	0	0
N	65,211	0.2	2	2	0
PC	17,580	0.1	7	0	0
SF	23,362	0.1	2	0	0
SNP	9,708	0.0	3	0	0
Others	183,431	0.6	43[1]	1[2]	0
Total	28,771,124	100.0	1,868	625	2

[1] Including 4 AP, 4 ILP, 2 Irish LP, 2 SPGB, 1 MGC, 1 SCPGB

[2] Namely: J. MacLeod (Inverness-shire and Ross and Cromarty, Ross and Cromarty—Ind L). He joined the Liberal-Unionist Group in May 1951.

Table 1.18 GENERAL ELECTION 1951

	Total votes	% share of total votes	Candidates	M.P.s Elected	Unopposed Returns
ENGLAND					
C	10,855,287	45.6	463	259	0
NL & C	767,417	3.2	39	12	0
(Total C)	(11,622,704)	(48.8)	(502)	(271)	(0)
L	537,434	2.3	91	2	0
Lab	11,630,467	48.8	506	233	0
Com	7,745	0.0	5	0	0
Others	27,745	0.1	8	0	0
Total	**23,826,095**	**100.0**	**1,112**	**506**	**0**
WALES					
C	421,525	27.6	30	5	0
NL & C	49,744	3.3	3	1	0
(Total C)	(471,269)	(30.9)	(33)	(6)	(0)
L	116,821	7.6	9	3	0
Lab	925,848	60.5	36	27	0
Com	2,948	0.2	1	0	0
PC	10,920	0.7	4	0	0
Others	1,643	0.1	1	0	0
Total	**1,529,449**	**100.0**	**84**	**36**	**0**
SCOTLAND					
C	1,108,321	39.9	57	29	0
NL & C	240,977	8.7	13	6	0
(Total C)	(1,349,298)	(48.6)	(70)	(35)	(0)
L	76,291	2.7	9	1	0
Lab	1,330,244	47.9	71	35	0
Com	10,947	0.4	4	0	0
SNP	7,299	0.3	2	0	0
Others	3,758	0.1	4	0	0
Total	**2,777,837**	**100.0**	**160**	**71**	**0**
NORTHERN IRELAND					
C	274,928	59.3	12	9	4
Lab	62,324	13.5	4	0	0
N	92,787	20.0	3	2	0
Others	33,174	7.2	1	1	0
Total	**463,213**	**100.0**	**20**	**12**	**4**
UNITED KINGDOM					
C	12,660,061	44.3	562	302	4
NL & C	1,058,138	3.7	55	19	0
(Total C)	(13,718,199)	(48.0)	(617)	(321)	(4)
L	730,546	2.6	109	6	0
Lab	13,948,883	48.8	617	295	0
Com	21,640	0.1	10	0	0
N	92,787	0.3	3	2	0
PC	10,920	0.0	4	0	0
SNP	7,299	0.0	2	0	0
Others	66,320	0.2	14[1]	1[2]	0
Total	**28,596,594**	**100.0**	**1,376**	**625**	**4**

[1] Including 3 ILP, 1 AP, 1 BEP, 1 Irish LP.

[2] Namely: J. Beattie (Belfast, West—Irish LP).

Table 1.19 GENERAL ELECTION 1955

	Total votes	% share of total votes	Candidates	M.P.s Elected
ENGLAND				
C	10,586,790	47.8	480	279
NL & C	578,646	2.6	29	14
(Total C)	(11,165,436)	(50.4)	(509)	(293)
L	571,034	2.6	95	2
Lab	10,355,892	46.8	510	216
Com	15,405	0.1	11	0
Others	28,363	0.1	9	0
Total	**22,136,130**	**100.0**	**1,134**	**511**
WALES				
C	383,132	26.7	28	5
NL & C	45,734	3.2	4	1
(Total C)	(428,866)	(29.9)	(32)	(6)
L	104,095	7.3	10	3
Lab	825,690	57.6	36	27
Com	4,544	0.3	1	0
PC	45,119	3.1	11	0
Others	25,410	1.8	1	0
Total	**1,433,724**	**100.0**	**91**	**36**
SCOTLAND				
C	1,056,209	41.5	59	30
NL & C	217,733	8.6	12	6
(Total C)	(1,273,942)	(50.1)	(71)	(36)
L	47,273	1.9	5	1
Lab	1,188,058	46.7	71	34
Com	13,195	0.5	5	0
SNP	12,112	0.5	2	0
Others	8,674	0.3	2	0
Total	**2,543,254**	**100.0**	**156**	**71**
NORTHERN IRELAND				
C	442,647	68.5	12	10
Lab	35,614	5.5	3	0
SF	152,310	23.5	12	2
Others	16,050	2.5	1	0
Total	**646,621**	**100.0**	**28**	**12**
UNITED KINGDOM				
C	12,468,778	46.6	579	324
NL & C	842,113	3.1	45	21
(Total C)	(13,310,891)	(49.7)	(624)	(345)
L	722,402	2.7	110	6
Lab	12,405,254	46.4	620	277
Com	33,144	0.1	17	0
PC	45,119	0.2	11	0
SF	152,310	0.6	12	2
SNP	12,112	0.0	2	0
Others	78,497	0.3	13[1]	0
Total	**26,759,729**	**100.0**	**1,409**	**630**

[1] Including 2 ILP, 1 Irish LP.

Table 1.20 GENERAL ELECTION 1959

	Total votes	% share of total votes	Candidates	M.P.s Elected
ENGLAND				
C	11,037,998	47.7	484	302
NL & C	521,242	2.2	25	13
(Total C)	(11,559,240)	(49.9)	(509)	(315)
L	1,449,593	6.3	191	3
Lab	10,085,097	43.6	511	193
Com	12,204	0.1	10	0
Others	21,635	0.1	13	0
Total	23,127,769	100.0	1,234	511
WALES				
C	441,461	29.6	31	6
NL & C	44,874	3.0	3	1
(Total C)	(486,335)	(32.6)	(34)	(7)
L	78,951	5.3	8	2
Lab	841,450	56.5	36	27
Com	6,542	0.4	2	0
PC	77,571	5.2	20	0
Others	408	0.0	1	0
Total	1,491,257	100.0	101	36
SCOTLAND				
C	1,060,609	39.7	59	25
NL & C	199,678	7.5	11	6
(Total C)	(1,260,287)	(47.2)	(70)	(31)
L	108,963	4.1	16	1
Lab	1,245,255	46.7	71	38
Com	12,150	0.5	6	0
SNP	21,738	0.8	5	0
Others	19,120	0.7	4	1
Total	2,667,513	100.0	172	71
NORTHERN IRELAND				
C	445,013	77.2	12	12
L	3,253	0.6	1	0
Lab	44,370	7.7	3	0
SF	63,415	11.0	12	0
Others	20,062	3.5	1	0
Total	576,113	100.0	29	12
UNITED KINGDOM				
C	12,985,081	46.6	586	345
NL & C	765,794	2.7	39	20
(Total C)	(13,750,875)	(49.3)	(625)	(365)
L	1,640,760	5.9	216	6
Lab	12,216,172	43.9	621	258
Com	30,896	0.1	18	0
PC	77,571	0.3	20	0
SF	63,415	0.2	12	0
SNP	21,738	0.1	5	0
Others	61,225	0.2	19[1]	1[2]
Total	27,862,652	100.0	1,536	630

[1] Including 2 ILP, 1 FP, 1 NI Ind Lab, 1 NLP, 1 SPGB, 1 UM

[2] Namely: Sir D. Robertson (Caithness and Sutherland—Ind C)

Table 1.21 GENERAL ELECTION 1964

	Total votes	% share of total votes	Candidates	M.P.s Elected
ENGLAND				
C	9,894,014	43.2	500	256
NL & C	212,014	0.9	11	6
(Total C)	(10,106,028)	(44.1)	(511)	(262)
L	2,775,752	12.1	323	3
Lab	9,982,360	43.5	511	246
Com	24,824	0.1	22	0
Others	48,287	0.2	42	0
Total	**22,937,251**	**100.0**	**1,409**	**511**
WALES				
C	398,960	27.6	34	6
NL & C	26,062	1.8	2	0
(Total C)	(425,022)	(29.4)	(36)	(6)
L	106,114	7.3	12	2
Lab	837,022	57.9	36	28
Com	9,377	0.6	5	0
PC	69,507	4.8	23	0
Total	**1,447,042**	**100.0**	**112**	**36**
SCOTLAND				
C	981,641	37.3	65	24
NL & C	88,054	3.3	6	0
(Total C)	(1,069,695)	(40.6)	(71)	(24)
L	200,063	7.6	26	4
Lab	1,283,667	48.7	71	43
Com	12,241	0.5	9	0
SNP	64,044	2.4	15	0
Others	4,829	0.2	5	0
Total	**2,634,539**	**100.0**	**197**	**71**
NORTHERN IRELAND				
C	401,897	63.0	12	12
L	17,354	2.7	4	0
Lab	102,759	16.1	10	0
Rep	101,628	15.9	12	0
Others	14,678	2.3	1	0
Total	**638,316**	**100.0**	**39**	**12**
UNITED KINGDOM				
C	11,676,512	42.2	611	298
NL & C	326,130	1.2	19	6
(Total C)	(12,002,642)	(43.4)	(630)	(304)
L	3,099,283	11.2	365	9
Lab	12,205,808	44.1	628	317
Com	46,442	0.2	36	0
PC	69,507	0.3	23	0
Rep	101,628	0.4	12	0
SNP	64,044	0.2	15	0
Others	67,794	0.2	48[1]	0
Total	**27,657,148**	**100.0**	**1,757**	**630**

[1] Including 3 Loyalists, 2 INDEC, 2 Pat P, 2 SPGB, 1 BNP, 1 FP, 1 N Dem P, 1 Rep LP

Table 1.22 GENERAL ELECTION 1966

	Total votes	% share of total votes	Candidates	M.P.s Elected
ENGLAND				
C	9,542,577	42.0	501	216
NL & C	149,779	0.7	9	3
(Total C)	(9,692,356)	(42.7)	(510)	(219)
L	2,036,793	9.0	273	6
Lab	10,886,408	48.0	511	286
Com	33,093	0.1	34	0
Others	44,045	0.2	35	0
Total	**22,692,695**	**100.0**	**1,363**	**511**
WALES				
C	396,795	27.9	36	3
L	89,108	6.3	11	1
Lab	863,692	60.6	36	32
Com	12,769	0.9	8	0
PC	61,071	4.3	20	0
Total	**1,423,435**	**100.0**	**111**	**36**
SCOTLAND				
C	960,675	37.7	71	20
L	172,447	6.8	24	5
Lab	1,273,916	49.9	71	46
Com	16,230	0.6	15	0
SNP	128,474	5.0	23	0
Others	638	0.0	2	0
Total	**2,552,380**	**100.0**	**206**	**71**
NORTHERN IRELAND				
C	368,629	61.8	12	11
L	29,109	4.9	3	0
Lab	72,613	12.2	4	0
N	22,167	3.7	1	0
Rep	62,782	10.5	5	0
Others	40,937	6.9	2	1
Total	**596,237**	**100.0**	**27**	**12**
UNITED KINGDOM				
C	11,268,676	41.4	620	250
NL & C	149,779	0.5	9	3
(Total C)	(11,418,455)	(41.9)	(629)	(253)
L	2,327,457	8.5	311	12
Lab	13,096,629	48.1	622	364
Com	62,092	0.2	57	0
N	22,167	0.1	1	0
PC	61,071	0.2	20	0
Rep	62,782	0.2	5	0
SNP	128,474	0.5	23	0
Others	85,620	0.3	39[1]	1[2]
Total	**27,264,747**	**100.0**	**1,707**	**630**

[1] Including 4 UM, 3 BNP, 2 SPGB, 1 FP, 1 ILP, 1 N Dem P, 1 Pat P, 1 RA, 1 Rep LP, 1 Unity

[2] Namely: G. Fitt (Belfast, West—Rep LP)

Table 1.23 GENERAL ELECTION 1970

	Total votes	% share of total votes	Candidates	M.P.s Elected
ENGLAND				
C	11,282,524	48.3	510	292
L	1,853,616	7.9	282	2
Lab	10,131,555	43.4	511	217
Com	20,103	0.1	35	0
Others	73,098	0.3	65	0
Total	**23,360,896**	**100.0**	**1,403**	**511**
WALES				
C	419,884	27.7	36	7
L	103,747	6.8	19	1
Lab	781,941	51.6	36	27
Com	6,459	0.4	8	0
PC	175,016	11.5	36	0
Others	29,507	2.0	3	1
Total	**1,516,554**	**100.0**	**138**	**36**
SCOTLAND				
C	1,020,674	38.0	70	23
L	147,667	5.5	27	3
Lab	1,197,068	44.5	71	44
Com	11,408	0.4	15	0
SNP	306,802	11.4	65	1
Others	4,616	0.2	8	0
Total	**2,688,235**	**100.0**	**256**	**71**
NORTHERN IRELAND				
C	422,041	54.2	12	8
L	12,005	1.5	4	0
Lab	98,194	12.6	7	0
Others (pro—C)	53,090	6.8	5	1
Others (anti—C)	193,783	24.9	12	3
Total	**779,113**	**100.0**	**40**	**12**
UNITED KINGDOM				
C	13,145,123	46.4	628	330
L	2,117,035	7.5	332	6
Lab	12,208,758	43.1	625	288
Com	37,970	0.1	58	0
PC	175,016	0.6	36	0
SNP	306,802	1.1	65	1
Others	354,094	1.2	93[1]	5[2]
Total	**28,344,798**	**100.0**	**1,837**	**630**

[1] Including 10 NF, 5 DP, 5 Unity, 4 N Dem P, 2 Nat DP, 2 Prot U, 2 SPGB, 1 BM, 1 ILP, 1 MK, 1 Rep LP, 1 VNP

[2] Namely: S.O. Davies (Merthyr Tydfil—Ind Lab); Miss B.J. Devlin (Mid-Ulster—Unity); G. Fitt (Belfast West—Rep LP); F. McManus (Fermanagh and South Tyrone—Unity); Rev. I.R.K. Paisley (Antrim, North—Prot U)

Table 1.24 GENERAL ELECTION 1974 (February)

	Total votes	% share of total votes	Candidates	M.P.s Elected
ENGLAND				
C	10,508,977	40.2	516	268
L	5,574,934	21.3	452	9
Lab	9,842,468	37.6	516	237
Com	13,379	0.1	23	0
NF	76,865	0.3	54	0
Others	124,995	0.5	113	2
Total	26,141,618	100.0	1,674	516
WALES				
C	412,535	25.9	36	8
L	255,423	16.0	31	2
Lab	745,547	46.8	36	24
Com	4,293	0.3	6	0
PC	171,374	10.7	36	2
Others	4,671	0.3	3	0
Total	1,593,843	100.0	148	36
SCOTLAND				
C	950,668	32.9	71	21
L	229,162	8.0	34	3
Lab	1,057,601	36.6	71	40
Com	15,071	0.5	15	0
SNP	633,180	21.9	70	7
Others	1,393	0.1	4	0
Total	2,887,075	100.0	265	71
NORTHERN IRELAND				
APNI	22,660	3.2	3	0
NI Lab	17,284	2.4	5	0
UU	94,301	13.1	7	0
SDLP	160,437	22.4	12	1
(Total Pro-Sunningdale)	(294,682)	(41.1)	(27)	(1)
DUP	58,656	8.2	2	1
Rep	15,152	2.1	4	0
UU	232,103	32.3	7	7
VUPP	75,944	10.6	3	3
Others	41,089	5.7	5	0
(Total Anti-Sunningdale)	(422,944)	(58.9)	(21)	(11)
Total	717,626	100.0	48	12
UNITED KINGDOM				
C	11,872,180	37.9	623	297
L	6,059,519	19.3	517	14
Lab	11,645,616	37.2	623	301
Com	32,743	0.1	44	0
NF	76,865	0.2	54	0
PC	171,374	0.6	36	2
SNP	633,180	2.0	70	7
Others	848,685	2.7	168[1]	14[2]
Total	31,340,162	100.0	2,135[3]	635

[1] Including all candidates in Northern Ireland and 9 WRP, 6 CPE, 6 People, 6 IDA, 4 SD, 3 IMG, 1 BM, 1 MK, 1 N Dem P, 1 NIP

[2] The twelve members for Northern Ireland constituencies (7 UU, 3 VUPP, 1 DUP, 1 SDLP) and E.J. Milne (Blyth—Ind Lab); D. Taverne (Lincoln—Dem Lab)

[3] The number of persons seeking election was 2,133 as one candidate contested three constituencies

Table 1.25 GENERAL ELECTION 1974 (October)

	Total votes	% share of total votes	Candidates	M.P.s Elected
ENGLAND				
C	9,414,008	38.9	515	253
L	4,878,792	20.2	515	8
Lab	9,695,051	40.1	516	255
Com	7,032	0.0	17	0
NF	113,757	0.5	89	0
Others	82,429	0.3	114	0
Total	24,191,069	100.0	1,766	516
WALES				
C	367,230	23.9	36	8
L	239,057	15.5	36	2
Lab	761,447	49.5	36	23
Com	2,941	0.2	3	0
PC	166,321	10.8	36	3
Others	844	0.1	3	0
Total	1,537,840	100.0	150	36
SCOTLAND				
C	681,327	24.7	71	16
L	228,855	8.3	68	3
Lab	1,000,581	36.3	71	41
Com	7,453	0.3	9	0
NF	86	0.0	1	0
SNP	839,617	30.4	71	11
Others	182	0.0	2	0
Total	2,758,101	100.0	293	71
NORTHERN IRELAND				
DUP	59,451	8.5	2	1
UU	256,065	36.5	7	6
VUPP	92,262	13.1	3	3
(Total UUUC)	(407,778)	(58.1)	(12)	(10)
APNI	44,644	6.3	5	0
NI Lab	11,539	1.6	3	0
Rep	21,633	3.1	5	0
SDLP	154,193	22.0	9	1
UPNI	20,454	2.9	2	0
Others	41,853	6.0	7	1
Total	702,094	100.0	43	12
UNITED KINGDOM				
C	10,462,565	35.8	622	277
L	5,346,704	18.3	619	13
Lab	11,457,079	39.2	623	319
Com	17,426	0.1	29	0
NF	113,843	0.4	90	0
PC	166,321	0.6	36	3
SNP	839,617	2.9	71	11
Others	785,549	2.7	162[1]	12[2]
Total	29,189,104	100.0	2,252[3]	635

[1] Including all candidates in Northern Ireland and 25 CFMPB, 13 UDP, 10 WRP, 8 CPE, 7 ICRA, 5 People, 1 MK, 1 SPGB.

[2] The twelve members for Northern Ireland constituencies (6 UU, 3 VUPP, 1 DUP, 1 Ind Rep, 1 SDLP).

[3] The number of persons seeking election was 2,231 owing to the fact that one candidate contested twelve constituencies and another contested eleven constituencies.

Table 1.26   CANDIDATES AT GENERAL ELECTIONS (Summary)

Election	C[1]	%	Lab	%	L	%	Others	%	Total	Candidates per seat
1885	602	45.0	–	–	572	42.7	164	12.3	1,338	2.0
1886	563	50.5	–	–	449	40.3	103	9.2	1,115	1.7
1892	606	46.5	–	–	532	40.8	165	12.7	1,303	1.9
1895	588	49.8	–	–	447	37.9	145	12.3	1,180	1.8
1900	569	51.6	15	1.4	402	36.5	116	10.5	1,102	1.6
1906	556	43.7	50	3.9	536	42.1	131	10.3	1,273	1.9
1910 (J)	594	45.2	78	5.9	511	38.9	132	10.0	1,315	2.0
1910 (D)	548	46.0	56	4.7	467	39.2	120	10.1	1,191	1.8
1918	445	27.4	361	22.2	421	26.0	396	24.4	1,623	2.3
1922	482	33.4	414	28.7	485	33.7	60	4.2	1,441	2.3
1923	536	37.1	427	29.5	457	31.6	26	1.8	1,446	2.4
1924	534	37.4	514	36.0	339	23.8	41	2.8	1,428	2.3
1929	590	34.1	569	32.9	513	29.6	58	3.4	1,730	2.8
1931	583	45.1	516[2]	39.9	117[3]	9.1	76	5.9	1,292	2.1
1935	583	43.2	552	41.0	161	11.9	52	3.9	1,348	2.2
1945	618	36.7	603	35.8	306	18.2	156	9.3	1,683	2.6
1950	619	33.2	617	33.0	475	25.4	157	8.4	1,868	3.0
1951	617	44.8	617	44.8	109	8.0	33	2.4	1,376	2.2
1955	624	44.3	620	44.0	110	7.8	55	3.9	1,409	2.2
1959	625	40.7	621	40.4	216	14.1	74	4.8	1,536	2.4
1964	630	35.9	628	35.7	365	20.8	134	7.6	1,757	2.8
1966	629	36.9	622	36.4	311	18.2	145	8.5	1,707	2.7
1970	628	34.2	625	34.0	332	18.1	252	13.7	1,837	2.9
1974 (F)	623	29.2	623	29.2	517	24.2	372	17.4	2,135	3.4
1974 (O)	622	27.6	623	27.7	619	27.5	388	17.2	2,252	3.5

[1] Including Liberal Unionists, 1886-1910 (D) and National, National Liberal and National Labour, 1931-45.

[2] Including 25 unendorsed.

[3] Including Independent Liberals.

Table 1.27 MEMBERS ELECTED AT GENERAL ELECTIONS (Summary)

Election	C[1]	%	Lab	%	L	%	Others	%	Total	Overall majority[2]	
1885	249	37.2	—	—	319†	47.6	102	15.2	670	None	
1886	393†	58.7	—	—	191	28.5	86	12.8	670	C	116
1892	314†	46.9	—	—	271	40.4	85	12.7	670	None	
1895	411	61.4	—	—	177†	26.4	82	12.2	670	C	153
1900	402	60.0	2	0.3	183†	27.3	83	12.4	670	C	135
1906	156†	23.3	29	4.3	399	59.6	86	12.8	670	L	129
1910 (J)	272†	40.6	40	6.0	274	40.9	84	12.5	670	None	
1910 (D)	272†	40.6	42	6.3	271	40.4	85	12.7	670	None	
1918	382†	54.0	57	8.1	163	23.0	105	14.9	707	Co	283[3]
1922	344	55.9	142	23.1	115†	18.7	14	2.3	615	C	74
1923	258	41.9	191	31.1	158†	25.7	8	1.3	615	None	
1924	412	67.0	151	24.5	40†	6.5	12	2.0	615	C	210
1929	260†	42.3	287	46.6	59	9.6	9	1.5	615	None	
1931	522†	84.9	52[4]	8.5	36[5]	5.8	5	0.8	615	Nat	492
1935	429†	69.8	154	25.0	21	3.4	11	1.8	615	Nat	242
1945	210†	32.8	393	61.4	12	1.9	25	3.9	640	Lab	147
1950	298†	47.7	315	50.4	9	1.4	3	0.5	625	Lab	6
1951	321	51.3	295	47.2	6	1.0	3	0.5	625	C	16
1955	345†	54.8	277	44.0	6	0.9	2	0.3	630	C	59
1959	365	57.9	258	41.0	6	0.9	1	0.2	630	C	99
1964	304†	48.3	317	50.3	9	1.4	0	—	630	Lab	5
1966	253	40.1	364†	57.8	12	1.9	1	0.2	630	Lab	97
1970	330	52.3	288†	45.7	6	1.0	6	1.0	630	C	31
1974 (F)	297†	46.8	301	47.4	14	2.2	23	3.6	635	None	
1974 (O)	277†	43.6	319	50.2	13	2.1	26	4.1	635	Lab	4

[1] Including Liberal Unionists, 1886-1910 (D) and National, National Liberal and National Labour, 1931-45.

[2] This figure represents the majority of the Government over all other parties combined. The Speaker has been excluded when calculating the majority.

[3] Theoretical majority. Seventy-three Sinn Fein members did not take their seats.

[4] Including 6 unendorsed.

[5] Of this total, four Liberals opposed the National Government and are counted with the Opposition in calculating the overall majority.

†Including the Speaker.

Table 1.28 VOTES CAST AT GENERAL ELECTIONS (Summary)

Election	C[1]	%	Lab	%	L[2]	%	Others	%	Total
1885	2,020,927	43.5	—	—	2,199,998	47.4	417,310	9.1	4,638,235
1886	1,520,886	51.4	—	—	1,353,581	45.0	99,696	3.6	2,974,163
1892	2,159,150	47.0	—	—	2,088,019	45.1	351,150	7.9	4,598,319
1895	1,894,772	49.1	—	—	1,765,266	45.7	206,244	5.2	3,866,282
1900	1,767,958	50.3	62,698	1.3	1,572,323	45.0	120,503	3.4	3,523,482
1906	2,422,071	43.4	321,663	4.8	2,751,057	49.4	131,300	2.4	5,626,091
1910 (J)	3,104,407	46.8	505,657	7.0	2,866,157	43.5	191,179	2.7	6,667,400
1910 (D)	2,420,169	46.6	371,802	6.4	2,293,869	44.2	149,398	2.8	5,235,238
1918	4,144,192	38.6	2,245,777	20.8	2,785,374	25.6	1,611,475	15.0	10,786,818
1922	5,502,298	38.5	4,237,349	29.7	4,139,460	28.8	513,223	3.0	14,392,330
1923	5,514,541	38.0	4,439,780	30.7	4,301,481	29.7	291,893	1.6	14,547,695
1924	7,854,523	46.8	5,489,087	33.3	2,928,737	17.8	367,932	2.1	16,640,279
1929	8,656,225	38.1	8,370,417	37.1	5,308,738	23.6	312,995	1.2	22,648,375
1931	13,156,790	60.7	6,649,630[3]	30.8	1,476,123	7.0	373,830	1.5	21,656,373
1935	11,755,654	53.3	8,325,491	38.1	1,443,093	6.8	472,816	1.8	21,997,054
1945	9,972,010	39.6	11,967,746	48.0	2,252,430	9.0	903,009	3.4	25,095,195
1950	12,492,404	43.5	13,266,176	46.1	2,621,487	9.1	391,057	1.3	28,771,124
1951	13,718,199	48.0	13,948,883	48.8	730,546	2.6	198,966	0.6	28,596,594
1955	13,310,891	49.7	12,405,254	46.4	722,402	2.7	321,182	1.2	26,759,729
1959	13,750,875	49.3	12,216,172	43.9	1,640,760	5.9	254,845	0.9	27,862,652
1964	12,002,642	43.4	12,205,808	44.1	3,099,283	11.2	349,415	1.3	27,657,148
1966	11,418,455	41.9	13,096,629	48.1	2,327,457	8.5	422,206	1.5	27,264,747
1970	13,145,123	46.4	12,208,758	43.1	2,117,035	7.5	873,882	3.0	28,344,798
1974 (F)	11,872,180	37.9	11,645,616	37.2	6,059,519	19.3	1,762,847	5.6	31,340,162
1974 (O)	10,462,565	35.8	11,457,079	39.2	5,346,704	18.3	1,922,756	6.7	29,189,104

[1] Including Liberal Unionists, 1886-1910 (D) and National, National Liberal and National Labour, 1931-45.

[2] Including both Liberal and National Liberal candidates in 1922 and Independent Liberals in 1931.

[3] Including 324,893 (4.9%) votes cast for 25 unendorsed candidates (see Table 1.14, footnote[3]).

Table 1.29 **PARTY VOTES AS PERCENTAGES OF ELECTORATE 1950—1974**

Party	1950	1951	1955	1959	1964	1966	1970	1974(F)	1974(O)
Conservative	36.5	39.6	38.2	38.9	33.5	31.7	33.4	29.9	26.1
Labour	38.7	40.3	35.6	34.5	34.0	36.4	31.0	29.3	28.6
Liberal	7.6	2.1	2.1	4.6	8.6	6.5	5.4	15.2	13.3
Others	1.1	0.6	0.9	0.7	1.0	1.2	2.2	4.4	4.8
Non-voters	16.1	17.4	23.2	21.3	22.9	24.2	28.0	21.2	27.2

Table 1.30 **CONSERVATIVE AND LABOUR VOTES AS PERCENTAGES OF TWO-PARTY VOTES 1950—1974**

Party	1950	1951	1955	1959	1964	1966	1970	1974(F)	1974(O)
Conservaitve	48.5	49.6	51.8	53.0	49.6	46.6	51.8	50.5	47.7
Labour	51.5	50.4	48.2	47.0	50.4	53.4	48.2	49.5	52.3

Table 1.31 **CONSERVATIVE, LABOUR AND LIBERAL VOTES AS PERCENTAGES OF THREE-PARTY VOTES 1950—1974**

Party	1950	1951	1955	1959	1964	1966	1970	1974(F)	1974(O)
Conservative	44.0	48.3	50.4	49.8	44.0	42.5	47.9	40.1	38.4
Labour	46.8	49.1	46.9	44.3	44.7	48.8	44.4	39.4	42.0
Liberal	9.2	2.6	2.7	5.9	11.3	8.7	7.7	20.5	19.6

Table 1.32 OVERALL SWING TO CONSERVATIVES AT GENERAL ELECTIONS

Although the usefulness of swing figures prior to the General Election of 1950 is extremely limited due in part to the varying number of seats contested by the main parties, the following table shows the overall swing from Labour to Conservative[1] in voting between elections. A separate figure is not given for Northern Ireland (where a conventional calculation of swing would be misleading) and the votes in University seats have been excluded except in the United Kingdom column.

Election	England	Wales	Scotland	United Kingdom
1922	− 3.6	0.0	− 8.5	− 4.5
1923	− 1.3	− 0.7	1.4	− 0.7
1924	2.3	4.3	2.0	3.1
1929	− 6.4	− 4.8	− 3.1	− 6.2
1931	15.6	4.5	14.6	14.4
1935	− 8.4	0.5	− 4.8	− 7.2
1945	− 12.1	− 11.4	− 9.7	− 11.8
1950	2.9	2.0	2.5	2.9
1951	1.2	0.5	1.0	0.9
1955	1.8	0.9	1.3	2.0
1959	1.3	1.9	− 1.4	1.0
1964	− 2.8	− 2.3	− 4.3	− 3.0
1966	− 2.9	− 2.1	− 2.0	− 2.7
1970	5.1	4.4	2.8	4.7
1974 (F)	− 1.2	1.5	1.4	− 1.3
1974 (O)	− 1.9	− 2.4	− 4.0	− 2.1

[1] Including National, National Liberal and National Labour, 1931—45.

Table 1.33 REPRESENTATION OF THE COUNTIES 1950—1974

The following table shows the party representation by "old" counties (including both borough and county constituencies) after each General Election since 1950.

In April 1974, England and Wales were divided into 53 new administrative counties and a year later Scotland was divided into 9 administrative regions. Until the next revision of constituency boundaries takes place in the early 1980's, many of the existing constituencies will have parts in several of the new counties and regions and this precludes the compiling of an analysis of seats based on the new administrative units.

When using this table it should be noted that substantial boundary changes took place at the General Elections of 1955 and February 1974, see Table 11.11.

ENGLAND	1950	1951	1955	1959	1964	1966	1970	1974(F)	1974(O)
C	253	271	293	315	262	219	292	268	253
Lab	251	233	216	193	246	286	217	237	255
L	2	2	2	3	3	6	2	9	8
Others	0	0	0	0	0	0	0	2	0
Total	506	506	511	511	511	511	511	516	516
BEDFORDSHIRE									
C	3	4	4	4	3	1	4	3	3
Lab	1	0	0	0	1	3	0	2	2
BERKSHIRE									
C	4	5	4	5	5	4	5	6	6
Lab	2	1	1	0	0	1	0	0	0
BUCKINGHAMSHIRE									
C	2	4	4	4	4	3	4	5	5
Lab	3	1	1	1	1	2	1	1	1
CAMBRIDGESHIRE (& ISLE OF ELY)									
C	3	3	3	3	3	2	3	2	2
Lab	0	0	0	0	0	1	0	0	0
L	0	0	0	0	0	0	0	1	1
CHESHIRE									
C	12	12	13	13	11	9	12	10	11
Lab	3	3	3	3	5	6	4	6	6
L	0	0	0	0	0	1	0	1	0
CORNWALL									
C	4	4	4	4	3	2	4	3	3
Lab	1	1	1	1	1	1	0	0	0
L	0	0	0	0	1	2	1	2	2
CUMBERLAND									
C	1	1	2	2	1	1	1	1	1
Lab	3	3	2	2	3	3	3	3	3
DERBYSHIRE									
C	2	2	2	3	2	1	4	3	3
Lab	8	8	8	7	8	9	6	7	7
DEVON									
C	8	9	10	9	9	7	8	8	8
Lab	2	1	0	0	0	2	1	1	1
L	0	0	0	1	1	1	1	1	1
DORSET									
C	4	4	4	4	4	4	4	4	4
DURHAM									
C	0	1	2	3	0	0	0	0	0
Lab	18	17	16	15	18	18	18	16	16

REPRESENTATION OF THE COUNTIES 1950–1974 (Cont.)

	1950	1951	1955	1959	1964	1966	1970	1974(F)	1974(O)
ESSEX									
C	12	12	16	16	15	11	16	11	11
Lab	12	12	10	10	11	15	10	3	3
GLOUCESTERSHIRE									
C	5	5	5	7	7	5	8	7	6
Lab	7	7	7	5	5	7	4	5	6
HAMPSHIRE (& ISLE OF WIGHT)									
C	12	12	14	14	14	12	13	14	13
Lab	2	2	1	1	1	3	2	2	3
L	0	0	0	0	0	0	0	1	1
HEREFORDSHIRE									
C	2	2	2	2	2	2	2	2	2
HERTFORDSHIRE									
C	6	6	8	8	6	6	6	7	5
Lab	1	1	0	0	2	2	2	2	4
HUNTINGDON (& PETERBOROUGH[1])									
C	1	1	1	1	1	1	1	2	1
Lab	0	0	0	0	0	0	0	0	1
KENT									
C	14	14	15	16	12	11	18	13	12
Lab	4	4	4	3	6	7	1	2	3
L	0	0	0	0	1	1	0	0	0
LANCASHIRE									
C	25	29	30	28	18	14	25	17	13
Lab	39	34	31	33	44	48	37	42	46
L	0	1	1	1	0	0	0	1	1
LEICESTERSHIRE									
C	3	3	3	3	3	3	5	5	4
Lab	5	5	5	5	5	5	3	3	4
LINCOLNSHIRE									
C	6	6	6	6	6	6	6	6	6
Lab	3	3	3	3	3	3	3	2	3
Others	0	0	0	0	0	0	0	1	0
LONDON[2]									
C	12	14	15	18	10	6	9	42	41
Lab	31	29	27	24	32	36	33	50	51
MIDDLESEX									
C	17	17	18	21	18	15	17	—	—
Lab	11	11	11	8	11	14	12	—	—
NORFOLK									
C	3	6	5	5	4	3	7	5	5
Lab	5	2	3	3	4	5	1	2	2
NORTHAMPTONSHIRE									
C	2	2	2	3	2	2	3	3	3
Lab	3	3	3	2	3	3	2	2	2
NORTHUMBERLAND									
C	4	4	4	5	4	4	4	3	3
Lab	6	6	6	5	6	6	6	5	6
L	0	0	0	0	0	0	0	1	1
Others	0	0	0	0	0	0	0	1	0
NOTTINGHAMSHIRE									
C	2	2	4	5	3	1	3	3	3
Lab	8	8	6	5	7	9	7	7	7

REPRESENTATION OF THE COUNTIES 1950—1974 (Cont.)

	1950	1951	1955	1959	1964	1966	1970	1974(F)	1974(O)
OXFORDSHIRE									
C	3	3	3	3	3	2	3	4	3
Lab	0	0	·0	0	0	1	0	0	1
SHROPSHIRE									
C	3	3	4	4	4	3	4	3	3
Lab	1	1	0	0	0	1	0	1	1
SOMERSET									
C	7	7	7	7	7	7	7	7	7
STAFFORDSHIRE									
C	3	3	4	5	6	5	8	6	5
Lab	15	15	15	14	13	14	11	14	15
SUFFOLK									
C	2	3	3	4	4	4	5	5	4
Lab	2	2	2	1	1	1	0	0	1
L	1	0	0	0	0	0	0	0	0
SURREY									
C	19	19	20	20	20	19	20	11	11
Lab	0	0	0	0	0	1	0	0	0
SUSSEX									
C	11	11	12	12	11	11	12	14	14
Lab	0	0	0	0	1	1	0	0	0
WARWICKSHIRE									
C	8	8	8	14	10	8	11	7	6
Lab	14	14	15	9	13	15	12	16	17
WESTMORLAND									
C	1	1	1	1	1	1	1	1	1
WILTSHIRE									
C	4	4	4	4	4	4	4	4	4
Lab	1	1	1	1	1	1	1	1	1
WORCESTERSHIRE									
C	4	4	4	4	4	4	5	5	5
Lab	2	2	2	2	2	2	1	2	2
YORKSHIRE									
C	19	21	23	25	18	15	20	16	16
Lab	38	36	32	30	38	40	36	40	40
L	1	1	1	1	0	1	0	1	1
WALES AND MONMOUTHSHIRE									
C	4	6	6	7	6	3	7	8	8
Lab	27	27	27	27	28	32	27	24	23
L	5	3	3	2	2	1	1	2	2
PC	0	0	0	0	0	0	0	2	3
Others	0	0	0	0	0	0	1	0	0
Total	36	36	36	36	36	36	36	36	36
ANGLESEY									
Lab	0	1	1	1	1	1	1	1	1
L	1	0	0	0	0	0	0	0	0
BRECONSHIRE & RADNORSHIRE									
Lab	1	1	1	1	1	1	1	1	1
CAERNARVONSHIRE									
C	0	1	1	1	1	0	1	1	1
Lab	2	1	1	1	1	2	1	0	0
PC	0	0	0	0	0	0	0	1	1

REPRESENTATION OF THE COUNTIES 1950–1974 (Cont.)

	1950	1951	1955	1959	1964	1966	1970	1974(F)	1974(O)
CARDIGANSHIRE									
Lab	0	0	0	0	0	1	1	0	0
L	1	1	1	1	1	0	0	1	1
CARMARTHENSHIRE									
Lab	1	1	1	2	2	2	2	2	1
L	1	1	1	0	0	0	0	0	0
PC	0	0	0	0	0	0	0	0	1
DENBIGHSHIRE									
C	1	1	1	1	1	1	1	1	1
Lab	1	1	1	1	1	1	1	1	1
FLINTSHIRE									
C	1	1	1	1	1	1	1	1	1
Lab	1	1	1	1	1	1	1	1	1
GLAMORGANSHIRE									
C	1	2	2	3	2	1	2	3	3
Lab	15	14	14	13	14	15	13	13	13
Others	0	0	0	0	0	0	1	0	0
MERIONETHSHIRE									
Lab	0	1	1	1	1	1	1	0	0
L	1	0	0	0	0	0	0	0	0
PC	0	0	0	0	0	0	0	1	1
MONMOUTHSHIRE									
C	1	1	1	1	1	0	1	1	1
Lab	5	5	5	5	5	6	5	5	5
MONTGOMERYSHIRE									
L	1	1	1	1	1	1	1	1	1
PEMBROKESHIRE									
C	0	0	0	0	0	0	1	1	1
Lab	1	1	1	1	1	1	0	0	0
SCOTLAND									
C	31	35	36	31	24	20	23	21	16
Lab	37	35	34	38	43	46	44	40	41
L	2	1	1	1	4	5	3	3	3
SNP	0	0	0	0	0	0	1	7	11
Others	1	0	0	1	0	0	0	0	0
Total	71	71	71	71	71	71	71	71	71
ABERDEENSHIRE									
C	3	3	3	3	3	1	3	2	2
Lab	1	1	1	1	1	2	1	1	1
L	0	0	0	0	0	1	0	0	0
SNP	0	0	0	0	0	0	0	1	1
ANGUS & KINCARDINESHIRE									
C	2	2	2	2	2	2	2	2	1
Lab	2	2	2	2	2	2	2	1	1
SNP	0	0	0	0	0	0	0	1	2
ARGYLL									
C	1	1	1	1	1	1	1	0	0
SNP	0	0	0	0	0	0	0	1	1
AYRSHIRE & BUTE									
C	2	2	3	2	2	2	2	2	2
Lab	3	3	2	3	3	3	3	3	3

REPRESENTATION OF THE COUNTIES 1950–1974 (Cont.)

	1950	1951	1955	1959	1964	1966	1970	1974(F)	1974(O)
BANFFSHIRE									
C	1	1	1	1	1	1	1	0	0
SNP	0	0	0	0	0	0	0	1	1
BERWICKSHIRE & EAST LOTHIAN									
C	0	1	1	1	1	0	0	1	0
Lab	1	0	0	0	0	1	1	0	1
CAITHNESS & SUTHERLAND									
C	1	1	1	0	0	0	0	0	0
Lab	0	0	0	0	0	1	1	1	1
L	0	0	0	0	1	0	0	0	0
Others	0	0	0	1	0	0	0	0	0
DUMFRIESSHIRE									
C	1	1	1	1	1	1	1	1	1
DUNBARTONSHIRE									
C	0	0	0	0	0	0	0	1	0
Lab	2	2	2	2	2	2	2	2	2
SNP	0	0	0	0	0	0	0	0	1
FIFE									
C	1	1	1	1	1	1	1	1	1
Lab	3	3	3	3	3	3	3	3	3
INVERNESS-SHIRE & ROSS & CROMARTY									
C	1	2	2	2	0	0	1	1	1
Lab	1	1	1	1	1	1	0	0	0
L	0	0	0	0	2	2	1	1	1
SNP	0	0	0	0	0	0	1	1	1
Others	1	0	0	0	0	0	0	0	0
KIRKCUDBRIGHTSHIRE & WIGTOWNSHIRE									
C	1	1	1	1	1	1	1	1	0
SNP	0	0	0	0	0	0	0	0	1
LANARKSHIRE									
C	8	9	9	6	2	2	2	2	2
Lab	14	13	13	16	20	20	20	19	19
MIDLOTHIAN (& PEEBLESSHIRE[3])									
C	4	4	4	4	4	4	4	4	4
Lab	4	4	4	4	4	4	4	4	4
MORAY & NAIRNSHIRE									
C	1	1	1	1	1	1	1	0	0
SNP	0	0	0	0	0	0	0	1	1
ORKNEY & SHETLAND									
L	1	1	1	1	1	1	1	1	1
PERTHSHIRE & KINROSS-SHIRE									
C	2	2	2	2	2	2	2	2	1
SNP	0	0	0	0	0	0	0	0	1
RENFREWSHIRE									
C	2	2	2	2	1	1	1	1	1
Lab	2	2	2	2	3	3	3	3	3
ROXBURGHSHIRE, SELKIRKSHIRE (& PEEBLESSHIRE[4])									
C	0	1	1	1	1	0	0	0	0
L	1	0	0	0	0	1	1	1	1

REPRESENTATION OF THE COUNTIES 1950–1974 (Cont.)

	1950	1951	1955	1959	1964	1966	1970	1974(F)	1974(O)
STIRLINGSHIRE & CLACKMANNANSHIRE									
Lab	3	3	3	3	3	3	3	2	2
SNP	0	0	0	0	0	0	0	1	1
WESTLOTHIAN									
Lab	1	1	1	1	1	1	1	1	1
NORTHERN IRELAND									
C	10	9	10	12	12	11	8	–	–
UU	–	–	–	–	–	–	–	11	10
N	2	2	0	0	0	0	0	0	0
SF	0	0	2	0	0	0	0	0	0
SDLP	0	0	0	0	0	0	0	1	1
Others	0	1	0	0	0	1	4	0	1
Total	12	12	12	12	12	12	12	12	12
ANTRIM									
C	6	5	6	6	6	5	4	–	–
UU	–	–	–	–	–	–	–	5	5
SDLP	0	0	0	0	0	0	0	1	1
Others	0	1	0	0	0	1	2	0	0
ARMAGH									
C	1	1	1	1	1	1	1	–	–
UU	–	–	–	–	–	–	–	1	1
DOWN									
C	2	2	2	2	2	2	2	–	–
UU	–	–	–	–	–	–	–	2	2
FERMANAGH & TYRONE									
C	0	0	0	2	2	2	0	–	–
UU	–	–	–	–	–	–	–	2	1
N	2	2	0	0	0	0	0	0	0
SF	0	0	2	0	0	0	0	0	0
Others	0	0	0	0	0	0	2	0	1
LONDONDERRY									
C	1	1	1	1	1	1	1	–	–
UU	–	–	–	–	–	–	–	1	1
UNITED KINGDOM									
C	298	321	345	365	304	253	330	297	277
Lab	315	295	277	258	317	364	288	301	319
L	9	6	6	6	9	12	6	14	13
N	2	2	0	0	0	0	0	0	0
PC	0	0	0	0	0	0	0	2	3
SF	0	0	2	0	0	0	0	0	0
SDLP	0	0	0	0	0	0	0	1	1
SNP	0	0	0	0	0	0	1	7	11
UU	–	–	–	–	–	–	–	11	10
Others	1	1	0	1	0	1	5	2	1
Total	625	625	630	630	630	630	630	635	635

[1] From 1974 only. Previously included in Northamptonshire.

[2] The area of the London County Council and from 1974 the Greater London Council.

[3] Until 1955 only. Subsequently included in Roxburghshire and Selkirkshire.

[4] From 1955 only. Previously included in Midlothian.

Table 1.34 REPRESENTATION OF THE MAJOR TOWNS 1950–1974

The following table shows the party representation in the major towns after each General Election since 1950.

When using this table it should be noted that substantial boundary changes took place at the General Elections of 1955 and February 1974, see Table 11.11.

	1950	1951	1955	1959	1964	1966	1970	1974(F)	1974(O)
ENGLAND									
BIRMINGHAM									
C	4	4	4	7	5	4	6	3	2
Lab	9	9	9	6	8	9	7	9	10
BRADFORD									
C	1	1	2	2	1	0	1	0	0
Lab	3	3	2	2	3	4	3	3	3
BRISTOL									
C	2	2	1	3	3	1	3	2	1
Lab	4	4	5	3	3	5	3	3	4
COVENTRY									
C	0	0	0	1	0	0	0	0	0
Lab	3	3	3	2	3	3	3	4	4
CROYDON[1]									
C	3	3	3	3	3	2	3	–	–
Lab	0	0	0	0	0	1	0	–	–
HARROW[1]									
C	3	3	3	3	3	2	3	–	–
Lab	0	0	0	0	0	1	0	–	–
KINGSTON UPON HULL									
C	2	2	1	1	0	0	0	0	0
Lab	2	2	2	2	3	3	3	3	3
LEEDS									
C	2	2	2	2	2	2	2	2	2
Lab	5	5	4	4	4	4	4	4	4
LEICESTER									
C	1	1	1	1	1	1	2	1	0
Lab	3	3	3	3	3	3	2	2	3
LIVERPOOL									
C	5	5	6	6	2	2	2	1	1
Lab	4	4	3	3	7	7	7	7	7
LONDON[2]									
C	12	14	15	18	10	6	9	6	6
Lab	31	29	27	24	32	36	33	29	29
MANCHESTER									
C	3	4	4	4	2	2	2	1	1
Lab	6	5	5	5	7	7	7	7	7
NEWCASTLE UPON TYNE									
C	1	1	1	2	1	1	1	1	1
Lab	3	3	3	2	3	3	3	3	3
NOTTINGHAM									
C	0	0	2	3	1	0	1	0	0
Lab	4	4	2	1	3	4	3	3	3
PLYMOUTH									
C	0	1	2	2	2	1	1	2	2
Lab	2	1	0	0	0	1	1	1	1

REPRESENTATION OF THE MAJOR TOWNS 1950–1974 (Cont.)

	1950	1951	1955	1959	1964	1966	1970	1974(F)	1974(O)
PORTSMOUTH									
C	3	3	3	3	3	2	2	1	1
Lab	0	0	0	0	0	1	1	1	1
SHEFFIELD									
C	2	2	2	2	2	1	2	1	1
Lab	5	5	4	4	4	5	4	5	5
STOKE-ON-TRENT									
Lab	3	3	3	3	3	3	3	3	3
TEESSIDE[3]									
Lab	–	–	–	–	–	–	–	4	4
WOLVERHAMPTON									
C	1	1	1	1	1	1	1	1	1
Lab	1	1	1	1	1	1	1	2	2
WALES									
CARDIFF									
C	1	1	1	1	1	0	1	2	2
Lab	2	2	2	2	2	3	2	2	2
SCOTLAND									
EDINBURGH									
C	4	4	4	4	4	4	4	4	4
Lab	3	3	3	3	3	3	3	3	3
GLASGOW									
C	7	7	7	5	2	2	2	2	2
Lab	8	8	8	10	13	13	12	11	11
NORTHERN IRELAND									
BELFAST									
C	4	3	4	4	4	3	3	–	–
UU	–	–	–	–	–	–	–	3	3
SDLP	0	0	0	0	0	0	0	1	1
Others	0	1	0	0	0	1	1	0	0

[1] Now within the area of the Greater London Council.

[2] Prior to 1974, the 28 boroughs within the area of the London County Council plus the City of London. Since 1974, the 12 Inner London Boroughs within the area of the Great London Council plus the City of London.

[3] An amalgamation of Middlesbrough, Redcar, Stockton-on-Tees and Thornaby-on-Tees.

Table 2.01 CONTESTED BY-ELECTIONS 1885—1945

The following table lists all contested by-elections and the party designation of the successful candidate. Where a seat changed hands this is indicated by an asterisk and the designation of the party gaining the seat and of the party losing the seat is given. For example (Lab/C) indicates a Labour gain from Conservative.

GENERAL ELECTION 1885—GENERAL ELECTION 1886

Date	1886
27/1	Croydon (C)
29/1	*Edinburgh, South (L/Ind L)
1/2	Armagh, Mid (C)
11/2	Galway Borough (N)
11/2	Hackney, South (L)
11/2	Monaghan, North
12/2	Newcastle upon Tyne (L)
13/2	Great Grimsby (L)
27/2	Cardiff Boroughs (L)
2/3	Flintshire (L)
26/3	Cheshire, Altrincham (C)
6/4	Barrow-in-Furness (L)
14/4	*Ipswich (two seats) (C/L & C/L)
21/4	Bradford, Central (L)

GENERAL ELECTION 1886—GENERAL ELECTION 1892

Date	1886
12/8	Tower Hamlets, St. George (C)
16/8	Lancashire, Newton (C)
20/8	Lancashire, Blackpool (C)
20/8	Leith Burghs (L)
20/8	Staffordshire, Burton (L)
25/8	King's Lynn (C)
23/12	Middlesex, Brentford (C)

	1887
26/1	Liverpool, Exchange (L)
2/2	Donegal, South (N)
9/2	St. George, Hanover Square (LU/C)
11/2	Antrim, North (C)
19/2	*Burnley (L/LU)
24/3	Derbyshire, Ilkeston (L)
23/4	Taunton (C)
18/5	Cornwall, St. Austell (L)
1/7	*Lincolnshire, Spalding (L/C)
7/7	Dublin University (C)
8/7	Paddington, North (C)
9/7	*Coventry (L/C)
18/7	Hampshire, Basingstoke (C)
19/7	Lambeth, Brixton (C)
19/7	Middlesex, Hornsey (C)
29/7	Gloucestershire, Forest of Dean (L)
2/8	Glasgow, Bridgeton (L)
13/8	*Cheshire, Northwich (L/LU)
30/8	Huntingdonshire, Ramsey (C)
1/12	Camberwell, Dulwich (C)

	1888
5/1	Winchester (C)
16/2	Dundee (L)
17/2	Southwark, West (L)
18/2	*Edinburgh, West (L/LU)[1]
23/2	*Yorkshire, Doncaster (LU/L)
29/2	Deptford (C)
27/3	Glamorganshire, Gower (L)
27/4	Lanarkshire, Mid (L)
12/5	Dublin, St. Stephen's Green (N)
23/5	*Southampton (L/C)
15/6	*Ayr Burghs (L/LU)
29/6	Kent, Isle of Thanet (C)
26/10	*Merthyr Tydfil (Ind L/L)
16/11	Dewsbury (L)

Date	
29/11	Finsbury, Holborn (C)
14/12	Maidstone (C)
18/12	Colchester (C)
21/12	Stockton-on-Tees (L)

	1889
18/1	*Lanarkshire, Govan (L/C)
19/2	Perthshire, Eastern (L)
11/3	Yorkshire, Barnsley (L)
15/3	*Lambeth, Kennington (L/C)
22/3	Lancashire, Gorton (L)
30/3	Middlesex, Enfield (C)
15/4	Birmingham, Central (LU)
16/4	*Rochester (L/C)
5/7	Fife, Western (L)
17/7	Carmarthenshire, Western (L)
19/7	Marylebone, East (C)
26/9	Lincolnshire, Sleaford (C)
7/10	*Peterborough (L/LU)
8/10	Elginshire and Nairnshire (L)
11/10	*Buckinghamshire, Buckingham (L/C)
25/10	Brighton (C)

	1890
11/2	Lanarkshire, Partick (LU)
4/3	*St. Pancras, North (L/C)
7/3	Lincolnshire, Stamford (C)
14/3	Stoke-on-Trent (L)
25/3	*Ayr Burghs (C/L)
2/4	Windsor (C)
10/4	*Caernarvon Boroughs (L/C)
9/5	Bristol, East (L)
2/7	*Barrow-in-Furness (L/LU)
17/7	Durham, Mid (L-Lab)
22/10	*Lancashire, Eccles (L/C)
15/12	Nottinghamshire, Bassetlaw (C)
22/12	Kilkenny, North (N)

	1891
21/1	*The Hartlepools (L/LU)
12/2	Northampton (L)
20/3	Aston Manor (C)
2/4	Sligo, North (N)
21/4	Oxfordshire, Woodstock (C/LU)
24/4	Whitehaven (C)
5/5	*Suffolk, Stowmarket (L/C)
7/5	Dorset, Southern (L)
8/5	*Leicestershire, Harborough (L/C)
28/5	Buckinghamshire, Buckingham (L)
1/6	Paisley (L)
7/7	Carlow (N)
23/7	*Cambridgeshire, Wisbech (L/C)
12/8	Walsall (L)
26/8	Lewisham (C)
8/10	Manchester, North-East (C)
9/10	Bute (C)
27/10	Strand (C)
6/11	Cork City (N)
13/11	*Devon, South Molton (L/LU)
27/11	Dorset, Eastern (C)
23/12	Waterford Borough (N)

[1] Resigned seat on joining the Liberal Party but re-elected at by-election.

CONTESTED BY-ELECTIONS 1885–1945 (Cont.)

GENERAL ELECTION 1886–GENERAL ELECTION 1892

Date	1892
23/1	*Lancashire, Rossendale (L/LU)
3/3	Surrey, Chertsey (C)
4/3	Derbyshire, Southern (L)
9/3	Belfast, East (C)
11/3	Kirkcaldy Burghs (L)
11/5	Hackney, North (C)

GENERAL ELECTION 1892–GENERAL ELECTION 1895

Date	1892
24/8	Derby (L)
25/8	Newcastle upon Tyne (L)
22/9	Leeds, South (L)
29/9	Bedfordshire, Luton (L)
13/10	*Gloucestershire, Cirencester (C/L)
10/12	Aberdeenshire, Eastern (L)

	1893
10/1	Liverpool, West Derby (C)
4/2	*Huddersfield (C/L)
6/2	Burnley (L)
9/2	Halifax (L)
9/2	*Walsall (L/C)
13/2	*Pontefract (L/C)
17/2	*Northumberland, Hexham (L/C)
18/2	Meath, South (N)
21/2	Meath, North (N)
22/2	Stockport (C)
23/2	*Gloucestershire, Cirencester (L/C)
24/2	Gateshead (L)
24/2	Sussex, Horsham (C)
6/3	*Great Grimsby (LU/L)
15/3	Banffshire (L)
15/6	*Linlithgowshire (C/L)
26/6	Pontefract (L)
15/8	*Hereford (C/L)
21/12	Lancashire, Accrington (L)

	1894
11/1	Lincolnshire, Horncastle (C)
26/3	Leith Burghs (L)
27/3	Hawick Burghs (L)
29/3	Berwickshire (L)
29/3	Montgomeryshire (L)
2/4	Essex, Romford (C)
3/4	Cambridgeshire, Wisbech (L)
5/4	Lanarkshire, Mid (L)
7/5	Hackney, South (L)
5/7	Sheffield, Attercliffe (L)
29/8	Leicester (two seats) (L-Lab/L & L)
17/10	Birkenhead (C)
17/11	*Forfarshire (C/L)
7/12	*Lincolnshire, Brigg (C/L)

	1895
22/1	Worcestershire, Evesham (C)
19/2	*Colchester (L/C)
21/3	Bristol, East (L)
20/4	Oxford (C)
23/4	Norfolk, Mid (LU)
26/4	Wicklow, East (N)
30/4	Leeds, East (L)
14/5	Dorset, Western (C)
14/5	*Newington, Walworth (C/L)
23/5	Warwick and Leamington (LU)
29/5	Edinburgh, West (LU)
13/6	*Inverness-shire (C/L-Crf)
27/6	Cork City (N)

GENERAL ELECTION 1895–GENERAL ELECTION 1900

Date	1895
2/9	Dublin, St. Stephen's Green (LU)
4/9	Kerry, South (N)
11/9	Limerick Borough (N)
2/12	Dublin University (LU)

	1896
22/1	Belfast, North (C)
28/1	St. Pancras, South (LU)
30/1	Lambeth, Brixton (C)
22/2	Montrose Burghs (L)
22/2	*Southampton (L/C)
26/2	Staffordshire, Lichfield (L)
27/3	Kerry, East (N)
19/3	Louth, South (N)
1/5	Aberdeen, North (L)
2/6	*Somerset, Frome (L/C)
2/6	*Wick Burghs (L/LU)
10/11	Bradford, East (C)

	1897
12/1	Yorkshire, Cleveland (L)
27/1	Salisbury (C)
30/1	Forfarshire (L)
1/2	Essex, Romford (C)
3/2	*Essex, Walthamstow (L-Lab/C)
15/2	Glasgow, Bridgeton (L)
18/2	Surrey, Chertsey (C)
3/3	Halifax (L)
8/6	Hampshire, Petersfield (C)
6/8	Sheffield, Brightside (L-Lab/L)
28/9	Denbighshire, Eastern (L)
28/10	Yorkshire, Barnsley (L)
4/11	*Lancashire, Middleton (L/C)
10/11	Liverpool, Exchange (LU)
15/11	Deptford (C)

	1898
12/1	Plymouth (L)
13/1	*York (C/L)
21/1	Dublin, St. Stephen's Green (C)
3/2	*Durham, South-Eastern (L/LU)
3/2	Wolverhampton, South (LU)
15/2	Pembrokeshire (L)
24/2	*Wiltshire, Cricklade (L/LU)
9/3	*Tower Hamlets, Stepney (L-Lab/C)
26/3	Maidstone (C)
30/3	Berkshire, Wokingham (C)
10/5	Staffordshire, Western (LU)
12/5	*Norfolk, Southern (L/LU)
22/6	Hertfordshire, Hertford (C)
30/6	*Durham (LU/L)
13/7	Gravesend (C)
25/7	*Reading (L/C)
2/8	*Great Grimsby (LU/L) [1]
3/8	Cornwall, Launceston (L)
24/8	*Lancashire, Southport (L/C)
7/9	Down, North (C)
17/9	Darlington (LU)
1/11	Fermanagh, North (C)

	1899
16/2	Londonderry City (N)
21/2	Lanarkshire, North-Western (L)
23/2	Yorkshire, Rotherham (L)
1/3	Hythe (C)
8/3	Yorkshire, Elland (L)
16/3	Norfolk, Northern (L)
5/4	Middlesex, Harrow (C)

[1] Resigned seat on joining the Liberal Unionist Party but re-elected at by-election.

CONTESTED BY-ELECTIONS 1885—1945 (Cont.)

Date	1899 (cont.)
30/5	Lancashire, Southport (L)
19/6	*Edinburgh, South (L/LU)
23/6	Edinburgh, East (L)
5/7	*Yorkshire, Osgoldcross (Ind L/L)[1]
6/7	*Oldham (two seats) (L/C & L/C)
12/7	St. Pancras, East (C)
27/10	Tower Hamlets, Bow and Bromley (C)
6/11	Exeter (C)
20/12	Clackmannanshire and Kinross-shire (L)

Date	1900
6/2	London University (LU)
6/2	York (C)
12/2	Armagh, Mid (C)
13/2	Lancashire, Rossendale (L)
16/2	Nottinghamshire, Newark (C)
26/2	Mayo, South (N)
3/5	Portsmouth (L)
23/5	Isle of Wight (C)
25/5	Manchester, South (LU)

GENERAL ELECTION 1900—GENERAL ELECTION 1906

Date	1900
21/12	Lancashire, Blackpool (C)

	1901
26/2	Lancashire, Stretford (C)
1/3	Maidstone (L)
7/5	Monmouth Boroughs (C)
24/5	Shropshire, Oswestry (C)
31/5	Essex, Saffron Walden (L)
25/6	Warwickshire, Stratford-on-Avon (C)
26/8	Hampshire, Andover (C)
26/9	*Lanarkshire, North-Eastern (LU/L)
21/11	*Galway Borough (N/C)

	1902
24/1	Hampstead (C)
28/1	Dewsbury (L)
3/2	Sheffield, Ecclesall (C)
5/2	*Down, East (Ind/C)
25/3	Wakefield (C/LU)
10/5	*Bury (L/C)
29/7	*Leeds, North (L/C)
18/8	*Belfast, South (Ind/C)
21/8	Kent, Sevenoaks (C)
22/10	*Devonport (C/L)
5/11	Yorkshire, Cleveland (L)
6/11	Liverpool, East Toxteth (C)
18/11	*Orkney and Shetland (Ind L/LU)[2]

	1903
2/1	*Cambridgeshire, Newmarket (L/C)
20/1	Liverpool, West Derby (C)
5/2	Antrim, South (C)
28/2	Dublin University (C)
11/3	*Woolwich (Lab/C)
17/3	*Sussex, Rye (L/C)
20/3	*Fermanagh, North (Ind/C)
26/3	Surrey, Chertsey (C)
8/4	Cornwall, Camborne (L)
14/5	Preston (C)
24/7	*Durham, Barnard Castle (Lab/L)
26/8	*Argyll (L/C)
17/9	*St. Andrews Burghs (L/LU)
23/9	Rochester (C)

Date	
9/10	Meath, South (N)
23/10	Belfast, West (LU)
23/10	Warwick and Leamington (LU)
4/11	Lancashire, Chorley (C)
15/12	Camberwell, Dulwich (C)
15/12	Lewisham (C)
22/12	Shropshire, Ludlow (LU)

	1904
7/1	Devon, Ashburton (L)
15/1	*Norwich (L/C)
20/1	Gateshead (L-Lab/L)
30/1	*Ayr Burghs (L/C)
12/2	*Hertfordshire, St. Albans (L/C)
26/2	Birmingham, South (LU)
1/3	Yorkshire, Normanton (L-Lab)
16/3	*Dorset, Eastern (L/C)
21/3	Dublin, St. Stephen's Green (N)
17/6	Leicestershire, Harborough (L)
20/6	*Devonport (L/C)
2/7	Yorkshire, Sowerby (L)
6/7	Surrey, Chertsey (C)
26/7	*Shropshire, Oswestry (L/C)
6/8	Reading (L)
10/8	*Lanarkshire, North-Eastern (L/LU)
7/10	Kent, Isle of Thanet (C)
3/11	Monmouthshire, Western (L-Lab/L)
11/11	Sussex, Horsham (C)

	1905
7/1	*Stalybridge (L/C)
12/1	Tower Hamlets, Mile End (LU/C)
26/1	*Dorset, Northern (L/C)
22/2	Liverpool, Everton (C)
2/3	*Westmorland, Appleby (L/LU)
3/3	*Bute (L/C)
5/4	*Brighton (L/C)
1/6	*Yorkshire, Whitby (L/C)
2/6	Sussex, Chichester (C)
29/6	*Finsbury, East (L/C)
3/7	Staffordshire, Kingswinford (C)
10/7	Down, West (C)
14/7	Carlisle (L)
8/9	Elgin Burghs (L)
14/9	Belfast, North (C)
13/10	*Yorkshire, Barkston Ash (L/C)
26/10	Hampstead (C)
6/12	Hampshire, New Forest (C)

GENERAL ELECTION 1906—GENERAL ELECTION 1910(J)

Date	1906
27/2	City of London (C)
12/3	Hampshire, Basingstoke (C)
30/3	Leicester (L/L-Lab)
6/4	Suffolk, Eye (L)
15/5	Camberwell, Dulwich (C)
24/7	Cornwall, Bodmin (L)
25/7	Tyrone, East (N)
3/8	*Cumberland, Cockermouth (C/L)
14/8	Denbighshire, Eastern (L)
3/11	Galway Borough (N)
16/11	Armagh, North (C)
28/11	Huddersfield (L)

[1] Resigned seat on leaving the Liberal Party but re-elected at by-election.
[2] Resigned seat on leaving the Liberal Unionist Party but re-elected at by-election.

CONTESTED BY-ELECTIONS 1885–1945 (Cont.)

Date	1907
30/1	Derbyshire, North-Eastern (L-Lab/L)
16/2	Banffshire (L)
20/2	Aberdeen, South (L)
26/2	*Lincolnshire, Brigg (C/L)
8/3	Tyrone, North (L)
27/3	Northumberland, Hexham (L)
17/4	Belfast, North (C)
10/5	Tower Hamlets, Stepney (C)
14/5	Surrey, Wimbledon (C)
11/6	Rutlandshire (C)
4/7	*Durham, Jarrow (Lab/L)
18/7	*Yorkshire, Colne Valley (Ind Lab/L)
31/7	Staffordshire, North-Western (L-Lab/L)
24/8	Bury St. Edmunds (C)
6/9	Down, West (C)
27/9	Liverpool, Kirkdale (C)
29/11	Kingston upon Hull, West (L)
	1908
17/1	*Devon, Ashburton (C/L)
31/1	*Herefordshire, Ross (LU/L)
7/2	Worcester (C)
13/2	Leeds, South (L)
21/2	Leitrim, North (N)
3/3	Hastings (C)
20/3	Down, West (C)
24/3	*Camberwell, Peckham (C/L)
23/4	Dewsbury (L)
24/4	*Manchester, North-West (C/L)
25/4	Kincardineshire (L)
5/5	Wolverhampton, East (L)
9/5	Dundee (L)
12/5	Montrose Burghs (L)
14/5	Shropshire, Newport (C)
22/5	Stirling Burghs (L)
20/6	*Yorkshire, Pudsey (C/L)
16/7	Pembrokeshire (L)
1/8	*Shoreditch, Haggerston (C/L-Lab)
25/9	*Newcastle upon Tyne (C/L)
1/12	Essex, Chelmsford (C)
	1909
23/2	Taunton (C)
27/2	Forfarshire (L)
2/3	*Glasgow, Central (C/L)
4/3	Edinburgh, South (L)
5/3	Hawick Burghs (L)
29/3	Croydon (C/LU)
2/4	Denbighshire, Eastern (L)
16/4	Edinburgh, East (L)
1/5	Cork City (Ind N)
4/5	*Sheffield, Attercliffe (Lab/L)
4/5	*Warwickshire, Stratford-on-Avon (C/L)
10/6	Limerick, East (N)
9/7	Yorkshire, Cleveland (L)
15/7	*Derbyshire, Mid (Lab/L)
20/7	Dumfries Burghs (L)
22/7	Derbyshire, High Peak (L)
28/10	*Southwark, Bermondsey (C/L)
5/11	Armagh, South (N)

GENERAL ELECTION 1910(J)–GENERAL ELECTION 1910(D)

	1910
1/3	Tower Hamlets, St. George (L)
7/3	Derbyshire, Ilkeston (L)
31/3	Glamorganshire, Mid (L)
29/4	Edinburgh, South (L)
30/4	Cheshire, Crewe (L)

Date	
20/6	The Hartlepools (L)
30/6	Dorset, Eastern (L)
20/7	Liverpool, Kirkdale (C)
27/10	South Shields (L)
1/11	Essex, Walthamstow (L)

GENERAL ELECTION 1910(D)–GENERAL ELECTION 1918

	1911
11/2	Cambridge University (C)
16/2	Lincolnshire, Horncastle (C)
22/2	Wiltshire, Westbury (L)
24/2	Gloucestershire, Forest of Dean (L)
9/3	Lanarkshire, North-Eastern (L)
27/3	Lancashire, Bootle (C)
19/4	Haddingtonshire (L)
28/4	*Cheltenham (C/L)
6/5	Devon, Barnstaple (L)
14/6	Ross and Cromarty (L)
5/7	Kingston upon Hull, Central (C)
6/7	Glasgow, Tradeston (L)
8/7	West Ham, North (L)
20/7	Bedfordshire, Luton (L)
21/7	Somerset, Wellington (C)
29/7	Bethnal Green, South-West (L)
2/8	Lancashire, Middleton (L)
26/9	Kilmarnock Burghs (L)
6/10	Tyrone, North (L)
27/10	Yorkshire, Keighley (L)
3/11	Bristol, East (L)
13/11	*Oldham (C/L)
21/11	*Somerset, Southern (C/L)
23/11	Hertfordshire, Hitchin (C)
20/12	*Ayrshire, Northern (C/L)
22/12	Lanarkshire, Govan (L)
	1912
24/1	Carmarthen Boroughs (L)
2/2	Edinburgh, East (L)
26/2	Glasgow, St. Rollox (L)
5/3	*Manchester, South (C/L)
19/4	Nottingham, East (C)
24/5	*Hackney, South (L/Ind L)
31/5	Norfolk, North-Western (L)
11/6	Hythe (C)
20/6	Yorkshire, Holmfirth (L)
1/7	Derbyshire, Ilkeston (L)
13/7	*Hanley (L/Lab)
26/7	*Cheshire, Crewe (C/L)
8/8	*Manchester, North-West (C/L)
22/8	Carmarthenshire, Eastern (L)
10/9	*Edinburghshire (C/L)
11/11	Taunton (C)
23/11	Bolton (L)
26/11	*Tower Hamlets, Bow and Bromley (C/Lab)
	1913
21/1	Flint Boroughs (L)
30/1	*Londonderry City (L/C)
19/2	Lancashire, Chorley (C)
18/3	Durham, Houghton-le-Spring (L)
18/3	Westmorland, Kendal (Ind C/C)
22/4	Shrewsbury (C)
30/4	Tower Hamlets, Whitechapel (L)
16/5	*Cambridgeshire, Newmarket (C/L)
28/5	Cheshire, Altrincham (C)
12/6	Wandsworth (C)
27/6	Leicester (L)
20/8	*Derbyshire, Chesterfield (L-Lab/Lab)

CONTESTED BY-ELECTIONS 1885—1945 (Cont.)

Date	1913 (cont.)
7/11	Linlithgowshire (L)
8/11	*Reading (C/L)
11/11	Yorkshire, Keighley (L)
8/12	Wick Burghs (L)
12/12	*Lanarkshire, Southern (C/L)

	1914
30/1	Durham, North-Western (L)
18/2	Buckinghamshire, Wycombe (C)
19/2	*Bethnal Green, South-West (C/L)
19/2	Tower Hamlets, Poplar (L)
26/2	*Leith Burghs (C/L)
12/5	Great Grimsby (C)
20/5	*Derbyshire, North-Eastern (C/Lab)
23/5	*Ipswich (C/L)
9/12	King's, Tullamore (Ind N/N)

	1915
11/6	Dublin, College Green (N)
17/6	Tipperary, North (N)
16/7	Glasgow, Central (C)
1/10	Dublin, Harbour (N)
25/11	*Merthyr Tydfil (Ind Lab/Lab)
9/12	Yorkshire, Cleveland (L)

	1916
10/1	Newington, West (L)
25/1	Tower Hamlets, Mile End (C)
24/2	Louth, North (N)
9/3	*Hertfordshire, Hertford (Ind/C)
23/3	Leicestershire, Harborough (L)
29/3	Cheshire, Hyde (L)
19/4	Surrey, Wimbledon (C)
28/4	Queen's, Ossory (N)
16/5	Gloucestershire, Tewkesbury (C)
22/5	Londonderry, South (C)
16/8	Northumberland, Berwick-upon-Tweed (L)
20/9	Nottinghamshire, Mansfield (L)
11/10	Ayrshire, Northern (C)
19/10	Winchester (C)
15/11	Cork, West (N)

	1917
31/1	Dublin University (C)
3/2	*Roscommon, North (SF/N)
13/2	Lancashire, Rossendale (L)
20/3	Stockton-on-Tees (L)
3/4	Aberdeen, South (L)
9/5	*Longford, South (SF/N)
28/6	Liverpool, Abercromby (C)
10/7	*Clare, East (SF/N)
12/7	Monmouthshire, Southern (L)
30/7	Dundee (L)
10/8	*Kilkenny City (SF/N)
23/10	Islington, East (L)
2/11	*Salford, North (Ind Lab/L-Lab)

	1918
31/1	Lancashire, Prestwich (L)
5/2	Armagh, South (N)
22/3	Waterford Borough (N)
3/4	Tyrone, East (N)
26/4	Yorkshire, Keighley (L)
4/5	Herefordshire, Ross (C)
28/5	Northumberland, Wansbeck (L/L-Lab)
7/6	Gravesend (C)
20/6	*Cavan, East (SF/N)
21/6	Battersea and Clapham, Clapham (C)
16/7	Finsbury, East (L)

GENERAL ELECTION 1918—GENERAL ELECTION 1922

Date	1919
26/2	Liverpool, West Derby (Co C)
1/3	*Leyton, West (L/Co C)
4/3	Londonderry, North (C)
19/3	Oxford University (Co C)
29/3	*Kingston upon Hull, Central (L/Co C)
16/4	*Aberdeenshire and Kincardineshire, Central (L/Co C)
27/5	*Antrim, East (Ind C/C)
10/7	Swansea, East (Co L)
16/7	*Lanarkshire, Bothwell (Lab/Co C)
30/8	*Lancashire, Widnes (Lab/Co C)
6/9	Yorkshire, Pontefract (Co L)
7/10	Manchester, Rusholme (Co C)
13/11	Durham, Chester-le-Street (Lab)
14/11	Croydon, South (Co C)
15/11	Kent, Isle of Thanet (C/Co C)
15/11	Plymouth, Sutton (Co C)
10/12	Hertfordshire, St. Albans (Co C)
17/12	Bromley (Co C)
20/12	*Yorkshire, Spen Valley (Lab/Co L)

	1920
31/1	Ashton-under-Lyne (Co C)
7/2	*Shropshire, The Wrekin (Ind/Co L)
12/2	Paisley (L)
25/2	Lincolnshire, Horncastle (Co C)
10/3	Argyll (Co L)
27/3	*Kent, Dartford (Lab/Co L)
27/3	Stockport (two seats) (Co L & Co C/Co Lab)
31/3	Camberwell, North-West (Co L)
31/3	Hampshire, Basingstoke (Co C)
1/4	Northampton (Co L)
9/4	Edinburgh, North (Co C)
9/4	Edinburgh, South (Co C)
24/4	Sunderland (Co L)
3/6	*Lincolnshire, Louth (L/Co C)
17/6	Nelson and Colne (Lab)
27/7	*Norfolk, Southern (Lab/Co L)
28/7	Suffolk, Woodbridge (Co C)
25/9	Ilford (Co C)
20/11	Shropshire, The Wrekin (Ind)
21/12	Monmouthshire, Abertillery (Lab)
21/12	Rhondda, West (Lab)

	1921
11/1	Herefordshire, Hereford (Co C)
12/1	*Kent, Dover (Ind/Co C)
18/2	Cardiganshire (Co L)
2/3	*Woolwich, East (Co C/Lab)
3/3	*Dudley (Lab/Co L)
4/3	*Kirkcaldy Burghs (Lab/Co L)
5/3	*Yorkshire, Penistone (Lab/L)
8/4	Somerset, Taunton (Co C)
19/4	Worcestershire, Bewdley (Co C)
23/4	Bedfordshire, Bedford (Co L)
4/5	Hastings (Co C)
13/5	Cumberland, Penrith and Cockermouth (Co C)
7/6	*Westminster, St. George's (AWL/Co C)
8/6	*Lancashire, Heywood and Radcliffe (Lab/Co L)
16/6	Hertfordshire, Hertford (AWL & Ind/Ind)
24/8	Glamorganshire, Caerphilly (Lab)
25/8	Westminster, Abbey (C/Co C)
13/9	Lewisham, West (C/Co C)
22/9	Lincolnshire, Louth (L)
5/10	Lancashire, Westhoughton (Lab)
10/11	Hornsey (C/Co C)
14/12	*Southwark, South-East (Lab/Co L)

CONTESTED BY-ELECTIONS 1885–1945 (Cont.)

Date	1922
17/1	Warwickshire, Tamworth (Co C)
18/2	*Manchester, Clayton (Lab/C)
20/2	*Camberwell, North (Lab/Co C)
24/2	*Cornwall, Bodmin (L/Co C)
7/3	Wolverhampton, West (Co C)
16/3	Cambridge (C/Co C)
16/3	Inverness-shire and Ross and Cromarty, Inverness (Co L)
24/3	Surrey, Chertsey (C/Co C)
30/3	*Leicester, East (Lab/Co L)
19/5	City of London (C/Co C)
29/6	Nottingham, East (Co C)
20/7	Glamorganshire, Gower (Lab)
25/7	*Glamorganshire, Pontypridd (Lab/Co L)
18/8	*Hackney, South (Co C/Ind)
18/10	*Newport (C/Co L)

GENERAL ELECTION 1922–GENERAL ELECTION 1923

	1922
13/12	Portsmouth, South (C)

	1923
17/1	Newcastle upon Tyne, East (Lab)
8/2	Stepney, Whitechapel and St. George's (Lab)
28/2	Darlington (C)
3/3	*Surrey, Mitcham (Lab/C)
3/3	*Willesden, East (L/C)
6/3	*Liverpool, Edge Hill (Lab/C)
7/4	*Anglesey (L/Ind Lab)
19/4	Shropshire, Ludlow (C)
31/5	*Northumberland, Berwick-upon-Tweed (C/NL)
21/6	*Devon, Tiverton (L/C)
21/6	Morpeth (Lab)
26/7	Leeds, Central (C)
13/8	Portsmouth, South (C)
30/10	Somerset, Yeovil (C)
30/10	Lincolnshire, Rutland and Stamford (C)

GENERAL ELECTION 1923–GENERAL ELECTION 1924

	1924
1/2	City of London (C)
28/2	Burnley (Lab)
19/3	Westminster, Abbey (C)
22/5	*Liverpool, West Toxteth (Lab/C)
23/5	Glasgow, Kelvingrove (C)
5/6	*Oxford (C/L)
9/7	Sussex, Lewes (C)
31/7	*Lincolnshire, Holland with Boston (C/Lab)
14/8	Carmarthenshire, Carmarthen (L)

GENERAL ELECTION 1924–GENERAL ELECTION 1929

	1924
22/12	Dundee (Lab)

	1925
27/2	Walsall (C)
12/6	Ayr Burghs (C)
17/6	Sussex, Eastbourne (C)
24/6	Oldham (L)
14/7	Gloucestershire, Forest of Dean (Lab)
17/9	*Stockport (Lab/C)
17/11	Galloway (C)
1/12	Suffolk, Bury St. Edmunds (C)
5/12	Yorkshire, Ripon (C)

Date	1926
29/1	Dunbartonshire (C)
29/1	Renfrewshire, Eastern (C)
17/2	*Darlington (Lab/C)
8/3	*Combined English Universities (C/L)
26/3	Lanarkshire, Bothwell (Lab)
29/4	*East Ham, North (Lab/C)
5/5	Yorkshire, Buckrose (C)
28/5	*Hammersmith, North (Lab/C)
21/7	Wallsend (Lab)
17/9	Cumberland, Northern (C)
25/11	Yorkshire, Howdenshire (C)
29/11	*Kingston-upon-Hull, Central (Lab/L[1])
30/11	Essex, Chelmsford (C)
21/12	Smethwick (Lab)

	1927
23/2	*Worcestershire, Stourbridge (Lab/C)
23/3	Leith (L)
28/3	*Southwark, North (L/Lab)
26/4	Combined Scottish Universities (C)
31/5	*Leicestershire, Bosworth (L/C)
16/6	Wiltshire, Westbury (C)
27/6	Lambeth, Brixton (C)
19/11	Southend-on-Sea (C)
24/11	Kent, Canterbury (C)

	1928
9/1	*Northampton (Lab/C)
25/1	Kent, Faversham (C)
2/2	Bristol, West (C)
9/2	*Lancashire, Lancaster (L/C)
23/2	Ilford (C)
6/3	*Cornwall, St. Ives (L/C)
7/3	Middlesbrough, West (L)
4/4	*Linlithgowshire (Lab/C)
23/4	Stoke-on-Trent, Hanley (Lab)
30/4	St. Marylebone (C)
28/6	Holborn (C)
28/6	*Carmarthenshire, Carmarthen (L/C[2])
4/7	Surrey, Epsom (C)
13/7	*Halifax (Lab/L)
16/7	Sheffield, Hallam (C)
16/8	Aberdeen, North (Lab)
26/9	Cheltenham (C)
11/10	Devon, Tavistock (C)
29/10	*Ashton-under-Lyne (Lab/C)

	1929
29/1	*Midlothian and Peeblesshire, Northern (Lab/C)
7/2	*Battersea, South (Lab/C)
7/2	Durham, Bishop Auckland (Lab)
13/2	Northumberland, Wansbeck (Lab)
19/3	Liverpool, East Toxteth (C)
20/3	*Cheshire, Eddisbury (L/C)
21/3	Bath (C)
21/3	*Lincolnshire, Holland with Boston (L/C)
21/3	*Lanarkshire, Northern (Lab/C)

GENERAL ELECTION 1929–GENERAL ELECTION 1931

	1929
31/7	*Preston (Lab/L[1])
1/8	Leeds, South-East (Lab)
8/8	Middlesex, Twickenham (C)
27/11	Ayrshire and Bute, Kilmarnock (Lab)
2/12	Warwickshire, Tamworth (C)

[1] Resigned seat on joining the Labour Party but re-elected at by-election.

[2] Elected as a Liberal but subsequently joined Conservative Party.

CONTESTED BY-ELECTIONS 1885–1945 (Cont.)

Date	1930
6/2	Sheffield, Brightside (Lab)
6/5	*Fulham, West (C/Lab)
27/5	Nottingham, Central (C)
26/6	Glasgow, Shettleston (Lab)
9/7	Norfolk, Northern (Lab)
2/9	Bromley (C)
30/10	*Paddington, South (EC/C)
6/11	*Yorkshire, Shipley (C/Lab)
28/11	Renfrewshire, Eastern (C)
3/12	Stepney, Whitechapel and St. George's (Lab)

Date	1931
16/1	Bristol, East (Lab)
5/2	Liverpool, East Toxteth (C)
19/2	Islington, East (Lab)
20/2	Hampshire, Fareham (C)
11/3	Wiltshire, Salisbury (C)
19/3	Westminster, St. George's (C)
19/3	Glamorganshire, Pontypridd (Lab)
26/3	*Sunderland (C/Lab)
15/4	Woolwich, East (Lab)
30/4	*Ashton-under-Lyne (C/Lab)
6/5	Yorkshire, Scarborough and Whitby (C)
7/5	Glasgow, St. Rollox (Lab)
19/5	Glamorganshire, Ogmore (Lab)
21/5	Gloucestershire, Stroud (C)
21/5	Lanarkshire, Rutherglen (Lab)
8/6	Gateshead (Lab)
22/6	Manchester, Ardwick (Lab)
23/6	Liverpool, Wavertree (C)

GENERAL ELECTION 1931–GENERAL ELECTION 1935

	1932
9/2	Croydon, South (C)
9/2	Hampshire, New Forest and Christchurch (C)
25/2	Oxfordshire, Henley (C)
17/3	Dunbartonshire (C)
21/4	*Wakefield (Lab/C)
28/4	St. Marylebone (C)
8/6	Camberwell, Dulwich (C)
28/6	Montrose Burghs (NL)
22/7	Cornwall, Northern (L)
26/7	*Wednesbury (Lab/C)
16/9	Middlesex, Twickenham (C)
22/9	Cardiganshire (L)

	1933
19/1	Liverpool, Exchange (C)
2/2	Fife, Eastern (NL)
27/2	*Rotherham (Lab/C)
17/3	Kent, Ashford (C)
28/3	Rhondda, East (Lab)
8/6	Hertfordshire, Hitchin (C)
14/6	Cheshire, Altrincham (C)
1/9	Derbyshire, Clay Cross (Lab)
25/10	*Fulham, East (Lab/C)
2/11	Ayrshire and Bute, Kilmarnock (N Lab)
7/11	Yorkshire, Skipton (C)
21/11	Lincolnshire, Rutland and Stamford (C)
21/11	Manchester, Rusholme (C)
28/11	Leicestershire, Harborough (C)

	1934
8/2	Cambridge (C)
15/2	Suffolk, Lowestoft (C)
19/2	Portsmouth, North (C)
7/3	Combined Scottish Universities (L)
19/4	Hampshire, Basingstoke (C)

Date	
24/4	*Hammersmith, North (Lab/C)
14/5	*West Ham, Upton (Lab/C)
5/6	Merthyr Tydfil, Merthyr (Lab)
14/6	Monmouthshire, Monmouth (C)
22/6	Middlesex, Twickenham (C)
26/6	Somerset, West-super-Mare (C)
27/6	Fermanagh and Tyrone (N)
26/7	Nottinghamshire, Rushcliffe (C)
23/10	*Lambeth, North (Lab/L)
25/10	*Wiltshire, Swindon (Lab/C)
28/11	Wandsworth, Putney (C)

	1935
6/2	*Liverpool, Wavertree (Lab/C)
14/3	Lambeth, Norwood (C)
16/4	Perthshire and Kinross-shire, Perth (NL/C)
2/5	Edinburgh, West (C)
21/5	Aberdeen, South (C)
17/6	Combined Scottish Universities (C)
16/7	*Liverpool, West Toxteth (Lab/C)
12/9	Dumfriesshire (NL)

GENERAL ELECTION 1935–GENERAL ELECTION 1945

	1936
27/1	Combined Scottish Universities (N Lab/C)
10/2	Inverness-shire and Ross and Cromarty, Ross and Cromarty (N Lab/NL)
18/3	*Dunbartonshire (Lab/C)
26/3	Carmarthenshire, Llanelly (Lab)
6/5	*Camberwell, Peckham (Lab/C)
18/6	Sussex, Lewes (C)
9/7	*Derby (Lab/N Lab)
23/7	Wandsworth, Balham and Tooting (C)
23/7	Sussex, East Grinstead (C)
20/10	Birmingham, Erdington (C)
5/11	Derbyshire, Clay Cross (Lab)
25/11	Preston (C)
26/11	*Greenock (Lab/NL)

	1937
4/2	St. Pancras, North (C)
18/2	Manchester, Gorton (Lab)
23/2	*Oxford University (Ind/C)
25/2	Richmond (Surrey) (C)
15/3	*Combined English Universities (Ind Prog/C)
23/3	Kent, Tonbridge (C)
23/3	Surrey, Farnham (C)
28/4	Cheshire, Stalybridge and Hyde (C)
29/4	Birmingham, West (C)
29/4	*Wandsworth, Central (Lab/C)
6/5	York (C)
10/6	Glasgow, Hillhead (C)
11/6	Buckinghamshire, Buckingham (C)
15/6	Plymouth, Drake (C)
22/6	*Cheltenham (Ind C/C)
22/6	Hertfordshire, Hemel Hempstead (C)
24/6	Lincolnshire, Holland with Boston (NL)
24/6	Worcestershire, Bewdley (C)
29/6	Ilford (C)
30/6	Cornwall, St. Ives (NL)
1/7	Kingston upon Thames (C)
2/7	Surrey, Chertsey (C)
13/7	Dorset, Northern (C)
7/9	Glasgow, Springburn (Lab)
13/10	*Islington, North (Lab/C)
24/11	Hastings (C)

CONTESTED BY-ELECTIONS 1885—1945 (Cont.)

Date	1938
27/1	Lancashire, Farnworth (Lab)
11/2	Glamorganshire, Pontypridd (Lab)
16/2	*Ipswich (Lab/C)
21/2	Combined Scottish Universities (Nat/N Lab)
6/4	*Fulham, West (Lab/C)
5/5	*Staffordshire, Lichfield (Lab/N Lab)
19/5	Buckinghamshire, Aylesbury (C)
2/6	Derbyshire, Western (C)
9/6	Staffordshire, Stafford (C)
16/6	Barnsley (Lab)
28/7	Willesden, East (C)
27/10	Oxford (C)
7/11	*Kent, Dartford (Lab/C)
16/11	Walsall (NL)
17/11	Yorkshire, Doncaster (Lab)
17/11	*Somerset, Bridgwater (Ind Prog/C)
24/11	Lewisham, West (C)
30/11	Lancashire, Fylde (C)
21/12	*Perthshire and Kinross-shire, Kinross and Western (C/Ind C)

Date	1939
26/1	Norfolk, Eastern (NL)
15/2	Yorkshire, Holderness (C)
23/2	Yorkshire, Ripon (C)
9/3	Batley and Morley (Lab)
30/3	Aberdeenshire and Kincardineshire, Kincardine and Western (C)
20/4	Ayrshire and Bute, South Ayrshire (Lab)
10/5	Sheffield, Hallam (C)
17/5	Birmingham, Aston (C)
17/5	*Southwark, North (Lab/NL)
17/5	Westminster, Abbey (C)
24/5	*Lambeth, Kennington (Lab/C)
4/7	Glamorganshire, Caerphilly (Lab)
13/7	Cornwall, Northern (L)
20/7	Hythe (C)
25/7	Monmouthshire, Monmouth (C)
27/7	Yorkshire, Colne Valley (Lab)
1/8	*Breconshire and Radnorshire (Lab/Nat)
13/10	Stirlingshire and Clackmannanshire, Clackmannan and Eastern (Lab)
8/12	Lancashire, Stretford (C)

Date	1940
10/2	Southwark, Central (Lab)
19/2	*Cambridge University (Ind C/C)
22/2	West Ham, Silvertown (Lab)
6/3	Northamptonshire, Kettering (C)
13/3	Leeds, North-East (C)
10/4	Argyll (C)
17/4	Battersea, North (Lab)
30/4	Glasgow, Pollok (C)
9/5	Renfrewshire, Eastern (C)
22/5	Lancashire, Middleton and Prestwich (C)
7/6	*Newcastle upon Tyne, North (Ind C/C)
12/6	Poplar, Bow and Bromley (Lab)
19/6	Croydon, North (C)
6/12	Northampton (C)

	1941
27/2	Dunbartonshire (Lab)
8/5	Birmingham, King's Norton (C)
28/5	Hornsey (C)

Date	
23/7	Dudley (C)
24/9	Yorkshire, Scarborough and Whitby (C)
26/9	Shropshire, The Wrekin (C)
15/10	Lancashire, Lancaster (C)
27/11	Hampstead (C)
2/12	Middlesex, Harrow (C)
11/12	Edinburgh, Central (C)

	1942
25/3	*Lincolnshire, Grantham (Ind/C)
13/4	Cardiff, East (Nat/C)
28/4	Glasgow, Cathcart (C)
29/4	*Wallasey (Ind/C)
29/4	*Warwickshire, Rugby (Ind/C)
8/5	Wandsworth, Putney (C)
18/5	Sussex, Chichester (C)
10/6	Glamorganshire, Llandaff and Barry (C)
25/6	*Essex, Maldon (Ind Lab/C)
30/6	Berkshire, Windsor (C)
8/7	Wiltshire, Salisbury (C)
12/8	Poplar, South Poplar (Lab)
17/10	Manchester, Clayton (Lab)

	1943
25/1	University of Wales (L)
29/1	Lanarkshire, Hamilton (Lab)
9/2	*Belfast, West (NI Lab/C)
10/2	Kent, Ashford (C)
11/2	Antrim (C)
11/2	Midlothian and Peeblesshire, Northern (C)
12/2	Norfolk, King's Lynn (C)
16/2	Portsmouth, North (C)
18/2	Bristol, Central (C)
23/2	Hertfordshire, Watford (C)
7/4	*Cheshire, Eddisbury (CW/NL)
20/4	Northamptonshire, Daventry (C)
1/6	The Hartlepools (C)
8/6	Nottinghamshire, Newark (C)
9/6	Birmingham, Aston (C)
24/8	Wiltshire, Chippenham (C)
15/10	Northamptonshire, Peterborough (C)
10/11	Woolwich, West (C)
14/12	Middlesex, Acton (C)
15/12	Lancashire, Darwen (C)

	1944
7/1	*Yorkshire, Skipton (CW/C)
3/2	Brighton (C)
17/2	Kirkcaldy Burghs (Lab)
17/2	*Derbyshire, Western (Ind Lab/C)
29/2	Suffolk, Bury St. Edmunds (C)
30/3	Camberwell, North (Lab)
14/4	Derbyshire, Clay Cross (Lab)
8/7	Manchester, Rusholme (C)
20/9	Wolverhampton, Bilston (Lab)
17/10	Northumberland, Berwick-upon-Tweed (L)

	1945
9/4	*Combined Scottish Universities (Ind/NL)
12/4	*Lanarkshire, Motherwell (SNP/Lab)
26/4	Caernarvon Boroughs (L)
26/4	*Essex, Chelmsford (CW/C)
15/5	Glamorganshire, Neath (Lab)
17/5	Newport (C)

Table 2.02 CONTESTED BY-ELECTIONS 1945–1975

The following table lists all contested by-elections from the General Election of 1945 until the end of December 1975.

By-election percentages are shown in bold type and the previous General Election percentages in light type.

The column headed 'Nationalist' gives the percentage of votes cast for Plaid Cymru (in Wales), Scottish National Party (in Scotland), Sinn Fein, Nationalist, Republican and Unity candidates (in Northern Ireland).

The column headed 'Swing' shows the average of the Conservative percentage gain and Labour percentage loss between the previous General Election and the by-election — a minus sign indicating a swing to Labour. Swing figures are only given where Conservative and Labour candidates shared the top two places in the poll at both the General Election and the by-election.

Percentage figures for the 1945 General Election at the Combined English and Combined Scottish Universities have been omitted as these elections were conducted by Proportional Representation (single transferable vote) and the figures would not be comparable.

Seats which changed hands are indicated by an asterisk placed before the name of the constituency.

GENERAL ELECTION 1945–GENERAL ELECTION 1950

CONSTITUENCY AND (DATE)	Turnout %	C %	Lab %	L %	Com %	Nation-alist %	Others %	Swing to C %
1945								
Smethwick	**65.4**	**31.2**	**68.8**	**–**	**–**	**–**	**–**	**– 2.9**
(1/10)	72.4	34.1	65.9	–	–	–	–	–
Ashton-under-Lyne	**70.5**	**35.0**	**54.1**	**10.9**	**–**	**–**	**–**	**– 3.1**
(2/10)	78.6	43.6	56.4	–	–	–	–	–
Edinburgh, East	**51.0**	**38.4**	**61.6**	**–**	**–**	**–**	**–**	**– 2.0**
(3/10)	69.4	37.3	56.4	–	–	6.3	–	–
Monmouthshire, Monmouth	**66.7**	**52.7**	**47.3**	**–**	**–**	**–**	**–**	**0.8**
(30/10)	72.0	51.9	48.1	–	–	–	–	–
City of London	**51.6**	**75.0**	**–**	**25.0**	**–**	**–**	**–**	**–**
(31/10)	63.9	78.8	–	11.0	–	–	10.2	–
Bromley	**60.6**	**49.6**	**39.1**	**11.3**	**–**	**–**	**–**	**– 0.2**
(14/11)	70.9	45.0	34.1	20.9	–	–	–	–
Bournemouth	**56.5**	**46.8**	**33.7**	**19.5**	**–**	**–**	**–**	**–**
(15/11)	71.2	55.5	21.7	22.8	–	–	–	–
Kensington, South	**36.8**	**81.7**	**–**	**18.3**	**–**	**–**	**–**	**–**
(20/11)	67.9	69.8	18.9	11.3	–	–	–	–
Tottenham, North	**39.5**	**36.4**	**63.6**	**–**	**–**	**–**	**–**	**8.2**
(13/12)	70.3	28.2	71.8	–	–	–	–	–
1946								
Preston	**64.9**	**44.4**	**55.6**	**–**	**–**	**–**	**–**	**– 2.3**
(31/1)	80.2	41.8	48.3	6.1	3.8	–	–	–
Ayrshire and Bute, South Ayrshire	**69.0**	**36.4**	**63.6**	**–**	**–**	**–**	**–**	**– 2.3**
(7/2)	75.0	38.7	61.3	–	–	–	–	–
Glasgow, Cathcart	**55.6**	**52.5**	**37.1**	**–**	**–**	**10.4**	**–**	**– 1.1**
(12/2)	67.6	58.8	41.2	–	–	–	–	–
Lancashire, Heywood and Radcliffe	**75.6**	**49.5**	**50.5**	**–**	**–**	**–**	**–**	**0.5**
(21/2)	76.4	49.0	51.0	–	–	–	–	–
*Combined English Universities	**42.1**	**30.0**[1]	**–**	**–**	**–**	**–**	**70.0**[2]	**–**
(13-18/3)	50.0	–	–	–	–	–	–	–
Glamorganshire, Ogmore	**33.1**	**–**	**70.6**	**–**	**–**	**29.4**	**–**	**–**
(4/6)	75.6	18.0	76.4	–	–	5.6	–	–
*Down	**66.6**	**51.4**[3]	**29.3**	**–**	**–**	**–**	**19.3**	**–**
(6/6)	49.3	40.5	–	–	–	–	59.5	–
Bexley	**61.2**	**47.5**	**52.5**	**–**	**–**	**–**	**–**	**11.0**
(22/7)	76.7	29.8	56.9	13.3	–	–	–	–
Monmouthshire, Pontypool	**64.8**	**26.8**	**73.2**	**–**	**–**	**–**	**–**	**4.1**
(23/7)	77.0	22.7	77.3	–	–	–	–	–
Battersea, North	**55.4**	**29.6**	**68.9**	**–**	**–**	**–**	**1.5**	**4.2**
(25/7)	70.9	26.1	73.9	–	–	–	–	–

CONTESTED BY-ELECTIONS 1945-1975 (Cont.)

CONSTITUENCY AND (DATE)	Turnout %	C %	Lab %	L %	Com %	Nation- alist %	Others %	Swing to C %
Glasgow, Bridgeton	53.3	21.6	28.0	–	–	–	50.4[4]	–
(29/8)	58.2	33.6	–	–	–	–	66.4[5]	–
Bermondsey, Rotherhithe	50.9	9.7	65.0	25.3	–	–	–	–
(19/11)	68.1	20.9	79.1	–	–	–	–	–
Paddington, North	53.9	43.2	55.6	–	–	–	1.2	5.8
(20/11)	71.0	37.1	61.2	–	–	–	1.7	–
*Combined Scottish Universities	50.7	68.2[6]	11.5	8.0	–	–	12.3	–
(22-27/11)	51.6	–	–	–	–	–	–	–
Aberdeen, South	65.6	54.8	45.2	–	–	–	–	2.6
(26/11)	71.9	46.8	42.3	10.9	–	–	–	–
Merthyr Tydfil, Aberdare	65.7	11.7	68.3	–	–	20.0	–	–
(5/12)	76.1	15.7	84.3	–	–	–	–	–
Ayrshire and Bute, Kilmarnock	68.4	32.5	59.7	–	–	7.8	–	– 4.2
(5/12)	76.1	40.6	59.4	–	–	–	–	–
1947								
Yorkshire, Normanton	54.6	17.8	79.8	–	–	–	2.4	3.3
(11/2)	79.9	15.7	84.3	–	–	–	–	–
Durham, Jarrow	73.4	37.5	59.3	–	–	–	3.2	5.1
(7/5)	76.0	34.0	66.0	–	–	–	–	–
Liverpool, Edge Hill	62.7	42.6	52.1	4.4	–	–	0.9	10.2
(11/9)	66.1	35.1	64.9	–	–	–	–	–
Islington, West	51.4	26.6	57.2	16.0	–	–	0.2	8.5
(25/9)	60.1	26.2	73.8	–	–	–	–	–
Kent, Gravesend	77.3	48.2	51.8	–	–	–	–	6.8
(26/11)	74.5	35.3	52.5	12.2	–	–	–	–
Yorkshire, Howdenshire	67.0	64.0	25.5	10.5	–	–	–	5.8
(27/11)	71.1	56.0	29.2	14.8	–	–	–	–
Edinburgh, East	63.0	34.3	50.6	10.1	–	5.0	–	1.4
(27/11)	69.4	37.3	56.4	–	–	6.3	–	–
Surrey, Epsom	70.5	61.0	31.5	7.5	–	–	–	8.6
(4/12)	74.6	50.0	37.8	12.2	–	–	–	–
1948								
*Glasgow, Camlachie	56.8	43.7	42.1	1.2	–	–	13.0[7]	–
(28/1)	65.0	42.3	–	–	–	–	57.7[8]	–
Paisley	76.0	43.2[9]	56.8	–	–	–	–	4.6
(18/2)	73.9	32.7	55.6	10.0	–	–	1.7	–
Wigan	81.4	35.7	59.0	–	3.4	–	1.9	6.5
(4/3)	80.4	31.8	68.2	–	–	–	–	–
Armagh	86.9	60.1	–	–	–	39.9	–	–
(5/3)	–	–	–	–	–	–	–	–
Croydon, North	74.8	54.0	36.6	9.4	–	–	–	8.2
(11/3)	73.2	41.1	40.1	18.8	–	–	–	–
Lincolnshire, Brigg	77.1	45.4	54.6	–	–	–	–	4.3
(24/3)	74.6	41.1	58.9	–	–	–	–	–
Southwark, Central	48.7	34.6	65.4	–	–	–	–	6.5
(29/4)	62.6	28.1	71.9	–	–	–	–	–
Glasgow, Gorbals	50.0	28.6	54.5	–	16.9	–	–	17.0
(30/9)	56.8	20.0	80.0	–	–	–	–	–
Stirling and Falkirk Burghs	72.9	42.8	49.0	–	–	8.2	–	3.0
(7/10)	71.5	43.9	56.1	–	–	–	–	–
Edmonton	62.7	46.6	53.4	–	–	–	–	16.2
(13/11)	69.0	29.0	68.2	–	–	–	2.8	–
Glasgow, Hillhead	56.7	68.4	31.6	–	–	–	–	5.9
(25/11)	65.8	58.5	33.6	7.9	–	–	–	–
1949								
Batley and Morley	81.3	40.7	59.3	–	–	–	–	5.5
(17/2)	80.7	28.4	58.1	13.5	–	–	–	–
Hammersmith, South	60.6	47.2	52.8	–	–	–	–	5.2
(24/2)	65.7	42.0	58.0	–	–	–	–	–
St. Pancras, North	65.1	39.5	57.5	–	3.0	–	–	5.5
(10/3)	71.0	34.7	63.8	–	–	–	1.5	–
Yorkshire, Sowerby	80.7	46.9	53.1	–	–	–	–	6.8
(16/3)	81.9	30.9	50.8	18.3	–	–	–	–

CONTESTED BY-ELECTIONS 1945-1975 (Cont.)

CONSTITUENCY AND (DATE)	Turnout %	C %	Lab %	L %	Com %	Nation-alist %	Others %	Swing to C %
Leeds, West	**65.1**	**44.8**	**55.2**	—	—	—	—	**10.5**
(21/7)	75.2	27.6	59.1	13.3	—	—	—	—
Bradford, South	**74.4**	**42.4**	**51.3**	—	—	—	**6.3**	**5.2**
(8/12)	76.7	33.1	52.5	14.4	—	—	—	—

[1] C gain from Ind   [4] ILP 34.3, Others 16.1   [7] ILP 6.4, Others 6.6

[2] Total polled by four candidates   [5] ILP   [8] Elected as ILP but subsequently took Labour Whip

[3] C gain from Ind C   [6] C gain from Ind   [9] Nat

GENERAL ELECTION 1950—GENERAL ELECTION 1951

CONSTITUENCY AND (DATE)	Turnout %	C %	Lab %	L %	Com %	Nation-alist %	Others %	Swing to C %
1950								
Sheffield, Neepsend	62.9	26.8	70.9	—	2.3	—	—	0.8
(5/4)	83.8	27.2	72.8	—	—	—	—	—
Dunbartonshire, West	83.4	49.6	50.4	—	—	—	—	0.4
(25/4)	85.5	47.8	49.3	—	2.9	—	—	—
Brighouse and Spenborough	85.4	49.5	50.5	—	—	—	—	1.7
(4/5)	88.0	47.8	52.2	—	—	—	—	—
Leicester, North-East	63.0	42.1	57.9	—	—	—	—	3.7
(28/9)	85.8	33.3	56.5	9.5	0.7	—	—	—
Glasgow, Scotstoun	73.7	50.8	47.3	—	—	—	1.9	1.5
(25/10)	84.6	46.5	46.0	4.9	2.6	—	—	—
Oxford	69.3	57.5	42.5	—	—	—	—	4.4
(2/11)	84.9	46.9	40.7	11.6	0.8	—	—	—
Birmingham, Handsworth	63.2	60.7	38.1	—	—	—	1.2	5.6
(16/11)	83.1	50.5	39.2	10.3	—	—	—	—
Belfast, West	79.9	50.7	—	—	—	—	49.3[1]	—
(29/11)	83.6	51.5	—	—	—	2.2	46.3[1]	—
Bristol, South-East	61.1	35.2	56.7	8.1	—	—	—	7.1
(30/11)	85.0	26.8	62.6	9.5	1.1	—	—	—
Monmouthshire, Abertillery	71.1	13.5	86.5	—	—	—	—	0.5
(30/11)	84.6	12.9	87.1	—	—	—	—	—
1951								
Bristol, West	53.6	81.4	18.6	—	—	—	—	16.9
(15/2)	82.4	58.9	30.0	11.1	—	—	—	—
Lancashire, Ormskirk	64.7	71.5	26.5	—	—	—	2.0	6.2
(5/4)	83.9	66.3	33.7	—	—	—	—	—
Harrow, West	68.0	72.0	28.0	—	—	—	—	7.5
(21/4)	86.7	58.6	29.5	11.9	—	—	—	—
Woolwich, East	66.8	39.3	60.7	—	—	—	—	3.6
(14/6)	83.3	33.0	61.5	3.5	1.4	—	0.6	—
Lancashire, Westhoughton	76.5	39.6	60.4	—	—	—	—	1.8
(21/6)	88.2	37.7	62.3	—	—	—	—	—

[1] Irish LP.

CONTESTED BY-ELECTIONS 1945-1975 (Cont.)

GENERAL ELECTION 1951—GENERAL ELECTION 1955

CONSTITUENCY AND (DATE)	Turnout %	C %	Lab %	L %	Com %	Nation- alist %	Others %	Swing to C %
1952								
Bournemouth East and Christchurch	63.8	61.8	23.4	10.1	—	—	4.7	0.1
(6/2)	80.8	63.3	25.1	11.6	—	—	—	—
Southport	61.0	62.0	28.5	9.5	—	—	—	− 0.9
(6/2)	77.7	60.2	24.8	15.0	—	—	—	—
Leeds, South-East	55.7	36.8	63.2	—	—	—	—	− 2.7
(7/2)	84.4	39.5	60.5	—	—	—	—	—
Dundee, East	71.5	35.6	56.3	—	—	7.4	0.7	− 6.5
(17/7)	87.2	46.2	53.8	—	—	—	—	—
Yorkshire, Cleveland	71.4	45.9	54.1	—	—	—	—	0.7
(23/10)	85.1	45.2	54.8	—	—	—	—	—
Belfast, South	47.1	75.1	24.9	—	—	—	—	− 0.7
(4/11)	73.8	75.8	24.2	—	—	—	—	—
Buckinghamshire, Wycombe	83.9	52.0	48.0	—	—	—	—	0.4
(4/11)	86.2	51.7	48.3	—	—	—	—	—
Birmingham, Small Heath	46.6	33.0	67.0	—	—	—	—	− 0.7
(27/11)	77.2	30.9	63.4	5.7	—	—	—	—
Lancashire, Farnworth	71.0	40.1	59.9	—	—	—	—	− 0.7
(27/11)	86.8	40.8	59.2	—	—	—	—	—
1953								
Kent, Canterbury	49.2	67.1	32.9	—	—	—	—	2.1
(12/2)	80.1	61.1	31.0	7.9	—	—	—	—
Kent, Isle of Thanet	58.7	61.3	38.7	—	—	—	—	− 0.3
(12/3)	78.0	61.6	38.4	—	—	—	—	—
Barnsley	57.9	27.1	72.9	—	—	—	—	3.4
(31/3)	77.2	17.3	69.7	13.0	—	—	—	—
Stoke-on-Trent, North	50.5	24.5	75.5	—	—	—	—	− 4.0
(31/3)	83.8	28.6	71.4	—	—	—	—	—
Hayes and Harlington	45.0	36.1	63.9	—	—	—	—	0.9
(1/4)	82.2	35.2	64.8	—	—	—	—	—
*Sunderland, South	72.7	48.6	46.1	5.3	—	—	—	1.5
(13/5)	82.2	49.7	50.3	—	—	—	—	—
Berkshire, Abingdon	75.9	53.2	39.7	7.1	—	—	—	1.3
(30/6)	80.0	55.5	44.5	—	—	—	—	—
Birmingham, Edgbaston	50.2	67.6	32.4	—	—	—	—	3.4
(2/7)	76.1	64.3	35.7	—	—	—	—	—
Nottinghamshire, Broxtowe	63.5	25.9	74.1	—	—	—	—	− 1.4
(17/9)	84.1	27.3	72.7	—	—	—	—	—
Crosby	62.5	68.1	27.6	—	—	—	4.3	− 0.7
(12/11)	79.8	70.9	29.1	—	—	—	—	—
Lancashire, Ormskirk	54.1	65.4	34.6	—	—	—	—	− 2.0
(12/11)	78.7	67.4	32.6	—	—	—	—	—
Holborn and St. Pancras South	56.2	45.6	52.1	2.3	—	—	—	− 1.1
(19/11)	73.7	45.8	50.2	4.0	—	—	—	—
Paddington, North	60.3	45.3	53.8	—	—	—	0.9	1.4
(3/12)	81.0	44.3	55.7	—	—	—	—	—
1954								
Ilford, North	45.4	59.8	32.3	7.9	—	—	—	5.0
(3/2)	84.8	55.5	38.0	6.5	—	—	—	—
Essex, Harwich	58.8	59.1	40.9	—	—	—	—	0.1
(11/2)	78.8	58.9	41.1	—	—	—	—	—
Kingston-upon-Hull, Haltemprice	45.7	61.8	38.2	—	—	—	—	3.6
(11/2)	82.8	58.1	41.9	—	—	—	—	—
Bournemouth, West	45.1	69.7	30.3	—	—	—	—	4.2
(18/2)	77.7	65.5	34.5	—	—	—	—	—
Sussex, Arundel and Shoreham	54.2	68.5	31.5	—	—	—	—	1.1
(9/3)	78.0	67.4	32.6	—	—	—	—	—
Yorkshire, Harrogate	55.3	70.8	29.2	—	—	—	—	0.2
(11/3)	78.7	70.6	29.4	—	—	—	—	—
Edinburgh, East	61.8	42.4	57.6	—	—	—	—	− 3.6
(8/4)	83.8	45.9	54.1	—	—	—	—	—

CONTESTED BY-ELECTIONS 1945-1975 (Cont.)

CONSTITUENCY AND (DATE)	Turnout %	C %	Lab %	L %	Com %	Nation-alist %	Others %	Swing to C %
Lanarkshire, Motherwell	70.5	39.3	56.4	–	4.3	–	–	– 1.3
(14/4)	84.7	42.7	57.3	–	–	–	–	–
Croydon, East	57.5	56.6	35.4	8.0	–	–	–	1.8
(30/9)	84.2	58.8	41.2	–	–	–	–	–
Shoreditch and Finsbury	40.7	21.8	78.2	–	–	–	–	– 5.6
(21/10)	73.2	27.4	72.6	–	–	–	–	–
Wakefield	68.6	41.9	58.1	–	–	–	–	0.1
(21/10)	85.3	41.7	58.3	–	–	–	–	–
Hampshire, Aldershot	58.7	60.1	39.9	–	–	–	–	– 0.3
(28/10)	77.8	60.3	39.7	–	–	–	–	–
Aberdare	69.7	14.5	69.5	–	–	16.0	–	–
(28/10)	86.1	15.4	78.5	–	–	6.1	–	–
Sutton and Cheam	55.6	66.5	33.5	–	–	–	–	3.8
(4/11)	81.7	62.8	37.2	–	–	–	–	–
Northumberland, Morpeth	73.0	28.7	71.3	–	–	–	–	0.6
(4/11)	85.5	28.1	71.9	–	–	–	–	–
Liverpool, West Derby	58.9	53.2	46.8	–	–	–	–	1.5
(18/11)	80.3	51.6	48.4	–	–	–	–	–
Inverness-shire and Ross and Cromarty, Inverness	49.2	41.4	22.6	36.0	–	–	–	–
(21/12)	69.3	64.5	35.5	–	–	–	–	–
1955								
Norfolk, South	66.6	51.5	48.5	–	–	–	–	– 3.0
(13/1)	82.4	54.5	45.5	–	–	–	–	–
Kent, Orpington	55.4	65.8	34.2	–	–	–	–	3.2
(20/1)	82.0	62.7	37.3	–	–	–	–	–
Twickenham	47.3	64.0	36.0	–	–	–	–	2.0
(25/1)	81.3	62.1	37.9	–	–	–	–	–
Edinburgh, North	46.4	59.4	40.6	–	–	–	–	0.6
(27/1)	80.0	58.8	41.2	–	–	–	–	–
Stockport, South	64.6	54.3	45.7	–	–	–	–	0.1
(3/2)	84.2	54.2	45.8	–	–	–	–	–
Denbighshire, Wrexham	62.4	30.8	57.9	–	–	11.3	–	– 0.2
(17/3)	84.8	34.8	61.6	–	–	3.6	–	–

GENERAL ELECTION 1955—GENERAL ELECTION 1959

CONSTITUENCY AND (DATE)	Turnout %	C %	Lab %	L %	Com %	Nation-alist %	Others %	Swing to C %
1955								
Mid-Ulster	89.7	49.3	–	–	–	50.7[1]	–	–
(11/8)	88.6	49.8	–	–	–	50.2	–	–
Gateshead, West	42.3	33.5	66.5	–	–	–	–	– 1.1
(7/12)	72.5	34.7	65.3	–	–	–	–	–
Greenock	75.3	46.3	53.7	–	–	–	–	– 2.3
(8/12)	77.9	48.6	51.4	–	–	–	–	–
Torquay	62.6	51.0	25.2	23.8	–	–	–	– 4.6
(15/12)	75.5	60.4	25.4	14.2	–	–	–	–
1956								
Durham, Blaydon	56.5	30.1	69.9	–	–	–	–	– 3.5
(2/2)	80.7	33.5	66.5	–	–	–	–	–
Leeds, North-East	39.9	63.2	36.8	–	–	–	–	1.7
(9/2)	73.1	61.4	38.6	–	–	–	–	–
Herefordshire, Hereford	61.5	44.3	19.3	36.4	–	–	–	–
(14/2)	78.8	51.8	23.4	24.8	–	–	–	–
Lincolnshire, Gainsborough	61.9	40.8	37.6	21.6	–	–	–	– 4.2
(14/2)	76.8	55.8	44.2	–	–	–	–	–
Somerset, Taunton	75.0	50.8	49.2	–	–	–	–	– 5.4
(14/2)	85.5	52.1	39.5	8.4	–	–	–	–

CONTESTED BY-ELECTIONS 1945-1975 (Cont.)

CONSTITUENCY AND (DATE)	Turnout %	C %	Lab %	L %	Com %	Nation-alist %	Others %	Swing to C %
Walthamstow, West	52.0	20.2	64.7	14.7	—	—	0.4	− 6.5
(1/3)	72.5	34.3	65.7	—	—	—	—	—
*Mid-Ulster	88.4	—	—	—	—	51.7[2]	48.3[3]	—
(8/5)	88.6	49.8	—	—	—	50.2[4]	—	—
Kent, Tonbridge	60.6	52.0	48.0	—	—	—	—	− 8.4
(7/6)	75.5	60.4	39.6	—	—	—	—	—
Newport	72.1	39.9	56.3	—	—	3.8	—	− 4.5
(6/7)	81.6	46.3	53.7	—	—	—	—	—
Durham, Chester-le-Street	64.9	19.2	80.8	—	—	—	—	− 4.5
(27/9)	79.6	23.7	76.3	—	—	—	—	—
Cheshire, City of Chester	71.5	51.7	36.2	12.1	—	—	—	− 4.7
(15/11)	77.9	56.7	31.6	11.7	—	—	—	—
Leicestershire, Melton	56.5	53.3	46.7	—	—	—	—	− 7.6
(19/12)	80.9	60.9	39.1	—	—	—	—	—
1957								
*Lewisham, North	70.8	46.5	49.5	—	—	—	4.0	− 5.4
(14/2)	77.9	54.0	46.0	—	—	—	—	—
Wednesbury	60.0	28.0	62.1	—	—	—	9.9	− 6.8
(28/2)	72.9	39.6	60.4	—	—	—	—	—
*Carmarthenshire, Carmarthen	87.5	—	47.3	41.2	—	11.5	—	—
(28/2)	85.1	—	42.7	49.5	—	7.8	—	—
Bristol, West	61.1	70.2	29.8	—	—	—	—	− 5.0
(7/3)	74.6	75.3	24.7	—	—	—	—	—
Warwickshire, Warwick and Leamington	77.9	52.3	47.7	—	—	—	—	−12.2
(7/3)	78.8	64.5	35.5	—	—	—	—	—
Beckenham	64.7	62.9	37.1	—	—	—	—	− 6.0
(21/3)	76.5	69.0	31.0	—	—	—	—	—
Newcastle upon Tyne, North	64.1	60.2	39.8	—	—	—	—	− 3.6
(21/3)	77.6	63.8	36.2	—	—	—	—	—
Edinburgh, South	65.8	45.6	30.9	23.5	—	—	—	−10.2
(29/5)	77.2	67.5	32.5	—	—	—	—	—
East Ham, North	57.3	29.4	56.3	—	—	—	14.3	− 4.3
(30/5)	74.9	40.9	59.1	—	—	—	—	—
Hornsey	63.0	53.5	46.5	—	—	—	—	− 8.0
(30/5)	76.3	60.2	37.2	—	2.6	—	—	—
Dorset, North	75.8	45.1	18.3	36.1	—	—	0.5	—
(27/6)	82.2	52.1	15.5	32.4	—	—	—	—
Gloucester	71.0	28.6	51.3	20.1	—	—	—	−10.5
(12/9)	80.9	49.1	50.9	—	—	—	—	—
Ipswich	75.6	32.7	45.8	21.5	—	—	—	− 3.7
(24/10)	80.5	47.1	52.9	—	—	—	—	—
Leicester, South-East	56.4	61.0	39.0	—	—	—	—	− 3.3
(28/11)	78.5	64.2	35.8	—	—	—	—	—
*Liverpool, Garston	49.7	49.2	35.6	15.2	—	—	—	− 6.7
(5/12)	71.0	63.5[5]	36.5	—	—	—	—	—
1958								
*Rochdale	80.2	19.8	44.7	35.5	—	—	—	—
(12/2)	82.8	51.5	48.5	—	—	—	—	—
*Glasgow, Kelvingrove	60.5	41.6	48.0	—	—	—	10.4	− 8.6
(13/3)	67.6	55.4	44.6	—	—	—	—	—
*Devon, Torrington	80.6	37.4	24.6	38.0	—	—	—	—
(27/3)	69.2	65.1	34.9	—	—	—	—	—
Islington, North	35.6	29.3	67.7	—	—	—	3.0	− 8.9
(15/5)	64.7	39.7	60.3	—	—	—	—	—
*Ealing, South	64.5	50.3	32.5	17.2	—	—	—	− 5.5
(12/6)	77.9	59.5[5]	30.9	9.6	—	—	—	—
St. Helens	54.6	35.3	64.7	—	—	—	—	− 0.4
(12/6)	73.5	35.7	64.3	—	—	—	—	—
Wigan	70.3	26.5	71.0	—	2.5	—	—	− 6.1
(12/6)	80.3	32.2	64.4	—	3.4	—	—	—
Somerset, Weston-super-Mare	72.2	49.3	26.2	24.5	—	—	—	− 1.1
(12/6)	73.8	62.7	37.3	—	—	—	—	—
Argyll	67.1	46.8	25.7	27.5	—	—	—	—
(12/6)	66.6	67.6	32.4	—	—	—	—	—

CONTESTED BY-ELECTIONS 1945-1975 (Cont.)

CONSTITUENCY AND (DATE)	Turnout %	C %	Lab %	L %	Com %	Nation-alist %	Others %	Swing to C %
Lancashire, Morecambe and								
Lonsdale	63.8	65.3	34.7	—	—	—	—	− 5.9
(6/11)	74.4	71.2	28.8	—	—	—	—	—
Sussex, Chichester	51.7	70.9	29.1	—	—	—	—	0.1
(6/11)	71.8	70.8	29.2	—	—	—	—	—
Monmouthshire, Pontypool	61.7	21.5	68.5	—	—	10.0	—	− 0.6
(10/11)	77.1	27.1	72.9	—	—	—	—	—
Aberdeenshire, East	65.9	48.6	27.1	24.3	—	—	—	− 7.8
(20/11)	59.8	68.5	31.5	—	—	—	—	—
Shoreditch and Finsbury	24.9	24.0	76.0	—	—	—	—	− 2.6
(27/11)	61.6	26.5	73.5	—	—	—	—	—
1959								
Southend, West	42.9	55.6	20.2	24.2	—	—	—	—
(29/1)	74.1	64.2	20.8	15.0	—	—	—	—
Harrow, East	68.9	52.8	46.2	—	—	—	1.0	− 1.1
(19/3)	82.6	54.4	45.6	—	—	—	—	—
Belfast, East	57.9	57.8	42.2	—	—	—	—	− 8.3
(19/3)	70.4	62.5	30.2	—	—	7.3	—	—
Norfolk, South-West	75.2	46.4	51.0	—	—	—	2.6	− 2.0
(25/3)	82.6	49.7	50.3	—	—	—	—	—
Kircudbrightshire and								
Wigtownshire, Galloway	72.7	50.4	23.9	25.7	—	—	—	—
(9/4)	69.1	66.9	33.1	—	—	—	—	—
Yorkshire, Penistone	65.0	35.9	64.1	—	—	—	—	− 1.8
(11/6)	80.0	37.7	62.3	—	—	—	—	—
Cumberland, Whitehaven	79.2	41.4	58.6	—	—	—	—	− 0.6
(18/6)	83.8	42.0	58.0	—	—	—	—	—

[1] T.J. Mitchell (SF). Subsequently Election Court awarded the seat to the Conservative candidate.

[2] SF 40.8, N 10.9

[3] Ind C

[4] At 1955 by-election seat retained by Sinn Fein but subsequently Election Court declared Conservative candidate to have been elected.

[5] Ind C at time of resignation.

GENERAL ELECTION 1959—GENERAL ELECTION 1964

CONSTITUENCY AND (DATE)	Turnout %	C %	Lab %	L %	Com %	Nation-alist %	Others %	Swing to C %
1960								
*Brighouse and Spenborough	82.4	50.8	49.2	—	—	—	—	0.8
(17/3)	85.5	49.9	50.1	—	—	—	—	—
Harrow, West	61.6	55.7	18.2	21.4	—	—	4.7	—
(17/3)	79.2	70.9	29.1	—	—	—	—	—
Edinburgh, North	53.8	54.2	30.3	15.5	—	—	—	− 2.1
(19/5)	73.9	64.0	36.0	—	—	—	—	—
Bolton, East	68.2	37.8	36.2	24.8	—	—	1.2	− 2.0
(16/11)	80.9	52.8	47.2	—	—	—	—	—
Bedfordshire, Mid	71.1	45.4	29.2	24.8	—	—	0.6	2.4
(16/11)	84.5	46.8	35.4	17.8	—	—	—	—
Devon, Tiverton	68.4	45.7	17.6	36.7	—	—	—	—
(16/11)	80.7	55.6	25.2	19.2	—	—	—	—
Hampshire, Petersfield	53.6	54.4	16.6	29.0	—	—	—	—
(16/11)	73.6	60.9	21.3	17.8	—	—	—	—
Shropshire, Ludlow	63.6	46.4	26.3	27.3	—	—	—	—
(16/11)	76.2	60.3	39.7	—	—	—	—	—
Surrey, Carshalton	54.2	51.7	20.7	27.6	—	—	—	—
(16/11)	82.5	54.0	30.5	15.5	—	—	—	—

CONTESTED BY-ELECTIONS 1945-1975 (Cont.)

CONSTITUENCY AND (DATE)	Turnout %	C %	Lab %	L %	Com %	Nation-alist %	Others %	Swing to C %
Monmouthshire, Ebbw Vale	76.1	12.7	68.8	11.5	–	–	7.0	3.0
(17/11)	85.8	19.0	81.0	–	–	–	–	–
Blyth	54.1	21.6	68.9	–	–	–	9.5	1.0
(24/11)	82.6	25.4	74.6	–	–	–	–	–
1961								
Worcester	64.2	39.7	30.2	30.1	–	–	–	– 2.9
(16/3)	79.3	57.7	42.3	–	–	–	–	–
Cambridgeshire	62.4	45.9	30.1	24.0	–	–	–	0.0
(16/3)	78.0	57.9	42.1	–	–	–	–	–
Derbyshire, High Peak	72.5	37.4	32.1	30.5	–	–	–	– 3.4
(16/3)	82.7	46.0	34.0	20.0	–	–	–	–
Essex, Colchester	64.9	47.2	33.1	19.7	–	–	–	– 0.8
(16/3)	82.4	51.6	35.9	12.5	–	–	–	–
Birmingham, Small Heath	42.6	28.8	59.2	12.0	–	–	–	– 7.8
(23/3)	65.7	42.6	57.4	–	–	–	–	–
Warrington	56.7	31.6	55.9	12.5	–	–	–	– 5.8
(20/4)	76.9	43.7	56.3	–	–	–	–	–
Paisley	68.1	13.2	45.4	41.4	–	–	–	–
(20/4)	78.9	42.7	57.3	–	–	–	–	–
Bristol, South-East	56.7	30.5	69.5[1]	–	–	–	–	–13.2
(4/5)	81.4	43.8	56.2	–	–	–	–	–
Manchester, Moss Side	46.7	41.2	25.8	27.8	–	–	5.2	–
(7/11)	69.2	62.3	37.7	–	–	–	–	–
Fife, East	67.3	47.5	26.4	26.1	–	–	–	– 9.4
(8/11)	75.2	69.9	30.1	–	–	–	–	–
Shropshire, Oswestry	60.8	40.8	28.0	28.4	–	–	2.8	–
(8/11)	74.2	55.9	28.0	16.1	–	–	–	–
Glasgow, Bridgeton	41.9	20.7	57.5	–	–	18.7	3.1	– 5.0
(16/11)	68.5	36.6	63.4	–	–	–	–	–
1962								
Lincoln	75.0	30.2	50.5	18.2	–	–	1.1	– 5.0
(8/3)	84.2	44.9	55.1	–	–	–	–	–
Blackpool, North	55.2	38.3	26.4	35.3	–	–	–	–
(13/3)	74.8	57.8	21.6	20.6	–	–	–	–
Middlesbrough, East	52.2	14.8	60.5	22.9	–	–	1.8	–
(14/3)	76.2	38.5	61.5	–	–	–	–	–
*Kent, Orpington	80.3	34.7	12.4	52.9	–	–	–	–
(14/3)	82.8	56.6	22.2	21.2	–	–	–	–
Pontefract	63.3	19.4	77.3	–	–	–	3.3	– 2.6
(22/3)	84.3	23.6	76.4	–	–	–	–	–
Stockton-on-Tees	81.5	27.8	45.3	26.9	–	–	–	– 5.0
(5/4)	83.9	46.3	53.7	–	–	–	–	–
Derby, North	60.5	22.5	49.4	25.4	–	–	2.7	–
(17/4)	76.7	47.2	52.8	–	–	–	–	–
Montgomeryshire	85.1	21.9	20.6	51.3	–	6.2	–	–
(15/5)	83.8	31.3	26.6	42.1	–	–	–	–
*Middlesbrough, West	72.2	33.7	39.7	25.8	–	–	0.8	–12.7
(6/6)	84.5	54.9	35.4	9.7	–	–	–	–
Derbyshire, West	79.4	36.1	27.3	32.5	–	–	4.1	–
(6/6)	81.9	61.3	38.7	–	–	–	–	–
West Lothian	71.1	11.4	50.9	10.8	3.6	23.3	–	–
(14/6)	77.9	39.7	60.3	–	–	–	–	–
Leicester, North-East	60.8	24.2	41.5	34.3	–	–	–	–
(12/7)	78.4	48.1	51.9	–	–	–	–	–
*Dorset, South	70.2	31.8	33.5	21.7	–	–	13.0	– 8.4
(22/11)	78.8	49.8	34.7	15.5	–	–	–	–
Norfolk, Central	60.2	37.7	37.0	22.5	–	–	2.8	– 7.5
(22/11)	79.9	50.3	34.8	14.9	–	–	–	–
Northamptonshire, South	69.0	41.2	38.6	19.3	–	–	0.9	– 5.7
(22/11)	82.7	57.0	43.0	–	–	–	–	–
Wiltshire, Chippenham	68.0	36.9	29.1	32.5	–	–	1.5	–
(22/11)	80.2	52.1	31.0	16.9	–	–	–	–
*Glasgow, Woodside	54.7	30.1	36.1	21.7	–	11.1	1.0	– 6.1
(22/11)	75.2	49.2	43.1	7.7	–	–	–	–

CONTESTED BY-ELECTIONS 1945-1975 (Cont.)

CONSTITUENCY AND (DATE)	Turnout %	C %	Lab %	L %	Com %	Nation-alist %	Others %	Swing to C %
1963								
Yorkshire, Colne Valley	78.9	15.4	44.4	39.5	–	–	0.7	–
(21/3)	84.1	29.9	44.3	25.8	–	–	–	–
Rotherham	56.3	28.4	69.3	–	–	–	2.3	– 7.6
(28/3)	78.9	37.2	62.8	–	–	–	–	–
Swansea, East	55.9	7.3	61.2	15.8	2.5	5.2	8.0	–
(28/3)	80.1	22.0	67.5	–	–	10.5	–	–
Leeds, South	60.5	20.1	63.0	14.7	2.2	–	–	– 7.7
(20/6)	79.0	31.0	58.6	10.4	–	–	–	–
Deptford	44.1	19.2	58.3	22.5	–	–	–	–
(4/7)	69.3	38.1	61.9	–	–	–	–	–
West Bromwich	55.2	23.6	58.8	17.6	–	–	–	–10.2
(4/7)	72.5	42.6	57.4	–	–	–	–	–
Warwickshire, Stratford	69.4	43.5	34.1	21.0	–	–	1.4	–13.7
(15/8)	76.9	68.5	31.5	–	–	–	–	–
*Bristol, South-East	42.2	–	79.7	–	–	–	20.3	–
(20/8)	81.4	43.8	56.2[2]	–	–	–	–	–
Belfast, South	48.3	64.3	25.8	9.9	–	–	–	– 4.9
(22/10)	72.1	69.9	21.6	7.5	–	1.0	–	–
*Luton	74.0	39.5	48.0	11.4	1.1	–	–	– 9.4
(7/11)	82.5	55.1	44.9	–	–	–	–	–
Perthshire and Kinross-shire, Kinross and West Perthshire	76.1	57.4	15.2	19.5	–	7.3	0.6	–
(7/11)	71.0	68.2	16.8	–	–	15.0	–	–
Dundee, West	71.6	39.4	50.6	–	2.6	7.4	–	– 4.9
(21/11)	82.9	48.3	49.6	–	2.1	–	–	–
St. Marylebone	44.2	54.9	31.8	13.3	–	–	–	– 8.9
(5/12)	65.5	64.5	23.6	11.9	–	–	–	–
Manchester, Openshaw	46.1	29.2	65.9	–	4.9	–	–	– 8.2
(5/12)	76.0	39.8	60.2	–	–	–	–	–
Suffolk, Sudbury and Woodbridge	70.5	49.6	37.0	13.4	–	–	–	– 3.7
(5/12)	81.1	53.0	33.0	14.0	–	–	–	–
Dumfriesshire	71.6	40.9	38.5	10.9	–	9.7	–	– 7.2
(12/12)	77.4	58.4	41.6	–	–	–	–	–
1964								
Hampshire, Winchester	68.7	52.2	34.6	13.2	–	–	–	– 8.5
(14/5)	76.7	67.3	32.7	–	–	–	–	–
*Lanarkshire, Rutherglen	82.0	44.5	55.5	–	–	–	–	– 7.6
(14/5)	85.8	52.1	47.9	–	–	–	–	–
Suffolk, Bury St. Edmunds	74.6	49.0	43.5	7.5	–	–	–	– 6.0
(14/5)	78.6	58.7	41.3	–	–	–	–	–
Wiltshire, Devizes	75.8	46.8	42.9	10.3	–	–	–	– 2.8
(14/5)	79.2	51.4	41.9	–	–	–	6.7	–
Kent, Faversham	74.8	44.1	55.1	–	–	–	0.8	– 5.2
(4/6)	83.8	49.7	50.3	–	–	–	–	–
Liverpool, Scotland	42.0	25.7	74.3	–	–	–	–	–12.5
(11/6)	62.5	38.2	61.8	–	–	–	–	–

[1] Viscount Stansgate (Anthony Wedgwood Benn). Subsequently Election Court awarded the seat to the Conservative candidate.

[2] At 1961 by-election seat retained by Labour but subsequently Election Court declared Conservative candidate to have been elected.

CONTESTED BY-ELECTIONS 1945-1975 (Cont.)

GENERAL ELECTION 1964—GENERAL ELECTION 1966

CONSTITUENCY AND (DATE)	Turnout %	C %	Lab %	L %	Com %	Nation-alist %	Others %	Swing to C%
1965								
*Leyton	57.7	42.8	42.4	14.0	—	—	0.8	8.7
(21/1)	70.2	33.5	50.3	16.2	—	—	—	—
Warwickshire, Nuneaton	60.8	34.9	49.0	16.1	—	—	—	4.9
(21/1)	80.1	29.1	52.8	18.1	—	—	—	—
Altrincham and Sale	62.0	50.0	29.0	19.4	—	—	1.6	1.1
(4/2)	81.2	46.8	28.0	25.2	—	—	—	—
Sussex, East Grinstead	64.5	55.0	13.5	31.5	—	—	—	—
(4/2)	78.0	53.2	19.8	27.0	—	—	—	—
Wiltshire, Salisbury	69.1	48.2	37.4	12.9	—	—	1.5	− 1.5
(4/2)	78.6	48.3	34.4	17.3	—	—	—	—
Essex, Saffron Walden	76.1	48.6	39.5	11.9	—	—	—	− 1.4
(23/3)	82.4	49.4	37.4	13.2	—	—	—	—
*Roxburghshire, Selkirkshire and Peeblesshire	82.2	38.6	11.3	49.2	—	—	0.9	—
(24/3)	82.2	42.8	15.8	38.9	—	2.5	—	—
Monmouthshire, Abertillery	63.2	14.3	79.0	—	—	6.7	—	3.6
(1/4)	75.5	14.1	85.9	—	—	—	—	—
Birmingham, Hall Green	52.4	54.8	28.8	16.4	—	—	—	2.7
(6/5)	75.8	52.6	31.8	15.6	—	—	—	—
Hove	58.5	62.2	20.6	16.9	—	—	0.3	2.4
(22/7)	69.6	68.4	31.6	—	—	—	—	—
Cities of London and Westminster	41.8	59.5	32.9	6.3	—	—	1.3	− 0.6
(4/11)	59.7	58.3	30.6	11.1	—	—	—	—
Erith and Crayford	72.0	37.4	55.4	7.2	—	—	—	1.3
(11/11)	79.6	32.5	53.1	14.4	—	—	—	—
1966								
Kingston-upon-Hull, North	76.3	40.8	52.2	6.3	—	—	0.7	− 4.5
(27/1)	77.2	40.8	43.3	15.9	—	—	—	—

GENERAL ELECTION 1966—GENERAL ELECTION 1970

CONSTITUENCY AND (DATE)	Turnout %	C %	Lab %	L %	Com %	Nation-alist %	Others %	Swing to C %
1966								
*Carmarthenshire, Carmarthen	74.9	7.1	33.1	20.8	—	39.0	—	—
(14/7)	83.0	11.6	46.2	26.1	—	16.1	—	—
1967								
Warwickshire, Nuneaton	66.1	32.7	42.1	17.6	—	—	7.6	6.5
(9/3)	79.7	31.6	53.9	14.5	—	—	—	—
Rhondda, West	82.2	4.3	49.0	—	6.8	39.9	—	—
(9/3)	80.3	7.8	76.1	—	7.4	8.7	—	—
*Glasgow, Pollok	75.7	36.9	31.2	1.9	1.8	28.2	—	5.3
(9/3)	79.0	47.6	52.4	—	—	—	—	—
Devon, Honiton	72.6	57.0	20.4	22.6	—	—	—	—
(16/3)	78.6	54.5	26.7	18.8	—	—	—	—
Staffordshire, Brierley Hill	68.0	53.8	36.2	7.8	—	—	2.2	7.6
(27/4)	79.0	51.2	48.8	—	—	—	—	—
*Cambridge	65.7	51.6	36.6	11.8	—	—	—	8.6
(21/9)	80.0	43.4	45.5	10.2	—	—	0.9	—
*Walthamstow, West	54.0	37.0	36.7	22.9	—	—	3.4	18.4
(21/9)	71.0	24.8	61.1	14.1	—	—	—	—
*Leicester, South-West	57.5	51.6	35.9	12.5	—	—	—	16.5
(2/11)	74.0	41.3	58.7	—	—	—	—	—
Manchester, Gorton	72.4	44.5	45.9	5.9	1.0	—	2.7	9.4
(2/11)	72.6	39.9	60.1	—	—	—	—	—
*Lanarkshire, Hamilton	73.7	12.5	41.5	—	—	46.0	—	—
(2/11)	73.3	28.8	71.2	—	—	—	—	—

CONTESTED BY-ELECTIONS 1945-1975 (Cont.)

CONSTITUENCY AND (DATE)	Turnout %	C %	Lab %	L %	Com %	Nation-alist %	Others %	Swing to C %
Derbyshire, West	64.5	56.6	18.4	19.8	–	–	5.2	–
(23/11)	83.4	49.6	37.2	13.2	–	–	–	–
1968								
Kensington, South	40.0	75.4	8.6	12.6	–	–	3.4	–
(14/3)	58.1	65.1	19.8	15.1	–	–	–	–
*Acton	59.7	48.6	33.9	11.4	–	–	6.1	15.1
(28/3)	73.9	42.3	57.7	–	–	–	–	–
*Dudley	63.5	58.1	34.0	7.9	–	–	–	21.1
(28/3)	73.9	40.9	59.1	–	–	–	–	–
*Warwickshire, Meriden	66.0	64.8	35.2	–	–	–	–	18.5
(28/3)	85.7	46.4	53.6	–	–	–	–	–
Warwickshire, Warwick and								
Leamington	58.5	68.3	16.5	15.2	–	–	–	18.1
(28/3)	78.9	51.6	36.1	12.3	–	–	–	–
*Oldham, West	54.7	46.5	33.6	6.7	–	–	13.2	17.7
(13/6)	70.9	38.8	61.2	–	–	–	–	–
Sheffield, Brightside	49.8	34.8	55.1	–	4.2	–	5.9	17.1
(13/6)	66.2	21.3	75.9	–	2.8	–	–	–
*Nelson and Colne	74.2	48.9	38.4	9.0	–	–	3.7	11.4
(27/6)	80.9	37.0	49.3	–	–	–	13.7	–
Glamorganshire, Caerphilly	75.9	10.4	45.6	3.6	–	40.4	–	–
(18/7)	76.7	14.6	74.3	–	–	11.1	–	–
Nottinghamshire, Bassetlaw	68.0	47.9	49.7	–	–	–	2.4	10.8
(31/10)	73.4	38.4	61.6	–	–	–	–	–
Hampshire, New Forest	55.9	66.3	13.8	19.9	–	–	–	–
(7/11)	74.2	51.2	26.7	22.1	·	–	–	–
1969								
Brighton, Pavilion	45.1	70.6	18.6	10.8	–	–	–	17.8
(27/3)	70.3	58.1	41.9	–	–	–	–	–
*Walthamstow, East	51.2	63.1	36.9	–	–	–	–	15.9
(27/3)	80.1	42.3	47.9	9.8	–	–	–	–
Somerset, Weston-super-Mare	60.8	65.7	14.6	19.7	–	–	–	–
(27/3)	78.5	52.1	28.8	19.1	–	–	–	–
*Mid-Ulster	91.5	46.7	–	–	–	53.3	–	–
(17/4)	83.9	52.2	–	–	–	47.8	–	–
Sussex, Chichester	53.4	74.2	12.2	13.6	–	–	–	–
(22/5)	73.2	57.2	25.1	17.7	–	–	–	–
*Birmingham, Ladywood	51.9	16.8	25.5	54.3	–	–	3.4	–
(26/6)	59.7	17.4	58.9	23.7	–	–	–	–
Islington, North	32.8	38.9	49.2	10.2	–	–	1.7	9.2
(30/10)	54.2	30.7	59.4	9.9	–	–	–	–
Paddington, North	46.3	48.3	51.7	–	–	–	–	11.4
(30/10)	66.4	32.3	58.4	9.3	–	–	–	–
Newcastle-under-Lyme	72.3	43.9	46.1	6.4	–	–	3.6	10.7
(30/10)	79.9	38.2	61.8	–	–	–	–	–
*Swindon	69.8	41.8	40.5	15.3	1.3	–	1.1	12.9
(30/10)	73.5	36.7	61.3	–	2.0	–	–	–
Glasgow, Gorbals	58.5	18.6	53.4	–	2.5	25.0	0.5	–
(30/10)	61.7	22.8	73.1	–	4.1	–	–	–
Lincolnshire, Louth	44.7	57.9	19.9	17.8	–	–	4.4	14.3
(4/12)	75.0	46.3	36.9	16.8	–	–	–	–
*Northamptonshire,								
Wellingborough	69.6	54.4	39.8	–	–	–	5.8	9.7
(4/12)	86.5	47.6	52.4	–	–	–	–	–
1970								
Somerset, Bridgwater	70.3	55.5	31.9	12.6	–	–	–	8.6
(12/3)	80.2	44.4	38.1	17.5	–	–	–	–
Ayrshire and Bute, South								
Ayrshire	76.3	25.6	54.0	–	–	20.4	–	3.0
(19/3)	75.1	32.8	67.2	–	–	–	–	–

CONTESTED BY-ELECTIONS 1945-1975 (Cont.)

GENERAL ELECTION 1970—GENERAL ELECTION 1974 (February)

CONSTITUENCY AND (DATE)	Turnout %	C %	Lab %	L %	Com %	Nation-alist %	Others %	Swing to C %
1970								
St. Marylebone	35.3	63.4	27.0	6.2	–	–	3.4	1.9
(22/10)	59.8	62.1	29.3	8.6	–	–	–	
Enfield, West	49.9	57.3	26.0	12.3	–	–	4.4	−0.3
(19/11)	71.2	57.9	26.2	12.8	–	–	3.1	
1971								
Liverpool, Scotland	37.7	18.4	71.3	–	–	–	10.3	−1.7
(1/4)	50.7	25.2	74.8	–	–	–	–	
Sussex, Arundel and Shoreham	53.1	64.1	20.9	14.7	–	–	0.3	2.6
(1/4)	72.0	60.8	22.9	16.3	–	–	–	
Southampton, Itchen	50.1	31.6	55.4	5.4	–	–	7.6	–
(27/5)	54.2	–	67.2	–	–	–	32.8	
*Worcestershire, Bromsgrove	67.0	48.4	51.6	–	–	–	–	−10.1
(27/5)	76.6	58.5	41.5	–	–	–	–	
Yorkshire, Goole	55.6	31.1	68.9	–	–	–	–	−8.7
(27/5)	69.5	39.8	60.2	–	–	–	–	
Hayes and Harlington	42.3	25.3	74.7	–	–	–	–	−16.5
(17/6)	67.2	41.2	57.7	–	1.1	–	–	
Greenwich	39.2	28.0	66.7	–	–	–	5.3	−8.9
(8/7)	64.0	36.3	57.3	6.4	–	–	–	
Stirling and Falkirk Burghs	60.0	18.9	46.5	–	–	34.6	–	–
(16/9)	73.1	34.8	50.7	–	–	14.5	–	
Lancashire, Widnes	45.4	30.9	69.1	–	–	–	–	−11.5
(23/9)	68.8	42.3	57.7	–	–	–	–	
Cheshire, Macclesfield	75.6	44.7	42.7	10.7	–	–	1.9	−8.4
(30/9)	76.4	52.1	33.3	14.6	–	–	–	
1972								
*Merthyr Tydfil	79.5	7.4	48.5	2.4	4.7	37.0	–	–
(13/4)	77.9	9.8	28.7	–	–	9.6	51.9[1]	
*Southwark	32.1	18.1	79.3	–	–	–	2.6	−11.1
(4/5)	48.2	28.2	67.3[2]	–	4.5	–	–	
Kingston upon Thames	53.6	52.3	31.0	11.3	–	–	5.4	−1.9
(4/5)	69.2	56.6	31.7	11.7	–	–	–	
*Rochdale	69.1	17.7	31.1	42.3	–	–	8.9	–
(26/10)	72.8	28.0	41.6	30.4	–	–	–	
Middlesex, Uxbridge	54.3	39.9	36.6	10.3	–	–	13.2	−2.2
(7/12)	74.9	49.3	41.7	9.0	–	–	–	
*Sutton and Cheam	56.3	31.9	8.7	53.6	–	–	5.8	–
(7/12)	67.6	58.1	27.3	14.6	–	–	–	
1973								
*Lincoln	72.6	17.5	23.3	–	–	–	59.2[3]	–
(1/3)	74.5	39.0	51.0	–	–	–	10.0	
Durham, Chester-le-Street	72.3	8.4	53.0	38.6	–	–	–	–
(1/3)	73.7	28.4	71.6	–	–	–	–	
Dundee, East	70.6	25.2	32.7	8.3	–	30.2	3.6	–
(1/3)	76.1	42.4	48.3	–	–	8.9	0.4	
West Bromwich	43.6	25.4	53.2	–	–	–	21.4	−8.7
(24/5)	62.2	44.8	55.2	–	–	–	–	
Lancashire, Westhoughton	63.4	42.3	57.0	–	–	–	0.7	−1.9
(24/5)	76.9	44.6	55.4	–	–	–	–	
Manchester, Exchange	43.7	7.1	55.3	36.5	–	–	1.1	–
(27/6)	57.0	27.8	68.5	–	–	–	3.7	
*Isle of Ely	65.8	35.0	26.7	38.3	–	–	–	–
(26/7)	71.9	59.9	40.1	–	–	–	–	
*Yorkshire, Ripon	64.3	40.5	13.9	43.5	–	–	2.1	–
(26/7)	73.7	60.7	26.2	13.1	–	–	–	
Hove	62.4	47.8	11.6	37.3	–	–	3.3	–
(8/11)	66.8	68.7	31.3	–	–	–	–	

CONTESTED BY-ELECTIONS 1945-1975 (Cont.)

CONSTITUENCY AND (DATE)	Turnout %	C %	Lab %	L %	Com %	Nation- alist %	Others %	Swing to C %
*Northumberland, Berwick- upon-Tweed	75.0	39.7	19.8	39.9	—	—	0.6	—
(8/11)	73.7	50.7	27.4	21.9	—	—	—	
Edinburgh, North	54.4	38.7	24.0	18.4	—	18.9	—	−0.5
(8/11)	70.1	52.8	37.1	10.1	—	—	—	
*Glasgow, Govan	51.7	11.7	38.2	8.2	—	41.9	—	—
(8/11)	63.3	28.2	60.0	—	1.5	10.3	—	

[1] Ind Lab

[2] Ind Lab at time of resignation.

[3] Dem Lab 58.2, Others 1.0

GENERAL ELECTION 1974 (February)—GENERAL ELECTION 1974 (October)

CONSTITUENCY AND (DATE)	Turnout %	C %	Lab %	L %	Com %	Nation- alist %	Others %	Swing to C %
1974								
Newham, South	25.9	11.1	62.7	12.5	—	—	13.7	—
(23/5)	63.2	12.2	66.1	14.8	—	—	6.9	

GENERAL ELECTION 1974 (October)—DECEMBER 1975

CONSTITUENCY AND (DATE)	Turnout %	C %	Lab %	L %	Com %	Nation- alist %	Others %	Swing to C %
1975								
*Greenwich, Woolwich West	62.3	48.8	42.1	5.3	—	—	3.8	7.6
(26/6)	73.9	38.6	47.1	14.3	—	—	—	

Table 2.03 UNCONTESTED BY-ELECTIONS

The following table lists all uncontested by-elections with the date and party designation of the successful candidate. Where a seat changed hands this is indicated by an asterisk before the name of the constituency and the designation of the party gaining the seat and of the party losing the seat is given. For example (Lab/C) indicates a Labour gain from Conservative.

GENERAL ELECTION 1885–GENERAL ELECTION 1886

Date	1886
29/1	Carlow (N)
9/2	Birmingham, West (L)
9/2	Derby (L)
9/2	Edinburgh, South (L)
9/2	Sheffield, Brightside (L)
10/2	Edinburghshire (L)
10/2	Hawick Burghs (L)
10/2	Stirling Burghs (L)
12/2	Elgin Burghs (L)
12/2	Leeds, South (L)
12/2	Northamptonshire, Mid (L)
12/2	Queen's, Ossory (N)
12/2	Staffordshire, North-Western (L)
13/2	Banffshire (L)
13/2	Bedfordshire, Luton (L)
13/2	Berwickshire (L)
13/2	Clackmannanshire and Kinross-shire (L)
24/2	Grantham (L)
24/2	Somerset, Southern (L)
1/3	Battersea and Clapham, Battersea (L)
3/4	Halifax (L)
7/4	Norwich (C)
19/4	Lancashire, Clitheroe (L)

GENERAL ELECTION 1886–GENERAL ELECTION 1892

Date	1886
11/8	Birmingham, East (C)
11/8	Brighton (C)
11/8	Bristol, West (C)
11/8	Croydon (C)
11/8	Hampstead (C)
11/8	Lewisham (C)
11/8	Liverpool, Walton (C)
11/8	Manchester, East (C)
11/8	Marylebone, East (C)
11/8	Paddington, South (C)
11/8	Plymouth (C)
11/8	Sheffield, Ecclesall (C)
11/8	Strand (C)
12/8	Bute (C)
12/8	Devon, Tiverton (C)
12/8	Isle of Wight (C)
12/8	Lincolnshire, Horncastle (C)
12/8	Middlesex, Ealing (C)
12/8	Middlesex, Enfield (C)
12/8	Wigtownshire (C)
13/8	Cambridge University (C)
13/8	Down, West (C)
13/8	Dublin University (two seats) (C & C)
13/8	Edinburgh and St. Andrews Universities (C)
13/8	Leicestershire, Melton (C)
16/8	Northamptonshire, Northern (C)
29/11	Brighton (C)

Date	1887
2/2	Kent, Dartford (C)
5/2	Longford, North (N)
7/2	Sligo, South (N)
16/5	Cork, North-East (N)
9/7	Cornwall, St. Ives (LU)

Date	
27/7	City of London (C)
24/8	Carlow (N)
21/9	Kerry, South (N)
17/11	Cambridge University (C)

Date	1888
3/2	Dublin University (C)
3/2	Liverpool, Walton (C)
20/2	Bristol, West (C)
28/2	Hampstead (C)
14/3	Merthyr Tydfil (L)
14/3	Sussex, Chichester (C)
21/3	Leicestershire, Melton (C)
17/4	Limerick Borough (N)
30/6	Longford, South (N)
6/7	Sligo, South (N)
10/8	Liverpool, West Derby (C)
6/11	Edinburgh and St. Andrews Universities (C)

Date	1889
27/2	Burnley (L)
3/6	Cork, South-East (N)
12/7	Dover (C)
12/8	Belfast, North (C)
25/9	Dundee (L)

Date	1890
20/2	Glamorganshire, Mid (L)
24/2	Waterford, West (N)
26/3	Cavan, West (N)
14/5	Galway, East (N)
15/5	Tipperary, Mid (N)
25/5	Down, East (C)
30/5	Donegal, West (N)
25/6	Donegal, North (N)
8/8	Carmarthenshire, Eastern (L)
12/11	Edinburgh and St. Andrews Universities (C)

Date	1891
18/4	City of London (C)
12/5	Strand (C)
2/6	Derbyshire, Western (LU)
3/6	City of London (C)
9/10	Cambridge University (C)
29/10	Kilkenny, North (N)
23/11	Leeds, North (C)
9/12	Sussex, Chichester (C)
17/12	Armagh, Mid (C)

Date	1892
15/2	Liverpool, Everton (C)
11/3	Wexford, North (N)
30/3	Worcestershire, Eastern (LU)
30/4	Essex, Chelmsford (C)

GENERAL ELECTION 1892–GENERAL ELECTION 1895

Date	1892
12/8	Finsbury, Holborn (C)
23/8	Aberdeen, South (L)
23/8	Bradford, Central (L)
23/8	Bury St. Edmunds (C)
23/8	Cornwall, St. Austell (L)
23/8	Hackney, South (L)

UNCONTESTED BY-ELECTIONS (Cont.)

Date	1892 (Cont.)
23/8	Sheffield, Brightside (L)
23/8	Southwark, West (L)
23/8	Wolverhampton, East (L)
24/8	Edinburghshire (L)
24/8	Forfarshire (L)
24/8	Glasgow, Bridgeton (L)
24/8	Northamptonshire, Mid (L)
24/8	Nottingham, East (L)
25/8	Clackmannanshire and Kinross-shire (L)
25/8	Elgin Burghs (L)
25/8	Fife, Eastern (L)
25/8	Stirling Burghs (L)
25/8	Stoke-on-Trent (L)
25/8	Yorkshire, Rotherham (L)
26/8	Merionethshire (L)
9/9	Dundee (L)
19/9	Essex, Saffron Walden (L)

Date	1893
8/2	Cork, North-East (N)
8/2	Rochester (C)
24/2	Tipperary, Mid (N)
19/6	Swansea, District (L)
28/6	Cork, North-East (N)
28/6	Cork, South-East (N)
4/7	Cardiganshire (L)
8/8	Mayo, West (N)
30/11	Wexford, South (N)
14/12	Brighton (C)

Date	1894
16/3	Leeds, West (L)
7/5	Dumfries Burghs (L)
16/8	Sussex, Chichester (C)
7/9	Kilkenny, South (N)
26/10	Sutherland (L-Crf)
14/11	York (L)

Date	1895
10/2	Paddington, South (C)
24/5	Croydon (C)
7/6	Lancashire, Chorley (C)
29/6	St. George, Hanover Square (C)
1/7	Birmingham, West (LU)
1/7	Bristol, West (C)
1/7	Manchester, East (C)
5/7	Croydon (C)
6/7	Lancashire, Blackpool (C)
6/7	Lincolnshire, Sleaford (C)
8/7	Middlesex, Ealing (C)

GENERAL ELECTION 1895—GENERAL ELECTION 1900

	1895
22/8	Cavan, West (N)
31/8	Inverness Burghs (LU)
11/9	Waterford, West (N)
28/11	Kensington, South (C)
29/11	Liverpool, East Toxteth (C)
30/11	Middlesex, Harrow (C)

	1896
21/2	Buckinghamshire, Wycombe (C)
6/4	Dublin, College Green (N)
24/4	Kerry, North (N)
12/5	Edinburgh and St. Andrews Universities (C)

	1897
15/7	Roscommon, South (N)

	1898
21/1	Armagh, Mid (C)

Date	
3/2	Marylebone, West (C/LU)
15/2	Birmingham, Edgbaston (C/LU)
11/5	Nottinghamshire, Newark (C)
19/7	Down, West (C)
20/10	Lancashire, Ormskirk (C)
4/11	Oxford (C)
9/12	Liverpool, Kirkdale (C)

	1899
6/1	Buckinghamshire, Aylesbury (LU)
16/1	Lancashire, Newton (C)
23/1	Surrey, Epsom (C)
14/2	Birmingham, North (LU)
25/2	Antrim, North (C)
2/5	Merionethshire (L)
11/5	Oxford University (LU/C)
7/12	Somerset, Wells (C)

	1900
16/2	Plymouth (C)
7/3	Sligo, North (N)
20/3	Lambeth, Brixton (C)
23/3	Finsbury, Holborn (C)
3/5	Edinburgh and St. Andrews Universities (C)
16/5	Dublin University (C)
17/7	Wiltshire, Wilton (C)

GENERAL ELECTION 1900—GENERAL ELECTION 1906

	1900
8/12	Dover (C)
8/12	Preston (C)
10/12	Somerset, Wellington (C)
10/12	Suffolk, Woodbridge (C)
10/12	Surrey, Guildford (C)
11/12	Derbyshire, Western (LU)
21/12	Monaghan, North (N)

	1901
17/5	Cork, Mid (N)
12/7	Berkshire, Wokingham (C)

	1902
19/2	Down, South (N)
26/2	Kilkenny, North (N)
4/3	Monaghan, South (N)
25/4	Donegal, West (N)
25/4	Woolwich (C)
1/8	*Lancashire, Clitheroe (Lab/L)
14/8	Devon, Tiverton (C)
15/8	Worcestershire, Eastern (LU)

	1903
26/2	Perthshire, Eastern (L)
9/3	Galway, Borough (N)
22/5	Kildare, South (N)
3/10	Leitrim, North (N)
24/10	Lancashire, Westhoughton (C)
28/10	Hampshire, Fareham (C)
28/10	Londonderry City (C)

	1904
9/2	City of London (C)
15/3	Lancashire, Rossendale (L)
6/4	*Isle of Wight (Ind C/C)[1]
10/6	Cavan, West (N)
19/8	Cork City (N)

	1905
14/2	Kildare, North (N)
14/6	Cork City (N)
15/6	Donegal, North (N)

[1] Resigned seat on leaving the Conservative Party but re-elected unopposed.

UNCONTESTED BY-ELECTIONS (Cont.)

Date	1905 (Cont.)
27/11	Yorkshire, Normanton (L-Lab)

GENERAL ELECTION 1906—GENERAL ELECTION 1910 (J)

Date	1906
26/2	Wiltshire, Westbury (L)
28/2	Aberdeenshire, Eastern (L)
28/2	Galway, North (N)
28/2	Leitrim, North (N)
3/3	Kilkenny, North (N)
5/6	Caernarvonshire, Eifion (L)
15/6	City of London (C)
15/6	St. George, Hanover Square (LU/C)
8/10	Glamorganshire, Mid (L)
31/12	Cork, Mid (Ind N)

Date	1907
12/2	Perth (L)
19/2	Monmouthshire, Northern (L)
6/3	Halifax (L)
13/4	Westmeath, South (N)
5/6	Middlesex, Hornsey (C)
20/6	Monaghan, North (N)
29/7	Kilkenny, South (N)
29/7	Wicklow, East (N)
21/8	Anglesey (L)
6/9	Longford, South (N)

Date	1908
3/2	Carlow (N)
5/2	Cornwall, St. Austell (L)
7/2	Glamorganshire, Mid (L)
26/2	Carmarthenshire, Western (L)
29/2	Worcestershire, Bewdley (C)
15/4	Derbyshire, Western (LU)
21/4	Sheffield, Central (C)

Date	1909
16/1	Warwickshire, Tamworth (C)
17/5	Edinburgh, West (LU)
5/8	Sligo, North (N)
10/8	Kilkenny, South (N)
3/9	Clare, West (N)

GENERAL ELECTION 1910(J)—GENERAL ELECTION 1910(D)

Date	1910
28/2	Swansea, District (L)
1/3	Yorkshire, Rotherham (L)
2/3	Cork, North-East (Ind N)
2/3	Devon, Barnstaple (L)
10/3	Yorkshire, Shipley (L)
12/3	Reading (L)
29/3	Wicklow, West (N)
28/4	Down, North (C)
28/4	Lanarkshire, Govan (L)
14/6	Dublin, Harbour (N)
17/6	Sussex, Lewes (C)

GENERAL ELECTION 1910(D)—GENERAL ELECTION 1918

Date	1911
11/2	Caernarvonshire, Arfon (L)
15/3	Louth, North (N)
23/3	Middlesex, Brentford (C)
29/4	Dorset, Eastern (L)
3/5	Birmingham, South (LU)
26/6	Brighton (C)
7/7	Kent, St. Augustine's (C)
13/7	Wicklow, East (N)
15/7	Cork, East (N)

Date	
15/7	Cork, North-East (Ind N)

Date	1912
8/3	Hereford (LU/C)
16/3	Essex, South-Eastern (C)
18/3	Herefordshire, Leominster (C)
21/3	Surrey, Epsom (C)
30/4	Gloucestershire, Forest of Dean (L)

Date	1913
15/2	Antrim, East (C)
15/2	Waterford, East (N)
9/6	Queen's, Leix (N)
23/6	Dover (C)
15/7	St. George, Hanover Square (C)
4/11	Cork, North (Ind N)

Date	1914
18/2	Cork City (Ind N)
6/4	Belfast, East (C)
8/4	Fife, Eastern (L)
30/6	Oxford University (C)
14/7	Birmingham, West (C)
16/7	Worcestershire, Eastern (C)
21/7	Galway, North (N)
13/8	Swansea, District (L)
20/8	Wicklow, West (N)
22/9	Bolton (Lab)
22/9	The Hartlepools (L)
29/6	Brighton (C)
30/11	Londonderry City (L)
4/12	Galway, East (N)
28/12	Sheffield, Attercliffe (Lab)

Date	1915
6/2	Norwich (L)
6/2	Swansea, District (L)
9/2	Scarborough (L)
9/2	Yorkshire, Shipley (L)
10/2	Yorkshire, Howdenshire (C)
12/2	Wigtownshire (C)
12/2	Yorkshire, Thirsk & Malton (C)
13/2	Cambridgeshire, Chesterton (L)
13/2	Essex, Saffron Walden (L)
15/2	Liverpool, Kirkdale (C)
17/2	Antrim, Mid (C)
22/2	Maidstone (C)
17/3	Carmarthen Boroughs (L)
29/4	Durham, Mid (L-Lab)
28/5	Kilmarnock Burghs (L)
9/6	Preston (C)
29/6	Yorkshire, Keighley (L)
6/7	Caernarvonshire, Arfon (L)
27/10	Westmorland, Appleby (C)
10/11	Lancashire, Heywood (L)
10/11	Middlesex, Uxbridge (C)
12/11	Cardiff Boroughs (C)
16/11	Surrey, Kingston (C)
24/11	Cornwall, St. Austell (L)
24/11	St. Helens (C)
30/11	Devon, Tiverton (C)

Date	1916
11/1	St. George, Hanover Square (C)
15/1	Portsmouth (C)
17/1	Staffordshire, North-Western (Lab)
20/1	Cambridgeshire, Chesterton (L)
21/1	Bradford, Central (L)
26/1	Yorkshire, Rotherham (L)
21/2	Liverpool, East Toxteth (C)

UNCONTESTED BY-ELECTIONS (Cont.)

Date	1916 (Cont.)
28/2	Tyrone, South (C)
29/2	Bolton (L)
29/2	Chester (C)
29/2	Worcestershire, Droitwich (C)
2/3	Cumberland, Cockermouth (L)
18/3	South Shields (L)
25/4	Dublin University (C)
22/5	Lancashire, Widnes (C)
18/7	Berwickshire (L)
7/8	Exeter (C)
15/8	Cornwall, Bodmin (C)
25/8	Yorkshire, Colne Valley (L)
29/8	Berkshire, Abingdon (C)
16/10	St. Pancras, West (C)
27/10	Fermanagh, North (C)
6/12	Middlesex, Hornsey (C)
23/12	Ashton-under-Lyne (C)
23/12	*Sheffield, Hallam (L/C)
28/12	Tower Hamlets, Whitechapel (L)
29/12	Derby (L)
29/12	Edinburgh and St. Andrews Universities (C)

	1917
2/1	Inverness-shire (L)
5/2	Yorkshire, Rotherham (L-Lab/L)
21/2	Perthshire, Western (C)
23/2	Warwickshire, Tamworth (C)
30/3	Oxford (C)
9/4	Belfast, South (C)
30/4	Middlesex, Ealing (C)
12/5	Edinburgh, South (L)
20/6	Oxfordshire, Henley (C)
28/6	Essex, Epping (C)
2/7	Belfast, South (C)
2/7	Fulham (C)
6/7	Dublin, South (N)
25/7	Cambridge (C)
27/7	Cambridgeshire, Chesterton (L)
10/8	Edinburgh and St. Andrews Universities (C)
25/8	Norwich (Lab)
5/10	Dublin University (C)
25/10	Hampshire, Basingstoke (C)
25/10	Lincolnshire, Spalding (L)
22/11	Armagh, North (C)
14/12	Cambridgeshire, Wisbech (L)
14/12	Southampton (L)

	1918
22/3	Manchester, South (C)
23/1	Armagh, Mid (C)
19/4	*King's, Tullamore (SF/Ind N)
25/4	Birmingham, West (C)
7/5	Exeter (C)
13/5	Newcastle upon Tyne (L)
18/6	Somerset, Bridgwater (C)
16/7	Manchester, North-East (Lab)
18/7	Hampshire, Fareham (C)
29/7	Sussex, East Grinstead (C)
9/8	Canterbury (C)
24/9	Oxfordshire, Banbury (L)
4/10	St. George, Hanover Square (C)
15/10	Bath (C)
23/10	Norfolk, Mid (C)
25/10	Elgin Burghs (L)
28/10	Lancashire, Prestwich (L)
28/10	South Shields (L)
6/11	Wiltshire, Wilton (C)

GENERAL ELECTION 1918—GENERAL ELECTION 1922

Date	1919
28/7	Dublin University (C)

	1920
26/7	Monmouthshire, Ebbw Vale (Lab)
9/11	Hertfordshire, Hemel Hempstead (C)
22/11	Lancashire, Middleton and Prestwich (Co L)

	1921
4/3	Birmingham, Moseley (Co C)
31/3	Birmingham, West (Co C)
9/4	Bristol, West (Co C)
14/4	Glasgow, Pollok (Co C)
16/4	Dorset, Eastern (Co L)
19/4	Cheshire, Eddisbury (Co C)
23/4	Sussex, Chichester (Co C)
14/5	Berkshire, Abingdon (Co C)
17/5	Orkney and Shetland (Co L)
20/6	Down, North (C)
23/6	Belfast, Duncairn (C)
23/6	Armagh, Mid (C)
2/7	Down, Mid (C)
8/7	Down, West (C)
29/8	Londonderry, South (C)

	1922
4/1	Shropshire, Ludlow (Co C)
18/1	Londonderry, South (C)
17/2	Down, West (C)
21/2	Down, North (C)
13/3	Liverpool, Exchange (Co C)
9/5	Wandsworth, Clapham (C/Co C)
2/6	Londonderry, North (C)
10/6	Berkshire, Newbury (Co C)
21/6	Moray and Nairnshire (Co L)
22/6	Oxfordshire, Banbury (Co L)
21/7	Down, North (C)

GENERAL ELECTION 1922—GENERAL ELECTION 1923

There were no uncontested by-elections

GENERAL ELECTION 1923—GENERAL ELECTION 1924

	1924
12/3	Kent, Dover (C)

GENERAL ELECTION 1924—GENERAL ELECTION 1929

	1926
13/2	Cambridge University (C)
	1929
29/1	Londonderry (C)

GENERAL ELECTION 1929—GENERAL ELECTION 1931

	1929
14/12	*Liverpool, Scotland (Lab/N)
	1931
7/3	Fermanagh and Tyrone (N)
25/8	Surrey, Guildford (C)

GENERAL ELECTION 1931—GENERAL ELECTION 1935

	1932
13/4	Richmond (Surrey) (C)
28/4	Sussex, Eastbourne (C)
12/7	Westminster, Abbey (C)

UNCONTESTED BY-ELECTIONS (Cont.)

Date	1933
8/5	Yorkshire, Normanton (Lab)
22/12	Yorkshire, Wentworth (Lab)

Date	1934
17/5	Yorkshire, Hemsworth (Lab)

	1935
23/2	Cambridge University (C)
29/3	Sussex, Eastbourne (C)
10/5	Warwickshire, Tamworth (C)
26/6	City of London (C)
6/7	Liverpool, West Derby (C)
20/7	Kent, Sevenoaks (C)

GENERAL ELECTION 1935—GENERAL ELECTION 1945

	1938
6/4	City of London (C)

	1939
10/5	Down (C)
12/7	Portsmouth, South (C)
6/10	Hampshire, Fareham (C)
7/10	Derbyshire, High Peak (C)
27/10	Lancashire, Ormskirk (N Lab)
28/10	Ashton-under-Lyne (Lab)
22/11	Cheshire, Macclesfield (C)
7/12	Wandsworth, Streatham (C)
13/12	Somerset, Wells (C)

	1940
1/2	Southampton (Nat/NL)
5/2	Swansea, East (Lab)
5/2	City of London (Nat/C)
8/2	Belfast, East (C)
7/3	Cheshire, City of Chester (C)
12/4	Lancashire, Lonsdale (C)
9/5	Brighton (C)
1/6	Yorkshire, Spen Valley (NL)
22/6	Wandsworth, Central (Lab)
27/6	Bournemouth (C)
5/7	Montrose Burghs (NL)
5/7	Newcastle upon Tyne, West (C)
19/7	Nottingham, Central (C)
20/7	Rochdale (Lab)
29/7	Northumberland, Wansbeck (C)
7/8	Middlesbrough, West (L)
19/8	Surrey, Mitcham (C)
28/8	Lancashire, Heywood and Radcliffe (C)
13/9	Bolton (C)
21/9	Manchester, Exchange (C)
25/9	Preston (C)
2/11	Queen's University of Belfast (C)
26/11	Hampshire, Aldershot (C)
27/11	Southampton (NL/Nat)
18/12	Birmingham, Edgbaston (C)

	1941
6/2	Yorkshire, Doncaster (Lab)
22/2	Dorset, Southern (C)
22/2	Hampshire, Petersfield (C)
10/3	Hertfordshire, Hitchin (C)
11/3	Cornwall, Bodmin (C)
26/3	Carmarthenshire, Carmarthen (Lab)
8/4	Great Yarmouth (NL)
9/4	Nottinghamshire, Mansfield (Lab)
16/4	West Bromwich (Lab)
21/6	Dorset, Western (C)
10/7	Greenock (Lab)
12/7	Edinburgh, West (C)
24/7	Yorkshire, Pontefract (Lab)
18/8	Northumberland, Berwick-upon-Tweed (L)
15/11	Brighton (C)

Date	1942
13/2	Yorkshire, Keighley (Lab)
2/3	Derbyshire, North-Eastern (Lab)
9/3	Warwickshire, Nuneaton (Lab)
11/3	Manchester, Gorton (Lab)
11/3	Newcastle-under-Lyme (Lab)
11/3	Wigan (Lab)
2/4	Devon, Tavistock (C)
21/7	Durham, Spennymoor (Lab)
7/8	Yorkshire, Rothwell (Lab)
8/8	Stepney, Whitechapel and St. George's (Lab)
27/8	Sheffield, Park (Lab)
20/10	Lancashire, Ince (Lab)

	1943
2/7	Staffordshire, Burton (C)
4/8	Buckinghamshire, Buckingham (C)
5/10	Hertfordshire, St. Albans (C)
15/11	Durham, Consett (Lab)

	1944
21/2	Sheffield, Attercliffe (Lab)
11/10	Chelsea (C)

	1945
14/5	Middlesbrough, West (L)

GENERAL ELECTION 1945—GENERAL ELECTION 1950

	1946
21/2	Yorkshire, Hemsworth (Lab)

GENERAL ELECTION 1950—GENERAL ELECTION 1951

	1951
19/5	Londonderry (C)

GENERAL ELECTION 1951—GENERAL ELECTION 1955

	1952
27/10	Antrim, North (C)

	1953
15/4	Down, North (C)

	1954
20/11	Armagh (C)

Note: There have been no uncontested by-elections since 1954.

Table 2.04   CONTESTED AND UNCONTESTED BY-ELECTIONS (Summary)

From	Contested	%	Uncontested	%	Total[1]	% of total seats
1885-86	15	39.5	23	60.5	38	5.7
1886-92	102	57.0	77	43.0	179	26.7
1892-95	53	51.5	50	48.5	103	15.4
1895-00	79	69.9	34	30.1	113	16.9
1900-06	81	71.1	33	28.9	114	17.0
1906-1910(J)	68	68.0	32	32.0	100	14.9
1910(J)-10(D)	10	47.6	11	52.4	21	3.1
1910(D)-18	115	46.6	132	53.4	247[2]	36.9
1918-22	78	72.2	30	27.8	108	15.3
1922-23	16	100.0	0	–	16	2.6
1923-24	9	90.0	1	10.0	10	1.6
1924-29	61	96.8	2	3.2	63	10.2
1929-31	33	91.7	3	8.3	36	5.9
1931-35	50	80.6	12	19.4	62	10.1
1935-45	150	68.5	69	31.5	219[3]	35.6
1945-50	51	98.1	1	1.9	52	8.1
1950-51	15	93.8	1	6.2	16	2.6
1951-55	45	93.8	3	6.2	48	7.7
1955-59	52	100.0	0	–	52	8.3
1959-64	62	100.0	0	–	62	9.8
1964-66	13	100.0	0	–	13	2.1
1966-70	38	100.0	0	–	38	6.0
1970-74(F)	30	100.0	0	–	30	4.8
1974(F)-74(O)	1	100.0	0	–	1	0.2

[1] Prior to 1926, by-elections could occur through M.P.s seeking re-election after appointment to certain ministerial and other offices. This considerably increased the number of by-elections during the period. See Table 2.05, footnote[1].

[2] From the outbreak of the First World War on August 4, 1914 until the Dissolution in 1918 there were 29 contested and 89 uncontested by-elections. The three major parties observed a truce during the war by nominating candidates only for seats which they had previously held. Twenty-two members of the House of Commons were killed or died on active service.

[3] From the outbreak of the Second World War on September 3, 1939 until the Dissolution in 1945 there were 75 contested and 66 uncontested by-elections. The three major parties observed a truce during the war by nominating candidates only for seats which they had previously held. Twenty-three members of the House of Commons were killed or died on active service.

Table 2.05 REASONS FOR BY-ELECTIONS

Cause of vacancy	Total	%	Cause of vacancy	Total	%
Death	700	40.2	Seeking re-election	20[4]	1.1
Resignation	512	29.4	Elected for two seats	14[5]	0.8
Ministerial appointment	205[1]	11.8	Disqualification	9[6]	0.5
Elevation to the Peerage	169[2]	9.7	Expulsion	6[7]	0.3
Succession to the Peerage	75	4.3	Bankruptcy	3[8]	0.2
Unseated	27[3]	1.6	Lunacy	1[9]	0.1

[1] Under the provisions of the Succession to the Crown Act, 1707 and a number of subsequent Acts, MPs appointed to certain ministerial and legal offices were required to seek re-election. For a list of the offices which if accepted by an MP were held to vacate his seat but did not debar him from seeking re-election see *Rogers on Elections* Volume 2 (18th edition, pp. 46-54, London 1906).
The Re-election of Ministers Act (1919) Amendment Act, 1926, removed the necessity of Ministers having to seek re-election upon appointment to certain offices.

[2] In cases where an MP resigned or accepted an appointment and *at the same time* was elevated to the Peerage, these have been counted as resignations and are not included in this total.

[3] Of this number 26 were unseated as the result of election petitions (see Table 11.13). The remaining case was that of the Hon. J.J. Astor (C), Kent, Dover, who in 1924 was unseated for having voted in the House of Commons before taking the Oath.

[4] The principal cause of MPs seeking re-election (i.e. resigning their seat and then seeking re-election at the resulting by-election) has been a change of party allegiance. Of the total, 13 were re-elected and 7 defeated. For a list from 1885-1918 see *British Parliamentary Election Results 1885-1918*, p. 591. Since 1918 the following have sought re-election: Hon. J.M. Kenworthy, Kingston-upon-Hull, Central, 1926; from Liberal to Labour—elected. Dr. L. Haden-Guest, Southwark North, 1927; from Labour to Constitutionalist — defeated. Sir W.A. Jowitt, Preston, 1929; from Liberal to Labour—elected. Duchess of Atholl, Perthshire and Kinross-shire, Kinross and Western, 1938; from Conservative to Independent—defeated. D. Taverne, Lincoln, 1973; from Labour to Democratic Labour—elected.

[5] All Irish Nationalists. For a list see *British Parliamentary Election Results 1885-1918*, p. 650.

[6] For a list from 1885-1918 see *British Parliamentary Election Results 1885-1918*, p. 591. Since 1918 the following have been disqualified:
W. Preston (C), Walsall, 1925; for holding contracts with the General Post Office.
Rev. J.G. MacManaway (C), Belfast, West, 1950; Minister of the Church of Ireland.
T.J. Mitchell (SF), Mid-Ulster, 1955; serving a term of imprisonment.
C. Beattie (C), Mid-Ulster, 1956; for holding an office of profit under the Crown.

[7] Namely:

1891, May 12	E.H. Verney (L), Buckinghamshire, Buckingham	
	Twelve months imprisonment for procuring a girl under 21 years of age for an immoral purpose.	
1892, Feb. 26	E.S.W. De Cobain (C), Belfast, East	
	In April 1891 a warrant was issued by the Royal Irish Constabulary for the arrest of De Cobain on charges alleging gross indecency. Before he could be arrested De Cobain went to France and twice failed to answer a summons from the House of Commons to appear before them. In January 1893 he returned to Belfast and was arrested a few weeks later. At Antrim Assizes in March 1893 he was convicted on 12 counts of gross indecency and sentenced to 12 months imprisonment with hard labour.	
1892, March 2	G.W. Hastings (LU), Worcestershire, Eastern.	
	Five years imprisonment for fraud.	
1922, August 1	H.W. Bottomley (Ind), Hackney, South.	
	Seven years imprisonment for fraud.	
1947, October 30	G. Allighan (Lab), Kent, Gravesend.	
	Contempt of the House of Commons and breach of privilege.	
1954, Dec. 16	P.A.D. Baker (C), Norfolk, South.	
	Seven years imprisonment for uttering forged documents.	

[8] Namely: P.A. McHugh (N), Leitrim, North, 1903; N.J. Murphy (N), Kilkenny, South, 1909; C.W.J. Homan (C), Ashton-under-Lyne, 1928.

[9] Namely: C. Leach (L), Yorkshire, Colne Valley, 1916.

Table 2.06 CANDIDATES AT BY-ELECTIONS

From	C	Lab	L	Com	ILP	N	PC	SNP	Others	Total
1885-86	15	—	33	—	—	5	—	—	2	55
1886-92	151	—	98	—	—	29	—	—	11	289
1892-95	63	—	75	—	3	15	—	—	5	161
1895-00	103	—	67	—	4	19	—	—	7	200
1900-06	93	7	70	—	0	19	—	—	12	201
1906-10(J)	72	13	66	—	0	22	—	—	17	190
1910(J)-10(D)	11	2	15	—	0	3	—	—	0	31
1910(D)-18	151	20	126	—	2	38	—	—	58	395
1918-22	76	56	69	1	0	0	—	—	21	223
1922-23	14	12	12	0	0	0	—	—	4	42
1923-24	10	8	7	0	0	0	—	—	1	26
1924-29	60	56	59	1	0	0	0	1	5	182
1929-31	32	31	14	7	1	1	0	3	7	96
1931-35	55	48	19	6	4	1	0	4	8	145
1935-45	176	98	20	4	11	0	3	7	112	431
1945-50	51	48	14	3	4	1	2	4	18	145
1950-51	16	14	1	1	2	0	0	0	2	36
1951-55	48	45	8	1	0	0	2	1	4	109
1955-59	50	50	19	1	3	1	3	0	11	138
1959-64	61	62	50	6	1	0	3	6	37	226
1964-66	13	13	12	0	0	0	1	0	10	49
1966-70	38	37	27	6	0	0	3	4	26	141
1970-74(F)	30	30	19	1	0	0	1	4	35	120
1974(F)-74(O)	1	1	1	0	0	0	0	0	2	5

Table 2.07 AVERAGE SWING AT BY-ELECTIONS 1945-1974

From	Total Swings to C	Total Swings to Lab	Average of individual Swings to C %	From	Total Swings to C	Total Swings to Lab	Average of individual Swings to C
1945-50	31	8	4.6	1959-64	4	35	− 5.8
1950-51	14	0	4.4	1964-66	7	4	1.5
1951-55	25	18	0.2	1966-70	25	0	12.6
1955-59	2	40	− 4.8	1970-74(F)	2	14	− 5.5
				1974(F)-74(O)	0	0	Nil

Table 3.01 CANDIDATES' EXPENSES[1]

Election	Agents[2]	Clerks[3]	Printing[4]	Meetings[5]	Rooms[6]	Miscel-laneous[7]	Personal Expenses[8]	Total[9]	Average[10]
	£	£	£	£	£	£	£	£	£
1885	220,150	103,119	284,190	28,080	35,517	62,729	56,502	790,287	610
1886	123,523	64,635	201,077	13,630	18,794	35,276	28,213	485,148	544
1892	192,874	98,999	310,379	19,627	29,709	60,03?	49,437	761,058	614
1895	151,177	82,500	259,248	13,786	24,090	47,194	40,001	617,996	624
1900	148,245	78,605	274,061	15,831	24,265	44,683	41,422	627,112	730
1906	196,656	130,051	418,596	30,456	46,137	71,670	65,355	958,921	827
1910(J)	195,177	146,100	469,949	43,946	54,232	93,020	65,801	1,068,225	861
1910(D)	156,611	104,915	335,160	33,446	39,627	71,272	49,929	790,960	769
1918†	—	—	—	—	—	—	—	—	—
1922	131,783	171,604	465,182	50,113	52,000	81,773	65,620	1,018,075	707
1923	124,631	167,296	436,411	58,529	52,647	82,334	60,492	982,340	679
1924	111,407	148,746	415,684	60,657	50,614	78,736	55,321	921,165	645
1929	138,148	188,043	577,344	68,221	66,852	106,715	68,184	1,213,507	701
1931	76,729	101,993	298,544	40,373	36,823	61,922	37,721	654,105	506
1935	83,699	107,020	340,493	41,628	40,484	68,047	40,722	722,093	536
1945	98,064	82,417	623,774	51,804	42,525	110,672	63,960	1,073,216	638
1950	90,536	65,321	714,870	67,415	53,893	114,057	64,032	1,170,124	626
1951	74,877	52,297	589,979	52,095	45,581	80,039	51,150	946,018	688
1955	78,808	51,923	557,055	37,333	42,096	85,205	52,257	904,677	642
1959	80,722	55,910	669,688	36,672	46,729	100,490	61,008	1,051,219	684
1964	85,616	51,683	824,085	40,950	51,578	104,665	70,626	1,229,203	700
1966	82,856	46,449	762,706	33,046	49,461	96,228	66,136	1,136,882	666
1970	86,061	50,480	1,046,373	30,296	50,759	128,827	73,184	1,465,980	798
1974(F)	102,996	49,926	1,591,994	37,517	64,043	162,184	87,747	2,096,407	982
1974(O)	103,010	46,528	1,748,728	41,585	67,164	161,499	92,714	2,261,228	1,004

[1] A limit on the amount a candidate could spend on an election campaign was first introduced by the Corrupt and Illegal Practices Prevention Act 1883. It fixed the legal maximum in a borough constituency at £350 where the number of electors on the register did not exceed 2,000. In boroughs with an electorate of over 2,000 the limit was £380 plus an additional £30 for each complete 1,000 electors above 2,000. In counties, the limit was £650 where the electorate did not exceed 2,000 and £710 in constituencies with over 2,000 electors plus an additional £60 for every complete 1,000 electors above 2,000.
By the Representation of the People Act, 1918, the maximum permitted expenditure became 5d. per elector in a borough constituency and 7d. (reduced to 6d. in 1929) in a county. The candidate's personal expenses and the fee, if any, paid to an election agent up to a maximum of £50 in a borough and £75 in a county, did not come within the statutory limit.
With the coming into force of the Representation of the People Act, 1949, the maximum permitted expenditure in Great Britain became £450 plus 1½d. per elector in a borough and 2d. in a county. Personal expenses were excluded from this limit. In Northern Ireland from 1950-57 the maximum permitted expenditure was 2d. per elector with personal expenses and election agent's fee (up to a maximum of £50 in a borough and £75 in a county) being excluded from this limit. By the Representation of the People (Amendment) Act, 1957, Northern Ireland adopted the scale laid down for Great Britain.
Under the Representation of the People Act, 1969, the maximum permitted expenditure by a candidate was raised to £750 plus 1s.0d. (5p) for every eight electors in a borough and 1s.0d. (5p) for every six electors in a county. Personal expenses were excluded from this limit.
The maximum limit on expenditure was again altered by the Representation of the People Act, 1974. This raised the basic figure to £1,075 plus 6p for every eight electors in a borough and 6p for every six electors in a county. Personal expenses are excluded from this limit.

[2] Fees paid to election agents, sub-agents and polling agents.

[3] Payments for clerks and messengers.

[4] The expenses of printing, of advertising, of publishing, issuing and distributing addresses and notices, and of stationery, postage, telegrams.

[5] Expenses of holding public meetings, including payments to speakers.

[6] Cost of hire of committee rooms.

[7] All expenses in respect of miscellaneous matters not included in the previous columns.

[8] The personal expenses of the candidate.

[9] This figure has not always been complete owing to the fact that at most elections a small number of candidates have failed to lodge a return of their expenses. The total expenditure at the General Elections of 1886, 1895, 1900, 1910(D), 1922, 1923, 1924, 1931 and 1935 was substantially reduced due to the high proportion of uncontested seats. The expenses of unopposed candidates were either nil or very small.

[10] Average expenditure per candidate to nearest £. This figure is distorted for some elections due to the number of uncontested seats. See footnote [9] above.

†No figures available.   Sources: Returns of Election Expenses (Home Office).

Table 3.02 RETURNING OFFICERS' EXPENSES

This table shows the costs incurred by Returning Officers in the conduct of General Elections. The figures from 1918 onwards are probably a slight overestimate of the actual expenses of each election as the cost of by-elections falling within the same financial year (April 1 to March 31) are included in the totals, separate figures not being published by the Treasury. This distortion may however be offset by the fact that disputes sometimes arise between Returning Officers and the Treasury as to expenses and as a result some payments to Returning Officers are delayed and would not be included in the figures for the financial year which included the General Election.

Returning Officers' expenses include the administrative costs of the election, printing, etc. Prior to 1918 these charges were paid by the candidates (the total charges in each constituency being divided equally among the candidates) in addition to their own election expenses (see Table 3.01).

The total cost to the taxpayer of a General Election is however considerably greater than figures given below would suggest. It is not possible to estimate the cost of diverting civil servants, local government staff, police officers, etc. from their normal duties to election work. A proportion of the annual cost (which since 1958 has been borne by ratepayers but partly recovered from government grants) of compiling the electoral register should also be allowed for in any attempt to estimate the cost of an election. The cost of compiling the 1973-74 register was estimated at about £6m and by now this figure must be considerably higher.

A further expenditure is the free delivery of the election address of each candidate, poll-cards and postal ballot papers. Since 1964, the Post Office has been able to recover this cost from the Treasury and figures supplied by the Post Office give their costs as: 1964—£990,275; 1966—£1,118,193; 1970—£1,648,854; 1974(F)—£2,896,180; 1974(O)— £3,331,684 (provisional).

Election	Returning Officers' expenses	Average per constituency[1]		Election	Returning Officers' expenses	Average per constituency[1]
	£	£			£	£
1885	235,907	352		1931	305,945	497
1886	138,938	207		1935	314,500	511
1892	197,542	295		1945	667,999	1,044
1895	156,742	234		1950	806,974	1,291
1900	150,279	224		1951	850,657	1,361
1906	206,335	308		1955	996,560	1,582
1910(J)	227,557	340		1959	1,147,856	1,822
1910(D)	187,753	280		1964	1,698,286	2,696
1918	490,716	694[2]		1966	1,551,496	2,463
1922	280,138	456		1970	2,078,165	3,299
1923	324,566	528		1974(F)	6,346,035	4,997[3]
1924	339,028	551		1974(O)		
1929	422,244	687				

[1] This figure is distorted for several elections prior to 1955 due to the number of uncontested constituencies in which expenses would be low.

[2] The high expenditure at this election was probably due to the considerable increase in the number of polling stations which must have necessitated the purchase of new ballot-boxes and other equipment.

[3] As the February election was at the end of the 1973-74 financial year, many of the accounts from Returning Officers were not paid by the Treasury until after April 1 and were therefore included in the expenditure figures for the year 1974-75. It is therefore not possible to provide separate figures for the two 1974 elections and the figure represents the total expenses in the financial years of 1973-74 and 1974-75.

Sources: 1885-1910; Returns of Election Expenses (Home Office).
1918; House of Commons Debates (1921), 142, c. 1893.
1922-66; Finance Accounts of the United Kingdom.
1970 onwards: Consolidated Fund and National Loans Fund Accounts (Supplementary Statements).

Table 4.01 ELECTORATE AND TURNOUT

	Total Electorate	Electorate in uncontested seats	% of total	Age of Register[1] (months)	Turnout %[2]
1885					
ENGLAND	4,094,674	42,595	1.0	—	81.9
WALES	282,242	33,095	11.7	—	82.2
SCOTLAND	560,580	30,462	0.1	—	82.0
IRELAND	737,965	146,461	19.9	—	75.0
UNIVERSITIES	32,569	25,709	78.9	—	77.2
UNITED KINGDOM	**5,708,030**	**278,322**	**4.9**	**4**	**81.2**
1886					
ENGLAND	4,094,674	1,265,691	30.9	—	74.1
WALES	282,242	107,350	38.0	—	74.5
SCOTLAND	560,580	80,772	14.4	—	72.3
IRELAND	737,965	493,550	66.9	—	79.8
UNIVERSITIES	32,569	25,835	79.3	—	55.8
UNITED KINGDOM	**5,708,030**	* **1,973,198**	**34.6**	**11½**	**74.2**
1892					
ENGLAND	4,478,524	301,868	6.7	—	78.7
WALES	314,647	40,010	12.7	—	75.6
SCOTLAND	589,520	—	—	—	78.3
IRELAND	740,536	171,499	23.2	—	67.7
UNIVERSITIES	37,314	32,962	88.3	—	56.2
UNITED KINGDOM	**6,160,541**	**546,339**	**8.9**	**11½**	**77.4**
1895					
ENGLAND	4,620,320	1,195,625	25.9	—	79.2
WALES	322,784	19,296	6.0	—	79.3
SCOTLAND	616,178	35,714	5.8	—	76.3
IRELAND	732,046	442,807	60.5	—	72.7
UNIVERSITIES	39,191	39,191	100.0	—	—
UNITED KINGDOM	**6,330,519**	**1,732,633**	**27.4**	**12**	**78.4**
1900					
ENGLAND	4,929,485	1,647,537	33.4	—	76.0
WALES	340,290	114,552	33.7	—	76.4
SCOTLAND	661,748	33,260	5.0	—	75.3
IRELAND	757,849	524,739	69.2	—	60.9
UNIVERSITIES	41,563	41,563	100.0	—	—
UNITED KINGDOM	**6,730,935**	**2,361,651**	**35.1**	**14½**	**75.1**
1906					
ENGLAND	5,416,537	227,095	4.2	—	83.6
WALES	387,535	148,487	38.3	—	82.6
SCOTLAND	728,725	7,464	1.0	—	80.9
IRELAND	686,661	522,612	76.1	—	82.1
UNIVERSITIES	45,150	11,290	25.0	—	67.0
UNITED KINGDOM	**7,264,608**	**916,948**	**12.6**	**6**	**83.2**
1910 (J)					
ENGLAND	5,774,892	54,348	0.9	—	87.7
WALES	425,744	—	—	—	84.9
SCOTLAND	762,184	—	—	—	84.7
IRELAND	683,767	420,304	61.5	—	80.3
UNIVERSITIES	48,154	19,060	39.6	—	71.3
UNITED KINGDOM	**7,694,741**	**493,712**	**6.4**	**6**	**86.8**
1910 (D)					
ENGLAND	5,774,892	1,025,512	17.8	—	82.1
WALES	425,744	123,423	29.0	—	78.3
SCOTLAND	779,012	90,057	11.6	—	81.8
IRELAND	683,767	419,489	61.4	—	74.8
UNIVERSITIES	46,566	40,496	87.9	—	73.1
UNITED KINGDOM	**7,709,981**	**1,698,977**	**22.0**	**16½[3]**	**81.6**

ELECTORATE AND TURNOUT (Cont.)

	Total Electorate	Electorate in uncontested seats	% of total	Age of Register[1] (months)	Turnout %[2]
1918[4]					
ENGLAND	16,021,600	2,023,222	12.6	–	55.7
WALES	1,170,974	367,641	31.4	–	65.9
SCOTLAND	2,205,383	216,015	9.8	–	55.1
IRELAND	1,926,274	474,778	24.6	–	69.5
UNIVERSITIES	68,091	–	–	–	60.2
UNITED KINGDOM	**21,392,322**	**3,081,656**	**14.4**	**5**	**57.2**
1922					
ENGLAND	16,726,739	1,272,920	7.6	–	72.8
WALES	1,235,579	111,898	9.1	–	79.4
SCOTLAND	2,231,532	82,053	3.7	–	70.4
N. IRELAND	608,877	447,468	73.5	–	77.2
UNIVERSITIES	71,729	32,355	45.1	–	65.9
UNITED KINGDOM	**20,874,456**	**1,946,694**	**9.3**	**● 5**	**73.0**
1923					
ENGLAND	17,079,822	951,223	5.6	–	71.1
WALES	1,258,973	166,044	13.2	–	77.3
SCOTLAND	2,250,826	105,500	4.7	–	67.9
N. IRELAND	615,320	404,818	65.8	–	76.5
UNIVERSITIES	78,120	34,109	43.6	–	72.6
UNITED KINGDOM	**21,283,061**	**1,661,694**	**7.8**	**6**	**71.1**
1924					
ENGLAND	17,471,109	611,975	3.5	–	77.4
WALES	1,287,543	301,355	23.4	–	80.0
SCOTLAND	2,279,893	72,258	3.2	–	75.1
N. IRELAND	610,064	87,744	14.4	–	66.7
UNIVERSITIES	82,379	3,104	3.8	–	66.9
UNITED KINGDOM	**21,730,988**	**1,076,436**	**5.0**	**4½**	**77.0**
1929[5]					
ENGLAND	23,424,580	129,401	0.6	–	76.6
WALES	1,598,509	–	–	–	82.4
SCOTLAND	2,940,456	–	–	–	73.5
N. IRELAND	771,946	199,989	25.9	–	63.8
UNIVERSITIES	119,257	3,361	2.8	–	65.8
UNITED KINGDOM	**28,854,748**	**332,751**	**1.2**	**6**	**76.3**
1931					
ENGLAND	24,423,766	1,660,748	6.8	–	76.1
WALES	1,625,118	251,865	15.5	–	79.3
SCOTLAND	2,992,433	291,440	9.7	–	77.4
N. IRELAND	773,302	521,178	67.4	–	74.5
UNIVERSITIES	137,742	97,011	70.4	–	69.8
UNITED KINGDOM	**29,952,361**	**2,822,242**	**9.4**	**5**	**76.4**
1935					
ENGLAND	25,618,571	811,794	3.2	–	70.7
WALES	1,669,793	529,638	31.7	–	76.4
SCOTLAND	3,115,917	42,079	1.4	–	72.6
N. IRELAND	805,220	403,947	50.2	–	72.0
UNIVERSITIES	164,948	30,663	18.6	–	57.9
UNITED KINGDOM	**31,374,449**	**1,818,121**	**5.8**	**5½**	**71.1**
1945					
ENGLAND	27,045,729	21,325	0.1	–	73.4
WALES	1,798,199	39,652	2.2	–	75.7
SCOTLAND	3,343,120	–	–	–	69.0
N. IRELAND	835,980	68,752	8.2	–	67.4
UNIVERSITIES	217,363	–	–	–	53.3
UNITED KINGDOM	**33,240,391**	**129,729**	**0.4**	**5**	**72.8**

ELECTORATE AND TURNOUT (Cont.)

	Total Electorate	Electorate in uncontested seats	% of total	Age of Register[1] (months)	Turnout %
1950					
ENGLAND	28,374,288	–	–	–	84.4
WALES	1,802,356	–	–	–	84.8
SCOTLAND	3,370,190	–	–	–	80.9
N. IRELAND	865,421	140,501	16.2	–	77.4
UNITED KINGDOM	**34,412,255**	**140,501**	**0.4**	**3**	**83.9**
1951					
ENGLAND	28,813,343	–	–	–	82.7
WALES	1,812,664	–	–	–	84.4
SCOTLAND	3,421,419	–	–	–	81.2
N. IRELAND	871,905	292,271	33.5	–	79.9
UNITED KINGDOM	**34,919,331**	**292,271**	**0.8**	**11**	**82.6**
1955					
ENGLAND	28,790,285	–	–	–	76.9
WALES	1,801,217	–	–	–	79.6
SCOTLAND	3,387,536	–	–	–	75.1
N. IRELAND	873,141	–	–	–	74.1
UNITED KINGDOM	**34,852,179**	–	–	**7½**	**76.8**
1959					
ENGLAND	29,303,126	–	–	–	78.9
WALES	1,805,686	–	–	–	82.6
SCOTLAND	3,413,732	–	–	–	78.1
N. IRELAND	874,760	–	–	–	65.9
UNITED KINGDOM	**35,397,304**	–	–	**12**	**78.7**
1964					
ENGLAND	29,804,627	–	–	–	77.0
WALES	1,805,454	–	–	–	80.1
SCOTLAND	3,393,421	–	–	–	77.6
N. IRELAND	890,552	–	–	–	71.7
UNITED KINGDOM	**35,894,054**	–	–	**12**	**77.1**
1966					
ENGLAND	29,894,141	–	–	–	75.9
WALES	1,800,925	–	–	–	79.0
SCOTLAND	3,359,891	–	–	–	76.0
N. IRELAND	902,288	–	–	–	66.1
UNITED KINGDOM	**35,957,245**	–	–	**5½**	**75.8**
1970[6]					
ENGLAND	32,737,025	–	–	–	71.4
WALES	1,958,778	–	–	–	77.4
SCOTLAND	3,629,017	–	–	–	74.1
N. IRELAND	1,017,193	–	–	–	76.6
UNITED KINGDOM	**39,342,013**	–	–	**8**	**72.0**
1974 (F)[7]					
ENGLAND	33,077,573	–	–	–	79.0
WALES	1,993,516	–	–	–	80.0
SCOTLAND	3,655,621	–	–	–	79.0
N. IRELAND	1,027,155	–	–	–	69.9
UNITED KINGDOM	**39,753,865**	–	–	**4½**	**78.8**
1974 (O)[7]					
ENGLAND	33,341,372	–	–	–	72.5
WALES	2,008,284	–	–	–	76.6
SCOTLAND	3,686,792	–	–	–	74.8
N. IRELAND	1,036,523	–	–	–	67.7
UNITED KINGDOM	**40,072,971**	–	–	**12**	**72.8**

[1] This figure is based on the qualifying date in England and Wales. The qualifying date in the other parts of the United Kingdom sometimes varied by a few weeks from that in England and Wales.

[2] This figure makes allowance, prior to 1950, for the two-member seats. Only the actual number (or an estimated figure in a few cases where details were not available) of electors voting in these seats have been counted. See Introductory Notes.

ELECTORATE AND TURNOUT (Cont.)

[3] In Scotland the election was contested on the November 1910 Register which had a qualifying date of July 31.

[4] Those who had served in the war were enfranchised at 19 years of age. Women were enfranchised at 30 years of age.

[5] Extension of the franchise to women at 21 years of age.

[6] Extension of the franchise to persons at 18 years of age.

[7] Estimated figure, see Introductory Notes. The forumula used was number of "dated names" multiplied by $\frac{12}{364}$ February 1974 and $\frac{236}{364}$ (October 1974).

Sources: Electorate 1918; House of Commons Papers, 1918 (138) xix, 925.
Electorate 1922—70; Returns of Election Expenses (Home Office).
Electorate 1974 (F) onwards; Parliamentary Research Services.

Table 4.02 BUSINESS ELECTORATE[1]

Election	Total	% of Total Electorate	Election	Total	% of Total Electorate
1918	159,013	0.9	1929	371,594	1.5
1922	199,904	1.1	1931	365,090	1.4
1923	208,694	1.1	1935	367,797	1.3
1924	211,257	1.1	1945[2]	48,974	0.2

[1] This table shows the number of persons on the Business Premises Register in England and Wales until the Business Vote was abolished in 1950. Figures for Scotland (except in 1945) and Northern Ireland were not published.

[2] The total for Scotland was 8,479 (0.3%).

Sources: 1918; House of Commons Papers, 1918 (138) xix, 925.
1922-45; Registrar-General's Statistical Reviews of England and Wales, Tables, Part 2, Civil.
Registrar-General for Scotland, Annual Report, 1945.

Table 4.03 MALE AND FEMALE ELECTORATE[1]

Election	Males	%	Females	%	Total
1918	12,913,166	60.4	8,479,156	39.6	21,392,322
1922	10,681,899	57.4	7,931,157	42.6	18,613,056[2]
1923	12,101,039	57.3	9,002,499	42.7	21,286,195[3]
1924	12,431,253	57.2	9,297,924	42.8	21,731,672[4]
1929[5]	13,657,434	47.3	15,193,925	52.7	28,851,359
1931	14,098,181	47.1	15,854,630	52.9	29,952,811
1935	14,801,402	47.2	16,571,821	52.8	31,373,223

[1] This table shows the number of men and women electors at each General Election until 1935. The compilation of statistics relating to the sex of electors ceased in 1938.

These statistics were compiled by the Registrar-General and are reproduced from the Statistical Abstract of the United Kingdom, No. 83, 1924-38. In some instances, the figure of total electorate is slightly different from that given (supplied by Returning Officers) in Home Office Returns of Election Expenses on which other tables in this book have been based. The discrepancies are however of no statistical significance.

[2] Excluding Scotland where, except for the City of Glasgow, statistics of male and female voters were not compiled.

[3] Including 182,657 electors in constituencies where statistics of male and female electors were not compiled.

[4] Including 2,495 electors in constituencies where statistics of male and female electors were not compiled.

[5] Extension of the franchise to women at 21 years of age.

Source: House of Commons Papers, 1939-40 (Cmd. 6232) x, 431.

Table 5.01   FORFEITED DEPOSITS—GENERAL ELECTIONS[1]

Election	C	Lab	L	Com	PC	SNP	Others	Total [2]	% of total opposed candidates
1918	3	6	44	—	—	—	108	161	10.6
1922	1	7	32	1	—	—	11	52	3.8
1923	0	17	8	0	—	—	2	27	1.9
1924	1	28	30	1	—	—	8	68	4.9
1929	18	35	25	21	1	2	11	113	6.6
1931	5	21[3]	6	21	1	2	29	85	6.9
1935	1	16	40	0	1	5	18	81	6.2
1945	6	2	76	12	6	6	74	182	10.8
1950	5	0	319	97	6	3	31	461	24.7
1951	3	1	66	10	4	1	11	96	7.0
1955	3	1	60	15	7	1	13	100	7.1
1959	2	1	55	17	14	3	24	116	7.6
1964	5	8	52	36	21	12	52	186	10.6
1966	9	3	104	57	18	10	36	237	13.9
1970	10	6	184	58	25	43	82	408	22.2
1974(F)	8	25	23	43	26	7	189	321	15.0
1974(O)	28	13	125	29	26	0	221	442	19.6

[1] Since 1918 a candidate has forfeited the deposit of £150 if he failed to poll more than one-eighth of the total votes cast, exclusive of spoilt papers. In the case of the two-member constituencies which existed until 1950, the number of votes was deemed to be the number of good ballot papers counted. The money from forfeited deposits goes to the Treasury but in the case of the University constituencies (where a candidate had to poll more than one-eighth of the first preference votes) the deposit was forfeited to the University. In the Combined Scottish Universities, the only three-member consitituency, the requirement was that a candidate must poll more than one-eighth of the first preference votes divided by three.
Where a candidate is nominated at a General Election in more than one constituency not more than one of the deposits can be returned irrespective of the number of votes polled. Eight deposits were forfeited in Ireland in 1918 owing to this rule.
Until 1950, the deposit was not returned to a successful candidate until he had taken the Oath as a Member of Parliament and, especially in 1918, Sinn Fein M.P.s must have forfeited their deposits through refusing to take their seats in the House of Commons.
Throught this table, forfeited deposits due to multiple candidatures or failure to take the Oath have been ignored.

[2] With a total of 3,136 forfeited deposits the Treasury benefited by £467,550 and the Universities by £2,850, a total of £470,400.

[3] Including 1 unendorsed.

Table 5.02   FORFEITED DEPOSITS—BY-ELECTIONS

From	C	Lab	L	Com	PC	SNP	Others	Total [1]	% of total opposed candidates
1918-22	1	0	2	1	—	—	8	12	6.2
1922-23	0	1	1	0	—	—	2	4	9.5
1923-24	0	0	2	0	—	—	0	2	8.0
1924-29	0	5	10	0	0	1	4	20	11.1
1929-31	0	0	2	6	0	1	2	11	11.8
1931-35	0	0	3	5	0	2	6	16	12.0
1935-45	0	1	2	3	0	2	43	51	14.1
1945-50	3	1	9	2	0	4	16	35	24.3
1950-51	0	0	1	1	0	0	3	5	14.3
1951-55	0	0	7	1	1	1	4	14	13.2
1955-59	0	0	1	1	3	0	12	17	12.3
1959-64	2	1	8	6	3	4	37	61	27.0
1964-66	0	1	4	0	1	0	10	16	32.7
1966-70	4	2	12	6	0	0	24	48	34.0
1970-74	4	2	9	1	0	0	33	49	40.8
1974(F)-1974(O)	1	0	0	0	0	0	2	3	60.0

[1] With a total of 364 forfeited deposits the Treasury benefited by £53,250 and the Universities by £1,350, a total of £54,600.

Table 6.01 **SEATS WHICH CHANGED HANDS AT GENERAL ELECTIONS 1950–1974**

	1950	1951	1955	1959	1964	1966	1970	1974(F)	1974(O)
C from L	0	2	0	1	0	0	5	2	2
Lab	10	21	11	28	5	0	68	1	0
DP	0	0	0	0	0	0	1	0	0
Irish LP	1	0	1	0	0	0	0	0	0
Ind	2	0	0	0	0	0	0	0	0
Inc C	0	0	0	0	0	0	1	0	0
Ind L	1	0	0	0	0	0	0	0	0
Lab from C	1	0	1	5	58	47	6	11	17
L	0	2	0	0	2	2	2	0	1
PC	0	0	0	0	0	0	1	0	0
SNP	0	0	0	0	0	0	1	0	0
Ind	0	1	0	0	0	0	0	0	0
Ind C	0	0	0	0	1	0	0	0	0
Ind Lab	1	0	0	0	0	0	0	0	2
L from C	2	0	0	1	3	3	0	2	1
Lab	0	1	0	0	0	1	0	2	0
Ind C	0	0	0	0	1	0	0	0	0
Irish LP from C	0	1	0	0	0	0	0	0	0
PC from Lab	0	0	0	0	0	0	0	2	1
Prot U from C	0	0	0	0	0	0	1	0	0
Rep LP from C	0	0	0	0	0	1	0	0	0
SF from N	0	0	2	0	0	0	0	0	0
SNP from Lab	0	0	0	0	0	0	1	2	0
C	0	0	0	0	0	0	0	4	4
Unity from C	0	0	0	0	0	0	1	0	0
UUUC from U	0	0	0	0	0	0	0	1	0
Unity	0	0	0	0	0	0	0	1	0
Ind	0	0	0	0	0	0	0	1	0
Ind Lab from Lab	0	0	0	0	0	0	1	1	0
Ind from UUUC	0	0	0	0	0	0	0	0	1
TOTAL	18	28	15	35	70	54	89	30	29

Table 6.02 **SEATS WHICH CHANGED HANDS AT BY-ELECTIONS 1950—1974**

	1950- 1951	1951- 1955	1955- 1959	1959- 1964	1964- 1966	1966- 1970	1970- 1974(F)	1974(F)- 1974(O)
C from Lab	0	1	0	1	1	12	0	0
Ind C	0	0	2	0	0	0	0	0
Lab from C	0	0	3	6	0	0	1	0
L	0	0	1	0	0	0	0	0
Ind Lab	0	0	0	0	0	0	2	0
L from C	0	0	1	1	1	0	4	0
Lab	0	0	0	0	0	1	1	0
PC from Lab	0	0	0	0	0	1	0	0
SNP from Lab	0	0	0	0	0	1	1	0
Unity from C	0	0	0	0	0	1	0	0
Ind C from C	0	0	1	0	0	0	0	0
Ind Lab from Lab	0	0	0	0	0	0	1	0
TOTAL	0	1	8	8	2	16	10	0

Table 6.03
GAINS AND LOSSES AT GENERAL ELECTIONS

Election	C net ±	Lab net ±	L net ±	Others net ±
1885[1]				
1886	+ 44		− 44	†
1892	− 49		+ 51	− 2
1895	+ 90		− 89	− 1
1900	+ 3	+ 2	− 4	− 1
1906	−211	+ 25	+ 185	+ 1
1910 (J)	+103	− 4	− 98	− 1
1910 (D)	†	+ 2	− 4	+ 2
1918[1]				
1922	− 18	+ 67	− 39	− 10
1923	− 88	+ 47	+ 42	− 1
1924	+ 155	− 42	−114	+ 1
1929	−140	+126	+ 14	†
1931	+217	−215	+ 6	− 8
1935	− 84	+ 94	− 12	+ 2
1945[2]	−187	+199	− 8	− 4
1950[3]	+ 11	− 8	+ 2	− 5
1951	+ 22	− 19	− 3	†
1955[4]	+ 11	− 10	†	− 1
1959	+ 23	− 23	†	†
1964	− 56	+ 56	+ 2	− 2
1966	− 51	+ 48	+ 2	+ 1
1970	+ 67	− 60	− 7	†
1974(F)[5]	− 14	+ 3	+ 2	+ 9
1974(O)	− 20	+ 19	− 2	+ 3

[1] Boundary changes. Calculation of gains and losses not applicable.

[2] Boundary changes. Calculations are based on the 593 constituencies with either unchanged boundaries or minor changes only.

[3] Boundary changes. Calculations are based on the 88 constituencies with either unchanged boundaries or minor changes only.

[4] Boundary changes. Calculations are based on the 454 constituencies with either unchanged boundaries or minor changes only.

[5] Boundary changes. Calculations are based on the 322 constituencies with either unchanged boundaries or minor changes only.

† No overall gain or loss.

Table 6.04
GAINS AND LOSSES AT BY-ELECTIONS

From	C net ±	Lab net ±	L net ±	Others net ±
1885-86	+ 2		− 1	− 1
1886-92	−20		+ 19	+ 1
1892-95	+ 4		− 4	†
1895-00	−11		+ 10	+ 1
1900-06	−25	+ 3	+ 17	+ 5
1906-10(J)	+ 11	+ 3	−16	+ 2
1910(J)-10(D)	†	†	†	†
1910(D)-18	+ 13	− 5	−10	+ 2
1918-22	−10	+ 13	− 6	+ 3
1922-23	− 3	+ 2	+ 2	− 1
1923-24	+ 1	†	− 1	†
1924-29	−16	+ 12	+ 4	†
1929-31	+ 3	− 2	− 1	†
1931-35	− 9	+ 10	− 1	†
1935-45	−28	+ 12	†	+ 16
1945-50	+ 4	− 1	†	− 3
1950-51	†	†	†	†
1951-55	+ 1	− 1	†	†
1955-59	− 3	+ 4	†	− 1
1959-64	− 6	+ 5	+ 1	†
1964-66	†	− 1	+ 1	†
1966-70	+ 11	−15	+ 1	+ 3
1970-74(F)	− 5	†	+ 5	†
1974 (F)-74(O)	†	†	†	†

† No overall gain or loss

Table 7.01 THE CONSERVATIVE VOTE[1]

Election	Candidates	Unopposed Returns	M.P.s Elected	Forfeited Deposits	Total votes	% of U.K. total
1885	602	10	249	—	2,020,927	43.5
1886	563	118	393	—	1,520,886	51.4
1892	606	40	314	—	2,159,150	47.0
1895	588	132	411	—	1,894,772	49.1
1900	569	163	402	—	1,767,958	50.3
1906	556	13	156	—	2,422,071	43.4
1910(J)	594	19	272	—	3,104,407	46.8
1910(D)	548	72	272	—	2,420,169	46.6
1918	445	41	382	3	4,144,192	38.6
1922	482	42	344	1	5,502,298	38.5
1923	536	35	258	0	5,514,541	38.0
1924	534	16	412	1	7,854,523	46.8
1929	590	4	260	18	8,656,225	38.1
1931	583	49	522	5	13,156,790	60.7
1935	583	23	429	1	11,755,654	53.3
1945	618	1	210	6	9,972,010	39.6
1950	619	2	298	5	12,492,404	43.5
1951	617	4	321	3	13,718,199	48.0
1955	624	0	345	3	13,310,891	49.7
1959	625	0	365	2	13,750,875	49.3
1964	630	0	304	5	12,002,642	43.4
1966	629	0	253	9	11,418,455	41.9
1970	628	0	330	10	13,145,123	46.4
1974(F)	623	0	297	8	11,872,180	37.9
1974(O)	622	0	277	28	10,462,565	35.8

[1] Including Liberal Unionists, 1886-1910(D) and National, National Liberal and National Labour 1931-45.

Table 7.02 THE LABOUR VOTE

Election	Candidates	Unopposed Returns	M.P.s Elected	Forfeited Deposits	Total Votes	% of U.K. total
1900	15[1]	0	2	—	62,698	1.3
1906	50	0	29	—	321,663	4.8
1910 (J)	78	0	40	—	505,657	7.0
1910(D)	56	3	42	—	371,802	6.4
1918	361	11	57	6	2,245,777	20.8
1922	414	4	142	7	4,237,349	29.7
1923	427	3	191	17	4,439,780	30.7
1924	514	9	151	28	5,489,087	33.3
1929	569	0	287	35	8,370,417	37.1
1931[2]	516	6	52	21	6,649,630	30.8
1935	552	13	154	16	8,325,491	38.0
1945	603	2	393	2	11,967,746	48.0
1950	617	0	315	0	13,266,176	46.1
1951	617	0	295	1	13,948,883	48.8
1955	620	0	277	1	12,405,254	46.4
1959	621	0	258	1	12,216,172	43.9
1964	628	0	317	8	12,205,808	44.1
1966	622	0	364	3	13,096,629	48.1
1970	625	0	288	6	12,208,758	43.1
1974(F)	623	0	301	25	11,645,616	37.2
1974(O)	623	0	319	13	11,457,079	39.2

[1] J. Keir Hardie is counted twice in this total. He contested both Preston and Merthyr Tydfil and was elected for the latter.

[2] Including twenty-five unendorsed candidates (see Table 1.14, footnote[3]) of whom six (including one unopposed) were elected, one deposit was forfeited and the total votes polled were 324,893 (4.9%).

Table 7.03 **SPONSORSHIP OF LABOUR CANDIDATES**

Election	Constituency Labour Parties[1]	%	ILP	%	Co-operative Party	%	Trade Unions[2]	%	Others[3]	%	Total
1900	–	–	9	60.0	–	–	3	20.0	3	20.0	15
1906	3	6.0	10	20.0	–	–	35	70.0	2	4.0	50
1910(J)†	?	–	14	17.9	–	–	?	–	2	2.6	78
1910(D)†	?	–	12	21.4	–	–	?	–	2	3.8	56
1918	144	39.9	50	13.9	–	–	163	45.1	4	1.1	361
1922†	?	–	55	13.2	11	2.7	?	–	0	–	414
1923†	?	–	89	20.8	10	2.3	?	–	0	–	427
1924†	?	–	87	16.9	10	1.9	?	–	0	–	514
1929	363	63.8	55	9.7	12	2.1	139	24.4	0	–	569
1931	341	69.4	–	–	18	3.7	132	26.9	0	–	491
1935	400	72.5	–	–	20	3.6	128	23.2	4	0.7	552
1945	443	73.5	–	–	34	5.6	126	20.9	0	–	603
1950	441	71.5	–	–	33	5.3	140	22.7	3	0.5	617
1951	441	71.5	–	–	38	6.1	137	22.2	1	0.2	617
1955	452	72.9	–	–	38	6.1	129	20.8	1	0.2	620
1959	461	74.2	–	–	30	4.8	129	20.8	1	0.2	621
1964	463	73.7	–	–	27	4.3	138	22.0	0	–	628
1966	460	73.9	–	–	24	3.9	138	22.2	0	–	622
1970	460	73.8	–	–	28	4.3	137	21.9	0	–	625
1974(F)	443	71.1	–	–	25	4.0	155	24.9	0	–	623
1974(O)	458	73.5	–	–	24	3.9	141	22.6	0	–	623

[1] Including (prior to February 1974) candidates of the Northern Ireland Labour Party if they received Labour Party endorsement.

[2] These figures are based on the Annual Conference Reports of the Labour Party but Martin Harrison in his book *Trade Unions and the Labour Party since 1945* (London, 1960) produces slightly modified figures as the result of an examination of union accounts.

[3] 1900:   Two sponsored by the Social Democratic Federation and one by a local trades council.
　　1906:   Sponsored by local trades councils.
　　1910(J): Sponsored by the Fabian Society.
　　1910(D): Sponsored by the Fabian Society.
　　1918:   Sponsored by the British Socialist Party.
　　1935:   Sponsored by the Scottish Socialist Party.
　　1950-59: Sponsored by the Royal Arsenal Co-operative Society.

† No complete figures are available.

Sources: Annual Conference Reports of the Labour Party, the Co-operative Party, the ILP and the Social Democratic Federation.
　　　　　　 Labour and Politics, 1900-1906 by Frank Bealey and Henry Pelling (London, 1958).
　　　　　　 The History of the Fabian Society by Edward R. Pease (London, 1916).

Table 7.04 **SPONSORSHIP OF LABOUR MEMBERS**

	Constituency Labour Parties	%	ILP	%	Co-operative Party	%	Trade Unions[1]	%	Others[2]	%	Total
Election											
1900	—	—	1	50.0	—	—	1	50.0	0	—	2
1906	1	3.5	7	24.1	—	—	21	72.4	0	—	29
1910(J)†	?	—	6	15.0	—	—	?	—	0	—	40
1910(D)†	?	—	8	19.0	—	—	?	—	1	2.4	42
1918	5	8.8	3	5.3	—	—	49	85.9	0	—	57
1922	18	12.7	32	22.5	4	2.8	86	60.6	2	1.4	142
1923	32	16.8	45	23.6	6	3.1	102	53.4	6	3.1	191
1924	27	17.9	27	17.9	5	3.3	88	58.2	4	2.7	151
1929	126	43.9	37	12.9	9	3.1	115	40.1	0	—	287
1931	13	28.3	—	—	1	2.2	32	69.5	0	—	46
1935	66	42.9	—	—	9	5.8	79	51.3	0	—	154
1945	249	63.3	—	—	23	5.9	121	30.8	0	—	393
1950	186	59.1	—	—	18	5.7	110	34.9	1	0.3	315
1951	174	59.0	—	—	16	5.4	104	35.3	1	0.3	295
1955	161	58.1	—	—	19	6.9	96	34.6	1	0.4	277
1959	148	57.4	—	—	16	6.2	93	36.0	1	0.4	258
1964	178	56.1	—	—	19	6.0	120	37.9	0	—	317
1966	214	58.8	—	—	18	4.9	132	36.3	0	—	364
1970	159	55.2	—	—	15	5.2	114	39.6	0	—	288
1974(F)	158	52.5	—	—	16	5.3	127	42.2	0	—	301
1974(O)	176	55.2	—	—	16	5.0	127	39.8	0	—	319

[1]These figures are based on the Annual Conference Reports of the Labour Party but Martin Harrison in his book *Trade Unions and the Labour Party since 1945* (London, 1960) produces slightly modified figures as the result of an examination of union accounts.

[2] 1910(D): Sponsored by the Fabian Society.
   1922: One sponsored by the Fabian Society and one by the Social Democratic Federation.
   1923: Two sponsored by the Fabian Society and four by the Social Democratic Federation.
   1924: One sponsored by the Fabian Society, and three by the Social Democratic Federation.
   1950-59: Sponsored by the Royal Arsenal Co-operative Society.

†No complete figures are available.

Sources: Annual Conference Reports of the Labour Party, the Co-operative Party, the ILP and the Social Democratic Federation.
   Labour and Politics, 1900-1906 by Frank Bealey and Henry Pelling (London, 1958).
   The History of the Fabian Society by Edward R. Pease (London, 1916).

Table 7.05 **THE LIBERAL VOTE**[1]

Election	Candidates	Unopposed Returns	M.P.s Elected	Forfeited Deposits	Total votes	% of U.K. total
1885	572	14	319	—	2,199,998	47.4
1886	449	40	191	—	1,353,581	45.0
1892	532	13	271	—	2,088,019	45.1
1895	447	11	177	—	1,765,266	45.7
1900	402	22	183	—	1,572,323	45.0
1906	536	27	399	—	2,751,057	49.4
1910(J)	511	1	274	—	2,866,157	43.5
1910(D)	467	35	271	—	2,293,869	44.2
1918	421	27	163	44	2,785,374	25.6
1922	485	10	115	32	4,139,460	28.8
1923	457	11	158	8	4,301,481	29.7
1924	339	6	40	30	2,928,737	17.8
1929	513	0	59	25	5,308,738	23.6
1931	117	5	36	6	1,476,123	7.0
1935	161	0	21	40	1,443,093	6.7
1945	306	0	12	76	2,252,430	9.0
1950	475	0	9	319	2,621,487	9.1
1951	109	0	6	66	730,546	2.6
1955	110	0	6	60	722,402	2.7
1959	216	0	6	55	1,640,760	5.9
1964	365	0	9	52	3,099,283	11.2
1966	311	0	12	104	2,327,457	8.5
1970	332	0	6	184	2,117,035	7.5
1974(F)	517	0	14	23	6,059,519	19.3
1974(O)	619	0	13	125	5,346,704	18.3

[1] Including both Liberal and National Liberal candidates in 1922 and Independent Liberals in 1931.

Table 7.06 **THE NATIONAL LIBERAL VOTE**[1]

Election	Candidates	Unopposed Returns	M.P.s Elected	Forfeited Deposits	Total votes	% of U.K. total
1931	41	7	35	0	809,302	3.7
1935	44	3	33	0	866,354	3.7
1945	49	0	11	0	737,732	2.9
1950	55	0	16^2	0	985,343	3.4
1951	55	0	19^2	0	1,058,138	3.7
1955	45	0	21^2	0	842,113	3.1
1959	39	0	20^2	0	765,794	2.7
1964	19	0	6^3	0	326,130	1.2
1966	9	0	3	0	149,779	0.5

[1] Only those candidates who actually *used* the National Liberal and Conservative (or one of the numerous variations) label have been included in this table. Between 1955 and 1966 the official lists of candidates issued by the National Liberal Organization included a number of candidates who did not use the joint label, preferring to run as straight Conservatives.
The National Liberal Organization was disbanded in May 1968.

[2] Excluding G.R.H. Nugent (Surrey, Guildford) who although elected as a Conservative joined the Liberal-Unionist Group, as an associate member.

[3] Excluding J.H. Osborn (Sheffield, Hallam) and Sir P.G. Roberts, Bt. (Sheffield, Heeley) who although elected as Conservatives joined the Liberal-Unionist Group as associate members.

Table 7.07 **THE COMMUNIST VOTE**[1]

Election	Candidates	M.P.s Elected[2]	Forfeited Deposits	Total votes	% of U.K. total
1922	5	1	1	33,637	0.2
1923	4	0	0	39,448	0.2
1924	8	1	1	55,346	0.3
1929	25	0	21	50,634	0.2
1931	26	0	21	74,824	0.3
1935	2	1	0	27,117	0.1
1945	21	2	12	102,780	0.4
1950	100	0	97	91,765	0.3
1951	10	0	10	21,640	0.1
1955	17	0	15	33,144	0.1
1959	18	0	17	30,896	0.1
1964	36	0	36	46,442	0.2
1966	57	0	57	62,092	0.2
1970	58	0	58	37,970	0.1
1974 (F)	44	0	43	32,743	0.1
1974 (O)	29	0	29	17,426	0.1

[1] Until 1924 it was possible for members of the Communist Party to secure adoption and endorsement as official Labour Party candidates. The following is a summary of these candidates who are not included in the above table:—

1922: S. Saklatvala (Battersea, North), polled 11,311 votes and was elected.

M.P. Price (Gloucester), polled 7,871 votes and was defeated. It appears that he was not an actual member of the Communist Party at this election but *The Communist* of November 25, 1922, described him as 'sympathetic'.

1923: W. Paul (Manchester, Rusholme), polled 5,366 votes and was defeated.

M.P. Price (Gloucester), polled 8,127 votes and was defeated.

S. Saklatvala (Battersea, North), polled 12,341 votes and was defeated.

J.J. Vaughan (Bethnal Green, South-West), polled 5,251 votes and was defeated.

Miss E.C. Wilkinson (Ashton-under-Lyne), polled 6,208 votes and was defeated.

[2] Namely:

W. Gallacher (Fife, Western), 1935-50;

C.J.L. Malone (Leyton, East), 1920-22 (elected as Co L in 1918 but joined the Communist Party when it was formed in 1920);

J.T.W. Newbold (Lanarkshire, Motherwell), 1922-23;

P. Piratin (Stepney, Mile-End), 1945-50;

S. Saklatvala (Battersea, North), 1922-23 (as Lab) and 1924-29.

Table 7.08 THE PLAID CYMRU VOTE

Election	Candidates	M.P.s Elected[1]	Forfeited Deposits	Total votes	% of Welsh total
1929	1	0	1	609	0.0
1931	2	0	1	2,050	0.2
1935	1	0	1	2,534	0.3
1945	7	0	6	16,017	1.2
1950	7	0	6	17,580	1.2
1951	4	0	4	10,920	0.7
1955	11	0	7	45,119	3.1
1959	20	0	14	77,571	5.2
1964	23	0	21	69,507	4.8
1966	20	0	18	61,071	4.3
1970	36	0	25	175,016	11.5
1974 (F)	36	2	26	171,374	10.7
1974 (O)	36	3	26	166,321	10.8

[1] Namely: G.R. Evans (Carmarthenshire, Carmarthen), 1966 (by-election) — 1970 and from 1974 (O);
D.E. Thomas (Merionethshire), from 1974 (F);
D.W. Wigley (Caernarvonshire, Caernarvon), from 1974 (F).

Table 7.09 THE SCOTTISH NATIONAL PARTY VOTE

Election	Candidates	M.P.s Elected[1]	Forfeited Deposits	Total votes	% of Scottish total
1929	2	0	2	3,313	0.1
1931	5	0	2	20,954	1.0
1935	8	0	5	29,517	1.3
1945	8	0	6	30,595	1.2
1950	3	0	3	9,708	0.4
1951	2	0	1	7,299	0.3
1955	2	0	1	12,112	0.5
1959	5	0	3	21,738	0.8
1964	15	0	12	64,044	2.4
1966	23	0	10	128,474	5.0
1970	65	1	43	306,802	11.4
1974 (F)	70	7	7	633,180	21.9
1974 (O)	71	11	0	839,617	30.4

[1] Namely: Mrs. M.A. Bain (Dunbartonshire, East), from 1974 (O);
G.D. Crawford (Perthshire and Kinross-shire, Perth and East Perthshire), from 1974 (O);
Mrs. W.M. Ewing (Lanarkshire, Hamilton), 1967 (by-election) — 1970 and (Moray and Nairnshire), from 1974 (F);
D. Henderson (Aberdeenshire, East) from 1974 (F);
I.S.M. MacCormick (Argyll), from 1974 (F);
Mrs. M. Macdonald (Glasgow, Govan), 1973 (by-election) — 1974 (F);
Dr. R.D. McIntyre (Lanarkshire, Motherwell), April (by-election) — June 1945;
G.N. Reid (Stirlingshire and Clackmannanshire, Clackmannan and East Stirlingshire), from 1974 (F);
D.J. Stewart (Inverness-shire and Ross and Cromarty, Western Isles), from 1970;
G.H. Thompson (Kirkcudbrightshire and Wigtownshire, Galloway), from 1974 (O);
H. Watt (Banffshire), from 1974 (F);
A.P. Welsh (Angus and Kincardineshire, South Angus), from 1974 (O);
R.G. Wilson (Dundee, East), from 1974 (F).

Table 7.10 THE NATIONALIST AND REPUBLICAN VOTE IN NORTHERN IRELAND

Election	CANDIDATES					M.P.s Elected[1]	Forfeited Deposits	Total votes	% of N.Ireland total
	N	SF	Rep	Others	Total				
1922	2	0	0	1	3	2	0	99,914	44.2
1923	2	0	0	0	2	2	0	87,671	27.3
1924	0	8	0	0	8	0	3	46,457	9.9
1929	3	0	0	0	3	2[2]	0	24,177	6.6
1931	3	0	0	0	3	2	0	123,053	38.9
1935	2	0	3	0	5	2	0	158,327	35.1
1945	3	0	0	0	3	2	0	148,078	18.8
1950	2	2	0	0	4	2	1	88,573	15.8
1951	3	0	0	0	3	2	0	92,787	20.0
1955	0	12	0	0	12	2[3]	5	152,310	23.5
1959	0	12	0	0	12	0	7	63,415	11.0
1964	0	0	12	1	13	0	7	116,306	18.2
1966	1	0	5	2	8	1	1	125,886	21.1
1970	0	0	0	11	11	3	5	190,462	24.5
1974(F)	0	0	4	3	7	0	6	38,407	5.4
1974(O)	0	0	5	1	6	1	4	54,428	7.8

[1] Those elected comprised:—

1935:	2 N
1950:	2 N
1966:	1 Rep LP
1970:	2 Unity, 1 Rep LP
1974(O):	1 Ind Rep

[2] Unopposed.

[3] Later unseated on petition.

Table 7.11
LIBERALS AND NATIONALISTS IN SECOND PLACE 1950–1974

The following table shows the number of constituencies (contested by *both* Conservative and Labour candidates) in which Liberal or Nationalist candidates took second place in the poll.

Election	L	PC	SNP
1950	17	0	0
1951	9	0	0
1955	11	1	1
1959	26	1	1
1964	55	0	1
1966	26	1	3
1970	26	8	9
1974 (F)	145	7	17
1974 (O)	102[1]	6[2]	42[3]

[1] Held by 92 Conservatives, 10 Labour.

[2] Held by 6 Labour.

[3] Held by 35 Labour, 5 Conservatives, 2 Liberals.

Table 8.01 POSTAL BALLOT PAPERS[1]

	No. issued	No. of covering envelopes returned before close of poll	No. rejected[2]	No. included in count
1945[3]				
ENGLAND	1,037,298	882,762	11,911	870,851
WALES	54,434	45,763	726	45,037
SCOTLAND	121,336	99,797	1,688	98,109
N. IRELAND	6,451	4,366	34	4,332
UNITED KINGDOM	**1,219,519**	**1,032,688**	**14,359**	**1,018,329**
1950				
ENGLAND	410,126	386,884	7,879	379,005
WALES	23,916	22,500	815	21,685
SCOTLAND	49,444	46,150	2,084	44,066
N. IRELAND	24,231	22,504	913	21,591
UNITED KINGDOM	**507,717**	**478,038**	**11,691**	**466,347**
1951				
ENGLAND	688,427	627,415	10,618	616,797
WALES	38,819	34,986	862	34,124
SCOTLAND	79,294	71,367	2,029	69,338
N. IRELAND	25,337	23,199	884	22,315
UNITED KINGDOM	**831,877**	**756,967**	**14,393**	**742,574**
1955				
ENGLAND	489,248	435,097	8,506	426,591
WALES	30,412	26,596	711	25,885
SCOTLAND	53,341	45,854	1,485	44,369
N. IRELAND	21,999	19,357	609	18,748
UNITED KINGDOM	**595,000**	**526,904**	**11,311**	**515,593**
1959				
ENGLAND	585,776	520,551	10,922	509,629
WALES	34,054	29,532	848	28,684
SCOTLAND	55,739	48,204	1,481	46,723
N. IRELAND	17,258	13,944	421	13,523
UNITED KINGDOM	**692,827**	**612,231**	**13,672**	**598,559**
1964				
ENGLAND	692,674	614,344	12,818	601,526
WALES	39,286	34,343	1,094	33,249
SCOTLAND	68,184	59,376	1,841	57,535
N. IRELAND	18,757	15,864	538	15,326
UNITED KINGDOM	**818,901**	**723,927**	**16,291**	**707,636**
1966				
ENGLAND	505,637	433,708	11,338	422,370
WALES	33,966	28,677	1,129	27,548
SCOTLAND	55,486	46,711	1,695	45,016
N. IRELAND	22,392	18,910	803	18,107
UNITED KINGDOM	**617,481**	**528,006**	**14,965**	**513,041**

POSTAL BALLOT PAPERS (Cont.)

	No. issued	No. of covering envelopes returned before close of poll	No. rejected[2]	No. included in count
1970				
ENGLAND	599,638	525,842	10,820	515,022
WALES	41,088	35,919	1,017	34,902
SCOTLAND	62,656	53,603	1,550	52,053
N. IRELAND	27,867	24,310	932	23,378
UNITED KINGDOM	731,249	639,674	14,319	625,355
1974(F)[4]				
ENGLAND	606,468	530,583	13,098	517,485
WALES	45,004	35,152	1,377	33,775
SCOTLAND	62,261	54,278	1,391	52,887
N. IRELAND	29,708	25,067	307	24,760
UNITED KINGDOM	743,441	645,080	16,173	628,907
1974(O)[5]				
ENGLAND	882,433	718,240	20,516	697,724
WALES	59,970	48,714	2,014	46,700
SCOTLAND	90,136	73,190	1,875	71,315
N. IRELAND	42,592	35,180	814	34,366
UNITED KINGDOM	1,075,131	875,324	25,219	850,105

[1] Statistics of postal voting were not compiled until the General Election of 1945. Prior to 1945, the only General Election in which there must have been a substantial number of postal votes was that of 1918. Between the wars only members of His Majesty's Forces serving in the United Kingdom and a few civilians could vote by post. The Representation of the People Act, 1949, considerably increased the categories of those eligible to vote by post.

[2] Number of cases in which the covering envelope or its contents were marked "empty", "rejected", "declaration rejected" or "vote rejected"

[3] These figures relate only to Service voters. In addition, a total of 1,381 civilian postal voters had their ballot papers included in constituency counts.

[4] Colums 2, 3 and 4 are exclusive of the figures for Ashford, Bassetlaw, Bath, Abertillery, Bedwellty, Ebbw Vale, Monmouth and Pontypool. The Returning Officers failed to make the statutory return to the Home Office.

[5] Columns 2, 3 and 4 are exclusive of the figures for Devizes and Northwich. The Returning Officers failed to make the statutory return to the Home Office.

Sources: 1945: House of Commons Papers, 1945-46 (22) xx, 609.
1950 onwards: Returns compiled by the Home Office and the Scottish Home and Health Department.

Table 8.02 **POSTAL BALLOT PAPERS (Summary)**

Election	Issued Postal Ballot Papers as % of total electorate	No. returned as % of No. issued	No. rejected as % of No. returned	Valid Postal Ballot Papers as % of total poll
1945[1]	3.7	84.7	1.4	4.2
1950	1.5	94.2	2.4	1.6
1951	2.4	91.0	1.9	2.6
1955	1.7	88.6	2.1	1.9
1959	2.0	88.4	2.2	2.1
1964	2.3	88.4	2.3	2.6
1966	1.7	85.5	2.8	1.9
1970	1.9	87.5	2.2	2.2
1974(F)	1.9	87.8	2.5	2.0
1974 (O)	2.7	81.7	2.9	2.9

[1] These figures relate only to Service voters.

Table 9.01 PUBLIC OPINION POLLS—VOTING FORECAST

This table shows the error in the final poll predictions of the public opinion polls forecasting the results of General Elections since 1945. As surveys are not normally carried out in Northern Ireland (Marplan in 1970 did cover Northern Ireland but their forecast has been adjusted to provide Great Britain only figures for the sake of uniformity) the figures relate only to Great Britain.

The final opinion poll findings were published in the following newspapers:

Business Decisions: *The Observer.*

Gallup Poll: *News Chronicle* (1945-59); *Daily Telegraph* (since 1964).

Louis Harris: *Daily Express.*

Marplan: *The Times* (1970); *Birmingham Evening Mail* (February 1974); *The Sun* (October 1974).

National Opinion Polls: *Daily Mail.*

Opinion Research Centre: *Evening Standard.*

Research Services: *Daily Graphic* (1951); *The Observer* (1964 and 1966).

+ indicates an overestimate   − indicates an underestimate

Election	Actual % share of total votes	Business Decisions	*Daily Express*	Gallup Poll	Louis Harris	Marplan	National Opinion Polls	Opinion Research Centre	Research Services
1945									
C	39.3			+1.7					
Lab	48.8	NO	NO	−1.8	NO	NO	NO	NO	NO
L	9.2	POLL	POLL	+1.3	POLL	POLL	POLL	POLL	POLL
Others	2.7			−1.2					
1950									
C	43.0		+1.5	+0.5					
Lab	46.8	NO	−2.8	−1.8	NO	NO	NO	NO	NO
L	9.3	POLL	+1.7	+1.2	POLL	POLL	POLL	POLL	POLL
Others	0.9		−0.4	+0.1					
1951									
C	47.8		+2.2	+1.7					+2.2
Lab	49.3	NO	−3.3	−2.3	NO	NO	NO	NO	−6.3
L	2.6	POLL	+0.9	+0.4	POLL	POLL	POLL	POLL	+4.1[1]
Others	0.3		+0.2	+0.2		.			−
1955									
C	49.3		+0.7	+1.7					
Lab	47.3	NO	0.0	+0.2	NO	NO	NO	NO	NO
L	2.8	POLL	−0.5	−1.3	POLL	POLL	POLL	POLL	POLL
Others	0.6		−0.2	−					
1959									
C	48.8		+0.3	−0.3			−0.8		
Lab	44.6	NO	+0.8	+1.9	NO	NO	−0.5	NO	NO
L	6.0	POLL	−1.0	−1.5	POLL	POLL	+1.3[1]	POLL	POLL
Others	0.6		−0.1	−0.1			−		
1964									
C	42.9		+1.6	+1.6			+1.4		+2.1
Lab	44.8	NO	−1.1	+1.7	NO	NO	+2.6	NO	+1.2
L	11.4	POLL	−0.4	−2.9	POLL	POLL	−3.5	POLL	−2.4
Others	0.9		−0.1	−0.4			−0.5		−
1966									
C	41.5		−3.8	−1.5			+0.1		+0.1
Lab	48.8	NO	+5.8	+2.2	NO	NO	+1.8	NO	+0.9
L	8.6	POLL	−0.9	−0.6	POLL	POLL	−1.2	POLL	−0.3
Others	1.1		−	−0.1			−0.7		−0.7
1970									
C	46.2		SEE	−4.2	−0.2	−5.2	−2.1	+0.3	
Lab	43.9	NO	HARRIS	+5.1	+4.1	+6.7	+4.3	+1.6	NO
L	7.6	POLL	POLL	−0.1	−2.6	−0.5	−1.2	−1.1	POLL
Others	2.3			−0.8	−1.3	−1.0	−1.0	−0.8	

PUBLIC OPINION POLLS—VOTING FORECAST (Cont.)

Election	Actual % share of total votes	Business Decisions	*Daily Express*	Gallup Poll	Louis Harris	Marplan	National Opinion Polls	Opinion Research Centre	Research Services
1974 (F)									
C	38.8	−3.8	SEE	+0.7	+1.4	−2.3	+0.7	+0.9	
Lab	38.0	−0.5	HARRIS	−0.5	−2.8	−3.5	−2.5	−1.3	NO
L	19.8	+3.7	POLL	+0.7	+2.2	+5.2	+2.2	+1.4	POLL
Others	3.4	+0.6		−0.9	−0.8	+0.6	−0.4	−1.0	
1974 (O)									
C	36.7	−1.2	SEE	−0.7	−2.1	−3.4	−5.7	−2.3	
Lab	40.2	−0.2	HARRIS	+1.3	+2.8	+2.8	+5.3	+1.6	NO
L	18.8	+1.2	POLL	+0.2	+0.5	+0.7	+0.7	+0.6	POLL
Others	4.3	+0.2		−0.8	−1.2	−0.1	−0.3	+0.1	

[1] These polls published a combined forecast of the Liberal and Others vote. This figure is therefore the error in prediction of the Liberal and Others vote combined.

Table 9.02 PUBLIC OPINION POLLS—WINNING PARTY AND LEAD FORECAST

Election	Party & Lead %		Business Decisions	Daily Express	Gallup Poll	Louis Harris	Marplan	National Opinion Polls	Opinion Research Centre	Research Services	Average Error
1945	Lab	9.5	—	—	− 3.5	—	—	—	—	—	3.5
1950	Lab	3.8	—	− 4.3	− 2.3	—	—	—	—	—	3.3
1951	Lab	1.5[1]	—	− 5.5	− 4.0	—	—	—	—	− 8.5	6.0
1955	C	2.0	—	+ 0.7	+ 1.5	—	—	—	—	—	1.1
1959	C	4.2	—	− 0.5	− 2.2	—	—	− 0.3	—	—	1.0
1964	Lab	1.9	—	− 2.7	− 0.1	—	—	+ 1.2	—	− 0.9	1.2
1966	Lab	7.3	—	+ 9.6	+ 3.7	—	—	+ 1.7	—	+ 0.8	4.0
1970	C	2.3	—	†	− 9.3	− 4.3	−11.9	− 6.4	− 1.3	—	6.6
1974(F)	C	0.8[2]	− 3.3	†	+ 1.2	+ 4.4	+ 1.2	+ 3.2	+ 2.2	—	2.6
1974(O)	Lab	3.5	+ 1.0	†	+ 2.0	+ 4.9	+ 6.2	+11.0	+ 3.9	—	4.8
Average error on lead	—		2.2	3.9	3.0	4.5	6.4	4.0	2.5	3.4	—

[1] Labour won 1.5% more votes in Great Britain than Conservatives but the latter obtained a parliamentary majority.

[2] Conservatives won 0.8% more votes in Great Britain than Labour but the latter formed a minority government.

† See Louis Harris.

Table 9.03 PUBLIC OPINION POLLS—OVERALL RECORD

Poll	No. of Elections covered	Minimum % error[1]	Maximum % error[1]	Average % error[2]
Opinion Research Centre	3	0.3	2.3	1.1
Gallup Poll	10	0.2	5.1	1.2
Daily Express	6	0.0[3]	5.8	1.3
Business Decisions	2	0.2	3.8	1.4
National Opinion Polls	6	0.1	5.7	1.7
Research Services	3	0.1	6.3	1.8
Louis Harris	3	0.2	4.1	1.8
Marplan	3	2.3	6.7	2.7

[1] These figures are based on the forecasts for Conservative and Labour votes only.

[2] These figures are based on the forecasts for Conservative, Labour, Liberal and Others.

[3] At the General Election of 1955 the Daily Express forecast exactly the Labour vote. No other opinion poll has equalled this achievement.

Table 10.01 **WOMEN CANDIDATES—GENERAL ELECTIONS**

Election	C	Lab	L	Com	PC	SNP	Others	Total	% of total candidates
1918	1	4	4	—	—	—	8	17	1.0
1922	5	10	16	0	—	—	2	33	2.3
1923	7	14	12	0	—	—	1	34	2.4
1924	12	22	6	0	—	—	1	41	2.9
1929	10	30	25	3	0	0	1	69	4.0
1931	16	36[1]	5	2	0	1	2	62	4.8
1935	19	33	11	0	0	0	4	67	5.0
1945	14	41	20	2	1	0	9	87	5.2
1950	29[2]	42	45	9	0	0	2	127[2]	6.8
1951	25	41	11	0	0	0	0	77	5.6
1955	33	43	14	1	1	0	0	92	6.5
1959	28	36	16	1	0	0	0	81	5.3
1964	24	33	24	4	1	0	4	90	5.1
1966	21	30	20	6	0	0	4	81	4.7
1970	26	29	23	6	0	10	5	99	5.4
1974 (F)	33	40	40	3	2	8	17	143	6.7
1974 (O)	30	50	49	2	1	8	21	161	7.1

[1] Including 6 unendorsed.

[2] Rt. Hon. Florence Horsbrugh (C) is counted twice in this total. She was defeated at Midlothian and Peebleshire but subsequently elected for Manchester, Moss Side where polling had been postponed due to the death of the Conservative candidate.

Table 10.02 **WOMEN ELECTED—GENERAL ELECTIONS**

Election	C	Lab	L	Com	PC	SNP	Others	Total	% of total M.P.s
1918	0	0	0	—	—	—	1[1]	1	0.1
1922	1	0	1	0	—	—	0	2	0.3
1923	3	3	2	0	—	—	0	8	1.3
1924	3	1	0	0	—	—	0	4	0.7
1929	3	9	1	0	0	0	1	14	2.3
1931	13	0	1	0	0	0	1	15	2.4
1935	6	1	1	0	0	0	1	9	1.5
1945	1	21	1	0	0	0	1	24	3.8
1950	6	14	1	0	0	0	0	21	3.4
1951	6	11	0	0	0	0	0	17	2.7
1955	10	14	0	0	0	0	0	24	3.8
1959	12	13	0	0	0	0	0	25	4.0
1964	11	18	0	0	0	0	0	29	4.6
1966	7	19	0	0	0	0	0	26	4.1
1970	15	10	0	0	0	0	1[2]	26	4.1
1974 (F)	9	13	0	0	0	1	0	23	3.6
1974 (O)	7	18	0	0	0	2	0	27	4.3

[1] Countess Markievicz (SF) who was elected for Dublin, St. Patrick's. She did not take her seat in the House of Commons.

[2] Miss B.J. Devlin (Mid-Ulster—Unity).

Table 10.03 WOMEN CANDIDATES—BY-ELECTIONS

From	C	Lab	L	Com	PC	SNP	Others	Total	% of total candidates
1918-22	1	2	1	0	—	—	0	4	1.8
1922-23	1	0	0	0	—	—	0	1	2.4
1923-24	0	0	0	0	—	—	0	0	—
1924-29	3	7	2	0	0	0	0	12	6.6
1929-31	1	3	2	1	0	1	1	9	9.4
1931-35	0	4	0	0	0	0	1	5	3.4
1935-45	5	4	2	1	0	0	13	25	5.8
1945-50	1	1	0	0	0	1	3	6	4.1
1950-51	0	0	1	0	0	0	0	1	2.8
1951-55	3	5	0	0	0	0	0	8	7.3
1955-59	4	3	2	0	1	0	1	11	8.0
1959-64	4	1	0	0	0	0	1	6	2.7
1964-66	0	0	2	0	0	0	0	2	4.1
1966-70	1	3	3	1	0	1	1	10	7.1
1970-74 (F)	0	3	0	0	0	1	3	7	5.8
1974(F)-74 (O)	0	0	0	0	0	0	0	0	—

Table 10.04 WOMEN ELECTED—BY-ELECTIONS

From	C	Lab	L	Com	PC	SNP	Others	Total	% of M.P.s elected
1918-22	1[1]	0	1[2]	0	—	—	0	2	1.9
1922-23	1	0	0	0	—	—	0	1	6.3
1923-24	0	0	0	0	—	—	0	0	—
1924-29	1	4	1	0	0	0	0	6	9.5
1929-31	0	2	0	0	0	0	0	2	5.6
1931-35	0	0	0	0	0	0	0	0	—
1935-45	3	3	0	0	0	0	0	6	2.7
1945-50	1	1	0	0	0	0	0	2	3.8
1950-51	0	0	0	0	0	0	0	0	—
1951-55	2	2	0	0	0	0	0	4	8.3
1955-59	2	2	0	0	0	0	0	4	7.7
1959-64	1	0	0	0	0	0	0	1	1.6
1964-66	0	0	0	0	0	0	0	0	—
1966-70	0	0	0	0	0	1	1[3]	2	5.3
1970-74 (F)	0	1	0	0	0	1	0	2	6.7
1974(F)-74(O)	0	0	0	0	0	0	0	0	—

[1] Viscountess Astor, the first woman to sit in the House of Commons. She was returned for Plymouth, Sutton at a by-election on November 15, 1919. The by-election was caused by the succession of her husband to the Peerage.

[2] Mrs. Margaret Wintringham, the first Liberal woman to be elected. She was returned for Lincolnshire, Louth at a by-election on September 22, 1921. The by-election was caused by the death of her husband.

[3] Miss B.J. Devlin (Mid-Ulster—Unity).

Table 11.01 **GENERAL ELECTION TIME-TABLE 1885—1910[1]**

Year	Parliament Dissolved	First nomination	First contest	Last contest[2]	Parliament Assembled
1885	November 18	November 23	November 24	December 18	January 12 (1886)
1886	June 26	June 30	July 1	July 27	August 5
1892	June 28	July 1	July 4	July 26	August 4
1895	July 8	July 12	July 13	August 7	August 12
1900	September 25	September 28	October 1	October 24	December 3
1906	January 8	January 11	January 12	February 8	February 13
1910 (J)	January 10	January 14	January 15	February 10	February 15
1910 (D)	November 28	December 2	December 3	December 19	January 31 (1911)

[1] General Elections from the First Reform Act to 1885 had taken place in 1832 (December); 1835 (January/February); 1837 (July/August); 1841 (June/July); 1847 (July/August); 1852 (July/August); 1857 (March/April); 1859 (April/May); 1865 (July); 1868 (November/December); 1874 (January/February); 1880 (April).

[2] The length of time between the first and last contested election is somewhat distorted by the fact that it was usual for the polling in the University constituencies and in Orkney and Shetland to be held a week or so after the other constituencies had completed polling. If University constituencies and Orkney and Shetland are excluded, the last polls were held on the following dates: 1885—December 9; 1886—July 17; 1892—July 19; 1895—July 29; 1900—October 15; 1906—January 29; 1910(J)—January 31; 1910(D)—December 19.

Table 11.02 **GENERAL ELECTION TIME-TABLE 1918—1974**

Year	Election Announced[1]	Parliament Dissolved	Nominations Closed	Polling Day[2]	Parliament Assembled
1918	November 14	November 25	December 4	Saturday, December 14[3]	February 4 (1919)
1922	October 23	October 26	November 4	Wednesday, November 15	November 20
1923	November 13	November 16	November 26	Thursday, December 6	January 8 (1924)
1924	October 9	October 9	October 18	Wednesday, October 29	December 2
1929	April 24	May 10	May 20	Thursday, May 30	June 25
1931	October 6	October 7	October 16	Tuesday, October 27	November 3
1935	October 23	October 25	November 4	Thursday, November 14	November 26
1945	May 23	June 15	June 25	Thursday, July 5[4]	August 1
1950	January 11	February 3	February 13	Thursday, February 23	March 1
1951	September 19	October 5	October 15	Thursday, October 25	October 31
1955	April 15	May 6	May 16	Thursday, May 26	June 7
1959	September 8	September 18	September 28	Thursday, October 8	October 20
1964	September 15	September 25	October 5	Thursday, October 15	October 27
1966	February 28	March 10	March 21	Thursday, March 31	April 18
1970	May 18	May 29	June 8	Thursday, June 18	June 29
1974 (F)	February 7	February 8	February 18	Thursday, February 28	March 6
1974 (O)	September 18	September 20	September 30	Thursday, October 10	October 22

[1] The method of informing the country of a Dissolution has been as follows:
Announcement made by the Leader of the House of Commons in the House of Commons: General Election of 1918.
Announcement by the Prime Minister in the House of Commons: General Elections of 1923, 1924, 1929, 1931, 1935.
Official announcement issued to the press during a parliamentary recess: General Elections of 1922, 1945, 1950, 1959, 1964, 1974 (O).
Official announcement issued to the press during a parliamentary session: General Elections of 1966, 1970, 1974 (F).
Broadcast (sound radio) by the Prime Minister during a parliamentary recess: General Elections of 1951 and 1955.

[2] The date of polling did not apply to the University constituencies (where the poll remained open for five days), Orkney and Shetland (where the poll remained open for two days until 1929), or in a few cases where polling in a constituency was postponed due to the death of a candidate after the close of nominations. Until 1950, hours of poll were from 8.00 a.m. until 8.00 p.m. but any candidate could request that (a) the poll commenced at 7.00 a.m.; (b) the poll closed at 9.00 p.m. or (c) the poll commenced at 7.00 a.m. and closed at 9.00 p.m. From 1950 until 1969, hours of poll were 7.00 a.m. to 9.00 p.m. and since 1970, 7.00 a.m. to 10.00 p.m.

[3] The counting of votes did not take place until December 28 as the ballot papers of His Majesty's Forces serving on the Western Front (who had been allowed to vote by post) had to be collected and dispatched to Britain.

[4] Due to the appointed polling day falling during the local holiday week in several constituencies, polling was delayed in twenty-two constituencies until July 12 and in one constituency until July 19. The counting of votes did not take place until July 26 as the ballot papers of His Majesty's Forces serving in certain countries overseas (who had been allowed to vote by post) had to be collected and dispatched to Britain by air.

Table 11.03   SEATS IN THE HOUSE OF COMMONS

	1885-1918[1]	1918-22[2]	1922-45[3]	1945-50[4]	1950-55[5]	1955-74 (F)[6]	Since 1974 (F)[7]
London Boroughs	59	62	62	62	43	42	92
English Boroughs	166	193	193	216	248	247	212
English Counties	231	230	230	232	215	222	212
ENGLAND	456	485	485	510	506	511	516
Welsh Boroughs	12	11	11	11	10	10	10
Welsh Counties	22	24	24	24	26	26	26
WALES	34	35	35	35	36	36	36
Scottish Burghs	31	33	33	33	32	32	29
Scottish Counties	39	38	38	38	39	39	42
SCOTLAND	70	71	71	71	71	71	71
Irish Boroughs	16	21	4	4	4	4	4
Irish Counties	85	80	8	8	8	8	8
IRELAND[8]	101	101	12	12	12	12	12
THE UNIVERSITIES[9]	9	15	12	12	0	0	0
UNITED KINGDOM	670	707	615	640	625	630	635

[1] Redistribution of Seats Act, 1885.

[2] Representation of the People Act, 1918.

[3] Government of Ireland Act, 1920.

[4] House of Commons (Redistribution of Seats) Act, 1944.

[5] Representation of the People Act, 1948.

[6] Statutory Instruments, 1955, Nos. 2-31 and 165-186.

[7] Statutory Instruments, 1970, Nos. 1674, 1675, 1678, 1680.

[8] The whole of Ireland until 1922, thereafter Northern Ireland only.

[9] The University seats were divided as follows: 1885-1918 — England 5; Scotland 2; Ireland 2. 1918-50 — England 7; Wales 1;
Scotland 3; Ireland (until 1922) 4; Northern Ireland (from 1922) 1.

Table 11.04   THE OVERNIGHT RESULTS

Since 1950 an increasing number of constituencies have commenced counting immediately after polling finished instead
of waiting until the next morning. The following is a summary of the strength of the parties and of gains and losses when
all the overnight counts had been completed. As the majority of overnight results come from urban constituencies, Labour
normally would expect a lead in the early results.

Election	Total Results	STATE OF PARTIES				PARTY GAINS AND LOSSES							
		C	Lab	L	Others	C +	C −	Lab +	Lab −	L +	L −	Others +	Others −
1950	264	102[1]	163	1	0	—		—		—		—	
1951	319	145[2]	175	2	1	11	1	0	12	1	0	1	0
1955	357	176	179	2	0	9	0	0	8	0	0	0	1
1959	388	205	180	3	0	21	4	3	21	1	0	0	0
1964	430	181	247	2	0	4	49	52	4	0	2	0	1
1966	461	151	304	5	1	0	43	42	1	2	1	1	0
1970	418	188	227	2	1	54	6	9	51	0	3	1	4
1974 (F)	442	177	255	5	5	2	12	10	5	2	1	4	0
1974 (O)	493	185	294	5	9	1	21	20	1	0	2	5	2

[1] Including 2 unopposed.

[2] Including 4 unopposed.

Table 11.05 MINISTERS DEFEATED 1918—1974

Election[1]	Ministry at Dissolution	Cabinet Ministers	Ministers not in the Cabinet	Law Officers	Junior Ministers[2]
1918	COALITION	0	0	0	0
1922	CONSERVATIVE	1	0	1	4
1923	CONSERVATIVE	2	2	1	2
1924	LABOUR	1	0	0	7
1929	CONSERVATIVE	1	0	2	5
1931	NATIONAL[3]	0	0	1	3
1935	NATIONAL	2	0	0	0
1945	NATIONAL[4]	5	8	0	19
1950	LABOUR	1	0	1	5
1951	LABOUR	0	0	0	2
1955	CONSERVATIVE	0	0	0	0
1959	CONSERVATIVE	0	0	0	2
1964	CONSERVATIVE	2	1	0	3
1966	LABOUR	0	0	0	0
1970	LABOUR	1	3	0	10
1974(F)	CONSERVATIVE	1	0	0	2
1974(O)	LABOUR	0	0	0	0

[1] At by-elections the following Ministers were defeated:

Rt. Hon. Sir A.S.T. Griffith-Boscawen (C), Minister of Agriculture and Fisheries (Dudley, 1921).

T.A. Lewis (L), Lord Commissioner of the Treasury (Glamorgan, Pontypridd, 1922).

Rt. Hon. Sir A.S.T. Griffith-Boscawen (C), Minister of Health (Surrey, Mitcham, 1923).

J.W. Hills (C), Financial Secretary to the Treasury (Liverpool, Edge Hill, 1923).

Hon. G.F. Stanley (C), Under-Secretary of State for the Home Department (Willesden, East, 1923).

Rt. Hon. P.C. Gordon Walker (Lab), Secretary of State for Foreign Affairs (Leyton, 1965).

With the exception of Sir A.S.T. Griffith-Boscawen who, after his defeat at Dudley in 1921, retained office and was elected at another by-election one month later, all defeated Ministers subsequently resigned office.

[2] Including the Treasurer, Comptroller and Vice-Chamberlain of H.M. Household.

[3] The defeated members of the former Labour Government were:—

Cabinet Ministers, 13; Ministers not in the Cabinet, 1; Junior Ministers, 20.

[4] The defeated members of the former Coalition Government were:—

Ministers not in the Cabinet, 10; Law Officers, 1; Junior Ministers, 14.

Table 11.06 SEATS WON ON A MINORITY VOTE[1]

Election	C	Lab	L	Others[2]	Total	% of total seats
1885	8	0	9	5	22	3.6
1886	0	0	0	0	0	—
1892	6	0	1	3	10	1.6
1895	5	0	8	2	15	2.4
1900	2	0	1	1	4	0.6
1906	11	2	9	5	27	4.4
1910(J)	8	0	21	1	30	4.9
1910(D)	1	0	10	2	13	2.1
1918	50	17	21	9	97	14.5
1922	88	54	28	3	173	30.0
1923	90	65	46	2	203	35.2
1924	80	33	7	4	124	21.5
1929	151	118	40	1	310	53.8
1931	21	4[3]	8	1	34	5.9
1935	32	17	7	2	58	10.1
1945	92	71	2	9	174	29.0
1950	106	76	5	0	187	29.9
1951	25	14	0	0	39	6.2
1955	25	11	1	0	37	5.9
1959	47	31	2	0	80	12.7
1964	154	71	7	0	232	36.8
1966	131	43	11	0	185	29.4
1970	68	48	6	2	124	19.7
1974(F)	229	150	9	20	408	64.3
1974(O)	224	131	11	14	380	59.8

[1] Only single-member seats are included in this table.

[2] Including:

	1892:	2 N
	1895:	2 N
	1906:	1 N
	1918:	4 NDP, 3 SF, 1 Co-op
	1922:	1 Com
	1935:	1 Com, 1 ILP
	1945:	2 Com, 1 CW, 1 ILP
	1970:	1 Prot U, 1 SNP
	1974(F):	5 SNP, 3 VUPP, 2 PC, 2UU, 1 SDLP
	1974(O):	9 SNP, 3 PC, 1 SDLP, 1 VUPP

[3] Including 1 unendorsed.

Table 11.07 **TYPES OF CONTESTS**

Election	SINGLE MEMBER SEATS WITH CANDIDATES NUMBERING:							Total Seats
	One	Two	Three	Four	Five	Six	Seven	
1885	35	538	39	4	0	0	0	616
1886	212	400	4	0	0	0	0	616
1892	57	527	30	2	0	0	0	616
1895	181	406	29	0	0	0	0	616
1900	229	379	7	1	0	0	0	616
1906	108	462	45	1	0	0	0	616
1910(J)	69	501	46	0	0	0	0	616
1910(D)	153	446	16	1	0	0	0	616
1918	101	311	211	36	10	1	0	670
1922	48	293	212	22	1	0	0	576
1923	41	280	254	1	0	0	0	576
1924	30	318	223	5	0	0	0	576
1929	5	98	447	26	0	0	0	576
1931	54	409	99	14	0	0	0	576
1935	34	389	146	7	0	0	0	576
1945	3	259	291	42	6	0	0	601
1950	2	113	405	100	5	0	0	625
1951	4	495	122	4	0	0	0	625
1955	0	489	133	8	0	0	0	630
1959	0	373	238	19	0	0	0	630
1964	0	194	379	53	4	0	0	630
1966	0	234	349	44	2	1	0	630
1970	0	185	328	103	13	1	0	630
1974(F)	0	38	370	191	32	3	1	635
1974(O)	0	0	346	238	44	7	0	635

Table 11.08 **SPOILT BALLOT PAPERS[1]**

	Want of official mark	Voting for more than one candidate	Writing or mark by which voter could be identified	Unmarked or void for uncertainty	Total	Average per constituency
1924						
ENGLAND & WALES	1,997	4,418	8,334	9,415	24,164	49
SCOTLAND	864	436	1,647	3,038	5,985	88
N. IRELAND	24	507	298	626	1,455	146
UNITED KINGDOM	2,885	5,361	10,279	13,079	31,604	54
1950						
SCOTLAND	1,849	986	1,136	1,295	5,266	74
1951						
SCOTLAND	1,193	646	1,254	1,574	4,667	66
1955						
SCOTLAND	921	671	1,158	1,841	4,591	65
1959						
SCOTLAND	927	796	878	1,615	4,216	59
1964						
ENGLAND	1,750	12,289	5,358	12,087	31,484	62
WALES	234	1,137	275	921	2,567	71
SCOTLAND	823	1,063	887	1,929	4,702	66
N. IRELAND	19	997	267	1,037	2,320	193
UNITED KINGDOM	2,826	15,486	6,787	15,974	41,073	65
1966						
ENGLAND	1,203	8,847	7,145	21,913	39,108	77
WALES	198	1,036	309	1,737	3,280	91
SCOTLAND	652	852	790	2,894	5,188	73
N. IRELAND	8	784	281	1,250	2,323	194
UNITED KINGDOM	2,061	11,519	8,525	27,794	49,899	79
1970						
ENGLAND	1,414	10,406	6,588	14,809	33,217	65
WALES	78	1,547	258	635	2,518	70
SCOTLAND	623	1,208	354	1,251	3,436	48
N. IRELAND	3	983	341	849	2,176	181
UNITED KINGDOM	2,118	14,144	7,541	17,544	41,347	66
1974 (F)						
ENGLAND	2,063	8,651	6,386	15,108	32,208	62
WALES	197	1,134	255	585	2,171	60
SCOTLAND	824	657	333	1,403	3,217	45
N. IRELAND	92	1,772	346	2,446	4,656	388
UNITED KINGDOM	3,176	12,214	7,320	19,542	42,252[2]	67
1974 (O)						
ENGLAND	2,095	8,543	4,599	9,892	25,129	49
WALES	225	1,201	214	502	2,142	60
SCOTLAND	582	983	196	869	2,630	37
N. IRELAND	36	2,765	1,000	4,004	7,805	650
UNITED KINGDOM	2,938	13,492	6,009	15,267	37,706[3]	59

[1] With the exception of the General Elections of 1880 and 1924, statistics relating to spoilt ballot papers were not compiled (except in Scotland from 1950) until the General Election of 1964.

[2] No returns received from 2 constituencies (Leigh and Ebbw Vale).

[3] No return received from Canterbury.

Sources: 1924: House of Commons Papers, 1926 (49) xxii, 619.
1950 onwards: Returns compiled by the Home Office and the Scottish Home and Health Department.

Table 11.09   UNOPPOSED RETURNS (Summary)

Election	Total Seats	C	Lab	L	N	Others[1]	Total	%
1885	670	10	—	14	19	0	43	6.4
1886	670	118	—	40	66	0	224	33.4
1892	670	40	—	13	9	1	63	9.4
1895	670	132	—	11	46	0	189	28.2
1900	670	163	0	22	58	0	243	36.3
1906	670	13	0	27	74	0	114	17.0
1910 (J)	670	19	0	1	55	0	75	11.2
1910 (D)	670	72	3	35	53	0	163	24.3
1918	707	41	11	27	1	27	107	15.1
1922	615	42	4	10	1	0	57	9.3
1923	615	35	3	11	1	0	50	8.1
1924	615	16	9	6	1	0	32	5.2
1929	615	4	0	0	3	0	7	1.1
1931	615	61	6[2]	0	0	0	67	10.9
1935	615	26	13	0	0	1	40	6.5
1945	640	1	2	0	0	0	3	0.5
1950	625	2	0	0	0	0	2	0.3
1951	625	4	0	0	0	0	4	0.6
1955	630	0	0	0	0	0	0	—
1959	630	0	0	0	0	0	0	—
1964	630	0	0	0	0	0	0	—
1966	630	0	0	0	0	0	0	—
1970	630	0	0	0	0	0	0	—
1974 (F)	635	0	0	0	0	0	0	—
1974 (O)	635	0	0	0	0	0	0	—

[1] Including:—   1918:   25 SF, 1 Co Lab.

[2] Including one unendorsed.

Table 11.10   POLLING DISTRICTS AND STATIONS

Election	Polling Districts[1]	Polling Stations[2]	Election	Polling Districts[1]	Polling Stations[2]
1922[3]	13,137	28,492	1951	26,348	48,212
1923	13,549	29,139	1955	27,797	49,510
1924	14,687	30,969	1959	28,951	49,817
1929	16,294	39,351	1964	30,255	49,637
1931	14,699	35,672	1966	30,470	49,565
1935	16,525	38,723	1970	30,864	49,687
1945	18,882	43,298	1974 (F)	31,287	48,631
1950	25,304	48,243	1974 (O)	31,171	48,384

[1] Each constituency is divided into a number of polling districts by the local authority (in Scotland by the Returning Officer).

[2] Each constituency polling district is further divided into a number of polling stations for the accommodation of electors. A separate room or separate booth may contain a separate polling station, or several polling stations may be constructed in the same room or booth. A Presiding Officer and clerks are appointed and separate equipment is provided for each polling station.

[3] No figures available prior to 1922.

Source: Returns of Election Expenses (Home Office).

Table 11.11 CONSTITUENCY BOUNDARY CHANGES[1]

Election	Unchanged	Minor changes[2]	Major changes[2]
1945	562	31	47
1950	80	8	537
1955	382	72	176
1974(F)	200	122	313

[1] Permanent Boundary Commissions (for England, Wales, Scotland and Northern Ireland) were created in 1944 and prior to the 1945 election they carried out a review of twenty abnormally large constituencies in England. Initial reports were published between September and December 1947 and the First Periodical Reports appeared between August and November 1954. The original rules laid down that each Commission must report not less than three or more than seven years from the date of their previous report but this was altered in 1958 to between ten and fifteen years. The Second Periodical Reports were published in June 1969 and the next reports cannot be published until June 1979 at the earliest or June 1884 at the latest. The Boundary Commissioners have indicated that it is their intention to report in the earlier part of this five year period.

[2] The Boundary Commissioners have been inconsistent in their classification of what they consider minor or major changes. The figures in each category prior to 1974 are based on the Commissioners reports but modified as the result of information from other sources. The 1974 figures have been especially calculated on the basis that only changes involving under 5% of the electorate should be classed as minor. Perhaps in future reports the Commissioners will consider the possibility of publishing in the reports or otherwise making available, the number of electors moving from one constituency to another. This information is essential in considering the effect of boundary changes yet it has never been included in the Periodical Reports and in 1974 had to be extracted from the complex forms which Electoral Registration Officers return annually to the Office of Population Censuses and Surveys.

Table 11.12 ILLITERATE VOTE[1]

Year	England	Wales	Scotland	Ireland	Total	% of total vote
1885	74,909	5,521	7,708	98,404	186,542	4.0
1886	35,541	3,046	4,836	36,722	80,145	2.7
1892	42,480	3,629	4,577	84,919	135,605	3.0
1895	24,852	3,669	4,062	40,357	72,940	1.9
1906	18,596	1,162	2,041	12,510	34,309	0.6
1910(J)	15,657	1,494	2,044	22,515	41,710	0.6

[1] Voters who are illiterate can have their ballot papers marked for them by Presiding Officers at polling stations. With the exception of the General Election of 1900, the Home Office published statistics of illiterate voters from 1885 until January 1910.

Source: Returns of Illiterate Voters (Home Office).

Table 11.13 **ELECTION PETITIONS**

General Elections	Void Elections [1]	Undue Elections [2]	Elections upheld [3]	Petitions withdrawn [4]	Total [5]
1885	4	1	4	3	12
1886	0	2	2	0	4
1892	5	1	6	1	13
1895	2	0	6	2	10
1900	2	0	3	2	7
1906	2	0	3	1	6
1910(J)	3	0	1	1	5
1910(D)	5	1	4	3	13
1922	1	0	1	0	2
1923	1	0	0	0	1
1929	0	0	1	0	1
1955	0	2	0	0	2
1959	0	0	1	0	1
1964	0	0	1	0	1
By-Elections					
1892-95	2	0	1	0	3
1895-1900	0	0	0	1	1
1959-64	0	1	0	0	1

The details of the petition trials[6] since 1918 are as follows:

Date	Constituency	Allegations	Result
Apr 1923	Derbyshire, North Eastern	Irregularities in the reception, rejection and counting of votes	Election upheld
May 1923	Northumberland, Berwick-upon-Tweed	Exceeding maximum permitted election expenses	Void election
May 1924	Oxford	Exceeding maximum permitted election expenses	Void election
Oct 1929	Plymouth, Drake	Bribery, etc.	Election upheld
Sep 1955	Fermanagh and South Tyrone	Elected member disqualified as a felon	Undue election
Oct 1955	Mid-Ulster	Elected member disqualified as a felon	Undue election
Apr 1960	Kensington, North	Irregularities by the Returning Officer	Election upheld
Jul 1961	Bristol, South-East	Elected member disqualified as a Peer	Undue election
Dec 1964	Perthshire and Kinross-shire, Kinross and West Perthshire	Corrupt and illegal practices (Failure to include cost of party political broadcasts in return of election expenses)	Election upheld

ELECTION PETITIONS (Cont.)

[1] A 'void' election was one in which the result was quashed and a new writ issued.

[2] An undue election was one in which the court found the successful candidate not duly elected and ruled that another candidate was entitled to be declared elected.

[3] An election 'upheld' was one in which the court dismissed the petition and found the Member duly elected.

[4] A petition withdrawn prior to the trial. Petitions which were withdrawn at the commencement of, or during a trial are counted as upheld.

[5] Where petitions were lodged against both members in a two-member seat this has been counted twice throughout the table.

[6] In addition, two petitions were lodged but not proceeded with due to the fact that no security for costs was lodged by the petitioners. The first followed the by-election at Croydon, North, in March 1948, when a Mr. H.W. Wicks petitioned that his nomination had been stopped by conspiracy. The second petition was at Leicestershire, Melton, following the General Election of 1959. This petition was lodged by a Mr. B.A. Abbott and alleged conspiracy.

Sources:
Journals of the House of Commons
O'Malley and Hardcastle's Reports on Election Petitions, Vols. 4, 5, 6, 7.
The Table, Vol. 24, pp. 59-76 (Fermanagh and South Tyrone: Mid-Ulster).
All England Law Reports, 1960, Vol. 2, p. 150 and *Weekly Law Reports,* 1960, Vol. 1, p. 762 (Kensington, North).
All England Law Reports, 1961, Vol. 3, p. 354 and *Weekly Law Reports,* 1961, Vol. 3, p. 577 (Bristol, South-East).
Scots Law Times, 1965, p. 186 (Kinross and West Pethshire).
House of Lords Record Office.
Public Record Office.
Royal Courts of Justice.

Appendix 1 REPRESENTATION OF CONSTITUENCIES 1885–1918

The following chart gives the party representation in each constituency from the General Election of 1885 until the Dissolution of the 1911-18 Parliament, except in Ireland where the representation is given through to the creation of the Irish Free State in 1922.

No distinction is made in Ireland between official Nationalists, Parnellite Nationalists and Independent Nationalists.

Where a constituency returned more than one member, the number of seats is given in brackets following the name of the constituency.

Changes which occurred at by-elections are shown in brackets *e.g.* Lab (C) indicates the seat was won by Labour at the General Election but subsequently lost to a Conservative.

LONDON—BOROUGHS

CONSTITUENCY	1885	1886	1892	1895	1900	1906	1910(J)	1910(D)
BATTERSEA AND CLAPHAM								
Battersea	L	L	Ind Lab	L/Lab	L/Lab	L/Lab	L/Lab	L/Lab
Clapham	L	C	C	C	C	C	C	C
BETHNAL GREEN								
North-East	L/Lab	L/Lab	L/Lab	C	C	L	L	L
South-West	L	L	L	L	C	L	L	L(C)
CAMBERWELL								
Dulwich	C	C	C	C	C	C	C	C
North	L	C	L	C	L	L	L	L
Peckham	C	C	C	C	C	L(C)	C	L
CHELSEA	L	C	C	C	C	L	C	C
CITY OF LONDON	C	C	C	C	C	C	C	C
[two seats]	C	C	C	C	C	C	C	C
DEPTFORD	C	C	C	C	C	Lab	Lab	Lab
FINSBURY								
Central	L	C	L	C	C	L/Lab	C	C
East	C	L/Lab	L/Lab	C	C(L)	L	L	L
Holborn	C	C	C	C	C	C	C	C
FULHAM	C	C	C	C	C	L	C	C
GREENWICH	C	C	C	C	C	L	C	C
HACKNEY								
Central	C	C	C	C	C	L	L	L
North	C	C	C	C	C	L	C	C
South	L	L	L	C	C	L	L	L[1] (L)
HAMMERSMITH	C	C	C	C	C	C	C	C
HAMPSTEAD	C	C	C	C	C	C	C	C
ISLINGTON								
East	L	C	C	C	C	L	L	L
North	C	C	C	C	C	L	L	C
South	L	C	C	C	C	L	L	L
West	L	LU	L	L	L	L	L	L
KENSINGTON								
North	C	C	L	C	C	L	C	C
South	C	C	C	C	C	C	C	C
LAMBETH								
Brixton	C	C	C	C	C	L	C	C
Kennington	C	C(L)	L	C	C	L	L	L
North	C	C	L	LU	C	L	C	C
Norwood	C	C	C	C	C	C	C	C
LEWISHAM	C	C	C	C	C	C	C	C
MARYLEBONE								
East	C	C	C	C	C	C	C	C
West	C	C	C	LU(C)	C	C	C	C

LONDON–BOROUGHS (Cont.)

CONSTITUENCY	1885	1886	1892	1895	1900	1906	1910(J)	1910(D)
NEWINGTON								
Walworth	C	C	L(C)	C	C	L	L	L
West	C	C	L	L	L	L	L	L
PADDINGTON								
North	C	C	C	C	C	L	C	C
South	C	C	C	C	C	C	C	C
ST. GEORGE, HANOVER SQUARE	C	C(LU)	LU	C	C	C(LU)	LU	LU(C)
ST. PANCRAS								
East	L	C	C	C	C	L	L/Lab	L/Lab
North	L	C(L)	L	C	C	L	L	L
South	L	LU	LU	LU	LU	L	LU	LU
West	L	L	C	C	C	L	L	C
SHOREDITCH								
Haggerston	L/Lab	L/Lab	L/Lab	C	L/Lab	L/Lab(C)	L	L
Hoxton	L	L	L	L	C	C	L	L
SOUTHWARK								
Bermondsey	L	C	L	C	C	L(C)	L	L
Rotherhithe	C	C	C	C	C	L	L	L
West	L	L	L	L	L	L	C	L
STRAND	C	C	C	C	C	C	C	C
TOWER HAMLETS								
Bow and Bromley	L	C	L	C	C	L	C	Lab(C)
Limehouse	C	C	L	C	C	L	L	L
Mile End	C	C	C	C	C(LU)	L	LU	LU(C)
Poplar	L	L	L	L	L	L	L	L
St. George	C	C	L	C	C	L	L	L
Stepney	L	C	C	C(L/Lab)	C	C	C	L
Whitechapel	L	L	L	L	L	L	L	L
WANDSWORTH	C	C	C	C	C	C	C	C
WESTMINSTER	C	C	C	C	C	C	C	C
WOOLWICH	C	C	C	C	C(Lab)	Lab	C	Lab

[1] Subsequently became an Independent Liberal.

ENGLAND–BOROUGHS

CONSTITUENCY	1885	1886	1892	1895	1900	1906	1910(J)	1910(D)
ASHTON-UNDER-LYNE	C	C	C	C	C	L	L	C
ASTON MANOR	L	C	C	C	C	C	C	C
BARROW-IN-FURNESS	L	LU(L)	C	C	C	Lab	Lab	Lab
BATH	C	LU	C	C	C	L	C	C
[two seats]	L	C	LU	LU	LU	L	C	C
BEDFORD	L	L	L	C	C	L	C	L
BIRKENHEAD	C	C	C	C	C	L/Lab	L/Lab	C
BIRMINGHAM								
Bordesley	L/Lab	LU	LU	LU	LU	LU	LU	LU
Central	L	LU	LU	LU	LU	LU	LU	LU
East	L	C	C	C	C	C	C	C
Edgbaston	L	LU	LU	LU(C)	C	C	C	C
North	L	LU	LU	LU	LU	LU	LU	LU
South	L	LU	LU	LU	LU	LU	LU	LU
West	L	LU	LU	LU	LU	LU	LU	LU(C)
BLACKBURN	C	C	C	C	C	C	L	Lab
[two seats]	C	C	C	C	C	Lab	Lab	L
BOLTON	C	C	C	C	C	L	L	L
[two seats]	C	C	C	L	L	Lab	Lab	Lab
BOSTON	L	C	L	C	C	L	C	C
BRADFORD								
Central	L	L	L	LU	LU	L	L	L

ENGLAND—BOROUGHS (Cont.)

CONSTITUENCY	1885	1886	1892	1895	1900	1906	1910(J)	1910(D)
BRADFORD (Cont.)								
East	L	C	L	C	C	L	L	L
West	L	L	L	C	C	Lab	Lab	Lab
BRIGHTON	C	C	C	C	C(L)	L	C	C
[two seats]	C	C	C	C	C	L	C	C
BRISTOL								
East	L	L	L	L	L	L	L	L
North	L	LU	L	LU	LU	L	L	L
South	L	C	C	C	C	L	L	L
West	C	C	C	C	C	C	C	C
BURNLEY	L	LU(L)	L	L	C	L/Lab	C	L
BURY	L	LU	LU	C	C(L)	L	L	L
BURY ST. EDMUNDS	C	C	C	C	C	C	C	C
CAMBRIDGE	C	C	C	C	C	L	C	C
CANTERBURY	C	C	C	C	C	C	C	Ind C
CARLISLE	L	L	L	L	L	L	L	L
CHATHAM	C	C	C	C	C	Lab	C	C
CHELTENHAM	C	C	C	C	C	L	C	L(C)
CHESTER	L	C	C	C	C	L	C	C
CHRISTCHURCH	C	C	C	C	C	L	C	C
COLCHESTER	C	C	C(L)	L	L	L	C	C
COVENTRY	C	C(L)	L	C	C	L	C	L
CROYDON	C	C	C	C	C	LU(C)	C	C
DARLINGTON	L	L	L	LU	LU	LU	L	LU
DERBY	L	L	L	C	L	L/Lab	L	L
[two seats]	L	L	L	C	Lab	L	Lab	Lab
DEVONPORT	C	C	L	L	L	L	C	C
[two seats]	C	C	L	L	L(C) (L)	L	C	C
DEWSBURY	L	L	L	L	L	L	L	L
DOVER	C	C	C	C	C	C	C	C
DUDLEY	L	C	C	C	C	L	L	C
DURHAM	C	C	L	L(LU)	LU	LU	LU	LU
EXETER	C	C	C	C	C	L	C	C
GATESHEAD	L	L	L	L	L(L/Lab)	L/Lab	L	L
GLOUCESTER	L	L	L	LU	L	L	C	C
GRANTHAM	L	C	C	C	L	L	L	L
GRAVESEND	C	C	C	C	C	C	C	C
GREAT GRIMSBY	L	LU	L(LU)	L(LU)	LU	LU	L	LU(C)
GREAT YARMOUTH	C	C	L	C	C	C	C	C
HALIFAX	L	L	L	C	LU	L	L	L
[two seats]	L	L	L	L	L	Lab	Lab	Lab
HANLEY	L	L	L	L	C	L/Lab	Lab	Lab(L)
HARTLEPOOLS, THE	L	LU(L)	L	LU	L	L	L	L
HASTINGS	L	C	C	C	L	C	C	C
HEREFORD	L	C	L(C)	C	C	C	C	C(LU)
HUDDERSFIELD	L	L	L(C)	L	L	L	L	L
HYTHE	Ind L	LU	Ind L	C	C	C	C	C
IPSWICH	L(C)	C	C	L	L	L	L	L
[two seats]	L(C)	C	C	C	C	I	L	L(C)
KIDDERMINSTER	L	C	C	C	C	L	C	C
KING'S LYNN	C	C	C	C	C	L	L	C
KINGSTON UPON HULL								
Central	C	C	C	C	C	C	C	C
East	L	C	L	C	C	L	L	L
West	L	L	L	L	L	L	L	L
LEEDS								
Central	C	C	C	C	C	L	L	L
East	C	L	L	L	C	Lab	Lab	Lab
North	C	C	C	C	C(L)	L	L	L
South	L	L	L	L	L	L	L	L
West	L	L	L	L	L	L	L	L
LEICESTER	L	L	L(L/Lab)	L/Lab	L/Lab	L/Lab(L)	L	L
[two seats]	L	L	L	L	C	Lab	Lab	Lab

ENGLAND—BOROUGHS (Cont.)

CONSTITUENCY	1885	1886	1892	1895	1900	1906	1910(J)	1910(D)
LINCOLN	L	C	L	LU	LU	L	L	L
LIVERPOOL								
Abercromby	C	C	C	C	C	L	C	C
East Toxteth	C	C	C	C	C	C	C	C
Everton	C	C	C	C	C	C	C	C
Exchange	C	L	L	LU	LU	L	L	C
Kirkdale	C	C	C	C	C	C	C	C
Scotland	N	N	N	N	N	N	N	N
Walton	C	C	C	C	C	C	C	C
West Derby	C	C	C	C	C	C	C	C
West Toxteth	C	C	C	C	C	C	C	C
MAIDSTONE	C	C	C	C	L	C	C	C
MANCHESTER								
East	C	C	C	C	C	L	Lab	Lab
North	C	L	L	L	L	L	L	L
North-East	C	C	C	C	C	Lab	Lab	Lab
North-West	C	C	C	C	C	L(C)	L	L(C)
South	L	L	L	LU	LU	L	L	L(C)
South-West	C	L	L	C	C	Lab	LU	L
MIDDLESBROUGH	L	L	Ind Lab	L/Lab	C	L/Lab	L	L
MORPETH	L/Lab	L/Lab	L/Lab	L/Lab	L/Lab	L/Lab	L/Lab	L/Lab
NEWCASTLE-UNDER-LYME	L	LU	L	L	LU	L	L	L
NEWCASTLE UPON TYNE	Ind L	L	C	C	C	Lab	L	L
[two seats]	L	L	L	C	C	L(C)	Lab	Lab
NORTHAMPTON	L	L	L	L	L	L	L	L
[two seats]	L	L	L	C	L	L	L	L
NORWICH	C	L	C	C	C(L)	Lab	L	L
[two seats]	L	C	L	C	C	L	Lab	Lab
NOTTINGHAM								
East	L	L	L	C	C	L	C	C
South	L	C	C	C	C	L/Lab	C	C
West	L	L/Lab	LU	L	L	L	L	L
OLDHAM	L	C	L	C(L)	L	L	L	L(C)
[two seats]	C	C	L	C(L)	C	L	L	L
OXFORD	C	C	C	C	C	C	C	C
PENRYN AND FALMOUTH	L	C	C	L	L	L	C	C
PETERBOROUGH	Ind L	LU(L)	L	LU	LU	L	L	L
PLYMOUTH	C	C	C	C	C	L	L	C
[two seats]	C	C	C	L	C	L	L	C
PONTEFRACT	C	C	C(L)	L	L	L	L	L
PORTSMOUTH	L	LU	L	L	C	L	C	C
[two seats]	L	C	L	L	C	L	LU	LU
PRESTON	C	C	C	C	C	Lab	C	C
[two seats]	C	C	C	C	C	L	C	C
READING	C	C	L	C(L)	L	L	L	L(C)
ROCHDALE	L	L	L	C	C	L	L	L
ROCHESTER	C	C(L)	C	C	C	L	C	L
ST. HELENS	C	C	C	C	C	Lab	Lab	C
SALFORD								
North	C	C	L	C	C	L/Lab	L/Lab	L/Lab (Ind Lab)
South	L	C	C	C	C	L	L	C
West	L	C	C	C	C	L	L	L
SALISBURY	L	C	C	C	C	L	C	C
SCARBOROUGH	C	L	C	L	L	L	L	L
SHEFFIELD								
Attercliffe	L	L	L	L	L	L(Lab)	Lab	Lab
Brightside	L	L	L	L(L/Lab)	C	L	L	L
Central	C	C	C	C	C	C	C	C
Ecclesall	C	C	C	C	C	C	C	C
Hallam	C	C	C	C	C	C	C	C(L)
SHREWSBURY	C	C	C	C	C	C	C	C
SOUTHAMPTON	C	C	C	C(L)	C	L	L	L
[two seats]	C	C(L)	L	LU	LU	L	L	L

ENGLAND—BOROUGHS (Cont.)

CONSTITUENCY	1885	1886	1892	1895	1900	1906	1910(J)	1910(D)
SOUTH SHIELDS	L	L	L	L	L	L	L	L
STAFFORD	L	C	L	L	L	L	L	L
STALYBRIDGE	C	C	C	C	C(L)	L	C	C
STOCKPORT	C	C	L	C	L	Lab	Lab	L
[two seats]	C	C	C	C	C	L	L	Lab
STOCKTON-ON-TEES	L	L	C	L	C	C	L	L
STOKE-ON-TRENT	L	L	L	LU	C	L/Lab	L/Lab	L/Lab
SUNDERLAND	L	L	L	C	C	L	Ind C	L
[two seats]	L	L	L	L	C	Lab	C	Lab
TAUNTON	C	C	C	C	C	C	C	C
TYNEMOUTH	C	C	C	C	C	L	L	L
WAKEFIELD	C	C	C	LU	LU(C)	C	C	L
WALSALL	L	L	C(L)	C	L	L	C	C
WARRINGTON	C	C	C	C	C	L	L	C
WARWICK AND LEAMINGTON	L	LU	LU	LU	LU	L	C	C
WEDNESBURY	C	L	C	C	C	L	C	C
WEST BROMWICH	L	C	C	C	C	L	C	C
WEST HAM								
North	L	C	L	C	C	L	L	L
South	L/Lab	C	Ind Lab	C	C	Lab	Lab	Lab
WHITEHAVEN	C	C	L	C	C	L	C	Lab
WIGAN	C	C	C	C	C	C	Lab	. C
WINCHESTER	C	C	C	C	C	C	C	C
WINDSOR	C	C	C	C	C	C	C	C
WOLVERHAMPTON								
East	L	L	L	L	L	L	L	L
South	L	LU	LU	LU	L	L	C	C
West	C	L	C	C	C	Lab	C	C
WORCESTER	C	C	C	C	C	C	C	C
YORK	L	L	C	C	C	L	L	C
[two seats]	L	L	L	L(C)	C	C	C	L

ENGLAND—COUNTIES

CONSTITUENCY	1885	1886	1892	1895	1900	1906	1910(J)	1910(D)
BEDFORDSHIRE								
Biggleswade	L	LU	L	LU	LU	L	L	L
Luton	L	L	L	L	L	L	L	L
BERKSHIRE								
Abingdon	C	C	C	C	C	L	C	C
Newbury	C	C	C	C	C	L	C	C
Wokingham	C	C	C	C	C	C	C	C
BUCKINGHAMSHIRE								
Aylesbury	L	LU	LU	LU	LU	LU	LU	LU
Buckingham	L	C(L)	l	C	C	L	L	L
Wycombe	C	C	C	C	C	L	C	C
CAMBRIDGESHIRE								
Chesterton	C	C	L	C	C	L	L	L
Newmarket	L	L	L	C	C(L)	L	C	L(C)
Wisbech	L	C(L)	L	C	L	L	L	L
CHESHIRE								
Altrincham	C	C	C	C	C	L	L	C
Crewe	L	L	L	C	L	L	L	L(C)
Eddisbury	C	C	C	C	C	L	C	C
Hyde	L	C	C	C	C	L	L	L
Knutsford	C	C	C	C	C	L	C	C
Macclesfield	L	C	C	C	C	L	L	L
Northwich	L	LU(L)	L	L	L	L	L	L
Wirral	C	C	C	C	C	L	C	C

ENGLAND—COUNTIES (Cont.)

CONSTITUENCY	1885	1886	1892	1895	1900	1906	1910(J)	1910(D)
CORNWALL								
Bodmin	L	LU	LU	LU	LU	L	L	LU(C)
Camborne	Ind L	L	L	LU	L	L	L	L
Launceston	L	L	L	L	L	L	L	L
St. Austell	L	L	L	L	L	L	L	L
St. Ives	L	LU	LU	LU	LU	L	L	L
Truro	L	LU	LU	LU	LU	L	L	L
CUMBERLAND								
Cockermouth	C	L	L	L	C	L(C)	C	L
Egremont	C	C	L	C	C	L	C	C
Eskdale	L	L	L	L	C	L	L	C
Penrith	L	C	C	C	C	C	C	C
DERBYSHIRE								
Chesterfield	L	LU	L	L	L	L/Lab	Lab	Lab (L/Lab)
High Peak	C	C	C	C	L	L	L	C
Ilkeston	L	L	L	L	L	L	L	L
Mid	L	L	L	L	L	L(Lab)	Lab	Lab
North-Eastern	L	L	L	L	L	L(L/Lab)	Lab	Lab (C)
Southern	L	L	L	C	C	L	L	L
Western	L	LU	LU	LU	LU	LU	LU	LU
DEVON								
Ashburton	L	L	L	L	L	L(C)	L	C
Barnstaple	L	LU	L	LU	L	L	L	L
Honiton	C	C	C	C	C	C	C	C
South Molton	L	LU(L)	L	L	L	L	L	L
Tavistock	L	LU	L	L	LU	L	L	LU
Tiverton	C	C	C	C	C	C	C	C
Torquay	L	C	C	C	L	L	L	LU
Totnes	L	LU	LU	LU	LU	LU	LU	LU
DORSET								
Eastern	L	C	C	C	C(L)	L	L	L
Northern	L	L	C	C	C(L)	L	C	C
Southern	L	C	C	C	C	L	C	C
Western	C	C	C	C	C	C	C	C
DURHAM								
Barnard Castle	L	L	L	L	L(Lab)	Lab	Lab	Lab
Bishop Auckland	L	L	L	L	L	L	L	L
Chester-le-Street	L	L	L	L	L	Ind Lab	Lab	Lab
Houghton-le-Spring	L/Lab	C	L	L	L	L	L	L
Jarrow	L	L	L	L	L	L(Lab)	L	L
Mid	L/Lab	L/Lab	L/Lab	L/Lab	L/Lab	L/Lab	L/Lab	L/Lab
North-Western	L	L	L	L	L	L	L	L
South-Eastern	L	LU	L	LU(L)	LU	LU	L	L
ESSEX								
Chelmsford	C	C	C	C	C	C	C	C
Epping	C	C	C	C	C	C	C	C
Harwich	C	C	C	C	C	L	C	C
Maldon	L	C	L	C	C	L	C	C
Romford	L	C	C	C	C	L	L	L
Saffron Walden	L	L	L	L	L	L	C	L
South-Eastern	C	C	C	C	C	L	C	C
Walthamstow	L	C	C	C(L/Lab)	C	L	L	L
GLOUCESTERSHIRE								
Cirencester	L	LU	L(C)(L)	C	C	L	C	C
Forest of Dean	L	L	L	L	L	L	L	L
Stroud	L	C	L	C	L	L	L	L
Tewkesbury	C	C	C	C	C	C	C	C
Thornbury	L	C	C	C	C	L	L	L
HAMPSHIRE								
Andover	C	C	C	C	C	C	C	C
Basingstoke	C	C	C	C	C	C	C	C
Fareham	C	C	C	C	C	C	C	C
New Forest	C	C	C	C	C	L	C	C
Petersfield	L	LU	C	C	C	C	C	C

ENGLAND—COUNTIES (Cont.)

CONSTITUENCY	1885	1886	1892	1895	1900	1906	1910(J)	1910(D)
HEREFORDSHIRE								
Leominster	L	C	C	C	C	L	C	C
Ross	L	LU	LU	LU	LU	L(LU)	LU	LU(C)
HERTFORDSHIRE								
Hertford	C	C	C	C	C	C	C	C(Ind)
Hitchin	C	C	C	C	C	L	C	C
St. Albans	C	C	C	C	C(L)	C	C	C
Watford	C	C	C	C	C	L	C	C
HUNTINGDONSHIRE								
Huntingdon	L	C	C	C	C	L	C	C
Ramsey	C	C	C	C	C	L	C	C
ISLE OF WIGHT	C	C	C	C	C(Ind C)	L	C	C
KENT								
Ashford	C	C	C	C	C	C	C	C
Dartford	C	C	C	C	C	L/Lab	C	L/Lab
Faversham	C	C	C	C	C	L	C	C
Isle of Thanet	C	C	C	C	C	C	C	C
Medway	C	C	C	C	C	C	C	C
St. Augustine's	C	C	C	C	C	C	C	C
Sevenoaks	C	C	C	C	C	C	C	C
Tunbridge	C	C	C	C	C	L	C	C
LANCASHIRE								
Accrington	L	C	L	L	L	L	L	L
Blackpool	C	C	C	C	C	C	C	C
Bootle	C	C	C	C	C	C	C	C
Chorley	C	C	C	C	C	C	C	C
Clitheroe	L	L	L	L	L(Lab)	Lab	Lab	Lab
Darwen	C	C	L	C	C	C	L	C
Eccles	C	C(L)	L	C	C	L	L	L
Gorton	L	L	L	C	C	Lab	Lab	Lab
Heywood	L	L	L	LU	LU	L	L	L
Ince	C	C	L/Lab	C	C	Lab	Lab	Lab
Lancaster	C	L	L	C	L	L	L	L
Leigh	L	L	L	L	L	L	L	L
Middleton	L	C	L	C(L)	C	L	L	L
Newton	C	C	C	C	C	Lab	Lab	C
North Lonsdale	C	C	L	LU	LU	C	C	C
Ormskirk	C	C	C	C	C	C	C	C
Prestwich	L	C	C	L	L	L	L	L
Radliffe-cum-Farnworth	L	L	L	C	L	L	L	L
Rossendale	L	LU(L)	L	L	L	L	L	L
Southport	L	C	C	C(L)	C	L	C	C
Stretford	L	C	C	C	C	L	L	L
Westhoughton	C	C	C	C	C	Lab	Lab	Lab
Widnes	C	C	C	C	C	C	C	C
LEICESTERSHIRE								
Bosworth	L	L	L	L	L	L	L	L
Harborough	L	C(L)	L	L	L	L	L	L
Loughborough	L	C	L	L	L	L	L	L
Melton	C	C	C	C	C	L	L	C
LINCOLNSHIRE								
Brigg	L	L	L(C)	L	L	L(C)	L	L
Gainsborough	L	C	L	L	C	L	L	L
Horncastle	C	C	C	C	C	C	C	C
Louth	L	C	L	L	L	L	C	L
Sleaford	C	C	C	C	C	L	C	C
Spalding	C	C(L)	L	LU	L	L	L	L
Stamford	C	C	C	C	C	C	C	C
MIDDLESEX								
Brentford	C	C	C	C	C	L	C	C
Ealing	C	C	C	C	C	C	C	C
Enfield	C	C	C	C	C	L	C	C
Harrow	C	C	C	C	C	L	C	C

ENGLAND—COUNTIES (Cont.)

CONSTITUENCY	1885	1886	1892	1895	1900	1906	1910(J)	1910(D)
MIDDLESEX (Cont.)								
Hornsey	C	C	C	C	C	C	C	C
Tottenham	C	C	C	C	C	L	L	L
Uxbridge	C	C	C	C	C	C	C	C
NORFOLK								
Eastern	C	C	L	L	L	L	L	L
Mid	L	LU	L	L	L	L	LU	LU(C)
Northern	L	L	L	L	L	L	L	L
North-Western	L/Lab	C	L/Lab	L/Lab	L	L	L	L
Southern	L	LU	LU	LU(L)	L	L	L	L
South-Western	C	C	C	C	C	L	L	L
NORTHAMPTONSHIRE								
Eastern	L	L	L	L	L	L	L	L
Mid	L	L	L	C	L	L	L	L
Northern	C	C	C	C	C	L/Lab	C	C
Southern	C	C	L	C	C	L	C	C
NORTHUMBERLAND								
Berwick-upon-Tweed	L	L	L	L	L	L	L	L
Hexham	L	L	C(L)	L	L	L	L	L
Tyneside	L	L	L	L	LU	L	L	L
Wansbeck	L/Lab	L/Lab	L/Lab	L/Lab	L/Lab	L/Lab	L/Lab	L/Lab(L)
NOTTINGHAMSHIRE								
Bassetlaw	C	C	C	C	C	L	C	C
Mansfield	L	L	L	L	L	L	L	L
Newark	C	C	C	C	C	C	C	C
Rushcliffe	L	L	L	L	L	L	L	L
OXFORDSHIRE								
Banbury	L	L	L	C	C	L	C	L
Henley	C	C	C	C	C	L	C	C
Woodstock	L	LU(C)	L	C	C	L	C	C
RUTLANDSHIRE	C	C	C	C	C	C	C	C
SHROPSHIRE								
Ludlow	L	LU	LU	LU	LU	LU	LU	LU
Newport	L	C	C	C	C	C	C	C
Oswestry	C	C	C	C	C(L)	C	C	C
Wellington	L	LU	LU	LU	LU	L	L	L
SOMERSET								
Bridgwater	C	C	C	C	C	L	C	C
Eastern	L	LU	LU	LU	LU	L	LU	LU
Frome	L	C	L	C(L)	L	L	L	L
Northern	C	C	L	C	C	L	L	L
Southern	L	L	L	L	L	L	L	L(C)
Wellington	L	C	C	C	C	C	C	C
Wells	C	C	C	C	C	L	C	C
STAFFORDSHIRE								
Burton	L	L	L	L	LU	LU	LU	LU
Handsworth	L	LU	LU	LU	LU	LU	LU	LU
Kingswinford	C	C	C	C	C	C	C	C
Leek	L	C	C	C	C	L	C	L
Lichfield	L	L	LU	L	L	L	L	L
North-Western	L	C	C	C	C	L(L/Lab)	Lab	Lab
Western	L	LU	LU	LU	LU	L	LU	LU
SUFFOLK								
Eye	L	L	L	L	L	L	L	L
Lowestoft	L	LU	C	C	C	L	C	L
Stowmarket	L	C(L)	L	C	C	L	C	C
Sudbury	L	LU	LU	LU	LU	L	C	C
Woodbridge	L	C	L	C	C	L	C	C
SURREY								
Chertsey	C	C	C	C	C	L	C	C
Epsom	C	C	C	C	C	C	C	C
Guildford	C	C	C	C	C	L	C	C

ENGLAND—COUNTIES (Cont.)

CONSTITUENCIES	1885	1886	1892	1895	1900	1906	1910(J)	1910(D)
SURREY (Cont.)								
Kingston	C	C	C	C	C	C	C	C
Reigate	C	C	C	C	C	L	C	C
Wimbledon	C	C	C	C	C	C	C	C
SUSSEX								
Chichester	C	C	C	C	C	C	C	C
Eastbourne	C	C	C	C	C	L	C	C
East Grinstead	C	C	C	C	C	L	C	C
Horsham	C	C	C	C	C	C	C	C
Lewes	C	C	C	C	C	C	C	C
Rye	C	C	C	C	C(L)	C	C	C
WARWICKSHIRE								
Nuneaton	L	C	C	C	C	L/Lab	Lab	Lab
Rugby	L	L	L	C	L	L	C	C
Stratford-on-Avon	L	C	C	C	C	L(C)	C	C
Tamworth	C	C	C	C	C	C	C	C
WESTMORLAND								
Appleby	C	C	C	C	L[1](L)	L	C	C
Kendal	C	C	C	C	C	L	C	C(Ind C)
WILTSHIRE								
Chippenham	L	C	C	C	C	L	C	C
Cricklade	L	LU	L	LU(L)	L	L	LU	L
Devizes	C	C	L	C	C	L	C	C
Westbury	L	L	L	C	L	L	L	L
Wilton	L	LU	C	C	C	L	C	C
WORCESTERSHIRE								
Bewdley	C	C	C	C	C	C	C	C
Droitwich	L	LU	LU	LU	LU	L	LU	LU(C)
Eastern	L	LU	LU	LU	LU	LU	LU	LU(C)
Evesham	C	C	C	C	C	C	C	C
Northern	L	LU	L	LU	LU	L	L	L
YORKSHIRE (EAST RIDING)								
Buckrose	C	C	L	L	L	L	L	L
Holderness	C	C	C	C	C	C	C	C
Howdenshire	C	C	C	C	C	C	C	C
YORKSHIRE (NORTH RIDING)								
Cleveland	L	L	L	L	L	L	L	L
Richmond	L	C	C	C	C	L	C	C
Thirsk and Malton	C	C	C	C	C	C	C	C
Whitby	C	C	C	C	C(L)	C	C	C
YORKSHIRE (WEST RIDING)								
Barkston Ash	C	C	C	C	C(L)	C	C	C
Barnsley	L	L	L	L	L	L	L	L
Colne Valley	L	LU	L	L	L	L(Ind Lab)	L	L
Doncaster	L	L(LU)	L	C	C	L	L	L
Elland	L	L	L	L	L	L	L	L
Hallamshire	L	L	L	L	L	L/Lab	Lab	Lab
Holmfirth	L	L	L	L	L	L	L	L
Keighley	L	L	L	L	L	L	L	L
Morley	L	L	L	L	L	L	L	L
Normanton	L/Lab	L/Lab	L/Lab	L/Lab	L/Lab	L/Lab	Lab	Lab
Osgoldcross	L	L	L	L(Ind L)	Ind L	L	L	L
Otley	L	L	L	C	L	L	L	L
Pudsey	L	L	L	L	L	L(C)	L	L
Ripon	L	C	C	C	C	L	C	C
Rotherham	L	L	L	L	L	L	L	L(L/Lab)
Shipley	L	L	L/Lab	LU	LU	L	L	L
Skipton	L	LU	L	LU	L	L	L	L
Sowerby	L	L	L	L	L	L	L	L
Spen Valley	L	L	L	L	L	L	L	L

[1] Subsequently became a Liberal Unionist.

WALES AND MONMOUTHSHIRE—BOROUGHS

CONSTITUENCY	1885	1886	1892	1895	1900	1906	1910(J)	1910(D)
CAERNARVON BOROUGHS	L	C(L)	L	L	L	L	L	L
CARDIFF BOROUGHS	L	L	L	C	L	L	L	C
CARMARTHEN BOROUGHS	L	L	L	LU	L	L	L	L
DENBIGH BOROUGHS	C	C	C	C	C	L/Lab	C	C
FLINT BOROUGHS	L	L	L	L	L	L	L	L
MERTHYR TYDFIL	L	L	L	L	L	L	L	L
[two seats]	L	L(Ind L)	L	L	Lab	Lab	Lab	Lab(Ind Lab)
MONMOUTH BOROUGHS	L	C	L	L	C	L	L	L
MONTGOMERY BOROUGHS	C	L	C	C	C	L	L	C
PEMBROKE AND HAVERFORD-								
WEST BOROUGHS	L	C	L	C	C	L	L	L
SWANSEA								
District	L	LU	L	L	L	L	L	L
Town	L	L	L	C	L	L	L	L

WALES AND MONMOUTHSHIRE—COUNTIES

CONSTITUENCY	1885	1886	1892	1895	1900	1906	1910(J)	1910(D)
ANGLESEY	L	L	L	L	L	L	L	L
BRECONSHIRE	L	L	L	L	L	L	L	L
CAERNARVONSHIRE								
Arfon	L	L	L	L	L	L	L	L
Eifion	L	L	L	L	L	L	L	L
CARDIGANSHIRE	L	L	L	L	L	L	L	L
CARMARTHENSHIRE								
Eastern	L	L	L	L	L	L	L	L
Western	L	L	L	L	L	L	L	L
DENBIGHSHIRE								
Eastern	L	L	L	L	L	L	L	L
Western	L	LU	L	L	L	L	L	L
FLINTSHIRE	L	L	L	L	L	L	L	L
GLAMORGANSHIRE								
Eastern	L	L	L	L	L	L	L	L/Lab
Gower	L	L	L	L	L	Ind L/Lab	Lab	Lab
Mid	L	L	L	L	L	L	L	L
Rhondda	Ind L/Lab	L/Lab	L/Lab	L/Lab	L/Lab	L/Lab	Lab	Lab
Southern	L	L	L	C	C	L/Lab	Lab	Lab
MERIONETHSHIRE	L	L	L	L	L	L	L	L
MONMOUTHSHIRE								
Northern	L	L	L	L	L	L	L	L
Southern	C	C	C	C	C	L	L	L
Western	L	L	L	L	L(L/Lab)	L/Lab	Lab	Lab
MONTGOMERYSHIRE	L	L	L	L	L	L	L	L
PEMBROKESHIRE	L	L	L	L	L	L	L	L
RADNORSHIRE	C	C	L	C	L	L	C	L

SCOTLAND—BURGHS

CONSTITUENCY	1885	1886	1892	1895	1900	1906	1910(J)	1910(D)
ABERDEEN								
North	L	L	L	L	L	L	L	L
South	L	L	L	L	L	L	L	L
AYR BURGHS	L	LU(L)(C)	L	C	C(L)	C	C	C

SCOTLAND—BURGHS (Cont.)

CONSTITUENCY	1885	1886	1892	1895	1900	1906	1910(J)	1910(D)
DUMFRIES BURGHS	L	L	L	L	L	L	L	L
DUNDEE	L	L	L	L	L	L	L	L
[two seats]	L	L	L	L	L	Lab	Lab	Lab
EDINBURGH								
Central	Ind L	L	L	L	L	L	L	L
East	Ind L	L	L	L	L	L	L	L
South	Ind L(L)	L	L	LU(L)	LU	L	L	L
West	L	LU(L)	LU	LU	LU	LU	LU	LU
ELGIN BURGHS	L	L	L	L	L	L	L	L
FALKIRK BURGHS	L	LU	L	LU	LU	L	L	L
GLASGOW								
Blackfriars and Hutchesontown	L	L	L	L	C	Lab	Lab	Lab
Bridgeton	L	L	L	L	C	L	L	L
Camlachie	L	L	LU	LU	LU	LU	LU	LU
Central	L	C	C	C	C	L(C)	C	C
College	L	L	L	C	C	L	L	L
St. Rollox	L	LU	L	C	LU	L	L	L
Tradeston	L	LU	LU	LU	LU	LU	Ind L	L
GREENOCK	L	LU	LU	LU	C	L	L	L
HAWICK BURGHS	L	L	L	L	L	L	L	L
INVERNESS BURGHS	L	LU	L	LU	LU	L	L	L
KILMARNOCK BURGHS	C	L	L	C	C	L	L	L
KIRKCALDY BURGHS	Ind L	L	L	L	L	L	L	L
LEITH BURGHS	L	L	L	L	L	L	L	L(C)
MONTROSE BURGHS	L	L	L	L	L	L	L	L
PAISLEY	L	L	L	L	L	L	L	L
PERTH	Ind L	L	C	L	L	L	L	L
ST. ANDREWS BURGHS	Ind L	LU	LU	LU	LU(L)	LU	L	LU
STIRLING BURGHS	L	L	L	L	L	L	L	L
WICK BURGHS	Ind L	L	LU	LU(L)	C	C	L	L

SCOTLAND—COUNTIES

CONSTITUENCY	1885	1886	1892	1895	1900	1906	1910(J)	1910(D)
ABERDEENSHIRE								
Eastern	L	L	L	L	LU	L	L	L
Western	L	L	L	L	L	L	L	L
ARGYLL	Ind L/Crf	C	L/Crf	C	C(L)	L	L	L
AYRSHIRE								
Northern	L	LU	LU	LU	LU	LU	L	L(C)
Southern	L	LU	L	LU	LU	L	L	L
BANFFSHIRE	L	L	L	L	L	L	L	L
BERWICKSHIRE	L	L	L	L	L	L	L	L
BUTE	C	C	C	C	C(L)	L	C	C
CAITHNESS	Ind L/Crf	L/Crf	L/Crf	L	L	L	L	L
CLACKMANNANSHIRE AND KINROSS-SHIRE	L	L	L	L	L	L	L	L
DUMFRIESSHIRE	L	LU	LU	L	LU	L	L	L
DUNBARTONSHIRE	C	C	L	C	C	L	L	L
EDINBURGHSHIRE[1]	L	L	L	L	L	L	L	L(C)
ELGINSHIRE AND NAIRNSHIRE	L	L	L	C	C	L	L	L
FIFE								
Eastern	L	L	L	L	L	L	L	L
Western	L	L	L	L	L	L	L	Lab
FORFARSHIRE	L	LU	L(C)	L	L	L	L	L

SCOTLAND—COUNTIES (Cont.)

CONSTITUENCY	1885	1886	1892	1895	1900	1906	1910(J)	1910(D)
HADDINGTONSHIRE	L	L	L	L	L	L	L	L
INVERNESS-SHIRE	Ind L/Crf	LU/Crf	L/Crf(C)	C	L	L	L	L
KINCARDINESHIRE	L	L	L	L	L	L	L	L
KIRKCUDBRIGHTSHIRE	C	C	C	C	C	L	C	L
LANARKSHIRE								
Govan	C	C(L)	L	L	L	C	L	L
Mid	L	L	L	L	L	L	L	L
North-Eastern	L	L	L	L	L(LU)(L)	L	L	L
North-Western	C	L/Lab	C	L	L	C	L	L
Partick	L	LU	LU	LU	LU	L	L	L
Southern	L	C	C	C	C	L	L	L(C)
LINLITHGOWSHIRE	L	L	L(C)	L	L	L	L	L
ORKNEY AND SHETLAND	L	L	L	L	LU(Ind L)	L	L	L
PEEBLESSHIRE AND SELKIRKSHIRE	L	LU	LU	LU	LU	L	L	L
PERTHSHIRE								
Eastern	L	L	L	L	L	L	L	L
Western	L	LU	LU	LU	LU	L	C	C
RENFREWSHIRE								
Eastern	L	C	C	C	C	L	C	C
Western	C	C	C	C	C	L	L	L
ROSS AND CROMARTY	Ind L/Crf	L/Crf	L/Crf	L	L	L	L	L
ROXBURGHSHIRE	L	LU	L	C	C	L	L	L
STIRLINGSHIRE	L	L	L	C	C	L	L	L
SUTHERLAND	L	L/Crf	L/Crf	L	LU	L	L	L
WIGTOWNSHIRE	C	C	C	C	C	C	C	C

[1] Subsequently the name of the county was changed to Midlothian.

IRELAND—BOROUGHS

CONSTITUENCY	1885	1886	1892	1895	1900	1906	1910(J)	1910(D)	1918
BELFAST									
Cromac	—	—	—	—	—	—	—	—	C
Duncairn	—	—	—	—	—	—	—	—	C
East	C	C	C	C	C	C	C	C	—
Falls	—	—	—	—	—	—	—	—	N
North	C	C	C	C	C	C	C	C	—
Ormeau	—	—	—	—	—	—	—	—	C
Pottinger	—	—	—	—	—	—	—	—	C
St. Anne's	—	—	—	—	—	—	—	—	C
Shankill	—	—	—	—	—	—	—	—	C
South	C	C	C	C	C(Ind C)	Ind C	C	C	—
Victoria	—	—	—	—	—	—	—	—	C
West	C	N	LU	LU	LU	N	N	N	—
Woodvale	—	—	—	—	—	—	—	—	C
CORK	N	N	N	N	N	N	N	N	SF
[two seats]	N	N	N	N	N	N	N	N	SF
DUBLIN									
Clontarf	—	—	—	—	—	—	—	—	SF
College Green	N	N	N	N	N	N	N	N	SF
Harbour	N	N	N	N	N	N	N	N	SF
St. James's	—	—	—	—	—	—	—	—	SF
St. Michan's	—	—	—	—	—	—	—	—	SF
St. Patrick's	N	N	N	N	N	N	N	N	SF
St. Stephen's Green	N	N	LU	LU(C)	N	N	N	N	SF
GALWAY	N	N	N	N	C(N)	N	N	N	—
KILKENNY	N	N	N	N	N	N	N	N(SF)	—

IRELAND—BOROUGHS (Cont.)

CONSTITUENCY	1885	1886	1892	1895	1900	1906	1910(J)	1910(D)	1918
LIMERICK	N	N	N	N	N	N	N	N	SF
LONDONDERRY	C	N	C	N	C	C	C	C(L)	SF
NEWRY	N	N	N	N	N	N	N	N	—
WATERFORD	N	N	N	N	N	N	N	N	N

IRELAND—COUNTIES

CONSTITUENCY	1885	1886	1892	1895	1900	1906	1910(J)	1910(D)	1918
ANTRIM									
East	C	C	C	C	C	C	C	C	C(Ind C)
Mid	C	C	C	C	C	C	C	C	C
North	C	C	C	C	C	L	LU	LU	C
South	C	C	C	C	C	C	C	C	C
ARMAGH									
Mid	C	C	C	C	C	C	C	C	C
North	C	C	C	C	C	C	C	C	C
South	N	N	N	N	N	N	N	N	N
CARLOW	N	N	N	N	N	N	N	N	SF
CAVAN									
East	N	N	N	N	N	N	N	N(SF)	SF
West	N	N	N	N	N	N	N	N	SF
CLARE									
East	N	N	N	N	N	N	N	N(SF)	SF
West	N	N	N	N	N	N	N	N	SF
CORK									
East	N	N	N	N	N	N	N	N	SF
Mid	N	N	N	N	N	N	N	N	SF
North	N	N	N	N	N	N	N	N	SF
North-East	N	N	N	N	N	N	N	N	SF
South	N	N	N	N	N	N	N	N	SF
South-East	N	N	N	N	N	N	N	N	SF
West	N	N	N	N	N	N	N	N	SF
DONEGAL									
East	N	N	N	N	N	N	N	N	N
North	N	N	N	N	N	N	N	N	SF
South	N	N	N	N	N	N	N	N	SF
West	N	N	N	N	N	N	N	N	SF
DOWN									
East	C	C	C	C	C(Ind)	C	C	C	C
Mid	—	—	—	—	—	—	—	—	C
North	C	C	C	C	C	C	C	C	C
South	N	N	N	N	N	N	N	N	N
West	C	C	C	C	C	C	C	C	C
DUBLIN									
North	N	N	N	N	N	N	N	N	SF
Pembroke	—	—	—	—	—	—	—	—	SF
Rathmines	—	—	—	—	—	—	—	—	C
South	N	N	C	C	N	C	C	N	SF
FERMANAGH									
North	N	N	C	C	C(Ind)	C	C	C	C
South	N	N	N	N	N	N	N	N	SF
GALWAY									
Connemara	N	N	N	N	N	N	N	N	SF
East	N	N	N	N	N	N	N	N	SF
North	N	N	N	N	N	N	N	N	SF
South	N	N	N	N	N	N	N	N	SF
KERRY									
East	N	N	N	N	N	N	N	N	SF
North	N	N	N	N	N	N	N	N	SF
South	N	N	N	N	N	N	N	N	SF
West	N	N	N	N	N	N	N	N	SF

IRELAND—COUNTIES (Cont.)

CONSTITUENCY	1885	1886	1892	1895	1900	1906	1910(J)	1910(D)	1918
KILDARE									
North	N	N	N	N	N	N	N	N	SF
South	N	N	N	N	N	N	N	N	SF
KILKENNY									
North	N	N	N	N	N	N	N	N	SF
South	N	N	N	N	N	N	N	N	SF
KING'S	—	—	—	—	—	—	—	—	SF
Birr	N	N	N	N	N	N	N	N	—
Tullamore	N	N	N	N	N	N	N	N(SF)	—
LEITRIM	—	—	—	—	—	—	—	—	SF
North	N	N	N	N	N	N	N	N	—
South	N	N	N	N	N	N	N	N	—
LIMERICK									
East	N	N	N	N	N	N	N	N	SF
West	N	N	N	N	N	N	N	N	SF
LONDONDERRY									
North	C	C	C	C	C	C	C	C	C
South	N	LU	LU	LU	LU	LU	LU	LU	C
LONGFORD	—	—	—	—	—	—	—	—	SF
North	N	N	N	N	N	N	N	N	—
South	N	N	N	N	N	N	N	N(SF)	—
LOUTH	—	—	—	—	—	—	—	—	SF
North	N	N	N	N	N	N	N	N	—
South	N	N	N	N	N	N	N	N	—
MAYO									
East	N	N	N	N	N	N	N	N	SF
North	N	N	N	N	N	N	N	N	SF
South	N	N	N	N	N	N	N	N	SF
West	N	N	N	N	N	N	N	N	SF
MEATH									
North	N	N	N	N	N	N	N	N	SF
South	N	N	N	N	N	N	N	N	SF
MONAGHAN									
North	N	N	N	N	N	N	N	N	SF
South	N	N	N	N	N	N	N	N	SF
QUEEN'S	—	—	—	—	—	—	—	—	SF
Leix	N	N	N	N	N	N	N	N	—
Ossory	N	N	N	N	N	N	N	N	—
ROSCOMMON									
North	N	N	N	N	N	N	N	N(SF)	SF
South	N	N	N	N	N	N	N	N	SF
SLIGO									
North	N	N	N	N	N	N	N	N	SF
South	N	N	N	N	N	N	N	N	SF
TIPPERARY									
East	N	N	N	N	N	N	N	N	SF
Mid	N	N	N	N	N	N	N	N	SF
North	N	N	N	N	N	N	N	N	SF
South	N	N	N	N	N	N	N	N	SF
TYRONE									
East	N	N	N	N	N	N	N	N	—
Mid	N	N	N	N	N	N	C	N	—
North	C	C	C	L	L	L	L	L	—
North-East	—	—	—	—	—	—	—	—	N
North-West	—	—	—	—	—	—	—	—	SF
South	N	LU	LU	LU	LU	L	LU	LU	C
WATERFORD	—	—	—	—	—	—	—	—	SF
East	N	N	N	N	N	N	N	N	—
West	N	N	N	N	N	N	N	N	—
WESTMEATH	—	—	—	—	—	—	—	—	SF
North	N	N	N	N	N	N	N	N	—
South	N	N	N	N	N	N	N	N	—
WEXFORD									
North	N	N	N	N	N	N	N	N	SF
South	N	N	N	N	N	N	N	N	SF

IRELAND—COUNTIES (Cont.)

CONSTITUENCY	1885	1886	1892	1895	1900	1906	1910(J)	1910(D)	1918
WICKLOW									
East	N	N	N	N	N	N	N	N	SF
West	N	N	N	N	N	N	N	N	SF

THE UNIVERSITIES

CONSTITUENCY	1885	1886	1892	1895	1900	1906	1910(J)	1910(D)	1918
CAMBRIDGE	C	C	C	C	C	C	C	C	—
[two seats]	C	C	C	C	C	C	C	C	—
LONDON	L	LU	LU	LU	LU	LU	LU	LU	—
OXFORD	C	C	C	C(LU)	LU	LU	LU	LU(C)	--
[two seats]	C	C	C	C	C	C	C	C	—
ABERDEEN AND GLASGOW	C	C	C	C	C	C	C	C	—
EDINBURGH AND ST. ANDREWS	C	C	C	C	C	C	LU	LU(C)	—
DUBLIN	C	C	C	C	C	C	C	C	C
[two seats]	C	C	C	C(LU)	LU(C)	C	C	C	Ind C
NATIONAL, DUBLIN	—	—	—	—	—	—	—	—	SF
QUEEN'S, BELFAST	--	—	—	—	—	—	—	—	C

Appendix 2 REPRESENTATION OF CONSTITUENCIES 1918–1949

The following chart gives the party representation in each constituency (for Ireland 1918-22 see Appendix 1) from the General Election of 1918 until the Dissolution of the 1945-50 Parliament.

At the General Election of 1918 and at by-elections between 1918 and 1922, no distinction is made between Coalition and non-Coalition members except in the case of the four Coalition Labour members.

At the General Election of 1922 no distinction is made between Liberal and National Liberal members.

Unionists (in Scotland) and Ulster Unionists (in Northern Ireland) are listed as Conservatives.

Labour and Co-operative members are listed as Labour.

Where a constituency returned more than one member, the number of seats is given in brackets following the name of the constituency.

Constituency boundary alterations which took place at the General Election of 1945 are indicated by one asterisk * (minor boundary alteration) or two asterisks ** (major boundary alteration) placed before the party abbreviation.

Changes which occurred at by-elections are shown in brackets, *e.g.* Lab (C) indicates the seat was won by Labour at the General Election but subsequently lost to a Conservative.

LONDON—BOROUGHS

CONSTITUENCY	1918	1922	1923	1924	1929	1931	1935	1945
BATTERSEA								
North	L	Lab	L	Com	Lab	C	Lab	Lab
South	C	C	C	C(Lab)	Lab	C	C	Lab
BERMONDSEY								
Rotherhithe	C	C	Lab	Lab	Lab	C	Lab	Lab
West	L	Lab	L	Lab	Lab	Lab	Lab	Lab
BETHNAL GREEN								
North-East	L	L	Lab	Lab	L	L	Lab	Lab
South-West	C	L	L	L	L	L	L	Lab
CAMBERWELL								
Dulwich	C	C	C	C	C	C	C	Lab
North	C(Lab)	Lab	Lab	Lab	Lab	C	Lab	Lab
North-West	L	L	L	C	Lab	C	C	Lab
Peckham	L	C	C	Lab	Lab	C	C(Lab)	Lab
CHELSEA	C	C	C	C	C	C	C	C
CITY OF LONDON	C	C	C	C	C	C	C(Nat)	Nat
[two seats]	C	C	C	C	C	C	C	C
DEPTFORD	Lab	Lab	Lab	Lab	Lab	C	Lab	Lab
FINSBURY	C	C	Lab	Lab	Lab	N Lab	Lab	Lab
FULHAM								
East	C	C	C	C	C	C(Lab)	C	Lab
West	C	C	C	C	Lab(C)	C	C(Lab)	Lab
GREENWICH	C	C	Lab	C	Lab	C	C	Lab
HACKNEY								
Central	L	L	L	C	Lab	C	Lab	Lab
North	C	C	L	C	C	C	C	Lab
South	Ind (C)	C	Lab	L	Lab	C	Lab	Lab
HAMMERSMITH								
North	C	C	Lab	C(Lab)	Lab	C(Lab)	Lab	Ind Lab
South	C	C	C	C	Lab	C	C	Lab
HAMPSTEAD	C	C	C	C	C	C	C	C
HOLBORN	C	C	C	C	C	C	C	C
ISLINGTON								
East	C	C	L	C	Lab	C	C	Lab
North	C	C	C	C	Lab	C	C(Lab)	Lab
South	C	C	Lab	Lab	Lab	C	Lab	Lab
West	C	C	Lab	Lab	Lab	C	Lab	Lab
KENSINGTON								
North	C	C	C	C	Lab	C	C	Lab
South	C	C	C	C	C	C	C	C
LAMBETH								
Brixton	C	C	L	C	C	C	C	Lab
Kennington	L	C	Lab	C	Lab	C	C(Lab)	Lab

LONDON—BOROUGHS (Cont.)

CONSTITUENCY	1918	1922	1923	1924	1929	1931	1935	1945
LAMBETH (Cont.)								
North	L	L	L	L	Lab	L(Lab)	Lab	Lab
Norwood	C	C	C	C	C	C	C	Lab
LEWISHAM								
East	C	C	C	C	C	C	C	Lab
West	C	C	C	C	C	C	C	Lab
PADDINGTON								
North	C	C	C	C	C	C	C	Lab
South	C	C	C	C	C(EC)	C	C	C
POPLAR								
Bow and Bromley	C	Lab	Lab	Lab	Lab	Lab	Lab	Lab
South Poplar	L	Lab	Lab	Lab	Lab	Lab	Lab	Lab
ST. MARYLEBONE	C	C	C	C	C	C	C	C
ST. PANCRAS								
North	C	C	Lab	C	Lab	C	C	Lab
South-East	C	C	Lab	C	Lab	C	C	Lab
South-West	C	C	C	C	Lab	C	C	Lab
SHOREDITCH	L	L	Lab	Lab	Lab	NL	Lab	Lab
SOUTHWARK								
Central	L	L	L	Lab	Lab	Nat	Lab	Lab
North	L	L	Lab	Lab(L)	Lab	NL	NL(Lab)	Lab
South-East	L(Lab)	L	Lab	Lab	Lab	C	Lab	Lab
STEPNEY								
Limehouse	L	Lab	Lab	Lab	Lab	Lab	Lab	Lab
Mile End	C	C	Lab	Lab	Lab	C	Lab	Com
Whitechapel and St. George's	L	Lab	Lab	Lab	Lab	L	Lab	Lab
STOKE NEWINGTON	C	C	L	C	C	C	C	Lab
WANDSWORTH								
Balham and Tooting	C	C	C	C	C	C	C	Lab
Central	C	C	C	C	Lab	C	C(Lab)	Lab
Clapham	C	C	C	C	C	C	C	Lab
Putney	C	C	C	C	C	C	C	C
Streatham	C	C	C	C	C	C	C	C
WESTMINSTER								
Abbey	C	C	C	C	C	C	C	C
St. George's	C(AWL)	Ind C	C	C	C	C	C	C
WOOLWICH								
East	Lab(C)	Lab	Lab	Lab	Lab	Lab	Lab	Lab
West	C	C	C	C	C	C	C	Lab

ENGLAND—BOROUGHS

CONSTITUENCY	1918	1922	1923	1924	1929	1931	1935	1945
ACCRINGTON	C	Lab	L	Const	Lab	C	C	Lab
ALTRINCHAM AND SALE	—	—	—	—	—	—	—	C
ASHTON-UNDER-LYNE	C	C	C	C(Lab)	Lab(C)	C	Lab	Lab
BARKING	—	—	—	—	—	—	—	Lab
BARNSLEY	L	Lab	Lab	Lab	Lab	NL	Lab	Lab
BARROW-IN-FURNESS	C	C	C	Lab	Lab	C	C	Lab
BATH	C	C	L	C	C	C	C	C
BATLEY AND MORLEY	L	Lab	Lab	L	Lab	C	Lab	Lab
BEXLEY	—	—	—	—	—	—	—	Lab
BIRKENHEAD								
East	C	L	L	C	L	L	L	Lab
West	C	C	Lab	C	Lab	C	C	Lab
BIRMINGHAM								
Acock's Green	—	—	—	—	—	—	—	Lab
Aston	C	C	C	C	Lab	C	C	Lab
Deritend	C	C	C	C	Lab	C	C	Lab
Duddeston	NDP	C	C	C	Lab	C	C	Lab
Edgbaston	C	C	C	C	C	C	C	C
Erdington	C	C	C	C	Lab	C	C	Lab

ENGLAND—BOROUGHS (Cont.)

CONSTITUENCY	1918	1922	1923	1924	1929	1931	1935	1945
BIRMINGHAM (Cont.)								
Handsworth	C	C	C	C	C	C	C	C
King's Norton	C	C	C	Lab	C	C	C	Lab
Ladywood	C	C	C	C	Lab	C	C	Lab
Moseley	C	C	C	C	C	C	C	**C
Sparkbrook	C	C	C	C	C	C	C	Lab
West Birmingham	C	C	C	C	C	C	C	Lab
Yardley	C	C	C	C	Lab	C	C	Lab
BLACKBURN	L	C	L	L	Lab	C	C	Lab
[two seats]	C	L	C	C	Lab	C	C	Lab
BLACKPOOL	C	C	L	C	C	C	C	—
North	—	—	—	—	—	—	—	C
South	—	—	—	—	—	—	—	C
BOLTON	L	C	Lab	C	Lab	C	C	Lab
[two seats]	Lab	L	C	C	Lab	C	C	Lab
BOOTLE	C	L	L	C	Lab	C	C	Lab
BOURNEMOUTH	Nat P	C	C	C	C	C	C	C
BRADFORD								
Central	C	Lab	Lab	C	Lab	C	Lab	Lab
East	NDP	Lab	Lab	L	Lab	C	C	Lab
North	C	C	L	C	Lab	C	C	Lab
South	C	L	L	Lab	Lab	L	L	Lab
BRIGHTON	C	C	C	C	C	C	C	C
[two seats]	C	C	C	C	C	C	C	?
BRISTOL								
Central	C	C	C	C	Lab	C	C	Lab
East	L	L	Lab	Lab	Lab	Lab	Lab	Lab
North	L	L	Lab	L	Lab	L	L	Lab
South	L	L	L	L	Lab	C	Lab	Lab
West	C	C	C	C	C	C	C	C
BROMLEY	C	C	C	C	C	C	C	*C
BURNLEY	Lab	Lab	Lab	Lab	Lab	Nat	Lab	Lab
BURY	C	C	C	C	C	C	C	C
CAMBRIDGE	C	C	C	C	C	C	C	Lab
CARLISLE	L	Lab	Lab	C	Lab	C	C	Lab
CHELTENHAM	C	C	C	C	C	C	C(Ind C)	Nat Ind
COVENTRY	C	C	Lab	C	Lab	C	C	—
East	—	—	—	—	—	—	—	Lab
West	—	—	—	—	—	—	—	Lab
CROYDON								
North	C	C	C	C	C	C	C	*C
South	C	C	C	C	C	C	C	*Lab
DAGENHAM	—	—	—	—	—	—	—	Lab
DARLINGTON	C	C	C	C(Lab)	Lab	C	C	Lab
DARTFORD	—	—	—	—	—	—	—	Lab
DERBY	Lab	Lab	Lab	Lab	Lab	N Lab	C	Lab
[two seats]	C	L	Lab	C	Lab	C	N Lab/ (Lab)	Lab
DEWSBURY	C	Lab	L	Lab	Lab	L	Lab	Lab
DUDLEY	C(Lab)	C	C	C	Lab	C	C	Lab
EALING	C	C	C	C	C	C	C	—
East	—	—	—	—	—	—	—	C
West	—	—	—	—	—	—	—	Lab
EAST HAM								
North	L	C	Lab	C(Lab)	Lab	C	C	Lab
South	NDP	Lab	Lab	Lab	Lab	C	Lab	Lab
ECCLES	C	Lab	Lab	C	Lab	C	C	Lab
EDMONTON	C	Lab	Lab	Lab	Lab	C	Lab	Lab
EXETER	C	C	C	C	Ind	C	C	C
GATESHEAD	C	Lab	L	Lab	Lab	NL	NL	Lab
GLOUCESTER	C	C	C	C	C	C	C	Lab
GREAT YARMOUTH	C	L	L	C	L	NL	NL	Lab
GRIMSBY	C	C	C	C	C	C	C	Lab
HALIFAX	L	L	L	L(Lab)	Lab	C	C	Lab
HARROW								
East	—	—	—	—	—	—	—	Lab
West	—	—	—	—	—	—	—	C

ENGLAND—BOROUGHS (Cont.)

CONSTITUENCY	1918	1922	1923	1924	1929	1931	1935	1945
HARTLEPOOLS, THE	C	L	L	C	C	C	C	Lab
HASTINGS	C	C	C	C	C	C	C	C
HENDON								
North	—	—	—	—	—	—	—	Lab
South	—	—	—	—	—	—	—	C
HESTON AND ISLEWORTH	—	—	—	—	—	—	—	Lab
HORNSEY	C	C	C	C	C	C	C	C
HUDDERSFIELD	L	L	Lab	Lab	Lab	NL	NL	Lab
HYTHE	C	C	C	C	C	C	C	C
ILFORD	C	C	C	C	C	C	C	—
North	—	—	—	—	—	—	—	Lab
South	—	—	—	—	—	—	—	Lab
IPSWICH	C	C	Lab	C	C	C	C(Lab)	Lab
KINGSTON UPON HULL								
Central	C(L)	L	L	L(Lab)	Lab	C	Lab	Lab
East	C	C	C	C	Lab	C	Lab	Lab
North-West	C	C	C	C	C	C	C	Lab
South-West	L	L	L	C	Lab	C	C	Lab
KINGSTON UPON THAMES	C	C	C	C	C	C	C	*C
LEEDS								
Central	L	C	C	C	Lab	N Lab	N Lab	Lab
North	L	C	C	C	C	C	C	C
North-East	C	C	C	C	C	C	C	Lab
South	L	Lab	Lab	Lab	Lab	C	Lab	Lab
South-East	Lab	Lab	Lab	Lab	Lab	Lab	Lab	Lab
West	L	L	Lab	Lab	Lab	C	C	Lab
LEICESTER								
East	L(Lab)	L	Lab	C	Lab	C	C	Lab
South	C	C	L	C	C	C	C	Lab
West	NDP	Lab	Lab	Lab	Lab	L	N Lab	Lab
LEIGH	L	Lab	Lab	Lab	Lab	Lab	Lab	Lab
LEYTON								
East	L	C	Lab	C	Lab	C	C	Lab
West	C(L)	C	C	C	Lab	C	Lab	Lab
LINCOLN	C	C	C	Lab	Lab	C	C	Lab
LIVERPOOL								
East Toxteth	C	C	C	C	C	C	C	C
Edge Hill	C	C(Lab)	Lab	Lab	Lab	C	C	Lab
Everton	C	C	C	C	Lab	C	Lab	Lab
Exchange	C	C	C	C	C	C	C	Lab
Fairfield	C	C	C	C	C	C	C	Lab
Kirkdale	C	C	C	C	Lab	C	C	Lab
Scotland	N	N	N	N	N(Lab)	Lab	Lab	Lab
Walton	C	C	C	C	C	C	C	Lab
Wavertree	C	C	L	C	C	C(Lab)	C	C
West Derby	C	C	L	C	C	C	C	C
West Toxteth	C	C	C(Lab)	Lab	Lab	C(Lab)	Lab	Lab
MANCHESTER								
Ardwick	C	Lab	Lab	Lab	Lab	C	Lab	Lab
Blackley	C	C	L	C	L	C	C	Lab
Clayton	C(Lab)	C	Lab	Lab	Lab	C	Lab	Lab
Exchange	C	C	L	C	C	C	C	Lab
Gorton	Lab	Lab	Lab	Lab	Lab	C	Lab	Lab
Hulme	C	C	C	C	Lab	C	C	Lab
Moss Side	C	C	L	C	C	C	C	Lab
Platting	Lab	Lab	Lab	Lab	Lab	C	Lab	Lab
Rusholme	C	C	L	C	C	C	C	Lab
Withington	C	C	L	C	L	C	C	C
MIDDLESBROUGH								
East	L	C	L	Lab	Lab	L	Lab	Lab
West	L	L	L	L	L	L	L	Lab
MITCHAM	—	—	—	—	—	—	—	Lab
MORPETH	Lab	Lab	Lab	Lab	Lab	C	Lab	Lab
NELSON AND COLNE	Lab	Lab	Lab	Lab	Lab	C	Lab	Lab
NEWCASTLE-UNDER-LYME	Ind L	Lab	Lab	Lab	Lab	Ind Lab	Lab	Lab

ENGLAND—BOROUGHS (Cont.)

CONSTITUENCY	1918	1922	1923	1924	1929	1931	1935	1945
NEWCASTLE UPON TYNE								
Central	C	Lab	Lab	Lab	Lab	C	C	Lab
East	L	Lab	L	Lab	L	NL	NL	Lab
North	C	C	C	C	C	C	C(Ind C)	C
West	L	Lab	L	Lab	Lab	C	C	Lab
NORTHAMPTON	L	L	Lab	C(Lab)	Lab	C	C	Lab
NORWICH	Co Lab	Ind	Lab	L	L	NL	NL	Lab
[two seats]	L	L	Lab	C	Lab	C	C	Lab
NOTTINGHAM								
Central	C	L	L	C	C	C	C	Lab
East	C	C	L	C	L	C	C	Lab
South	C	C	C	C	Lab	N Lab	N Lab	Lab
West	Lab	Lab	Lab	Lab	Lab	C	Lab	Lab
OLDHAM	C	L	Lab	C	Lab	C	C	Lab
[two seats]	L	Lab	L	L	Lab	C	NL	Lab
OXFORD	C	L	L (C)	C	C	C	C	C
PLYMOUTH								
Devonport	C	C	L	L	L	NL	NL	Lab
Drake	C	C	C	C	Lab	C	C	Lab
Sutton	C	C	C	C	C	C	C	Lab
PORTSMOUTH								
Central	L	C	L	C	Lab	C	C	Lab
North	C	C	C	C	C	C	C	Lab
South	C	C	C	C	C	C	C	C
PRESTON	Lab	Lab	Lab	Lab	Lab	C	C	Lab
[two seats]	C	L	L	C	L(Lab)	C	C	Lab
READING	C	C	Lab	C	Lab	C	C	Lab
RICHMOND (Surrey)	C	Ind C	C	C	C	C	C	C
ROCHDALE	C	Lab	L	Lab	Lab	C	Lab	Lab
ROCHESTER								
Chatham	C	C	C	C	Lab	C	C	Lab
Gillingham	C	C	C	C	C	C	C	Lab
ROMFORD	—	—	—	—	—	—	—	Lab
ROSSENDALE	C	C	C	C	Lab	C	C	Lab
ROTHERHAM	C	C	Lab	Lab	Lab	C(Lab)	Lab	Lab
ST. HELENS	Lab	Lab	Lab	Lab	Lab	C	Lab	Lab
SALFORD								
North	Lab	Lab	Lab	C	Lab	C	C	Lab
South	C	C	Lab	C	Lab	C	C	Lab
West	C	C	Lab	C	Lab	C	C	Lab
SHEFFIELD								
Attercliffe	L	Lab	Lab	Lab	Lab	C	Lab	Lab
Brightside	L	Lab	Lab	Lab	Lab	C	Lab	Lab
Central	C	C	C	C	Lab	C	C	Lab
Ecclesall	C	C	C	C	C	C	C	C
Hallam	C	C	C	C	C	C	C	C
Hillsborough	L	Lab	Lab	Lab	Lab	C	Lab	Lab
Park	L	L	C	C	Lab	C	Lab	Lab
SMETHWICK	Lab	Lab	Lab	Lab	Lab	C	C	Lab
SOUTHALL	—	—	—	—	—	—	—	Lab
SOUTHAMPTON	L	C	C	C	Lab	C	C	Lab
[two seats]	L	C	C	C	Lab	NL	NL	Lab
SOUTHEND-ON-SEA	C	C	C	C	C	C	C	C
SOUTHPORT	C	C	L	C	C	C	C	C
SOUTH SHIELDS	L	L	L	L	Lab	L	Lab	Lab
STOCKPORT	L	L	C	C(Lab)	Lab	C	C	C
[two seats]	Co Lab (C)	C	L	C	C	C	C	C
STOCKTON-ON-TEES	L	L	L	C	Lab	C	C	Lab
STOKE-ON-TRENT								
Burslem	Lab	Lab	L	Lab	Lab	Nat	Lab	Lab
Hanley	NDP	Lab	Lab	Lab	Lab	C	Lab	Lab
Stoke	L	L	L	Const	Lab	C	Lab	Lab
SUNDERLAND	L	C	C	C	Lab	C	NL	Lab
[two seats]	C	C	C	C	Lab (C)	C	C	Lab
SUTTON AND CHEAM	—	—	—	—	—	—	—	C

ENGLAND—BOROUGHS (Cont.)

CONSTITUENCY	1918	1922	1923	1924	1929	1931	1935	1945
TOTTENHAM								
North	C	Lab	Lab	Lab	Lab	C	Lab	Lab
South	C	C	Lab	C	Lab	N Lab	Lab	Lab
TWICKENHAM	—	—	—	—	—	—	—	C
TYNEMOUTH	C	C	C	C	C	C	C	Lab
WAKEFIELD	C	C	Lab	C	Lab	C(Lab)	Lab	Lab
WALLASEY	C	C	C	C	C	C	C(Ind)	C
WALLSEND	NDP	Lab	Lab	Lab	Lab	C	C	Lab
WALSALL	Nat P	L	L	C	Lab	Nat	NL	Lab
WALTHAMSTOW								
East	C	C	C	Const	Lab	C	C	Lab
West	NDP	Lab	Lab	L	Lab	Lab	Lab	Lab
WARRINGTON	C	C	Lab	C	Lab	C	C	Lab
WEDNESBURY	Lab	Lab	Lab	Lab	Lab	C(Lab)	Lab	Lab
WEMBLEY								
North	—	—	—	—	—	—	—	Lab
South	—	—	—	- -	—	—	—	Lab
WEST BROMWICH	Lab	Lab	Lab	Lab	Lab	C	Lab	Lab
WEST HAM								
Plaistow	Lab	Lab	Lab	Lab	Lab	Lab	Lab	Lab
Silvertown	NSP	Lab	Lab	Lab	Lab	Lab	Lab	Lab
Stratford	C	Lab	Lab	Lab	Lab	Lab	Lab	Lab
Upton	C	C	Lab	C	Lab	C(Lab)	Lab	Lab
WIGAN	Lab	Lab	Lab	Lab	Lab	Lab	Lab	Lab
WILLESDEN								
East	C	C(L)	L	C	C	C	C	*Lab
West	C	C	Lab	Lab	Lab	C	Lab	*Lab
WIMBLEDON	C	C	C	C	C	C	C	*Lab
WOLVERHAMPTON								
Bilston	C	C	C	Lab	Lab	C	C	Lab
East	L	L	L	L	L	L	L	Lab
West	C	C	C	C	Lab	C	C	Lab
WOODFORD	—	—	—	—	—	—	—	C
WORCESTER	C	L	C	C	C	C	C	C
YORK	C	C	C	C	Lab	C	C	Lab

ENGLAND—COUNTIES

CONSTITUENCY	1918	1922	1923	1924	1929	1931	1935	1945
BEDFORDSHIRE								
Bedford	L	C	C	C	C	C	C	Lab
Luton	L	C	L	C	L	NL	NL	Lab
Mid	C	L	L	C	L	C	C	C
BERKSHIRE								
Abingdon	C	C	L	C	C	C	C	C
Newbury	C	C	L	C	C	C	C	C
Windsor	C	C	C	C	C	C	C	C
BUCKINGHAMSHIRE								
Aylesbury	C	C	L	C	C	C	C	*C
Buckingham	C	C	C	C	C	C	C	Lab
Eton and Slough	—	—	—	—	—	—	—	Lab
Wycombe	C	C	L	C	C	C	C	**Lab
CAMBRIDGESHIRE	L	C	C	C	C	C	C	Lab
CHESHIRE								
Altrincham	C	C	L	C	C	C	C	—
Bucklow	—	—	—	—	—	—	—	C
City of Chester	C	C	C	C	C	C	C	C
Crewe	L	Lab	Lab	C	Lab	C	C	Lab
Eddisbury	C	C	C	C(L)	L	NL	NL(CW)	NL
Knutsford	C	C	C	C	C	C	C	*C

ENGLAND—COUNTIES (Cont.)

CONSTITUENCY	1918	1922	1923	1924	1929	1931	1935	1945
CHESHIRE (Cont.)								
Macclesfield	C	C	C	C	C	C	C	C
Northwich	C	C	C	C	C	C	C	C
Stalybridge and Hyde	C	C	L	C	Lab	C	C	Lab
Wirral	C	C	L	C	C	C	C	C
CORNWALL								
Bodmin	C(L)	L	L	C	L	L	C	C
Camborne	L	L	L	Const	L	C	C	C
Northern	L	L	L	C	L	L	L	L
Penryn and Falmouth	C	C	L	C	L	C	C	Lab
St. Ives	L	C	L	C(L)	L	NL	NL	NL
CUMBERLAND								
Northern	C	C	C	C	C	C	L	L
Penrith and Cockermouth	C	L	C	C	C	C	C	C
Whitehaven	C	Lab	Lab	C	Lab	C	Lab	Lab
Workington	Lab	Lab	Lab	Lab	Lab	Lab	Lab	Lab
DERBYSHIRE								
Belper	L	L	C	C	Lab	C	C	Lab
Chesterfield	L	L	L	L	Lab	C	Lab	Lab
Clay Cross	L	Lab	Lab	Lab	Lab	Lab	Lab	Lab
High Peak	C	C	C	C	C	C	C	C
Ilkeston	L	Lab	Lab	Lab	Lab	N Lab	Lab	Lab
North-Eastern	L	Lab	Lab	Lab	Lab	C	Lab	Lab
Southern	L	C	C	C	Lab	C	C	Lab
Western	L	L	C	C	C	C	C(Ind Lab)	Lab
DEVON								
Barnstaple	L	C	L	C	C	C	L	C
Honiton	C	C	C	C	C	C	C	C
South Molton	L	L	L	C	L	NL	NL	NL
Tavistock	C	L	L	C	C	C	C	C
Tiverton	C	C(L)	L	C	C	C	C	C
Torquay	C	C	L	C	C	C	C	C
Totnes	C	C	L	C	C	C	C	C
DORSET								
Eastern	L	Ind C	C	C	L	C	C	C
Northern	C	L	L	C	C	C	C	L
Southern	C	C	C	C	C	C	C	C
Western	C	C	C	C	C	C	C	C
DURHAM								
Barnard Castle	Lab	C	Lab	C	Lab	C	Lab	Lab
Bishop Auckland	Lab	Lab	Lab	Lab	Lab	NL	Lab	Lab
Blaydon	L	Lab	Lab	Lab	Lab	C	Lab	Lab
Chester-le-Street	Lab	Lab	Lab	Lab	Lab	Lab	Lab	Lab
Consett	L	Lab	Lab	Lab	Lab	NL	Lab	Lab
Durham	C	Lab	Lab	Lab	Lab	L	Lab	Lab
Houghton-le-Spring	Lab	Lab	Lab	Lab	Lab	C	Lab	Lab
Jarrow	L	Lab	Lab	Lab	Lab	C	Lab	Lab
Seaham	L	Lab	Lab	Lab	Lab	N Lab	Lab	Lab
Sedgefield	C	Lab	C	C	Lab	C	Lab	Lab
Spennymoor	L	Lab	Lab	Lab	Lab	Lab	Lab	Lab
ESSEX								
Chelmsford	C	C	L	C	C	C	C(CW)	*CW
Colchester	C	C	C	C	C	C	C	Lab
Epping	C	C	C	Cons	C	C	C	**Lab
Harwich	C	L	L	C	L	NL	NL	NL
Hornchurch	—	—	—	—	—	—	—	Lab
Maldon	C	C	Lab	C	C	C	C(Ind Lab)	*Lab
Romford	L	L	C	C	Lab	C	Lab	—
Saffron Walden	L	C	C	C	C	C	C	C
South-Eastern	C	C	Lab	C	Lab	C	C	**Lab
Thurrock	—	—	—	—	—	—	—	Lab
GLOUCESTERSHIRE								
Cirencester and Tewkesbury	C	C	C	C	C	C	C	C
Forest of Dean	Lab	Lab	Lab	Lab	Lab	N Lab	Lab	Lab
Stroud	L	C	L	C	C	C	C	Lab
Thornbury	L	C	L	C	C	C	C	Lab

ENGLAND—COUNTIES (Cont.)

CONSTITUENCY	1918	1922	1923	1924	1929	1931	1935	1945
HAMPSHIRE								
Aldershot	C	C	C	C	C	C	C	C
Basingstoke	C	C	L	C	C	C	C	C
Fareham	C	C	C	C	C	C	C	C
New Forest and								
Christchurch	C	C	C	C	C	C	C	C
Petersfield	C	C	C	C	C	C	C	C
Winchester	C	C	C	C	C	C	C	Lab
HEREFORDSHIRE								
Hereford	C	C	C	C	L	C	C	C
Leominster	C	C	C	C	C	C	C	C
HERTFORDSHIRE								
Barnet	—	—	—	—	—	—	—	Lab
Hemel Hempstead	C	C	L	C	C	C	C	*C
Hertford	Ind(AWL &Ind)	C	C	C	C	C	C	*C
Hitchin	C	C	C	C	C	C	C	*Lab
St. Albans	C	C	C	C	C	C	C	**Lab
Watford	C	C	C	C	C	C	C	*Lab
HUNTINGDONSHIRE	C	C	L	C	L	NL	NL	NL
ISLE OF ELY	L	C	L	C	L	L	L	C
ISLE OF WIGHT	C	L	L	C	C	C	C	C
KENT								
Ashford	C	C	C	C	L	C	C	C
Canterbury	C	C	C	C	C	C	C	C
Chislehurst	C	C	C	C	C	C	C	**Lab
Dartford	L(Lab)	Const	Lab	C	Lab	C	C(Lab)	—
Dover	C(Ind)	C	C	C	C	C	C	Lab
Faversham	C	C	C	C	C	C	C	Lab
Gravesend	C	C	Lab	C	C	C	C	Lab
Isle of Thanet	C	C	C	C	C	C	C	C
Maidstone	C	C	C	C	C	C	C	C
Orpington	—	—	—	—	—	—	—	C
Sevenoaks	C	C	L	C	C	C	C	*C
Tonbridge	C	C	C	C	C	C	C	C
LANCASHIRE								
Chorley	C	C	C	C	C	C	C	Lab
Clitheroe	Lab	C	C	C	C	C	C	Lab
Darwen	C	C	L	C	L	L	C	C
Farnworth	C	Lab	Lab	Lab	Lab	C	Lab	Lab
Fylde	C	C	C	C	C	C	C	*C
Heywood and Radcliffe	L(Lab)	L	L	Const	L	C	C	Lab
Ince	Lab	Lab	Lab	Lab	Lab	Lab	Lab	Lab
Lancaster	C	C	L	C(L)	C	C	C	C
Lonsdale	C	C	L	C	C	C	C	C
Middleton and Prestwich	L	L	C	C	C	C	C	C
Mossley	L	Ind	Ind	Ind	Lab	Nat Ind	Nat Ind	Lab
Newton	Lab	Lab	Lab	Lab	Lab	C	Lab	*Lab
Ormskirk	Lab	C	C	C	Lab	N Lab	N Lab	Lab
Royton	C	C	L	C	C	C	C	C
Stretford	L	L	L	Const	Ind	C	C	*Lab
Waterloo	C	C	C	C	C	C	C	C
Westhoughton	Lab	Lab	Lab	Lab	Lab	Lab	Lab	Lab
Widnes	C(Lab)	C	C	C	Lab	C	C	Lab
LEICESTERSHIRE								
Bosworth	L	C	L	C(L)	L	NL	NL	*Lab
Harborough	C	C	L	C	C	C	C	Lab
Loughborough	L	L	L	C	Lab	C	C	Lab
Melton	C	C	C	C	C	C	C	C
LINCOLNSHIRE—PARTS OF HOLLAND								
Holland with Boston	Lab	Lab	Lab(C)	C(L)	L	NL	NL	NL
LINCOLNSHIRE—PARTS OF KESTEVEN, AND RUTLANDSHIRE								
Grantham	C	L	C	C	C	C	C(Ind)	Ind
Rutland and Stamford	C	C	C	C	C	C	C	C

ENGLAND—COUNTIES (Cont.)

CONSTITUENCY	1918	1922	1923	1924	1929	1931	1935	1945
LINCOLNSHIRE—PARTS OF LINDSEY								
Brigg	C	C	C	C	Lab	C	Lab	Lab
Gainsborough	C	C	L	C	C	C	C	C
Horncastle	C	L	L	C	C	C	C	C
Louth	C(L)	L	L	C	C	C	C	C
MIDDLESEX								
Acton	C	C	C	C	Lab	C	C	*Lab
Brentford and Chiswick	C	C	C	C	C	C	C	*Lab
Enfield	C	C	Lab	C	Lab	C	C	*Lab
Finchley	C	C	L	C	C	C	C	*C
Harrow	C	Ind	Ind	C	C	C	C	—
Hendon	C	C	C	C	C	C	C	—
Spelthorne	C	C	C	C	C	C	C	*Lab
Twickenham	C	C	C	C	C	C	C	—
Uxbridge	C	C	C	C	C	C	C	**Lab
Wood Green	C	C	C	C	C	C	C	C
NORFOLK								
Eastern	C	C	L	C	L	NL	NL	NL
King's Lynn	C	C	L	C	C	C	C	Lab
Northern	Ind	Lab	Lab	Lab	Lab	C	C	Lab
Southern	L(Lab)	C	Lab	C	C	C	C	Lab
South-Western	L	L	C	C	Lab	C	C	Lab
NORTHAMPTONSHIRE								
Daventry	C	C	C	C	C	C	C	C
Kettering	Co-op	C	Lab	C	Lab	C	C	Lab
Peterborough	C	C	C	C	Lab	C	C	Lab
Wellingborough	Lab	L	Lab	Lab	Lab	C	C	Lab
NORTHUMBERLAND								
Berwick-upon-Tweed	L	L (C)	C	C	C	C	L	C
Hexham	C	C	L	C	C	C	C	C
Wansbeck	L	Lab	Lab	Lab	Lab	C	C	Lab
NOTTINGHAMSHIRE								
Bassetlaw	C	C	C	C	Lab	N Lab	Lab	Lab
Broxtowe	Lab	Lab	Lab	Lab	Lab	Lab	Lab	Lab
Mansfield	Lab	L	Lab	Lab	Lab	Lab	Lab	Lab
Newark	C	C	C	C	C	C	C	C
Rushcliffe	C	C	C	C	C	C	C	Lab
OXFORDSHIRE								
Banbury	L	C	C	C	C	C	C	C
Henley	C	C	C	C	C	C	C	C
SHROPSHIRE								
Ludlow	C	C	C	C	C	C	C	C
Oswestry	C	C	C	C	C	C	C	C
Shrewsbury	C	C	L	C	C	C	C	C
The Wrekin	L(Ind)	C	Lab	C	Lab	C	C	Lab
SOMERSET								
Bridgwater	C	C	L	C	C	C	C(Ind Prog)	Ind Prog
Frome	C	C	Lab	C	Lab	C	C	Lab
Taunton	C	L	L	C	C	C	C	Lab
Wells	C	C	L	C	C	C	C	C
Weston-super-Mare	C	C	L	C	C	C	C	C
Yeovil	C	C	C	C	C	C	C	C
STAFFORDSHIRE								
Burton	C	C	C	C	C	C	C	Lab
Cannock	Co Lab	Lab	Lab	Lab	Lab	C	Lab	Lab
Kingswinford	Lab	Lab	Lab	Lab	Lab	C	Lab	Lab
Leek	Lab	Lab	Lab	Lab	Lab	C	Lab	Lab
Lichfield	L	L	Lab	C	Lab	N Lab	N Lab/ (Lab)	*Lab
Stafford	C	C	C	C	C	C	C	Lab
Stone	C	C	C	C	C	C	C	C
SUFFOLK (EAST)								
Eye	L	L	C	C	L	NL	NL	L
Lowestoft	L	C	C	C	C	C	C	Lab
Woodbridge	C	C	C	C	C	C	C	C

ENGLAND—COUNTIES (Cont.)

CONSTITUENCY	1918	1922	1923	1924	1929	1931	1935	1945
SUFFOLK (WEST)								
Bury St. Edmunds	C	C	C	C	C	C	C	C
Sudbury	L	C	L	C	C	C	C	Lab
SURREY								
Carshalton	—	—	—	—	—	—	—	C
Chertsey	C	C	C	C	C	C	C	C
Eastern	C	C	C	C	C	C	C	*C
Epsom	C	C	C	C	C	C	C	**C
Farnham	C	C	C	C	C	C	C	C
Guildford	C	C	C	C	C	C	C	C
Mitcham	C	C(Lab)	C	C	C	C	C	—
Reigate	C	C	C	C	C	C	C	*C
SUSSEX (EAST)								
Eastbourne	C	C	C	C	C	C	C	C
East Grinstead	C	C	C	C	C	C	C	C
Lewes	C	C	C	C	C	C	C	C
Rye	C	C	C	C	C	C	C	C
SUSSEX (WEST)								
Chichester	C	C	L	C	C	C	C	*C
Horsham	—	—	—	—	—	—	—	C
Horsham and Worthing	C	C	C	C	C	C	C	—
Worthing	—	—	—	—	—	—	—	C
WARWICKSHIRE								
Nuneaton	C	C	L	C	Lab	C	Lab	**Lab
Rugby	C	C	L	C	C	C	C(Ind)	*Ind
Solihull	—	—	—	—	—	—	—	C
Sutton Coldfield	—	—	—	—	—	—	—	C
Tamworth	C	C	C	C	C	C	C	—
Warwick and Leamington	C	C	C	C	C	C	C	*C
WESTMORLAND	C	C	C	C	C	C	C	C
WILTSHIRE								
Chippenham	C	L	L	C	C	C	C	C
Devizes	C	C	L	C	C	C	C	C
Salisbury	C	C	L	C	C	C	C	C
Swindon	C	C	C	C	Lab	C(Lab)	C	Lab
Westbury	C	L	L	C	C	C	C	C
WORCESTERSHIRE	·							
Bewdley	C	C	C	C	C	C	C	C
Evesham	C	C	C	C	C	C	C	C
Kidderminster	C	C	C	C	C	C	C	Lab
Stourbridge	L	C	C	C(Lab)	Lab	C	C	Lab
YORKSHIRE (EAST RIDING)								
Buckrose	L	C	C	C	C	C	C	L
Holderness	C	L	C	C	C	C	C	C
Howdenshire	C	C	C	C	C	C	C	C
YORKSHIRE (NORTH RIDING)								
Cleveland	C	C	L	C	Lab	C	C	Lab
Richmond	C	C	C	C	C	C	C	C
Scarborough and Whitby	C	C	C	C	C	C	C	C
Thirsk and Malton	C	C	C	C	C	C	C	C
YORKSHIRE (WEST RIDING)								
Barkston Ash	C	C	C	C	C	C	C	C
Colne Valley	L	Lab	Lab	Lab	Lab	L	Lab	Lab
Doncaster	L	Lab	Lab	Lab	Lab	C	Lab	Lab
Don Valley	NDP	Lab	Lab	Lab	Lab	Lab	Lab	Lab
Elland	C	Lab	L	Lab	Lab	C	C	Lab
Hemsworth	Lab	Lab	Lab	Lab	Lab	Lab	Lab	Lab
Keighley	C	Lab	L	Lab	Lab	C	Lab	Lab
Normanton	Lab	Lab	Lab	Lab	Lab	Lab	Lab	Lab
Penistone	L(Lab)	L	L	Lab	Lab	C	Lab	Lab
Pontefract	L	Lab	Lab	C	Lab	C	Lab	Lab
Pudsey and Otley	L	C	C	C	C	C	C	C
Ripon	C	C	C	C	C	C	C	C
Rother Valley	Lab	Lab	Lab	Lab	Lab	Lab	Lab	Lab
Rothwell	Lab	Lab	Lab	Lab	Lab	Lab	Lab	Lab

ENGLAND—COUNTIES (Cont.)

CONSTITUENCY	1918	1922	1923	1924	1929	1931	1935	1945
YORKSHIRE (WEST RIDING) (Cont.)								
Shipley	L	L	Lab	Lab	Lab (C)	C	Lab	Lab
Skipton	C	C	C	C	C	C	C(CW)	C
Sowerby	Ind	C	L	C	Lab	C	C	Lab
Spen Valley	L(Lab)	L	L	L	L	NL	NL	Lab
Wentworth	Lab	Lab	Lab	Lab	Lab	Lab	Lab	Lab

WALES AND MONMOUTHSHIRE—BOROUGHS

CONSTITUENCY	1918	1922	1923	1924	1929	1931	1935	1945
CAERNARVON BOROUGHS	L	L	L	L	L	L[1]	L	C
CARDIFF								
Central	C	C	C	C	Lab	N Lab	N Lab	Lab
East	L	C	L	C	Lab	C	C(Nat)	Lab
South	C	C	Lab	C	Lab	C	C	Lab
MERTHYR TYDFIL								
Aberdare	NDP	Lab	Lab	Lab	Lab	Lab	Lab	Lab
Merthyr	L	Lab	Lab	Lab	Lab	ILP	Lab	Lab
NEWPORT	L(C)	C	C	C	Lab	C	C	Lab
RHONDDA								
East	Lab	Lab	Lab	Lab	Lab	Lab	Lab	Lab
West	Lab	Lab	Lab	Lab	Lab	Lab	Lab	Lab
SWANSEA								
East	L	Lab	Lab	Lab	Lab	Lab	Lab	Lab
West	L	L	Lab	L	Lab	NL	NL	Lab

[1] Anti-National Government.

WALES AND MONMOUTHSHIRE—COUNTIES

CONSTITUENCY	1918	1922	1923	1924	1929	1931	1935	1945
ANGLESEY	Ind Lab	Ind Lab/ (L)	L	L	L	L[1]	L	L
BRECONSHIRE AND RADNORSHIRE	L	L	L	C	Lab	C	Nat(Lab)	Lab
CAERNARVONSHIRE	L	Lab	L	L	L	L[1]	L	Lab
CARDIGANSHIRE	L	L	Ind L	L	L	L	L	L
CARMARTHENSHIRE								
Carmarthen	L	L	L	L	Lab	L	Lab	L
Llanelly	L	Lab	Lab	Lab	Lab	Lab	Lab	Lab
DENBIGHSHIRE								
Denbigh	L	L	L	L	L	NL	NL	NL
Wrexham	L	Lab	Lab	L	Lab	L	Lab	Lab
FLINTSHIRE	L	L	L	C	L	NL	C	C
GLAMORGANSHIRE								
Aberavon	L	Lab	Lab	Lab	Lab	Lab	Lab	Lab
Caerphilly	Lab	Lab	Lab	Lab	Lab	Lab	Lab	Lab
Gower	Lab	Lab	Lab	Lab	Lab	Lab	Lab	Lab

WALES AND MONMOUTHSHIRE—COUNTIES (Cont.)

CONSTITUENCY	1918	1922	1923	1924	1929	1931	1935	1945
GLAMORGANSHIRE (Cont.)								
Llandaff and Barry	C	C	C	C	Lab	C	C	Lab
Neath	L	Lab	Lab	Lab	Lab	Lab	Lab	Lab
Ogmore	Lab	Lab	Lab	Lab	Lab	Lab	Lab	Lab
Pontypridd	L(Lab)	Lab	Lab	Lab	Lab	Lab	Lab	Lab
MERIONETHSHIRE	L	L	L	L	L	L	L	L
MONMOUTHSHIRE								
Abertillery	Lab	Lab	Lab	Lab	Lab	Lab	Lab	Lab
Bedwellty	Lab	Lab	Lab	Lab	Lab	Lab	Lab	Lab
Ebbw Vale	Lab	Lab	Lab	Lab	Lab	Lab	Lab	Lab
Monmouth	C	C	C	C	C	C	C	C
Pontypool	Lab	Lab	Lab	Lab	Lab	Lab	Lab	Lab
MONTGOMERYSHIRE	L	L	L	L	L	NL	NL	L
PEMBROKESHIRE	L	L	L	C	L	L[1]	L	L

[1] Anti-National Government.

SCOTLAND—BURGHS

CONSTITUENCY	1918	1922	1923	1924	1929	1931	1935	1945
ABERDEEN								
North	Ind Lab	Lab	Lab	Lab	Lab	C	Lab	Lab
South	C	C	C	C	C	C	C	C
AYR BURGHS	C	C	C	C	C	C	C	C
DUMBARTON BURGHS	L	Lab	Lab	Lab	Lab	Ind Lab	Lab	Lab
DUNDEE	L	SPP	SPP	Lab	SPP	L	C	Lab
[two seats]	Lab	Lab	Lab	SPP	Lab	C	L	Lab
DUNFERMLINE BURGHS	L	Lab	Lab	Lab	Lab	NL	Lab	Lab
EDINBURGH								
Central	Lab	Lab	Lab	Lab	Lab	C	C	Lab
East	L	L	L	Lab	Lab	L	Lab	Lab
North	C	C	L	C	C	C	C	Lab
South	C	C	C	C	C	C	C	C
West	C	L	L	C	Lab	C	C	C
GLASGOW								
Bridgeton	L	Lab	Lab	Lab	Lab	ILP	ILP	ILP
Camlachie	C	Lab	Lab	Lab	Lab	C	ILP	ILP(C)
Cathcart	L	Lab	C	C	C	C	C	C
Central	C	C	C	C	C	C	C	C
Gorbals	Co Lab	Lab	Lab	Lab	Lab	Ind Lab	ILP	Lab
Govan	Lab	Lab	Lab	Lab	Ind Lab	Lab	Lab	Lab
Hillhead	C	C	C	C	C	C	C	C
Kelvingrove	C	C	C	C	C	C	C	Lab
Maryhill	C	Lab	Lab	C	Lab	C	Lab	Lab
Partick	L	L	Lab	C	Lab	C	C	C
Pollok	C	C	C	C	C	C	C	C
St. Rollox	C	Lab	Lab	Lab	Lab	Lab	Lab	Lab
Shettleston	C	Lab	Lab	Lab	Lab	ILP	ILP	ILP
Springburn	C	Lab	Lab	Lab	Lab	C	Lab	Lab
Tradeston	C	Lab	Lab	Lab	Lab	C	Lab	Lab
GREENOCK	L	L	L	L	L	NL	NL(Lab)	Lab
KIRKCALDY BURGHS	L(Lab)	L	Lab	Lab	Lab	C	Lab	Lab
LEITH	L	L	L	L	L	NL	NL	Lab
MONTROSE BURGHS	L	L	L	L	L	NL	NL	NL
PAISLEY	L	L	L	Lab	Lab	L	L	Lab
STIRLING AND FALKIRK BURGHS	L	Lab	L	Lab	Lab	C	Lab	Lab

SCOTLAND—COUNTIES

CONSTITUENCY	1918	1922	1923	1924	1929	1931	1935	1945
ABERDEENSHIRE AND KINCARDINESHIRE								
Central	C(L)	L	L	C	C	C	C	C
Eastern	L	L	L	C	C	C	C	C
Kincardine and Western	L	L	C	C	L	• C	C	C
ARGYLL	L	L	L	C	C	C	C	C
AYRSHIRE AND BUTE								
Bute and Northern	C	C	C	C	C	C	C	C
Kilmarnock	L	L	Lab	C	Lab	N Lab	N Lab	Lab
South Ayrshire	Lab	Lab	Lab	Lab	Lab	C	Lab	Lab
BANFFSHIRE	L	L	L	C	L	L	C	C
BERWICKSHIRE AND HADDINGTONSHIRE[1]	L	L	Lab	C	Lab	C	C	Lab
CAITHNESS AND SUTHERLAND	L	L	L	L	L	L	L	C
DUMFRIESSHIRE	C	L	L	C	L	L	NL	NL
DUNBARTONSHIRE	C	C	Lab	C	Lab	C	C(Lab)	Lab
FIFE								
Eastern	C	L	L	C	L	NL	NL	NL
Western	Lab	Lab	Lab	Lab	Lab	C	Com	Com
FORFARSHIRE[2]	C	L	L	C	C	C	C	C
GALLOWAY	L	L	L	C	L	C	C	Ind C
INVERNESS—SHIRE AND ROSS AND CROMARTY								
Inverness	L	L	L	L	L	NL	NL	Ind L
Ross and Cromarty	L	L	L	L	L	NL	NL(N Lab)	Ind L
Western Isles	L	L	L	L	L	NL	Lab	Lab
LANARKSHIRE								
Bothwell	C(Lab)	Lab	Lab	Lab	Lab	C	Lab	Lab
Coatbridge	C	Lab	Lab	Lab	Lab	C	Lab	Lab
Hamilton	Lab	Lab	Lab	Lab	Lab	Lab	Lab	Lab
Lanark	C	C	Lab	C	Lab	C	C	Lab
Motherwell	C	Com	C	Lab	Lab	C	Lab(SNP)	Lab
Northern	C	Lab	Lab	C(Lab)	Lab	C	C	Lab
Rutherglen	L	Lab	Lab	Lab	Lab	C	C	Lab
LINLITHGOWSHIRE[3]	C	Lab	Lab	C(Lab)	Lab	C	Lab	Lab
MIDLOTHIAN AND PEEBLESSHIRE								
Northern	C	C	Lab	C(Lab)	C	C	C	C
Peebles and Southern	L	Lab	Lab	Lab	Lab	C	C	Lab
MORAY AND NAIRNSHIRE	L	L	C	C	C	C	C	C
ORKNEY AND SHETLAND	L	L	L	L	L	L	C	C
PERTHSHIRE AND KINROSS—SHIRE								
Kinross and Western	L	L	C	C	C	C	C	C
Perth	L	C	L	C	C	C(NL)	C	C
RENFREWSHIRE								
Eastern	L	Lab	Lab	C	C	C	C	C
Western	L	Lab	Lab	C	Lab	C	C	Lab
ROXBURGHSHIRE AND SELKIRKSHIRE	L	L	C	C	C	C	C	C
STIRLINGSHIRE AND CLACKMANNANSHIRE								
Clackmannan and Eastern	C	Lab	Lab	Lab	Lab	C	Lab	Lab
Western	C	Lab	Lab	C	Lab	C	Lab	Lab

[1] Subsequently the name of the county was changed to East Lothian.

[2] Subsequently the name of the county was changed to Angus.

[3] Subsequently the name of the county was changed to West Lothian.

NORTHERN IRELAND—BOROUGHS

CONSTITUENCY	1918	1922	1923	1924	1929	1931	1935	1945
BELFAST								
East	—	C	C	C	C	C	C	C
North	—	C	C	C	C	C	C	C
South	—	C	C	C	C	C	C	C
West	—	C	C	C	C	C	C(NI Lab)	Ind Lab

NORTHERN IRELAND—COUNTIES

CONSTITUENCY	1918	1922	1923	1924	1929	1931	1935	1945
ANTRIM	—	C	C	C	C	C	C	C
[two seats]	—	C	C	C	C	C	C	C
ARMAGH	—	C	C	C	C	C	C	C
DOWN	—	C	C	C	C	C	C	Ind C(C)
[two seats]	—	C	C	C	C	C	C	C
FERMANAGH AND								
TYRONE	—	N	N	C	N	N	N	N
[two seats]	—	N	N	C	N	N	N	N
LONDONDERRY	—	C	C	C	C	C	C	C

THE UNIVERSITIES

CONSTITUENCY	1918	1922	1923	1924	1929	1931	1935	1945
CAMBRIDGE	C	C	C	C	C	C	C(Ind C)	C
[two seats]	C	Ind L	C	C	C	C	C	Ind
COMBINED ENGLISH	L	C	C	C	C	Ind	C(Ind Prog)	Ind (C)
[two seats]	C	L	L	L(C)	Ind	C	Ind	Ind
LONDON	C	C	C	Ind	Ind	Nat Ind	Nat Ind	Nat Ind
OXFORD	C	C	C	C	C	C	C(Ind)	Ind
[two seats]	C	C	C	C	C	C	Ind	Ind
WALES	L	L	CP	L	L	L	L	L
COMBINED SCOTTISH	C	C	C	C	C	C	C	Nat
[three seats]	L	L	L	L	L	L·	NL(Ind)	Ind(C)
	C	C	C	C	C	C	C(Nat)	C
QUEEN'S, BELFAST	—	C	C	C	C	C	C	C

Appendix 3 REPRESENTATION OF CONSTITUENCIES 1950–1974

The following chart gives the party representation in each constituency from the General Election of 1950 until the Dissolution of the 1970-74 Parliament.

Unionists (in Scotland until 1965), Ulster Unionists (in Northern Ireland) and joint National Liberal and Conservative members (until 1968) are listed as Conservatives. Labour and Co-operative members are listed as Labour.

The eighty constituencies unaffected by the boundary alterations which took place at the General Election of 1950 are indicated by a dagger † placed before the name of the constituency. In a further eight constituencies the changes were of a minor nature and are indicated by an asterisk * placed before the name of the constituency. Although their boundaries were unaltered, the borough constituencies of Acton, and Brentford and Chiswick were previously divisions of the county of Middlesex, Hornchurch of the county of Essex; Mitcham of the county of Surrey and Sutton Coldfield of the county of Warwickshire.

Boundary alterations which took place in a large number of constituencies at the General Election of 1955 and in a few constituencies at the General Elections of 1951, 1959 and 1964 are indicated by one asterisk * (minor boundary alteration) or two asterisks ** (major boundary alteration) placed before the party abbreviation.

Changes which occurred at by-elections are shown in brackets, *e.g.* Lab (C) indicates the seat was won by Labour at the General Election but subsequently lost to a Conservative.

LONDON—BOROUGHS

CONSTITUENCY	1950	1951	1955	1959	1964	1966	1970
BARONS COURT	—	—	Lab	C	Lab	Lab	Lab
BATTERSEA							
North	Lab	Lab	Lab	Lab	Lab	Lab	Lab
South	Lab	C	C	C	Lab	Lab	Lab
BERMONDSEY	Lab	Lab	Lab	Lab	Lab	Lab	Lab
BETHNAL GREEN	Lab	Lab	**Lab	Lab	Lab	Lab	Lab
CAMBERWELL							
Dulwich	Lab	C	C	C	Lab	Lab	Lab
Peckham	Lab	Lab	Lab	Lab	Lab	Lab	Lab
CHELSEA	C	C	C	C	C	C	C
CITIES OF LONDON AND							
WESTMINSTER	C	C	C	C	C	C	C
†DEPTFORD	Lab	Lab	Lab	Lab	Lab	Lab	Lab
FULHAM	—	—	Lab	Lab	Lab	Lab	Lab
†East	Lab	Lab	—	—	—	—	—
†West	Lab	Lab	—	—	—	—	—
†GREENWICH	Lab	Lab	Lab	Lab	Lab	Lab	Lab
HACKNEY							
Central	—	—	Lab	Lab	Lab	Lab	Lab
South	Lab	Lab	—	—	—	—	—
HAMMERSMITH							
North	Lab	Lab	**Lab	Lab	Lab	Lab	Lab
South	Lab	Lab	—	—	—	—	—
†HAMPSTEAD	C	C	C	C	C	Lab	C
HOLBORN AND ST. PANCRAS							
SOUTH	Lab	Lab	Lab	C	Lab	Lab	Lab
ISLINGTON							
†East	Lab	Lab	Lab	Lab	Lab	Lab	Lab
†North	Lab	Lab	Lab	Lab	Lab	Lab	Lab
South-West	Lab	Lab	Lab	Lab	Lab	Lab	Lab
KENSINGTON							
†North	Lab	Lab	Lab	Lab	Lab	Lab	Lab
South	C	C	C	C	C	C	C
LAMBETH							
Brixton	Lab	Lab	Lab	Lab	Lab	Lab	Lab
†Norwood	C	C	C	C	C	Lab	Lab
Vauxhall	Lab	Lab	Lab	Lab	Lab	Lab	Lab
LEWISHAM							
North	C	C	C(Lab)	C	C	Lab	Lab
South	Lab	Lab	Lab	Lab	Lab	Lab	Lab
West	C	C	C	C	C	Lab	C

LONDON—BOROUGHS (Cont.)

CONSTITUENCY	1950	1951	1955	1959	1964	1966	1970
PADDINGTON							
†North	Lab	Lab	Lab	Lab	Lab	Lab	Lab
†South	C	C	C	C	C	C	C
POPLAR	Lab	Lab	Lab	Lab	Lab	Lab	Lab
†ST. MARYLEBONE	C	C	C	C	C	C	C
ST. PANCRAS NORTH	Lab	Lab	Lab	Lab	Lab	Lab	Lab
SHOREDITCH AND FINSBURY	Lab	Lab	Lab	Lab	Lab	Lab	Lab
SOUTHWARK	Lab	Lab	Lab	Lab	Lab	Lab	Lab
STEPNEY	Lab	Lab	Lab	Lab	Lab	Lab	Lab
STOKE NEWINGTON AND HACKNEY NORTH	Lab	Lab	**Lab	Lab	Lab	Lab	Lab
WANDSWORTH							
Central	Lab	Lab	C	C	Lab	Lab	Lab
Clapham	Lab	Lab	Lab	C	Lab	Lab	C
Putney	C	C	C	C	*Lab	Lab	Lab
†Streatham	C	C	C	C	C	C	C
WOOLWICH							
East	Lab	Lab	*Lab	Lab	Lab	Lab	Lab
West	C	C	*C	C	Lab	Lab	Lab

ENGLAND—BOROUGHS

CONSTITUENCY	1950	1951	1955	1959	1964	1966	1970
ACCRINGTON	Lab	Lab	Lab	Lab	Lab	Lab	Lab
†ACTON	Lab	Lab	Lab	C	Lab	Lab(C)	Lab
†ALTRINCHAM AND SALE	C	C	C	C	C	C	C
ASHTON-UNDER-LYNE	Lab	*Lab	**Lab	Lab	Lab	Lab	Lab
†BARKING	Lab	Lab	Lab	Lab	Lab	Lab	Lab
BARNSLEY	Lab	Lab	Lab	Lab	*Lab	Lab	Lab
BARROW-IN-FURNESS	Lab	Lab	Lab	Lab	Lab	Lab	Lab
†BATH	C	*C	C	C	C	C	C
BATLEY AND MORLEY	Lab	Lab	Lab	Lab	Lab	Lab	Lab
BEBINGTON	C	C	C	C	C	Lab	C
BECKENHAM	C	C	C	C	C	C	C
BEXLEY	C	C	C	C	C	C	C
BILSTON	Lab	Lab	*Lab	Lab	Lab	Lab	Lab
BIRKENHEAD	Lab	Lab	Lab	Lab	Lab	Lab	Lab
BIRMINGHAM							
All Saints	—	—	Lab	C	Lab	Lab	Lab
Aston	Lab	Lab	**Lab	Lab	Lab	Lab	Lab
†Edgbaston	C	C	C	C	C	C	C
Erdington	Lab	Lab	—	—	—	—	—
Hall Green	C	C	**C	C	C	C	C
†Handsworth	C	C	**C	C	C	C	C
King's Norton	C	C	—	—	—	—	—
Ladywood	Lab	Lab	**Lab	Lab	Lab	Lab(L)	Lab
Northfield	Lab	Lab	**Lab	Lab	Lab	Lab	Lab
Perry Barr	Lab	Lab	Lab	Lab	C	Lab	C
Selly Oak	—	—	C	C	C	C	C
Small Heath	Lab	Lab	**Lab	Lab	Lab	Lab	Lab
Sparkbrook	Lab	Lab	**Lab	C	Lab	Lab	Lab
Stechford	Lab	Lab	**Lab	Lab	Lab	Lab	Lab
Yardley	Lab	Lab	**Lab	C	Lab	Lab	C
BLACKBURN	—	—	Lab	Lab	Lab	Lab	Lab
East	Lab	Lab	—	—	—	—	—
West	C	C	—	—	—	—	—
BLACKPOOL							
North	C	C	C	*C	*C	C	C
South	C	C	C	C	*C	C	C
BLYTH	Lab	Lab	Lab	Lab	Lab	Lab	Lab

ENGLAND—BOROUGHS (Cont.)

CONSTITUENCY	1950	1951	1955	1959	1964	1966	1970
BOLTON							
East	Lab	C	C	C	Lab	Lab	C
West	Lab	L	L	L	Lab	Lab	C
BOOTLE	Lab	*Lab	**Lab	Lab	Lab	Lab	Lab
BOURNEMOUTH							
East and Christchurch	C	C	C	C	*C	C	C
West	C	C	C	C	C	C	C
BRADFORD							
Central	Lab	Lab	—	—	—	—	—
East	Lab	Lab	**Lab	Lab	Lab	Lab	Lab
North	C	C	**C	*C	Lab	Lab	Lab
South	Lab	Lab	**Lab	Lab	Lab	Lab	Lab
West	—	—	C	C	C	Lab	C
†BRENTFORD AND CHISWICK	C	C	C	C	C	Lab	Lab
BRIGHOUSE AND							
SPENBOROUGH	Lab	Lab	**Lab	Lab(C)	Lab	Lab	C
BRIGHTON							
Kemptown	C	C	*C	C	Lab	Lab	C
Pavilion	C	C	*C	C	C	C	C
BRISTOL							
Central	Lab	Lab	**Lab	Lab	Lab	Lab	Lab
North-East	Lab	Lab	**Lab	C	C	Lab	C
North-West	C	C	**Lab	C	C	Lab	C
South	Lab	Lab	**Lab	Lab	Lab	Lab	Lab
South-East	Lab	Lab	**Lab	Lab[1] (Lab)	Lab	Lab	Lab
West	C	C	**C	C	C	C	C
BROMLEY	C	C	C	C	C	C	C
BURNLEY	Lab	Lab	Lab	Lab	Lab	Lab	Lab
BURY AND RADCLIFFE	C	C	C	C	Lab	Lab	C
CAMBRIDGE	C	C	C	C	C	Lab(C)	C
*CARLISLE	Lab	*Lab	C	C	Lab	Lab	Lab
CHELTENHAM	C	C	C	C	C	C	C
CHESTERFIELD	Lab	Lab	Lab	Lab	Lab	Lab	Lab
COVENTRY							
East	Lab	Lab	Lab	Lab	*Lab	Lab	Lab
North	Lab	Lab	Lab	Lab	*Lab	Lab	Lab
South	Lab	Lab	Lab	C	*Lab	Lab	Lab
CROSBY	C	C	**C	C	*C	C	C
CROYDON							
East	C	C	—	—	—	—	—
North	C	C	—	—	—	—	—
North-East	—	—	C	C	C	C	C
North-West	—	—	C	C	C	C	C
South	—	—	C	C	C	Lab	C
West	C	C	—	—	—	—	—
†DAGENHAM	Lab	Lab	Lab	Lab	Lab	Lab	Lab
DARLINGTON	Lab	C	C	C	Lab	Lab	Lab
DARTFORD	Lab	Lab	—	—	—	—	—
DERBY							
North	Lab	Lab	**Lab	Lab	Lab	Lab	Lab
South	Lab	Lab	**Lab	Lab	Lab	Lab	Lab
DEWSBURY	Lab	Lab	**Lab	Lab	Lab	Lab	Lab
DONCASTER	Lab	*C	C	C	Lab	Lab	Lab
DROYLSDEN	Lab	Lab	—	—	—	—	—
DUDLEY	Lab	Lab	*Lab	Lab	Lab	Lab(C)	Lab
EALING							
North	Lab	Lab	C	C	Lab	Lab	Lab
South	C	C	C	C	C	C	C
EAST HAM							
†North	Lab	Lab	Lab	Lab	Lab	Lab	Lab
†South	Lab	Lab	Lab	Lab	Lab	Lab	Lab
ECCLES	Lab	Lab	Lab	*Lab	*Lab	Lab	Lab
EDMONTON	Lab	Lab	Lab	Lab	Lab	Lab	Lab
ENFIELD							
East	Lab	Lab	Lab	Lab	Lab	Lab	Lab
West	C	C	C	C	C	C	C
ERITH AND CRAYFORD	—	—	Lab	Lab	Lab	Lab	Lab

ENGLAND—BOROUGHS (Cont.)

CONSTITUENCY	1950	1951	1955	1959	1964	1966	1970
ETON AND SLOUGH	Lab	Lab	Lab	Lab	C	Lab	Lab
EXETER	C	C	C	C	C	Lab	C
FELTHAM	—	—	Lab	Lab	Lab	Lab	Lab
FINCHLEY	C	C	C	C	C	C	C
GATESHEAD							
East	Lab	Lab	**Lab	Lab	*Lab	Lab	Lab
West	Lab	Lab	**Lab	Lab	*Lab	Lab	Lab
GILLINGHAM	C	C	C	C	C	C	C
GLOUCESTER	Lab	*Lab	*Lab	Lab	*Lab	Lab	C
GOSPORT AND FAREHAM	C	C	C	C	C	C	C
GRIMSBY	Lab	Lab	Lab	Lab	*Lab	Lab	Lab
HALIFAX	Lab	Lab	C	C	Lab	Lab	Lab
HARROW							
Central	C	C	**C	C	C	C	C
East	C	C	**C	C	C	Lab	C
West	C	C	**C	C	C	C	C
HARTLEPOOLS, THE	Lab	Lab	*Lab	C	Lab	Lab	Lab
HASTINGS	C	C	**C	C	C	C	C
HAYES AND HARLINGTON	Lab	Lab	Lab	Lab	Lab	Lab	Lab
HENDON							
†North	C	C	C	C	C	C	C
†South	C	C	C	C	C	C	C
†HESTON AND ISLEWORTH	C	C	**C	C	C	C	C
†HORNCHURCH	Lab	Lab	C	C	C	Lab	C
HORNSEY	C	C	C	C	C	C	C
HOVE	C	C	C	C	C	C	C
HUDDERSFIELD							
East	Lab	Lab	**Lab	Lab	Lab	Lab	Lab
West	L	L	**L	L	Lab	Lab	Lab
ILFORD							
*North	C	C	C	C	*C	C	C
*South	C	C	C	C	*C	Lab	C
IPSWICH	Lab	Lab	*Lab	Lab	Lab	Lab	C
JARROW	—	—	Lab	Lab	Lab	Lab	Lab
KEIGHLEY	Lab	Lab	Lab	C	Lab	Lab	C
KINGSTON UPON HULL							
Central	Lab	Lab	—	—	—	—	—
East	Lab	Lab	**Lab	*Lab	Lab	Lab	Lab
Haltemprice	C	C	—	—	—	—	—
North	C	C	**C	C	Lab	Lab	Lab
West	—	—	Lab	Lab	Lab	Lab	Lab
KINGSTON UPON THAMES	C	C	**C	C	*C	C	C
LEEDS							
Central	Lab	*Lab	—	—	—	—	—
East	—	—	Lab	Lab	*Lab	Lab	Lab
North	C	*C	—	—	—	—	—
North-East	Lab	*Lab	**C	C	*C	C	C
North-West	C	*C	**C	C	C	C	C
South	Lab	*Lab	Lab	Lab	Lab	Lab	Lab
South-East	Lab	*Lab	**Lab	Lab	Lab	Lab	Lab
West	Lab	*Lab	**Lab	Lab	Lab	Lab	Lab
LEICESTER							
North-East	Lab	Lab	Lab	Lab	Lab	Lab	Lab
North-West	Lab	Lab	Lab	Lab	Lab	Lab	Lab
South-East	C	C	**C	C	C	C	C
South-West	Lab	Lab	Lab	Lab	Lab	Lab(C)	C
LEIGH	Lab	Lab	Lab	Lab	Lab	Lab	Lab
LEYTON	Lab	Lab	Lab	Lab	Lab(C)	Lab	Lab
LINCOLN	Lab	Lab	Lab	Lab	*Lab	Lab	Lab(Ind Lab)
LIVERPOOL							
Edge Hill	Lab	Lab	**Lab	Lab	Lab	Lab	Lab
Exchange	Lab	Lab	**Lab	Lab	Lab	Lab	Lab
Garston	C	C	**C	C	C	C	C
Kirkdale	Lab	Lab	**C	C	Lab	Lab	Lab
Scotland	Lab	Lab	*Lab	Lab	Lab	Lab	Lab
Toxteth	C	C	*C	C	Lab	Lab	Lab

ENGLAND—BOROUGHS (Cont.)

CONSTITUENCY	1950	1951	1955	1959	1964	1966	1970
LIVERPOOL (Cont.)							
Walton	C	*C	**C	C	Lab	Lab	Lab
Wavertree	C	C	**C	C	C	C	C
West Derby	C	C	**C	C	*Lab	Lab	Lab
LUTON	C	C	C	C(Lab)	Lab	Lab	C
MANCHESTER							
Ardwick	Lab	Lab	**Lab	Lab	Lab	Lab	Lab
Blackley	Lab	C	C	C	Lab	Lab	Lab
Cheetham	Lab	Lab	**Lab	Lab	Lab	Lab	Lab
Clayton	Lab	Lab	—	—	—	—	—
Exchange	Lab	Lab	**Lab	Lab	Lab	Lab	Lab
Gorton	Lab	Lab	**Lab	Lab	Lab	Lab	Lab
Moss Side	C	C	C	C	C	C	C
Openshaw	—	—	Lab	Lab	Lab	Lab	Lab
Withington	C	C	**C	C	C	C	C
Wythenshawe	C	C	**C	C	Lab	Lab	Lab
MERTON AND MORDEN	C	C	C	C	C	C	C
MIDDLESBROUGH							
East	Lab	Lab	Lab	Lab	*Lab	Lab	Lab
West	Lab	C	C	C(Lab)	*Lab	Lab	C
†MITCHAM	C	C	C	C	C	C	C
†NELSON AND COLNE	Lab	Lab	Lab	Lab	Lab	Lab(C)	C
NEWCASTLE-UNDER-LYME	Lab	Lab	Lab	Lab	Lab	Lab	Lab
NEWCASTLE UPON TYNE							
Central	Lab	Lab	**Lab	Lab	Lab	Lab	Lab
East	Lab	Lab	Lab	C	Lab	Lab	Lab
North	C	C	C	C	C	C	C
West	Lab	Lab	**Lab	Lab	Lab	Lab	Lab
NORTHAMPTON	Lab	Lab	Lab	Lab	Lab	Lab	Lab
NORWICH							
North	Lab	*Lab	Lab	Lab	Lab	Lab	Lab
South	C	C	C	C	Lab	Lab	C
NOTTINGHAM							
Central	Lab	Lab	**C	*C	Lab	Lab	Lab
East	Lab	Lab	—	—	—	—	—
North	—	—	Lab	*Lab	Lab	Lab	Lab
North-West	Lab	Lab	—	—	—	—	—
South	Lab	Lab	**C	*C	C	Lab	C
*West	—	—	Lab	*C	Lab	Lab	Lab
OLDBURY AND HALESOWEN	Lab	Lab	Lab	Lab	Lab	Lab	C
OLDHAM							
East	Lab	*C	*C	Lab	Lab	Lab	Lab
West	Lab	*Lab	*Lab	Lab	Lab	Lab(C)	Lab
OXFORD	C	C	C	C	*C	Lab	C
PLYMOUTH							
Devonport	Lab	*Lab	**C	C	C	C	C
Sutton	Lab	*C	**C	C	C	Lab	Lab
PONTEFRACT	Lab	Lab	Lab	Lab	Lab	Lab	Lab
POOLE	C	C	C	C	C	C	C
PORTSMOUTH							
Langstone	C	C	*C	C	*C	C	C
South	C	C	*C	C	C	C	C
West	C	C	*C	C	C	Lab	Lab
PRESTON							
North	C	C	C	C	C	Lab	C
South	Lab	Lab	*C	C	*Lab	Lab	C
PUDSEY	C	C	C	C	C	C	C
READING	—	—	Lab	C	*C	Lab	C
North	Lab	C	—	—	—	—	—
South	Lab	Lab	—	—	—	—	—
RICHMOND (Surrey)	C	C	C	C	*C	C	C
ROCHDALE	Lab	C	C(Lab)	Lab	Lab	Lab	Lab(L)
ROCHESTER AND CHATHAM	Lab	Lab	*Lab	C	*Lab	Lab	C
ROMFORD	C	C	**Lab	Lab	Lab	Lab	Lab
ROSSENDALE	Lab	Lab	Lab	Lab	Lab	Lab	C
ROTHERHAM	Lab	Lab	Lab	Lab	Lab	Lab	Lab

ENGLAND—BOROUGHS (Cont.)

CONSTITUENCY	1950	1951	1955	1959	1964	1966	1970
ROWLEY REGIS AND TIPTON	Lab	Lab	*Lab	Lab	Lab	Lab	Lab
RUISLIP-NORTHWOOD	C	C	C	C	C	C	C
ST.HELENS	Lab	Lab	*Lab	Lab	Lab	Lab	Lab
SALFORD							
East	Lab	Lab	Lab	Lab	Lab	Lab	Lab
West	Lab	Lab	Lab	Lab	*Lab	Lab	Lab
SHEFFIELD							
Attercliffe	Lab	Lab	**Lab	Lab	Lab	Lab	Lab
Brightside	Lab	Lab	**Lab	Lab	Lab	Lab	Lab
Hallam	C	C	**C	C	C	C	C
Heeley	C	C	**C	C	C	Lab	C
Hillsborough	Lab	Lab	**Lab	Lab	Lab	Lab	Lab
Neepsend	Lab	Lab	—	—	—	—	—
Park	Lab	Lab	**Lab	Lab	Lab	Lab	Lab
SMETHWICK	Lab	Lab	Lab	Lab	C	Lab	Lab
SOUTHALL	Lab	Lab	Lab	Lab	Lab	Lab	Lab
SOUTHAMPTON							
Itchen	Lab	Lab	**Lab	Lab	Lab	Lab	Lab
Test	Lab	Lab	**C	C	C	Lab	C
SOUTHEND							
East	C	C	**C	C	C	C	C
West	C	C	**C	C	C	C	C
SOUTHGATE	C	C	C	C	C	C	C
†SOUTHPORT	C	C	C	C	C	C	C
SOUTH SHIELDS	Lab	*Lab	Lab	Lab	Lab	Lab	Lab
STOCKPORT							
North	C	C	C	C	Lab	Lab	C
South	C	C	*C	C	Lab	Lab	Lab
STOCKTON-ON-TEES	Lab	Lab	*Lab	Lab	Lab	Lab	Lab
STOKE-ON-TRENT							
Central	Lab	Lab	*Lab	Lab	Lab	Lab	Lab
North	Lab	Lab	*Lab	Lab	Lab	Lab	Lab
South	Lab	Lab	*Lab	Lab	Lab	Lab	Lab
STRETFORD	C	C	C	C	C	Lab	C
SUNDERLAND							
North	Lab	Lab	*Lab	Lab	Lab	Lab	Lab
South	Lab	Lab(C)	*C	C	Lab	Lab	Lab
SURBITON	—	—	C	C	C	C	C
†SUTTON AND CHEAM	C	C	C	C	C	C	C(L)
†SUTTON COLDFIELD	—	—	C	C	C	C	C
SWINDON	Lab	Lab	*Lab	Lab	Lab	Lab(C)	Lab
TORQUAY	C	C	C	C	C	C	C
TOTTENHAM	Lab	Lab	Lab	Lab	Lab	Lab	Lab
†TWICKENHAM	C	C	C	C	C	C	C
TYNEMOUTH	C	C	C	C	C	C	C
WAKEFIELD	Lab	Lab	**Lab	Lab	*Lab	Lab	Lab
WALLASEY	C	C	C	C	C	C	C
WALLSEND	Lab	Lab	Lab	Lab	Lab	Lab	Lab
WALSALL	Lab	Lab	—	—	—	—	—
North	—	—	Lab	Lab	*Lab	Lab	Lab
South	—	—	C	C	*C	C	C
WALTHAMSTOW							
†East	Lab	Lab	C	C	C	Lab(C)	C
†West	Lab	Lab	Lab	Lab	Lab	Lab(C)	Lab
WANSTEAD AND WOODFORD	—	—	—	—	*C	C	C
(formerly Woodford, q.v.)							
WARRINGTON	Lab	Lab	*Lab	Lab	Lab	Lab	Lab
WATFORD	Lab	Lab	C	C	Lab	Lab	Lab
WEDNESBURY	Lab	Lab	**Lab	Lab	Lab	Lab	Lab
WEMBLEY							
†North	C	C	C	C	C	C	C
†South	C	C	C	C	C	C	C
WEST BROMWICH	Lab	Lab	Lab	Lab	Lab	Lab	Lab
WEST HAM							
North	Lab	Lab	Lab	Lab	Lab	Lab	Lab
South	Lab	Lab	Lab	Lab	Lab	Lab	Lab
†WIGAN	Lab	Lab	Lab	Lab	Lab	Lab	Lab

ENGLAND—BOROUGHS (Cont.)

CONSTITUENCY	1950	1951	1955	1959	1964	1966	1970
WILLESDEN							
East	Lab	Lab	Lab	C	Lab	Lab	Lab
West	Lab	Lab	Lab	Lab	Lab	Lab	Lab
WIMBLEDON	C	C	**C	C	C	C	C
WOLVERHAMPTON							
North-East	Lab	Lab	**Lab	Lab	Lab	Lab	Lab
South-West	C	C	**C	C	C	C	C
†WOODFORD (Wanstead and							
Woodford from 1964, q.v.)	C	C	**C	C	—	—	—
WOOD GREEN	Lab	Lab	Lab	Lab	Lab	Lab	Lab
WORCESTER	C	C	*C	C	C	C	C
WORTHING	C	C	C	C	C	C	C
YORK	C	C	C	C	*C	Lab	Lab

[1] On petition following 1961 by-election, Labour member unseated, Conservative declared elected. Subsequently Conservative resigned and at by-election Labour regained seat.

ENGLAND—COUNTIES

CONSTITUENCY	1950	1951	1955	1959	1964	1966	1970
BEDFORDSHIRE							
Bedford	C	C	*C	C	C	Lab	C
Mid	C	C	*C	C	C	C	C
South	Lab	C	C	C	C	Lab	C
BERKSHIRE							
Abingdon	C	C	C	C	C	C	C
Newbury	C	C	**C	C	*C	C	C
Windsor	C	C	C	C	C	C	C
Wokingham	C	C	**C	C	*C	C	C
BUCKINGHAMSHIRE							
Aylesbury	C	C	C	C	C	C	C
Buckingham	Lab	C	C	C	Lab	Lab	C
South	C	C	C	C	C	C	C
†Wycombe	Lab	C	C	C	C	C	C
CAMBRIDGESHIRE	C	C	C	C	C	C	C
CHESHIRE							
Cheadle	C	C	*C	C	C	L	C
City of Chester	C	C	C	C	C	C	C
Crewe	Lab	Lab	**Lab	Lab	Lab	Lab	Lab
Knutsford	C	C	**C	C	C	C	C
Macclesfield	C	C	C	C	C	C	C
Nantwich	—	—	C	C	C	C	C
Northwich	C	C	**C	C	C	C	C
Runcorn	C	C	C	C	C	C	C
Stalybridge and Hyde	Lab	Lab	Lab	Lab	Lab	Lab	Lab
Wirral	C	C	C	C	C	C	C
CORNWALL							
Bodmin	C	C	C	C	L	L	C
Falmouth and Camborne	Lab	Lab	Lab	Lab	Lab	Lab	C
North	C	C	C	C	C	L	L
St. Ives	C	C	C	C	C	C	C
Truro	C	C	C	C	C	C	C
CUMBERLAND							
Penrith and the Border	C	*C	C	C	C	C	C
Whitehaven	Lab	Lab	Lab	Lab	Lab	Lab	Lab
Workington	Lab	Lab	Lab	Lab	Lab	Lab	Lab
DERBYSHIRE							
Belper	Lab	Lab	Lab	Lab	Lab	Lab	C
Bolsover	Lab	Lab	Lab	Lab	Lab	Lab	Lab
High Peak	C	C	C	C	C	Lab	C

ENGLAND—COUNTIES (Cont.)

CONSTITUENCY	1950	1951	1955	1959	1964	1966	1970
DERBYSHIRE (Cont.)							
Ilkeston	Lab	Lab	Lab	Lab	Lab	Lab	Lab
North-East	Lab	Lab	Lab	Lab	Lab	Lab	Lab
South-East	Lab	Lab	**Lab	C	Lab	Lab	C
West	C	C	C	C	C	C	C
DEVON							
Honiton	C	C	C	C	C	C	C
North	C	C	C	L	L	L	L
Tavistock	C	*C	C	C	C	C	C
Tiverton	C	C	C	C	C	C	C
Torrington	C	*C	C(L)	C	C	C	C
Totnes	C	C	C	C	C	C	C
DORSET							
North	C	C	C	C	C	C	C
South	C	C	C	C(Lab)	C	C	C
West	C	C	C	C	C	C	C
DURHAM							
Bishop Auckland	Lab	Lab	*Lab	Lab	Lab	Lab	Lab
Blaydon	Lab	Lab	Lab	Lab	Lab	Lab	Lab
Chester-le-Street	Lab	Lab	Lab	Lab	Lab	Lab	Lab
Consett	Lab	Lab	Lab	Lab	Lab	Lab	Lab
Durham	Lab	Lab	Lab	Lab	Lab	Lab	Lab
Easington	Lab	Lab	Lab	Lab	Lab	Lab	Lab
Houghton-le-Spring	Lab	Lab	*Lab	Lab	Lab	Lab	Lab
Jarrow	Lab	*Lab	—	—	—	—	--
North-West	Lab	Lab	Lab	Lab	Lab	Lab	Lab
Sedgefield	Lab	Lab	*Lab	Lab	Lab	Lab	Lab
ESSEX							
Billericay	C	C	**C	C	C	Lab	C
Chelmsford	C	C	**C	C	C	C	C
Chigwell	—	—	C	C	C	C	C
Colchester	C	C	C	*C	C	C	C
†Epping	C	C	C	C	Lab	Lab	C
Harwich	C	C	C	C	C	C	C
Maldon	Lab	Lab	C	*C	C	C	C
Saffron Walden	C	C	C	*C	C	C	C
South-East	—	—	C	C	C	C	C
†Thurrock	Lab	Lab	Lab	Lab	Lab	Lab	Lab
GLOUCESTERSHIRE							
Cirencester and Tewkesbury	C	C	**C	C	C	C	C
South	Lab	Lab	**C	C	C	C	C
Stroud	—	—	C	C	*C	C	C
Stroud and Thornbury	C	*C	—	—	—	—	—
West	Lab	*Lab	Lab	Lab	Lab	Lab	Lab
HAMPSHIRE							
Aldershot	C	C	C	C	C	C	C
Basingstoke	C	C	**C	C	C	C	C
Eastleigh	—	—	C	C	C	C	C
New Forest	C	C	**C	C	*C	C	C
Petersfield	C	C	**C	C	*C	C	C
Winchester	C	C	**C	C	C	C	C
HEREFORDSHIRE							
Hereford	C	C	C	C	C	C	C
Leominster	C	C	C	C	C	C	C
HERTFORDSHIRE							
Barnet	C	C	**C	C	C	C	C
East	—	—	C	C	C	C	C
Hemel Hempstead	C	C	C	C	C	C	C
Hertford	C	C	**C	C	C	C	C
Hitchin	C	C	**C	C	Lab	Lab	Lab
St. Albans	C	C	**C	C	C	C	C
South-West	C	C	C	C	C	C	C
†HUNTINGDONSHIRE	C	C	C	C	C	C	C
*ISLE OF ELY	C	C	C	C	C	C	C(L)
†ISLE OF WIGHT	C	C	C	C	C	C	C

ENGLAND—COUNTIES (Cont.)

CONSTITUENCY	1950	1951	1955	1959	1964	1966	1970
KENT							
Ashford	C	C	C	C	C	C	C
Canterbury	C	C	C	C	C	C	C
Chislehurst	C	C	**C	C	C	Lab	C
Dartford	—	—	Lab	Lab	Lab	Lab	C
Dover	C	C	C	C	Lab	Lab	C
Faversham	Lab	Lab	Lab	Lab	Lab	Lab	C
Folkestone and Hythe	C	C	C	C	C	C	C
Gravesend	Lab	Lab	**C	C	*Lab	Lab	C
Isle of Thanet	C	C	C	C	C	C	C
Maidstone	C	C	C	C	C	C	C
Orpington	C	C	**C	C(L)	L	L	C
Sevenoaks	C	C	C	C	C	C	C
Tonbridge	C	C	C	C	C	C	C
LANCASHIRE							
Chorley	Lab	Lab	**Lab	Lab	Lab	Lab	C
Clitheroe	C	C	C	C	C	C	C
Darwen	C	C	**C	C	C	C	C
Farnworth	Lab	Lab	Lab	*Lab	Lab	Lab	Lab
Heywood and Royton	C	C	C	C	Lab	Lab	Lab
Huyton	Lab	Lab	*Lab	Lab	*Lab	Lab	Lab
Ince	Lab	Lab	Lab	Lab	Lab	Lab	Lab
Lancaster	C	C	C	C	C	Lab	C
Middleton and Prestwich	C	C	C	C	C	Lab	C
Morecambe and Lonsdale	C	C	C	C	C	C	C
Newton	Lab	Lab	*Lab	Lab	Lab	Lab	Lab
North Fylde	C	C	C	*C	C	C	C
Ormskirk	C	*C	**C	C	*C	C	C
South Fylde	C	C	*C	C	*C	C	C
Westhoughton	Lab	Lab	Lab	Lab	Lab	Lab	Lab
Widnes	Lab	Lab	*Lab	Lab	Lab	Lab	Lab
LEICESTERSHIRE							
Bosworth	Lab	Lab	*Lab	Lab	Lab	Lab	C
Harborough	C	C	**C	C	C	C	C
Loughborough	Lab	Lab	*Lab	Lab	Lab	Lab	Lab
Melton	C	C	C	C	C	C	C
LINCOLNSHIRE—PARTS OF HOLLAND							
Holland with Boston	C	C	C	C	C	C	C
LINCOLNSHIRE—PARTS OF KESTEVEN, AND RUTLANDSHIRE							
Grantham	C	C	C	C	*C	C	C
Rutland and Stamford	C	C	C	C	C	C	C
LINCOLNSHIRE—PARTS OF LINDSEY							
Brigg	Lab	Lab	Lab	Lab	Lab	Lab	Lab
Gainsborough	C	C	C	C	C	C	C
Horncastle	C	C	C	C	C	C	C
Louth	C	C	C	C	*C	C	C
MIDDLESEX							
Spelthorne	C	C	**C	C	C	C	C
Uxbridge	Lab	Lab	Lab	C	C	Lab	C
NORFOLK							
Central	C	*C	C	C	C	C	C
King's Lynn	Lab	C	C	C	Lab	Lab	C
North	Lab	Lab	Lab	Lab	Lab	Lab	C
South	C	C	C	C	C	C	C
South-West	Lab	C	Lab	Lab	C	C	C
Yarmouth	Lab	C	C	C	C	Lab	C
NORTHAMPTONSHIRE							
Kettering	Lab	Lab	Lab	Lab	Lab	Lab	Lab
Peterborough	C	C	C	C	C	C	C
South	C	C	C	C	C	C	C
Wellingborough	Lab	Lab	Lab	C	Lab	Lab(C)	C

ENGLAND—COUNTIES (Cont.)

CONSTITUENCY	1950	1951	1955	1959	1964	1966	1970
NORTHUMBERLAND							
Berwick-upon-Tweed	C	C	C	C	C	C	C(L)
Hexham	C	C	C	C	C	C	C
Morpeth	Lab	Lab	Lab	Lab	Lab	Lab	Lab
NOTTINGHAMSHIRE							
Ashfield	—	—	Lab	Lab	Lab	Lab	Lab
†Bassetlaw	Lab	Lab	**Lab	Lab	Lab	Lab	Lab
Broxtowe	Lab	Lab	—	—	—	—	—
Carlton	C	C	C	C	C	C	C
Mansfield	Lab	Lab	**Lab	Lab	Lab	Lab	Lab
Newark	Lab	Lab	**Lab	Lab	Lab	Lab	Lab
Rushcliffe	C	C	**C	C	C	Lab	C
OXFORDSHIRE							
Banbury	C	C	C	C	C	C	C
Henley	C	C	C	C	*C	C	C
SHROPSHIRE							
Ludlow	C	C	C	C	C	C	C
Oswestry	C	C	C	C	C	C	C
Shrewsbury	C	C	C	C	C	C	C
The Wrekin	Lab	Lab	C	C	C	Lab	C
SOMERSET							
†Bridgwater	C	C	C	C	C	C	C
North	C	*C	*C	C	*C	C	C
†Taunton	C	C	C	C	C	C	C
Wells	C	C	C	C	*C	C	C
Weston-super-Mare	C	C	*C	C	C	C	C
†Yeovil	C	C	C	C	C	C	C
STAFFORDSHIRE							
Brierley Hill	Lab	Lab	*Lab	C	C	C	C
Burton	C	C	C	C	C	C	C
Cannock	Lab	Lab	**Lab	Lab	Lab	Lab	C
Leek	Lab	Lab	Lab	Lab	Lab	Lab	C
Lichfield and Tamworth	Lab	Lab	**Lab	Lab	Lab	Lab	C
Stafford and Stone	C	C	C	C	C	C	C
SUFFOLK							
Bury St. Edmunds	C	C	C	C	C	C	C
Eye	L	C	*C	C	C	C	C
Lowestoft	Lab	Lab	Lab	C	C	C	C
Sudbury and Woodbridge	C	C	*C	C	C	C	C
SURREY							
†Carshalton	C	C	C	C	C	C	C
Chertsey	C	C	C	C	C	C	C
Dorking	C	C	C	C	C	C	C
East	C	C	C	C	C	C	C
Epsom	C	C	C	C	C	C	C
Esher	C	C	C	C	C	C	C
Farnham	C	C	C	C	C	C	C
Guildford	C	C	C	C	*C	C	C
Reigate	C	C	C	C	C	C	C
Woking	C	C	C	C	*C	C	C
SUSSEX (EAST)							
Eastbourne	C	C	**C	C	C	C	C
East Grinstead	C	C	**C	C	C	C	C
Lewes	C	C	**C	C	C	C	C
Rye	—	—	C	C	C	C	C
SUSSEX (WEST)							
Arundel and Shoreham	C	C	C	C	C	C	C
Chichester	C	C	C	C	C	C	C
Horsham	C	C	*C	C	C	C	C
WARWICKSHIRE							
Meriden	—	—	Lab	C	*Lab	Lab(C)	C
†Nuneaton	Lab	Lab	**Lab	Lab	Lab	Lab	Lab
Rugby	Lab	Lab	Lab	C	*C	Lab	Lab
Solihull	C	C	C	C	C	C	C
Stratford	C	C	C	C	C	C	C
Sutton Coldfield	C	C	—	—	—	—	—
Warwick and Leamington	C	C	C	C	*C	C	C

ENGLAND—COUNTIES (Cont.)

CONSTITUENCY	1950	1951	1955	1959	1964	1966	1970
†WESTMORLAND	C	C	C	C	C	C	C
WILTSHIRE							
Chippenham	C	C	C	C	C	C	C
Devizes	C	C	*C	C	C	C	C
Salisbury	C	C	C	C	C	C	C
Westbury	C	C	C	C	C	C	C
WORCESTERSHIRE							
Bromsgrove	C	C	C	C	C	C	C(Lab)
Kidderminster	C	C	C	C	C	C	C
South	C	C	*C	C	C	C	C
YORKSHIRE (EAST RIDING)							
Beverley	C	C	—	—	—	—	—
Bridlington	C	C	**C	*C	C	C	C
Haltemprice	—	—	C	C	C	C	C
Howden	—	—	C	C	C	C	C
YORKSHIRE (NORTH RIDING)							
Cleveland	Lab	Lab	Lab	C	Lab	Lab	Lab
Richmond	C	C	C	C	C	C	C
Scarborough and Whitby	C	C	C	C	C	C	C
Thirsk and Malton	C	C	C	C	C	C	C
YORKSHIRE (WEST RIDING)							
Barkston Ash	C	C	C	C	*C	C	C
Colne Valley	Lab	Lab	**Lab	Lab	Lab	L	Lab
Dearne Valley	Lab	Lab	Lab	Lab	Lab	Lab	Lab
Don Valley	Lab	*Lab	Lab	Lab	Lab	Lab	Lab
Goole	Lab	Lab	Lab	Lab	Lab	Lab	Lab
Harrogate	C	C	C	C	C	C	C
Hemsworth	Lab	Lab	**Lab	Lab	Lab	Lab	Lab
Normanton	Lab	Lab	Lab	Lab	Lab	Lab	Lab
Penistone	Lab	Lab	**Lab	Lab	Lab	Lab	Lab
Ripon	C	C	C	C	C	C	C(L)
Rother Valley	Lab	Lab	Lab	Lab	Lab	Lab	Lab
Shipley	C	C	C	*C	C	C	C
Skipton	C	C	C	C	C	C	C
Sowerby	Lab	Lab	Lab	Lab	Lab	Lab	Lab

WALES AND MONMOUTHSHIRE—BOROUGHS

CONSTITUENCY	1950	1951	1955	1959	1964	1966	1970
ABERDARE	Lab	Lab	Lab	Lab	Lab	Lab	Lab
CARDIFF							
North	C	*C	C	C	C	Lab	C
South-East	Lab	*Lab	Lab	Lab	Lab	Lab	Lab
West	Lab	*Lab	Lab	Lab	Lab	Lab	Lab
MERTHYR TYDFIL	Lab	Lab	Lab	Lab	Lab	Lab	Ind Lab(Lab)
NEWPORT	Lab	Lab	*Lab	Lab	Lab	Lab	Lab
RHONDDA							
East	Lab	Lab	Lab	Lab	Lab	Lab	Lab
West	Lab	Lab	Lab	Lab	Lab	Lab	Lab
SWANSEA							
East	Lab	Lab	*Lab	Lab	Lab	Lab	Lab
West	Lab	Lab	*Lab	C	Lab	Lab	Lab

WALES AND MONMOUTHSHIRE—COUNTIES

CONSTITUENCY	1950	1951	1955	1959	1964	1966	1970
†ANGLESEY	L	Lab	Lab	Lab	Lab	Lab	Lab
†BRECONSHIRE AND RADNORSHIRE	Lab	Lab	Lab	Lab	Lab	Lab	Lab
CAERNARVONSHIRE							
Caernarvon	Lab	Lab	Lab	Lab	Lab	Lab	Lab
Conway	Lab	C	C	C	C	Lab	C
†CARDIGANSHIRE	L	L	L	L	L	Lab	Lab
CARMARTHENSHIRE							
Carmarthen	L	L	*L(Lab)	Lab	Lab	Lab(PC)	Lab
Llanelly	Lab	Lab	*Lab	Lab	Lab	Lab	Lab
DENBIGHSHIRE							
Denbigh	C	C	C	C	C	C	C
†Wrexham	Lab	Lab	Lab	Lab	Lab	Lab	Lab
FLINTSHIRE							
East Flint	Lab	Lab	Lab	Lab	Lab	Lab	Lab
West Flint	C	C	C	C	C	C	C
GLAMORGANSHIRE							
Aberavon	Lab	Lab	Lab	Lab	Lab	Lab	Lab
Barry	Lab	*C	C	C	C	C	C
Caerphilly	Lab	Lab	Lab	Lab	Lab	Lab	Lab
Gower	Lab	Lab	Lab	Lab	Lab	Lab	Lab
Neath	Lab	Lab	Lab	Lab	Lab	Lab	Lab
†Ogmore	Lab	Lab	Lab	Lab	Lab	Lab	Lab
†Pontypridd	Lab	Lab	Lab	Lab	Lab	Lab	Lab
†MERIONETHSHIRE	L	Lab	Lab	Lab	Lab	Lab	Lab
MONMOUTHSHIRE							
Abertillery	Lab	Lab	Lab	Lab	Lab	Lab	Lab
Bedwellty	Lab	Lab	Lab	Lab	Lab	Lab	Lab
†Ebbw Vale	Lab	Lab	Lab	Lab	Lab	Lab	Lab
Monmouth	C	*C	*C	C	C	Lab	C
Pontypool	Lab	Lab	Lab	Lab	Lab	Lab	Lab
†MONTGOMERYSHIRE	L	L	L	L	L	L	L
†PEMBROKESHIRE	Lab	Lab	Lab	Lab	Lab	Lab	C

SCOTLAND—BURGHS

CONSTITUENCY	1950	1951	1955	1959	1964	1966	1970
ABERDEEN							
North	Lab	Lab	*Lab	Lab	Lab	Lab	Lab
South	C	C	*C	C	C	Lab	C
COATBRIDGE AND AIRDRIE	Lab	Lab	*Lab	Lab	Lab	Lab	Lab
DUNDEE							
East	Lab	Lab	Lab	Lab	Lab	Lab	Lab
West	Lab	Lab	Lab	Lab	Lab	Lab	Lab
DUNFERMLINE BURGHS	Lab	Lab	Lab	Lab	*Lab	Lab	Lab
EDINBURGH							
Central	Lab	Lab	**Lab	Lab	Lab	Lab	Lab
East	Lab	Lab	*Lab	Lab	*Lab	Lab	Lab
Leith	Lab	Lab	Lab	Lab	Lab	Lab	Lab
North	C	C	**C	C	C	C	C
Pentlands	C	C	**C	C	*C	C	C
South	C	C	C	C	*C	C	C
West	C	C	C	C	*C	C	C
GLASGOW							
Bridgeton	Lab	Lab	**Lab	Lab	Lab	Lab	Lab
Camlachie	Lab	Lab	—	—	—	—	—
Cathcart	C	C	C	C	C	C	C
Central	Lab	Lab	**Lab	Lab	Lab	Lab	Lab

SCOTLAND—BURGHS (Cont.)

CONSTITUENCY	1950	1951	1955	1959	1964	1966	1970
GLASGOW (Cont.)							
Craigton	—	—	C	Lab	Lab	Lab	Lab
Gorbals	Lab	Lab	**Lab	Lab	Lab	Lab	Lab
Govan	C	C	**Lab	Lab	Lab	Lab	Lab(SNP)
Hillhead	C	C	**C	C	C	C	C
Kelvingrove	C	C	**C(Lab)	C	Lab	Lab	Lab
Maryhill	Lab	Lab	Lab	Lab	Lab	Lab	Lab
Pollok	C	C	**C	C	Lab	Lab(C)	Lab
Provan	—	—	Lab	Lab	Lab	Lab	Lab
Scotstoun	C	C	**C	Lab	Lab	Lab	Lab
Shettleston	Lab	Lab	Lab	Lab	Lab	Lab	Lab
Springburn	Lab	Lab	**Lab	Lab	Lab	Lab	Lab
Tradeston	Lab	Lab	—	—	—	—	—
Woodside	C	C	**C	C(Lab)	Lab	Lab	Lab
GREENOCK	Lab	Lab	*Lab	Lab	*Lab	Lab	Lab
KIRKCALDY BURGHS	Lab	*Lab	*Lab	Lab	Lab	Lab	Lab
PAISLEY	Lab	Lab	Lab	Lab	Lab	Lab	Lab
STIRLING AND FALKIRK BURGHS	Lab	Lab	*Lab	Lab	Lab	Lab	Lab

SCOTLAND—COUNTIES

CONSTITUENCY	1950	1951	1955	1959	1964	1966	1970
ABERDEENSHIRE							
East	C	C	**C	C	C	C	C
West	C	C	**C	C	C	L	C
ANGUS[1] AND KINCARDINE-SHIRE							
North Angus and Mearns	C	C	C	C	C	C	C
South Angus	C	C	C	C	C	C	C
ARGYLL	C	C	C	C	C	C	C
AYRSHIRE AND BUTE							
Ayr	C	C	C	C	C	C	C
Bute and North Ayrshire	C	C	*C	C	C	C	C
Central Ayrshire	Lab	Lab	*C	Lab	Lab	Lab	Lab
Kilmarnock	Lab	Lab	Lab	Lab	Lab	Lab	Lab
South Ayrshire	Lab	Lab	Lab	Lab	Lab	Lab	Lab
BANFFSHIRE	C	C	C	C	C	C	C
BERWICKSHIRE AND EAST LOTHIAN[2]	Lab	C	C	C	C	Lab	Lab
CAITHNESS AND SUTHERLAND	C	C	C	Ind C	L	Lab	Lab
DUMFRIESSHIRE	C	C	C	C	C	C	C
DUNBARTONSHIRE							
East	Lab	*Lab	Lab	Lab	Lab	Lab	Lab
West	Lab	*Lab	Lab	Lab	Lab	Lab	Lab
FIFE							
East	C	C	C	C	C	C	C
West	Lab	*Lab	*Lab	Lab	*Lab	Lab	Lab
INVERNESS-SHIRE AND ROSS AND CROMARTY							
†Inverness	C	C	C	C	L	L	L
†Ross and Cromarty	Ind L	C	C	C	L	L	C
†Western Isles	Lab	Lab	Lab	Lab	Lab	Lab	SNP
KIRKCUDBRIGHTSHIRE AND WIGTOWNSHIRE							
*Galloway	C	C	C	C	C	C	C

SCOTLAND—COUNTIES (Cont.)

CONSTITUENCY	1950	1951	1955	1959	1964	1966	1970
LANARKSHIRE							
Bothwell	Lab	Lab	*Lab	Lab	Lab	Lab	Lab
Hamilton	Lab	Lab	Lab	Lab	Lab	Lab(SNP)	Lab
†Lanark	C	C	C	Lab	Lab	Lab	Lab
Motherwell	Lab	Lab	*Lab	Lab	Lab	Lab	Lab
North	Lab	Lab	*Lab	Lab	Lab	Lab	Lab
Rutherglen	Lab	C	C	C(Lab)	Lab	Lab	Lab
MIDLOTHIAN	—	—	Lab	Lab	*Lab	Lab	Lab
MIDLOTHIAN AND PEEBLES-SHIRE	Lab	Lab	—	—	—	—	—
†MORAY AND NAIRNSHIRE	C	C	C	C	C	C	C
†ORKNEY AND SHETLAND	L	L	L	L	L	L	L
PERTHSHIRE AND KINROSS-SHIRE							
†Kinross and West Perthshire	C	C	C	C	C	C	C
†Perth and East Perthshire	C	C	C	C	C	C	C
RENFREWSHIRE							
East	C	*C	C	C	C	C	C
West	C	*C	*C	C	*Lab	Lab	Lab
†ROXBURGHSHIRE AND SELKIRKSHIRE	L	C	—	—	—	—	—
ROXBURGHSHIRE, SELKIRK-SHIRE AND PEEBLESSHIRE	—	—	C	C	C(L)	L	L
STIRLINGSHIRE AND CLACKMANNANSHIRE							
Clackmannan and East Stirlingshire	Lab	Lab	*Lab	Lab	Lab	Lab	Lab
West Stirlingshire	Lab	Lab	*Lab	Lab	Lab	Lab	Lab
†WEST LOTHIAN[3]	Lab	Lab	Lab	Lab	Lab	Lab	Lab

[1] Formerly Forfarshire.

[2] Formerly Haddingtonshire.

[3] Formerly Linlithgowshire.

NORTHERN IRELAND—BOROUGHS

CONSTITUENCY	1950	1951	1955	1959	1964	1966	1970
BELFAST							
†East	C	C	C	C	C	C	C
†North	C	C	C	C	C	C	C
†South	C	C	C	C	C	C	C
†West	C	Irish LP	C	C	C	Rep LP	Rep LP

NORTHERN IRELAND—COUNTIES

CONSTITUENCY	1950	1951	1955	1959	1964	1966	1970
ANTRIM							
North	C	C	C	C	C	C	Prot U
South	C	C	C	C	C	C	C
ARMAGH	C	C	C	C	C	C	C
DOWN							
North	C	C	C	C	C	C	C
South	C	C	C	C	C	C	C
FERMANAGH AND							
SOUTH TYRONE	N	N	SF[1]	C	C	C	Unity
LONDONDERRY	C	C	C	C	C	C	C
MID-ULSTER	N	N	SF[1] (Ind C)	C	C	C(Unity)	Unity

[1] On petition, Sinn Fein member unseated, Conservative declared elected.

Appendix 4   REPRESENTATION OF CONSTITUENCIES 1974–1975

The following chart gives the party representation in each constituency from the General Election of 1974 (February) until December 1975.

The 200 constituencies unaffected by the boundary alterations which took place at the General Election of 1974 (February) are indicated by a dagger † placed before the name of the constituency. In a further 122 constituencies, boundary changes were of a minor nature (involving less than a 5% change in the electorate) and an asterisk * is placed before the names of these constituencies.

Although their boundaries were unaltered, the following former county constituencies became borough constituencies: Blaydon (Durham); Epsom (Surrey); Farnworth (Lancashire); Middleton and Prestwich (Lancashire); Spelthorne (Middlesex); Thurrock (Essex); Windsor (Berkshire). Epsom was renamed Epsom and Ewell and Windsor became Windsor and Maidenhead.

In a further twelve constituencies, name changes took place without boundary alterations: (London Borough) – St. Marylebone became City of Westminster, St. Marylebone; (English Boroughs becoming Greater London Boroughs) – Hornsey became Haringey, Hornsey; Ilford South became Redbridge, Ilford South; Leyton became Waltham Forest, Leyton; Richmond became Richmond upon Thames, Richmond; Surbiton became Kingston upon Thames, Surbiton; Tottenham became Haringey, Tottenham; Wood Green became Haringey, Wood Green; (English Borough) – Pontefract became Pontefract and Castleford; (English Counties) – Brigg (Lincolnshire) became Brigg and Scunthorpe; Dover (Kent) became Dover and Deal; (Welsh County) – Llanelly (Carmarthenshire) became Llanelli.

Changes which occured at by-elections are shown in brackets, *e.g.* Lab (C) indicates that the seat was won by Labour at the General Election but subsequently lost to a Conservative.

GREATER LONDON BOROUGHS

Constituency	1974 (F)	1974 (O)	Constituency	1974 (F)	1974 (O)
BARKING			EALING		
*Barking	Lab	Lab	Acton	C	C
*Dagenham	Lab	Lab	North	Lab	Lab
BARNET			Southall	Lab	Lab
Chipping Barnet	C	C	ENFIELD		
Finchley	C	C	*Edmonton	Lab	Lab
Hendon, North	C	C	North	Lab	Lab
Hendon, South	C	C	Southgate	C	C
BEXLEY			GREENWICH		
Bexleyheath	C	C	Greenwich	Lab	Lab
*Erith and Crayford	Lab	Lab	Woolwich, East	Lab	Lab
Sidcup	C	C	*Woolwich, West	Lab	Lab (C)
BRENT			HACKNEY		
East	Lab	Lab	Central	Lab	Lab
North	C	C	North and Stoke Newington	Lab	Lab
South	Lab	Lab	South and Shoreditch	Lab	Lab
BROMLEY			HAMMERSMITH		
Beckenham	C	C	Fulham	Lab	Lab
Chislehurst	C	C	North	Lab	Lab
*Orpington	C	C	HARINGEY		
Ravensbourne	C	C	†Hornsey	C	C
CAMDEN			†Tottenham	Lab	Lab
*Hampstead	C	C	†Wood Green	Lab	Lab
Holborn and St. Pancras South	Lab	Lab	HARROW		
St. Pancras, North	Lab	Lab	*Central	C	C
CITIES OF LONDON AND WESTMINSTER			*East	C	C
*City of London and Westminster South	C	C	†West	C	C
Paddington	Lab	Lab	HAVERING		
†St. Marylebone	C	C	Hornchurch	Lab	Lab
CROYDON			Romford	C	C
Central	C	C	Upminster	C	C
*North-East	C	C	HILLINGDON		
*North-West	C	C	Hayes and Harlington	Lab	Lab
South	C	C			

GREATER LONDON BOROUGHS (Cont.)

Constituency	1974 (F)	1974 (O)
HILLINGDON (Cont.)		
*Ruislip-Northwood	C	C
Uxbridge	C	C
HOUNSLOW		
Brentford and Isleworth	C	C
Feltham and Heston	Lab	Lab
ISLINGTON		
Central	Lab	Lab
North	Lab	Lab
South and Finsbury	Lab	Lab
KENSINGTON AND CHELSEA		
Chelsea	C	C
Kensington	C	C
KINGSTON UPON THAMES		
†Kingston upon Thames	C	C
†Surbiton	C	C
LAMBETH		
Central	Lab	Lab
*Norwood	Lab	Lab
Streatham	C	C
Vauxhall	Lab	Lab
LEWISHAM		
Deptford	Lab	Lab
East	Lab	Lab
West	Lab	Lab
MERTON		
Mitcham and Morden	Lab	Lab
Wimbledon	C	C
NEWHAM		
North-East	Lab	Lab
*North-West	Lab	Lab
South	Lab	Lab
REDBRIDGE		
Ilford, North	C	Lab
†Ilford, South	Lab	Lab
Wanstead and Woodford	C	C
RICHMOND UPON THAMES		
†Richmond	C	C
*Twickenham	C	C
SOUTHWARK		
Bermondsey	Lab	Lab
Dulwich	Lab	Lab
Peckham	Lab	Lab
SUTTON		
Carshalton	C	C
*Sutton and Cheam	C	C
TOWER HAMLETS		
Bethnal Green and Bow	Lab	Lab
Stepney and Poplar	Lab	Lab
WALTHAM FOREST		
Chingford	C	C
*Leyton	Lab	Lab
Walthamstow	Lab	Lab
WANDSWORTH		
Battersea, North	Lab	Lab
Battersea, South	Lab	Lab
Putney	Lab	Lab
Tooting	Lab	Lab

Constituency	1974 (F)	1974 (O)
ENGLAND — BOROUGHS		
†ACCRINGTON	Lab	Lab
ALDRIDGE-BROWNHILLS	Lab	Lab
†ALTRINCHAM AND SALE	C	C
†ASHTON-UNDER-LYNE	Lab	Lab
†BARNSLEY	Lab	Lab
†BARROW-IN-FURNESS	Lab	Lab
BASILDON	Lab	Lab
*BATH	C	C
†BATLEY AND MORLEY	Lab	Lab
BEBINGTON AND ELLESMERE PORT	Lab	Lab
BIRKENHEAD	Lab	Lab
BIRMINGHAM		
Edgbaston	C	C
Erdington	Lab	Lab
Hall Green	C	C
Handsworth	Lab	Lab
Ladywood	Lab	Lab
Northfield	Lab	Lab
Perry Barr	Lab	Lab
Selly Oak	C	Lab
Small Heath	Lab	Lab
Sparkbrook	Lab	Lab
Stechford	Lab	Lab
Yardley	Lab	Lab
†BLACKBURN	Lab	Lab
BLACKPOOL		
†North	C	C
†South	C	C
†BLAYDON	Lab	Lab
*BLYTH	Ind Lab	Lab
BOLTON		
†East	Lab	Lab
†West	C	Lab
BOOTLE	Lab	Lab
BOURNEMOUTH		
East	C	C
West	C	C
BRADFORD		
North	Lab	Lab
South	Lab	Lab
West	Lab	Lab
†BRIGHOUSE AND SPENBOROUGH	Lab	Lab
BRIGHTON		
†Kemptown	C	C
†Pavilion	C	C
BRISTOL		
North-East	Lab	Lab
*North-West	C	Lab
*South	Lab	Lab
South-East	Lab	Lab
West	C	C
†BURNLEY	Lab	Lab
†BURY AND RADCLIFFE	C	Lab
†CAMBRIDGE	C	C
†CARLISLE	Lab	Lab
CHEADLE	C	C
†CHELTENHAM	C	C
CHERTSEY AND WALTON	C	C
†CHESTERFIELD	Lab	Lab
CHRISTCHURCH AND LYMINGTON	C	C
COVENTRY		
North-East	Lab	Lab
North-West	Lab	Lab

ENGLAND — BOROUGHS (Cont.)

Constituency	1974 (F)	1974 (O)	Constituency	1974 (F)	1974 (O)
COVENTRY (Cont.)			LIVERPOOL (Cont.)		
South-East	Lab	Lab	Toxteth	Lab	Lab
South-West	Lab	Lab	†Walton	Lab	Lab
CROSBY	C	C	†Wavertree	C	C
*DARLINGTON	Lab	Lab	†West Derby	Lab	Lab
DERBY			LUTON		
North	Lab	Lab	East	Lab	Lab
South	Lab	Lab	West	Lab	Lab
†DEWSBURY	Lab	Lab			
†DONCASTER	Lab	Lab	MANCHESTER		
DUDLEY			Ardwick	Lab	Lab
East	Lab	Lab	*Blackley	Lab	Lab
West	Lab	Lab	Central	Lab	Lab
†ECCLES	Lab	Lab	*Gorton	Lab	Lab
†EPSOM AND EWELL	C	C	Moss Side	Lab	Lab
ESHER	C	C	*Openshaw	Lab	Lab
†ETON AND SLOUGH	Lab	Lab	Withington	C	C
EXETER	C	C	Wythenshawe	Lab	Lab
			†MIDDLETON AND PRESTWICH	Lab	Lab
FAREHAM	C	C	†NELSON AND COLNE	C	Lab
†FARNWORTH	Lab	Lab	*NEWCASTLE-UNDER-LYME	Lab	Lab
			NEWCASTLE UPON TYNE		
GATESHEAD			†Central	Lab	Lab
†East	Lab	Lab	†East	Lab	Lab
†West	Lab	Lab	†North	C	C
†GILLINGHAM	C	C	†West	Lab	Lab
GLOUCESTER	C	C	NORTHAMPTON		
GOSPORT	C	C	North	Lab	Lab
*GRIMSBY	Lab	Lab	South	C	C
HALESOWEN AND STOURBRIDGE	C	C	NORWICH		
†HALIFAX	Lab	Lab	North	Lab	Lab
*HARTLEPOOL	Lab	Lab	South	Lab	Lab
†HASTINGS	C	C	NOTTINGHAM		
HAVANT AND WATERLOO	C	C	East	Lab	Lab
HAZEL GROVE	L	C	North	Lab	Lab
†HOVE	C	C	West	Lab	Lab
HUDDERSFIELD			*NUNEATON	Lab	Lab
†East	Lab	Lab	OLDHAM		
†West	Lab	Lab	†East	Lab	Lab
*INCE	Lab	Lab	†West	Lab	Lab
†IPSWICH	C	Lab	†OXFORD	C	Lab
*JARROW	Lab	Lab	PETERBOROUGH	C	Lab
†KEIGHLEY	Lab	Lab	PLYMOUTH		
KINGSTON UPON HULL			Devenport	Lab	Lab
Central	Lab	Lab	Drake	C	C
East	Lab	Lab	Sutton	C	C
*West	Lab	Lab	†PONTEFRACT AND CASTLEFORD	Lab	Lab
LEEDS			†POOLE	C	C
East	Lab	Lab	PORTSMOUTH		
North-East	C	C	North	Lab	Lab
North-West	C	C	South	C	C
South	Lab	Lab	PRESTON		
South-East	Lab	Lab	†North	Lab	Lab
*West	Lab	Lab	†South	Lab	Lab
LEICESTER			†PUDSEY	C	C
East	Lab	Lab	READING NORTH	C	C
South	C	Lab	REIGATE	C	C
West	Lab	Lab	†ROCHDALE	L	L
†LEIGH	Lab	Lab	†ROCHESTER AND CHATHAM	C	Lab
*LINCOLN	Dem Lab	Lab	†ROSSENDALE	C	Lab
LIVERPOOL			*ROTHERHAM	Lab	Lab
Edge Hill	Lab	Lab	†ST. HELENS	Lab	Lab
†Garston	Lab	Lab	SALFORD		
Kirkdale	Lab	Lab	†East	Lab	Lab
Scotland Exchange	Lab	Lab	†West	Lab	Lab

ENGLAND—BOROUGHS (Cont.)

Constituency	1974 (F)	1974 (O)
SHEFFIELD		
Attercliffe	Lab	Lab
Brightside	Lab	Lab
Hallam	C	C
Heeley	Lab	Lab
Hillsborough	Lab	Lab
Park	Lab	Lab
*SOLIHULL	C	C
SOUTHAMPTON		
†Itchen	Lab	Lab
*Test	C	Lab
SOUTHEND		
†East	C	C
†West	C	C
†SOUTHPORT	C	C
†SOUTH SHIELDS	Lab	Lab
†SPELTHORNE	C	C
STOCKPORT		
*North	Lab	Lab
*South	Lab	Lab
STOKE-ON-TRENT		
Central	Lab	Lab
*North	Lab	Lab
South	Lab	Lab
*STRETFORD	C	C
SUNDERLAND		
North	Lab	Lab
South	Lab	Lab
SUTTON COLDFIELD	C	C
*SWINDON	Lab	Lab
TEESSIDE		
Middlesbrough	Lab	Lab
Redcar	Lab	Lab
Stockton	Lab	Lab
Thornaby	Lab	Lab
THANET		
East	C	C
West	C	C
*THURROCK	Lab	Lab
*TORBAY	C	C
*TYNEMOUTH	C	C
*WAKEFIELD	Lab	Lab
WALLASEY	C	C
*WALLSEND	Lab	Lab
WALLSALL		
North	Lab	Lab
South	Lab	Lab
WARLEY		
East	Lab	Lab
West	Lab	Lab
*WARRINGTON	Lab	Lab
*WATFORD	Lab	Lab
WEST BROMWICH		
East	Lab	Lab
West	Lab	Lab
WIGAN	Lab	Lab
WOLVERHAMPTON		
North-East	Lab	Lab
South-East	Lab	Lab
South-West	C	C
WORCESTER	C	C
WORTHING	C	C
YORK	Lab	Lab

ENGLAND — COUNTIES

Constituency	1974 (F)	1974 (O)
BEDFORDSHIRE		
*Bedford	C	C
*Mid	C	C
South	C	C
BERKSHIRE		
*Abingdon	C	C
Newbury	C	C
Reading, South	C	C
†Windsor and Maidenhead	C	C
Wokingham	C	C
BUCKINGHAMSHIRE		
Aylesbury	C	C
Beaconsfield	C	C
*Buckingham	C	C
Chesham and Amersham	C	C
Wycombe	C	C
CAMBRIDGESHIRE AND ISLE OF ELY		
*Cambridgeshire	C	C
*Isle of Ely	L	L
CHESHIRE		
*City of Chester	C	C
*Crewe	Lab	Lab
Knutsford	C	C
*Macclesfield	C	C
*Nantwich	C	C
*Northwich	C	C
†Runcorn	C	C
†Stalybridge and Hyde	Lab	Lab
Wirral	C	C
CORNWALL		
*Bodmin	L	C
†Falmouth and Camborne	C	C
*North	L	L
†St. Ives	C	C
*Truro	C	L
CUMBERLAND		
†Penrith and the Border	C	C
†Whitehaven	Lab	Lab
†Workington	Lab	Lab
DERBYSHIRE		
Belper	Lab	Lab
†Bolsover	Lab	Lab
†High Peak	C	C
†Ilkeston	Lab	Lab
North-East	Lab	Lab
South-East	C	C
†West	C	C
DEVON		
*Honiton	C	C
North	L	L
Tiverton	C	C
*Totnes	C	C
West	C	C
DORSET		
*North	C	C
†South	C	C
*West	C	C
DURHAM		
Bishop Auckland	Lab	Lab
*Chester-le-Street	Lab	Lab
†Consett	Lab	Lab
Durham	Lab	Lab
Easington	Lab	Lab

ENGLAND – COUNTIES (Cont.)

Constituency	1974 (F)	1974 (O)
DURHAM (Cont.)		
Houghton-le-Spring	Lab	Lab
North-West	Lab	Lab
ESSEX		
Braintree	C	C
Brentwood and Ongar	C	C
Chelmsford	C	C
†Colchester	C	C
Epping Forest	C	C
Harlow	Lab	Lab
†Harwich	C	C
Maldon	C	C
*Saffron Walden	C	C
South-East	C	C
GLOUCESTERSHIRE		
*Cirencester and Tewkesbury	C	C
Kingswood	Lab	Lab
South	C	C
*Stroud	C	C
West	Lab	Lab
HAMPSHIRE		
Aldershot	C	C
Basingstoke	C	C
Eastleigh	C	C
New Forest	C	C
*Petersfield	C	C
Winchester	C	C
HEREFORDSHIRE		
*Hereford	C	C
*Leominster	C	C
HERTFORDSHIRE		
East	C	C
Hemel Hempstead	C	Lab
Hertford and Stevenage	Lab	Lab
Hitchin	C	C
St. Albans	C	C
South	C	C
South-West	C	C
Welwyn and Hatfield	C	Lab
HUNTINGDON AND PETERBOROUGH		
*Huntingdonshire	C	C
***ISLE OF WIGHT**	L	L
KENT		
Ashford	C	C
†Canterbury	C	C
Dartford	Lab	Lab
†Dover and Deal	C	C
†Faversham	C	C
†Folkestone and Hythe	C	C
*Gravesend	Lab	Lab
†Maidstone	C	C
Royal Tunbridge Wells	C	C
Sevenoaks	C	C
Tonbridge and Malling	C	C
LANCASHIRE		
†Chorley	Lab	Lab
†Clitheroe	C	C
†Darwen	C	C
†Heywood and Royton	Lab	Lab
Huyton	Lab	Lab
†Lancaster	C	C
†Morecambe and Lonsdale	C	C
*Newton	Lab	Lab
†North Fylde	C	C

Constituency	1974 (F)	1974 (O)
LANCASHIRE (Cont.)		
Ormskirk	Lab	Lab
†South Fylde	C	C
*Westhoughton	Lab	Lab
†Widnes	Lab	Lab
LEICESTERSHIRE		
Blaby	C	C
*Bosworth	C	C
Harborough	C	C
*Loughborough	Lab	Lab
Melton	C	C
LINCOLNSHIRE—PARTS OF HOLLAND		
*Holland with Boston	C	C
LINCOLNSHIRE—PARTS OF KESTEVEN AND RUTLANDSHIRE		
*Grantham	C	C
*Rutland and Stamford	C	C
LINCOLNSHIRE—PARTS OF LINDSEY		
†Brigg and Scunthorpe	Lab	Lab
*Gainsborough	C	C
†Horncastle	C	C
*Louth	C	C
NORFOLK		
North	C	C
North-West	C	C
South	C	C
†South-West	C	C
Yarmouth	C	C
NORTHAMPTONSHIRE		
Daventry	C	C
Kettering	Lab	Lab
Wellingborough	C	C
NORTHUMBERLAND		
†Berwick-upon-Tweed	L	L
*Hexham	C	C
†Morpeth	Lab	Lab
NOTTINGHAMSHIRE		
Ashfield	Lab	Lab
†Bassetlaw	Lab	Lab
Beeston	C	C
Carlton	C	C
†Mansfield	Lab	Lab
†Newark	Lab	Lab
Rushcliffe	C	C
OXFORDSHIRE		
Banbury	C	C
Henley	C	C
Mid-Oxon	C	C
SHROPSHIRE		
Ludlow	C	C
*Oswestry	C	C
*Shrewsbury	C	C
The Wrekin	Lab	Lab
SOMERSET		
†Bridgwater	C	C
*North	C	C
*Taunton	C	C
*Wells	C	C
†Weston-super-Mare	C	C
*Yeovil	C	C
STAFFORDSHIRE		
†Burton	C	C
Cannock	Lab	Lab
Leek	C	C
Lichfield and Tamworth	C	Lab
South-West	C	C

ENGLAND — COUNTIES (Cont.)

Constituency	1974 (F)	1974 (O)
STAFFORDSHIRE (Cont.)		
*Stafford and Stone	C	C
SUFFOLK		
†Bury St. Edmunds	C	C
†Eye	C	C
†Lowestoft	C	C
†Sudbury and Woodbridge	C	C
SURREY		
†Dorking	C	C
East	C	C
†Farnham	C	C
†Guildford	C	C
North-West	C	C
Woking	C	C
SUSSEX (EAST)		
Eastbourne	C	C
East Grinstead	C	C
Lewes	C	C
Mid	C	C
†Rye	C	C
SUSSEX (WEST)		
Arundel	C	C
Chichester	C	C
Horsham and Crawley	C	C
Shoreham	C	C
WARWICKSHIRE		
Meriden	Lab	Lab
*Rugby	Lab	Lab
*Stratford-on-Avon	C	C
*Warwick and Leamington	C	C
*WESTMORLAND	C	C
WILTSHIRE		
*Chippenham	C	C
*Devizes	C	C
†Salisbury	C	C
*Westbury	C	C
WORCESTERSHIRE		
Bromsgrove and Redditch	C	C
*Kidderminster	C	C
*South	C	C
YORKSHIRE (EAST RIDING)		
*Bridlington	C	C
*Haltemprice	C	C
*Howden	C	C
YORKSHIRE (NORTH RIDING)		
Cleveland and Whitby	C	C
Richmond	C	C
Scarborough	C	C
Thirsk and Malton	C	C
YORKSHIRE (WEST RIDING)		
†Barkston Ash	C	C
†Colne Valley	L	L
†Dearne Valley	Lab	Lab
†Don Valley	Lab	Lab
†Goole	Lab	Lab
†Harrogate	C	C
†Hemsworth	Lab	Lab
†Normanton	Lab	Lab
Penistone	Lab	Lab
†Ripon	C	C
*Rother Valley	Lab	Lab
†Shipley	C	C
†Skipton	C	C
†Sowerby	Lab	Lab

WALES AND MONMOUTHSHIRE —BOROUGHS

Constituency	1974 (F)	1974 (O)
†ABERDARE	Lab	Lab
CARDIFF		
North	C	C
North-West	C	C
South-East	Lab	Lab
West	Lab	Lab
†MERTHYR TYDFIL	Lab	Lab
NEWPORT	Lab	Lab
RHONDDA	Lab	Lab
SWANSEA		
†East	Lab	Lab
†West	Lab	Lab

WALES AND MONMOUTHSHIRE—COUNTIES

Constituency	1974 (F)	1974 (O)
†ANGLESEY	Lab	Lab
†BRECON AND RADNORSHIRE	Lab	Lab
CAERNARVONSHIRE		
†Caernarvon	PC	PC
†Conway	C	C
†CARDIGANSHIRE	L	L
CARMARTHENSHIRE		
†Carmarthen	Lab	PC
†Llanelli	Lab	Lab
DENBIGHSHIRE		
†Denbigh	C	C
†Wrexham	Lab	Lab
FLINTSHIRE		
†East	Lab	Lab
†West	C	C
GLAMORGANSHIRE		
*Aberavon	Lab	Lab
Barry	C	C
*Caerphilly	Lab	Lab
†Gower	Lab	Lab
†Neath	Lab	Lab
*Ogmore	Lab	Lab
†Pontypridd	Lab	Lab
†MERIONETHSHIRE	PC	PC
MONMOUTHSHIRE		
†Abertillery	Lab	Lab
†Bedwellty	Lab	Lab
†Ebbw Vale	Lab	Lab
Monmouth	C	C
†Pontpool	Lab	Lab
†MONTGOMERYSHIRE	L	L
†PEMBROKESHIRE	C	C

SCOTLAND —BURGHS

Constituency	1974 (F)	1974 (O)
ABERDEEN		
*North	Lab	Lab
*South	C	C
*COATBRIDGE AND AIRDRIE	Lab	Lab
DUNDEE		
†East	SNP	SNP
*West	Lab	Lab
EDINBURGH		
Central	Lab	Lab
*East	Lab	Lab
Leith	Lab	Lab
North	C	C
Pentlands	C	C
†South	C	C
West	C	C
GLASGOW		
Cathcart	C	C
Central	Lab	Lab
Craigton	Lab	Lab
Garscadden	Lab	Lab
Govan	Lab	Lab
Hillhead	C	C
Kelvingrove	Lab	Lab
Maryhill	Lab	Lab
†Pollok	Lab	Lab
Provan	Lab	Lab
Queen's Park	Lab	Lab
Shettleston	Lab	Lab
Springburn	Lab	Lab
GREENOCK AND PORT GLASGOW	Lab	Lab
*MOTHERWELL AND WISHAW	Lab	Lab
*PAISLEY	Lab	Lab
*STIRLING, FALKIRK AND GRANGEMOUTH	Lab	Lab

SCOTLAND — COUNTIES

Constituency	1974 (F)	1974 (O)
ABERDEENSHIRE		
†East	SNP	SNP
*West	C	C
ANGUS AND KINCARDINESHIRE		
*North Angus and Mearns	C	C
*South Angus	C	SNP
†ARGYLL	SNP	SNP
AYRSHIRE AND BUTE		
*Ayr	C	C
†Bute and North Ayrshire	C	C
Central Ayrshire	Lab	Lab
Kilmarnock	Lab	Lab
*South Ayrshire	Lab	Lab
†BANFFSHIRE	SNP	SNP
†BERWICKSHIRE AND EAST LOTHIAN	C	Lab
†CAITHNESS AND SUTHERLAND	Lab	Lab
†DUMFRIESSHIRE	C	C
DUNBARTONSHIRE		
Central	Lab	Lab
East	C	SNP
West	Lab	Lab
FIFE		
Central	Lab	Lab
Dunfermline	Lab	Lab

Constituency	1974 (F)	1974 (O)
FIFE (Cont.)		
*East	C	C
Kirkcaldy	Lab	Lab
INVERNESS-SHIRE AND ROSS AND CROMARTY		
†Inverness	L	L
†Ross and Cromarty	C	C
†Western Isles	SNP	SNP
KIRKCUDBRIGHTSHIRE AND WIGTOWNSHIRE		
†Galloway	C	SNP
LANARKSHIRE		
Bothwell	Lab	Lab
East Kilbride	Lab	Lab
Hamilton	Lab	Lab
Lanark	Lab	Lab
North	Lab	Lab
Rutherglen	Lab	Lab
*MIDLOTHIAN	Lab	Lab
†MORAY AND NAIRNSHIRE	SNP	SNP
†ORKNEY AND SHETLAND	L	L
PERTHSHIRE AND KINROSS-SHIRE		
*Kinross and West Perthshire	C	C
*Perth and East Perthshire	C	SNP
RENFREWSHIRE		
East	C	C
West	Lab	Lab
†ROXBURGHSHIRE, SELKIRKSHIRE AND PEEBLESSHIRE	L	L
STIRLINGSHIRE AND CLACKMANNANSHIRE		
*Clackmannan and East Stirlingshire	SNP	SNP
*West Stirlingshire	Lab	Lab
†WEST LOTHIAN	Lab	Lab

NORTHERN IRELAND — BOROUGHS

Constituency	1974 (F)	1974 (O)
BELFAST		
East	VUPP	VUPP
North	UU	UU
South	VUPP	VUPP
West	SDLP	SDLP

NORTHERN IRELAND — COUNTIES

Constituency	1974 (F)	1974 (O)
ANTRIM		
North	DUP	DUP
South	UU	UU
†ARMAGH	UU	UU
DOWN		
North	UU	UU
†South	UU	UU
†FERMANAGH AND SOUTH TYRONE	UU	Ind Rep
†LONDONDERRY	UU	UU
†MID-ULSTER	VUPP	VUPP

Appendix 5   RECORDS AND PRECEDENTS

The following records and precedents have (unless otherwise stated) been established since the introduction of universal suffrage in 1918. University seats and those in Ireland from 1918-22 have been ignored in compiling the records.

RECORDS

Largest Majorities—General Elections (Over 50,000)

Sir A.C. Rawson (Brighton[1], C), 1931	62,253
Rt. Hon. G.C. Tryon (Brighton[1], C), 1931	62,041
Rt. Hon. C.C. Craig (Antrim[1], C), 1924	58,354
Rt. Hon. R.W.H. O'Neill (Antrim[1], C), 1924	58,250
Rt. Hon. Sir P. Cunliffe-Lister (Middlesex, Hendon, C), 1931	51,000
J.B.H. Currie (Down, North, C), 1959	50,734
K. Cunningham (Antrim, South, C), 1959	50,041

Largest Majorities—By-Elections (Over 30,000)

E. Gates (Lancashire, Middleton and Prestwich, C), May 22, 1940	31,618

Smallest Majorities—General Elections (Under 10)

A.J. Flint (Derbyshire, Ilkeston, N Lab) 1931	2
Rt. Hon. F.D. Acland (Devon, Tiverton, L), 1923	3
W. Stamford (Leeds, West, Lab), 1924	3
Sir H. Nicholls, Bt. (Northamptonshire, Peterborough, C), 1966	3
G. Jones (Carmarthenshire, Carmarthen, Lab), 1974(F)	3
Lord Colum Crichton-Stuart (Cheshire, Northwich, C), 1929	4
Hon. G.R. Ward (Worcester, C), 1945	4
Ropner (Durham, Sedgefield, C), 1923	6
L. Gandar-Dower, (Caithness and Sutherland, C), 1945	6
J. Privett (Portsmouth, Central, C) 1922	7
H. Hobden (Brighton, Kemptown, Lab), 1964	7
A. Tyler (Cornwall, Bodmin, L), 1974(F)	9

Smallest Majorities—By-Elections (Under 50)

Sir H.C. Lowther (Cumberland, Penrith and Cockermouth, Co C), May 13, 1921	31
W. Nicholson (Westminster, Abbey, C), March 19, 1924	43

Largest Number of Votes Cast for a Candidate—General Elections (Over 65,000)

Sir A.C. Rawson (Brighton[1], C), 1931	75,205
Rt. Hon. G.C. Tryon (Brighton[1], C), 1931	74,993
Sir R. Blair (Middlesex, Hendon, C), 1935	69,762
F. Entwistle (Bolton[1], C), 1931	66,385
Rt. Hon. Sir P. Cunliffe-Lister (Middlesex, Hendon, C), 1931	66,305

Largest Number of Votes Cast for a Candidate—By-Elections (Over 50,000)

H. Mullan (Down[1], C), June 6, 1946	50,699

Smallest Number of Votes Cast for a Candidate—General Elections (Under 50)

Clyde (Glasgow, Govan, CFMPB) 1974(O)	27
Rao (Camden, Hampstead, Ind), 1974(O)	31
G. Boaks (City of London and Westminster South, Ind), 1974(F)	35
E. Eckley (City of London and Westminster South, Ind), 1974(F)	44
G. Boaks (Lambeth, Streatham, Ind), 1974(F)	45
Ralfe (Brighton, Kemptown, Ind), 1974(O)	47

Smallest Number of Votes Cast for a Candidate—By-Elections (Under 25)

Wort (Perthshire and Kinross-shire, Kinross and West Perthshire, Ind C), November 7, 1963	23

Highest Turnout—General Election

United Kingdom—Fermanagh and South Tyrone, 1951	93.4%
Great Britain—Lancashire, Darwen, 1924	92.7%

Highest Turnout—By-Election

United Kingdom—Mid-Ulster, April 17, 1969	91.5%
Great Britain—Ashton-under-Lyne, October 29, 1928	89.1%

160

Lowest Turnout—General Election

Lambeth, Kennington, 1918[2] 29.7%

Lowest Turnout—By-Election

Poplar, South Poplar, August 12, 1942[3] 9.3%

[1] Two-member seat.

[2] Polling had been delayed in this constituency due to the death of the Conservative candidate. This plus the fact that the 1918 electoral register was notoriously inaccurate helps to explain the very low turnout.

[3] If war-time by-elections are excluded, the 24.9% poll at the Shoreditch and Finsbury by-election on November 27, 1958, is the lowest turnout recorded.

PRECEDENTS

By-Elections

The ebb and flow of political support between General Elections was dramatically shown by the following by-election results:

Kent, Dartford (27/3/20) A Coalition majority of 9,370 at the previous (1918) General Election was turned into a Labour majority of 9,048.

Fulham, East (25/10/33). A Conservative majority of 14,521 at the previous (1931) General Election was turned into a Labour majority of 4,840.

Kent, Orpington (14/3/62). A Conservative majority of 14,760 at the previous (1959) General Election was turned into a Liberal majority of 7,855.

Leyton (21/1/65). A Labour majority of 7,926 at the previous (1964) General Election was turned into a Conservative majority of 205.

Walthamstow, West (21/9/67). A Labour majority of 8,725 at the previous (1966) General Election was turned into a Conservative majority of 62.

Dudley (28/3/68). A Labour majority of 10,022 at the previous (1966) General Election was turned into a Conservative majority of 11,656.

Warwickshire, Meriden (28/3/68). A Labour majority of 4,581 at the previous (1966) General Election was turned into a Conservative majority of 15,263.

Swindon (30/10/69). A Labour majority of 10,443 at the previous (1966) General Election was turned into a Conservative majority of 478.

Worcestershire, Bromsgrove (27/5/71). A Labour majority of 1,868 at the previous (1970) General Election was turned into a Conservative majority of 10,874.

Rochdale (26/10/72). A Labour majority of 5,171 at the previous (1970) General Election was turned into a Liberal majority of 5,093.

Sutton and Cheam (7/12/72). A Conservative majority of 12,696 at the previous (1970) General Election was turned into a Liberal majority of 7,417.

Isle of Ely (26/7/73). A Conservative majority of 9,606 at the previous (1970) General Election was turned into a Liberal majority of 1,470.

Yorkshire, Ripon (26/7/73) A Conservative majority of 12,064 at the previous (1970) General Election was turned into a Liberal majority of 946.

Northumberland, Berwick-upon-Tweed (8/11/73). A Conservative majority of 7,145 at the previous (1970) General Election was turned into a Liberal majority of 57.

Candidates

Anglesey is a Constituency which appears to attract candidates with the same surname. At the General Election of 1955 the Labour,

Liberal and Conservative candidates all shared Hughes as their sur names. At the General Election of 1964 the Conservative, Liberal and Plaid Cymru candidates all had the surname of Jones.

At Bermondsey, Rotherhithe at the General Election of 1918 and at Lincoln at the General Election of 1950, the successful candidate each polled exactly the same number of votes as the combined total votes of their opponents.

There is only one instance of a seven-cornered contest at a General Election—Haringey, Tottenham in 1974(F).

Three by-elections have provided seven-cornered contests—Dorset South (22/11/62), Perthshire and Kinross-shire, Kinross and West Perthshire (7/11/63), Middlesex, Uxbridge (7/12/72).

Counts

Northamptonshire, Peterborough claims the record for the largest number of recounts. At the General Election of 1966 the Conservative candidate, Sir Harmar Nicholls, Bt., was returned with majority of three votes after seven recounts. The first count gave the Labour candidate a majority of 163 and the first recount produced the same result. Uncounted ballot-papers were then discovered in a ballot-box and the recond recount gave Labour a majority of two votes. Third and fourth recounts reversed the position and gave Sir Harmar majorities of two and then six votes. A fifth recount put Labour back in the lead by a single vote but a sixth recount showed Sir Harmar ahead once again, this time with a majority of two vote The seventh and final recount added another vote to Sir Harmar majority.

There were thirty-eight spoilt ballot-papers and counting started at 9.00 a.m. but the result was not declared until 5.30 p.m.

Probably the longest time taken to count ballot-papers and declare result can be claimed by Derbyshire, North-Eastern. At the General Election of 1922 the count commenced at 10.00 a.m. on a Thurs day but was not completed until 1.00 p.m. the following day due to three recounts and four adjustments. The final outcome was majority of five votes for the Labour candidate but after a recount and scrutiny by an Election Court the majority was increased to fifteen votes.

At Derbyshire, Ilkeston at the General Election of 1931, counting commenced immediately after the close of poll and went on until 2.30 a.m. when after four recounts a fifth was demanded. The Returning Officer adjourned the count until 10.30 a.m. and the result—a National Labour majority of two votes—was finally declared at noon.

Electorate

The constituency with the largest ever electorate was Essex, Romford. At the General Election of 1935 there were 167,939

RECORDS AND PRECEDENTS (Cont.)

electors on the Register. At the same election Middlesex, Hendon claimed 164,786 electors. When the last pre-war Electoral Register was published in 1939 the figures had risen to 208,609 at Hendon and 207,101 at Romford. Both constituencies were divided in the redistribution which took place in 1945.

The constituency with the smallest electorate was the City of London, a two-member seat. At the General Election of 1945 there were only 10,851 electors on the Register of whom 6,608 qualified for a vote on account of business premises in the constituency.

Southwark, North holds the record for the smallest electorate in a single-member seat—14,108 electors at the General Election of 1945.

Expenses

The late James Maxton (Glasgow, Bridgeton, ILP) created a record when he retained his seat at the General Election of 1935 and only spent £54 in election expenses.

Forfeited Deposits

The Scottish Universities by-election (22-27/11/46) created an unusual record when out of five candidates, four forfeited their deposits.

From November 1947 until December 1954 no Liberal candidate was able to save his deposit at a by-election.

Historical

At Bewdley at the General Election of 1874, G. Griffith (L) received only one vote in a total poll of 910.

At Launceston at a by-election on July 3, 1874, H.S. Giffard (C) received one vote in a total poll of 651. He had been nominated without his consent.

At Ripon at a by-election on December 22, 1860, F.R. Lees who stood as a Temperance Chartist and Extreme Radical candidate received no votes at all. He did have a number of supporters but apparently they had been led to believe that his opponent, a Liberal, had been returned unopposed and that no poll was being held.

At St. Andrews Burghs at the General Election of 1885, both the Independent Liberal and Liberal candidates polled exactly the same number of votes. As the Returning Officer was not an elector in the constituency he was unable to give a casting vote and he declared both candidates to have been elected. An election petition was lodged and as the result of a scrutiny of the ballot papers the Independent Liberal was declared elected by a majority of two votes.

At Ashton-under-Lyne at the General Election of 1886, both the Conservative and Liberal candidates polled exactly the same number of votes but the Returning Officer gave his casting vote to the Conservative candidate who was declared elected.

At Gloucestershire, Cirencester at a by-election on October 13, 1892, a Conservative was elected with a majority of three votes over his Liberal opponent. As a result of an election petition and scrutiny of the ballot-papers the votes cast for each candidate were found to be equal and a new election was ordered.

At Durham at the General Election of 1895 a Liberal defeated a Liberal-Unionist by one vote. As the result of a subsequent recount prior to the hearing of an election petition, the Liberal majority was increased to three votes.

At Exeter at the General Election of December, 1910, a Liberal defeated a Conservative by four votes. As the result of an election petition and scrutiny of the ballot-papers the seat was awarded to the Conservative candidate who was found to have a majority of one vote.

The Ballot Act of 1872 brought about many changes in election law and provided for the written nomination of candidates and a secret ballot.

The first contested election under the new Act was a by-election at Pontefract on August 15, 1872. The election aroused great interest throughout the country and many people travelled to Pontefract to observe the first British parliamentary election by secret ballot. Polling took place between 8.00 a.m. and 4.00 p.m. and after the count (carried out personally by the Returning Officer) the result was declared just after 8.00 p.m. The Rt. Hon. H.C.E. Childers retained the seat for the Liberals with a majority of 80 votes over his Conservative opponent, Viscount Pollington. There were twenty-three spoilt papers and a turnout of 63.7% in this historic election.

Minorities

At each of the ten General Elections from 1918 to 1951, the successful candidate in the Lancashire, Darwen constituency was returned on a minority vote.

At the General Election of 1922, the successful Conservative candidate at Portsmouth, Central polled only 26.9% of the total votes cast.

Nationalists

The Scottish National Party and Plaid Cymru have each gained surpise victories at by-elections—

At Lanarkshire, Motherwell on April 12, 1945, Dr. R.D. McIntyre (SNP) won the seat from Labour with a majority of 617 votes. The Labour majority at the previous (1935) General Election had been 430 over a Conservative but at the by-election Dr. McIntyre had a straight-fight with Labour due to the electoral truce which existed during the war. The constituency had not previously been contested by a Scottish Nationalist.

At Lanarkshire, Hamilton on November 2, 1967, Mrs. W.M. Ewing (SNP) won the seat from Labour with a majority of 1,799. The Labour majority at the previous (1966) General Election had been 16,576 in a straight-fight with a Conservative. The Scottish National Party had not contested the seat since 1959 when their candidate had forfeited his deposit.

At Glasgow, Govan on November 8, 1973, Mrs. M. Macdonald (SNP) won the seat from Labour with a majority of 571. The Labour majority at the previous (1970) General Election had been 7,142 and the SNP candidate had forfeited his deposit.

At Carmarthenshire, Carmarthen on July 14, 1966, G.R. Evans (PC) won the seat from Labour with a majority of 2,436. The Labour majority at the previous (1966) General Election had been 9,233 in a four-cornered contest in which Evans had secured third place.

Opinion Polls

The first figures to be published of voting intentions in Britain appeared in the *News Chronicle* of March 9, 1939. They were from the British Institute of Public Opinion (now Gallup Poll) and forecast the result of a by-election that day at Batley and Morley.

The BIPO showed the Conservative candidate ahead of Labour with 50.7% to 49.3%. The actual result was a substantial Labour victory by 55.4% to 44.6%, a BIPO error of 6.1%.

Although this was the first published forecast, the BIPO had carried out voting intention surveys at four previous by-elections with a high decree of accuracy, the errors ranging between 0.6% and 1.1%.

Postal Votes

The record for the largest number of postal ballot-papers issued and included in a count is held by Fermanagh and South Tyrone. At the General Election of 1974(O) the number issued was 9,911 (13.9% of the electorate) of which 8,979 (14.2% of the total poll) were included in the count.

If Northern Ireland is excluded, Devon, North holds the record. At the General Election of 1974(O) the number issued was 4,109 (5.6% of the electorate) of which 3,298 (5.6% of the total poll) were included in the count.

Glasgow, Bridgeton holds the record for the smallest postal vote. At the General Election of 1950 there were only 115 postal ballot-

RECORDS AND PRECEDENTS (Cont.)

papers issued and 91 counted. At the General Election of 1966 the number issued increased to 127 but the number included in the count fell to a record low figure of 87.

Spoilt ballot papers

Since statistics relating to spoilt ballot-papers were first compiled for the United Kingdom in 1964, the record for the highest number of spoilt papers is held by Londonderry. At the General Election of 1974(O), 1,820 were rejected of which 1,477 were unmarked or void for uncertainty.

If Northern Ireland is excluded, the highest number of spoilt papers was at Barking, Dagenham at the General Election of 1974(F) when the total was 484. Of this number, 454 were unmarked or void for uncertainty, the majority having the word 'Liberal' written across them.

The lowest number of spoilt papers was at Edinburgh, Leith at the General Election of 1974(O) when only 9 were rejected.

Turnout

There was so much local interest in the result of the Ashton-under-Lyne by-election (29/10/28) that the Mayor arranged for coloured rockets indicating the party of the successful candidate to be fired from the roof of the Town Hall. The by-election resulted in a Labour victory and yellow rockets (the local Labour colour) were fired which could be seen throughout the town by the many people awaiting the result. Despite a steady downpour of rain throughout polling day the by-election achieved a turnout of 89.1%, a record for a by-election which has never been exceeded in Great Britain.

At the five General Elections from 1922 to 1931, the turnout at Lancashire, Darwen always exceeded 90.0%.

Camberwell, North holds the record for the smallest number of votes cast in a parliamentary election. At a by-election on March 30, 1944, two candidates polled a total of only 3,329 votes. The turnout was 11.2%.

Victory and Defeat

The most overwhelming victory ever recorded at a General Election was at Down, North in 1959. The Conservative candidate received 98.0% of the total votes cast. At a by-election on May 22, 1940 at Lancashire, Middleton and Prestwich, the Conservative candidate received 98.7% of the total votes cast.

When M.R. Bonham Carter gained a seat for the Liberals at Devon, Torrington (27/3/58) it was the first Liberal gain at a by-election for twenty-nine years. The previous occasion had been at Lincolnshire, Holland with Boston on March 21, 1929.

When N. MacDermot (Lab) won Lewisham, North (14/2/57) from the Conservatives it was the first time that Labour had gained a seat from the Conservatives at a by-election for over seventeen years. The previous occasion had been at Lambeth, Kennington on May 24, 1939.

One of the most humiliating defeats ever suffered by a Government at a by-election took place at Kent, Dartford on March 27, 1920. At the previous (1918) General Election a Coalition Liberal candidate had won the seat in a straight-fight with Labour with a majority of 9,370. At the five-cornered by-election contest Labour gained the seat with a majority of 9,048, the Coalition candidate (this time a Conservative) taking third place. The Coalition vote fell from 71.4% to 15.5% and the Labour vote went up from 28.6% to 50.2%.

When the Conservatives won Sunderland, South (13/5/53) it was the first occasion since 1924 that a Government had won a seat from the Opposition at a by-election and only two such previous victories had been recorded since 1918. These were Liverpool, West Toxteth (22/5/24) when Labour won the seat from the Conservatives and Woolwich, East (2/3/21) when the Conservatives won the seat from Labour.

There has been only one occasion since 1953 that a Government has won a seat from the Opposition at a by-election. This was at Brighouse and Spenborough (17/3/60) when a National Liberal and Conservative candidate won the seat from Labour.

Women

Dame Irene Ward (Tynemouth, C) was a member of the House of Commons longer than any other woman. She was first elected for Wallsend in 1931 and retained her seat until defeated in 1945. In 1950 she was elected for Tynemouth and retired in 1974(F). She fought a total of twelve contested elections.

The late Lady Megan Lloyd George was a member of the House of Commons for a total of thirty-one years and fought ten contested elections. She was Liberal member for Anglesey from 1929 until she was defeated in 1951. In 1957 she was elected at a by-election as Labour member for Carmarthenshire, Carmarthen and retained the seat until her death in 1966.

Miss Jennie Lee was first elected for Lanarkshire, Northern at a by-election in 1929 but was defeated at the General Election of 1931. She was elected for Staffordshire, Cannock in 1945 and retained the seat until she was defeated in 1970. She fought thirteen elections, a record for a woman candidate.

Appendix 6 WOMEN MEMBERS OF PARLIAMENT

The following is a complete list of women elected to the House of Commons since 1918 showing their party and period of service. A dagger † denotes a member of the present Parliament.

Adamson, Mrs. J.L. (Lab), 1938-46
Apsley, Lady (C), 1943-45
Astor, Viscountess[1] (C), 1919-45
Atholl, Duchess of (C), 1923-38
Bacon, Miss A.M. (Lab), 1945-70
†Bain, Mrs. M.A. (SNP), 1974(O)-
Bentham, Dr. Ethel (Lab), 1929-31
Bondfield, Miss M.G. (Lab), 1923-24 and 1926-31
†Boothroyd, Miss B. (Lab), 1973-
Braddock, Mrs. E.M. (Lab), 1945-70
Burton, Miss E.F. (Lab), 1950-59
†Butler, Mrs. J.S. (Lab), 1955-
†Castle, Mrs. B.A. (Lab), 1945-
Cazalet, Miss T., see Cazalet-Keir, Mrs. T.
Cazalet-Keir, Mrs. T. (C), 1931-45
†Chalker, Mrs. L. (C), 1974(F)-
Colman, Miss G.M. (Lab), 1945-50
†Colquhoun, Mrs. M.M. (Lab), 1974(F)-
Copeland, Mrs. I. (C), 1931-35
Corbet, Mrs. F.K. (Lab), 1945-74(F)
Cullen, Mrs. A. (Lab), 1948-69
Dalton, Mrs. F.R. (Lab), February-May, 1929
Davidson, Viscountess (C), 1937-59
Devlin, Miss B.J. see McAliskey, Mrs. B.J.
†Dunwoody, Hon. Mrs. G.P. (Lab), 1966-70 and 1974(F)-
Emmet, Hon. Mrs. E.V.E. (C), 1955-65
†Ewing, Mrs. W.M. (SNP), 1967-70 and 1974(F)-
Fenner, Mrs. P.E. (C), 1970-74(O)
Fisher, Mrs. D.M.G. (Lab), 1970-74(F)
†Fookes, Miss J.E. (C), 1970-
Ford, Mrs. P. (C), 1953-55
Gammans, Lady (C), 1957-66
Ganley, Mrs. C.S. (Lab), 1945-51
Gould, Mrs. B.A. (Lab), 1945-50
Grant, Lady, see Tweedsmuir, Lady
Graves, Miss F.M. (C), 1931-35
Hall, Miss J.V. (C), 1970-74(F)
Hamilton, Mrs. M.A. (Lab), 1929-31
Hardie, Mrs. A. (Lab), 1937-45
†Hart, Mrs. J.C.M. (Lab), 1959-
†Harvie Anderson, Miss M.B. (C), 1959-
†Hayman, Mrs. H.V. (Lab), 1974(O)-
Herbison, Miss M.M. (Lab), 1945-70
Hill, Mrs. E. (C), 1950-64
Holt, Miss M. (C), 1970-74(F)
Hornsby-Smith, Dame Patricia (C), 1950-66 and 1970-74(F)
Horsbrugh, Dame Florence (C), 1931-45 and 1950-59
Iveagh, Countess of (C), 1927-35
†Jackson, Miss M.M. (Lab), 1974(O)-
†Jeger, Mrs. L.M. (Lab), 1953-59 and 1964-
Jewson, Miss D. (Lab), 1923-24
Kellett, Mrs. M.E. see Kellett-Bowman, Mrs. M.E.
†Kellett-Bowman, Mrs. M.E. (C), 1970-
Kerr, Mrs. A.P. (Lab), 1964-70
†Knight, Mrs. J.C.J. (C), 1966-

Lawrence, Miss A.S. (Lab), 1923-24 and 1926-31
Lee, Miss J. (Lab), 1929-31 and 1945-70
†Lestor, Miss J. (Lab), 1966-
Lloyd George, Lady Megan (L), 1929-51 and (Lab), 1957-66
McAliskey, Mrs. B.J.[2] (Unity then Ind Soc), 1969-74(F)
McAlister, Mrs. M.A. (Lab), 1958-59
Macdonald, Mrs. M. (SNP), 1973-74(F)
McKay, Mrs. M. (Lab), 1964-70
McLaughlin, Mrs. F.P.A. (C), 1955-64
Mann, Mrs. J. (Lab), 1945-59
Manning, Mrs. E.L. (Lab), February-October, 1931 and 1945-50
Markievicz, Countess[3] (SF), 1918-22
†Maynard, Miss V.J. (Lab), 1974(O)-
Middleton, Mrs. L.A. (Lab), 1945-51
Middleweek, Miss H.V., see Hayman, Mrs. H.V.
†Miller, Mrs. M. (Lab), 1974(O)-
Monks, Mrs. C.M. (C), 1970-74(F)
Mosley, Lady Cynthia (Lab), 1929-31
Nichol, Mrs. M.E. (Lab), 1945-50 •
Noel-Buxton, Lady (Lab), 1930-31 and 1945-50
†Oppenheim, Mrs. S. (C), 1970-
Paton, Mrs. F.B. (Lab), 1945-50
Phillipson, Mrs. M. (C), 1923-29
Phillips, Dr. Marion (Lab), 1929-31
Pickford, Hon. Mary A. (C), 1931-34
Picton-Turberville, Miss E. (Lab), 1929-31
Pike, Miss I.M.P. (C), 1956-74(F)
Pitt, Dame Edith (C), 1953-64
Quennell, Miss J.M. (C), 1960-74(O)
Rathbone, Mrs. B.F., see Wright, Mrs. B.F.
Rathbone, Miss E.F. (Ind), 1929-46
Rees, Mrs. D.M. (Lab), 1950-51
†Richardson, Miss J. (Lab), 1974(F)-
Ridealgh, Mrs. M. (Lab), 1945-50
Runciman, Mrs. H. (L), 1928-29
Runge, Mrs. N.C. (C), 1931-35
Shaw, Mrs. C.M. (Lab), 1945-46
Shaw, Mrs. H.B. (C), 1931-45
†Short, Mrs. R. (Lab), 1964-
Slater, Mrs. H. (Lab), 1953-66
Summerskill, Dr. Edith (Lab), 1938-61
†Summerskill, Dr. Hon. Shirley C.W. (Lab), 1964-
Tate, Mrs. M.C. (C), 1931-45
†Taylor, Mrs. W.A. (Lab), 1974(O)-
Terrington, Lady (L), 1923-24
†Thatcher, Mrs. M.H. (C), 1959-
Tweedsmuir, Lady (C), 1946-66
Vickers, Dame Joan (C), 1955-74(F)
Ward, Dame Irene (C), 1931-45 and 1950-74(F)
Ward, Mrs. S.A. (C), 1931-35
White, Mrs. E.L. (Lab), 1950-70
Wilkinson, Miss E.C. (Lab), 1924-31 and 1935-47
†Williams, Mrs. S.V.T.B. (Lab), 1964-
Wills, Mrs. E.A. (Lab), 1945-50
Wintringham, Mrs. M. (L), 1921-24
†Wise, Mrs. A. (Lab), 1974(F)-
Wright, Mrs. B.F. (C), 1941-45

[1] The first woman to take her seat (December 1, 1919) in the House of Commons.

[2] The youngest woman to have been elected. Miss Devlin (as she was at the time) was twenty-one years of age and had been born on April 23, 1947. She was elected on April 17, 1969.

[3] The first woman to be elected (December 28, 1918) but she did not take her seat in the House of Commons.

Appendix 7 REASONS FOR HOLDING GENERAL ELECTIONS

1885
Resignation of the Liberal Government and request for a Dissolution after a defeat in the House of Commons on an amendment to the Finance Bill. The Marquess of Salisbury formed a minority Conservative Government but within five months he requested a Dissolution.

1886
Resignation of the Liberal Government and request for a Dissolution after a defeat in the House of Commons on the Irish Home Rule Bill.

1892
Request by the Prime Minister for a Dissolution on Parliament nearing the end of its statutory term of seven years.

1895
Resignation of the Liberal Government after a defeat in the House of Commons on the issue of the supply of cordite to the Army. The Marquess of Salisbury formed a minority Conservative Government and immediately requested a Dissolution.

1900
Request by the Prime Minister for a Dissolution to obtain a renewal of the electors' confidence in the Government at a time when it appeared that the South African War was drawing to a close.

1906
Resignation of the Conservative Government after a series of defeats in by-elections and internal disputes over tariff reform. Sir Henry Campbell-Bannerman formed a minority Liberal Government and immediately requested a Dissolution.

1910(J)
Request by the Prime Minister for a Dissolution after the House of Lords had rejected the Finance Bill.

1910(D)
Request by the Prime Minister for a Dissolution after a Constitutional Conference of Liberal and Conservative members had failed to agree on proposals to limit the power of the House of Lords.

1918
End of World War 1. Parliament should have been dissolved in 1915 but its life was extended due to the war.

1922
Lloyd George resigned as Prime Minister of a Coalition Government and Bonar Law formed a Conservative Government and immediately asked for a Dissolution.

1923
Bonar Law resigned as Prime Minister and was succeeded by Baldwin who within six months asked for a Dissolution to obtain a mandate for tariff reforms.

1924
Resignation of the Labour Government and request for a Dissolution after a defeat in the House of Commons on the issue of the Government's decision not to prosecute J.R. Campbell, editor of a Communist Party journal, under the Incitement to Mutiny Act.

1929
Request by the Prime Minister for a Dissolution on Parliament nearing the end of its statutory term of five years.

1931
Resignation of the Labour Government and formation of a National Government by Ramsay MacDonald who six weeks later asked for a Dissolution in order to obtain a new mandate.

1935
Request by the Prime Minister for a Dissolution on Parliament nearing the end of its statutory term of five years.

1945
End of War in Europe. Parliament should have been dissolved in 1940 but its life was extended due to the war.

1950
Request by the Prime Minister for a Dissolution on Parliament nearing the end of its statutory term of five years.

1951
Request by the Prime Minister for a Dissolution to obtain a renewal of the electors' confidence in the Government and an adequate parliamentary majority

1955
Winston Churchill resigned as Prime Minister and was succeeded by Sir Anthony Eden who immediately asked for a Dissolution.

1959
Request by the Prime Minister for a Dissolution on Parliament nearing the end of its statutory term of five years.

1964
Request by the Prime Minister for a Dissolution on Parliament nearing the end of its statutory term of five years.

1966
Request by the Prime Minister for a Dissolution to obtain a renewal of the electors' confidence in the Government and an adequate parliamentary majority.

1970
Request by the Prime Minister for a Dissolution on Parliament nearing the end of its statutory term of five years.

1974(F)
Request by the Prime Minister for a Dissolution to obtain a renewal of the electors' confidence in the Government on the eve of a strike by the National Union of Mineworkers.

1974(O)
Request by the Prime Minister for a Dissolution to obtain a renewal of the electors' confidence in the Government and an overall parliamentary majority.

Appendix 8   SEATS VACANT AT DISSOLUTIONS

1886
No seat vacant

1892
Essex, Epping (C)
Lambeth, Norwood (C)
Pembroke and Haverfordwest Boroughs (C)
Swansea Town (L)

1895
No seat vacant

1900
Armagh, South (N)

1906
Cambridge University (C)
Montgomeryshire (L)

1910 (J)
Ipswich (L)
Kensington, South (C)
Liverpool, Exchange (L)
Middlesex, Uxbridge (C)
Portsmouth (L)
Tipperary, Mid (N)

1910 (D)
Carmarthenshire, Western (L)
Kerry, East (Ind N)
Lancashire, Clitheroe (Lab)

1918
Belfast, North (C)
Cork, North-East (Ind N)
Fulham (C)
Staffordshire, Western (C)
Surrey, Kingston (C)
Surrey, Reigate (Nat P)

1922
Roxburghshire and Selkirkshire (Co L)

1923
Ayrshire and Bute, Kilmarnock (L)
Glasgow, Central (C)
University of Wales (NL)
Warwickshire, Warwick and Leamington (C)

1924
London University (C)

1929
Buckinghamshire, Aylesbury (C)
Cambridge University (C)
Carlisle (C)
Lancashire, Ince (Lab)
Nottinghamshire, Mansfield (Lab)
Preston (one seat) (C)
Willesden, East (C)
Yorkshire, Thirsk and Malton (C)

1931
Gateshead[1] (Lab)
Yorkshire, Hemsworth (Lab)

1935
Derbyshire, Clay Cross (Lab)
Essex, Harwich (NL)
Hammersmith, North (Lab)

[1] Member died on the day of Dissolution.

Holborn[1] (C)
Lancashire, Farnworth (C)
Roxburghshire and Selkirkshire (C)

1945
Antrim (one seat) (C)
Bradford, East (C)
Bristol, North (NL)
Cardiganshire (L)
Hythe (C)
Wednesbury (Lab)
Yorkshire, Rother Valley (Lab)

1950
Deptford (Lab)
Durham, Chester-le-Street (Lab)
Islington, North (Lab)
Manchester, Ardwick (Lab)
Rotherham (Lab)
Sheffield, Hillsborough (Lab)
Sheffield, Park (Lab)

1951
Droylsden (Lab)
Lanarkshire, Lanark (C)
Lincolnshire, Grantham (C)

1955
Glasgow, Pollok (C)
Kent, Gravesend (Lab)
Norwich, South (C)

1959
Birmingham, Sparkbrook (Lab)
Kensington, South (C)
Lancashire, Clitheroe (C)
Midlothian (Lab)
Nottingham, North (Lab)
Yorkshire, Richmond (C)

1964
Ashton-under-Lyne (Lab)
Bebington (C)
Berkshire, Newbury (C)
Blackpool, South (C)
Cheshire, Runcorn (C)
Edinburgh, Pentlands (C)
Norfolk, North (Lab)
Northamptonshire, Kettering (Lab)
Renfrewshire, West (NL & C)
Salford, West (Lab)
Shoreditch and Finsbury (Lab)
Southgate (C)
Surrey, Woking (C)
Westmorland (C)

1966
Birmingham, Edgbaston (C)
Cornwall, Falmouth and Camborne (Lab)

1970
Northumberland, Morpeth (Lab)
Twickenham (C)

1974 (F)
Worcestershire, South (C)

1974 (O)
Newcastle upon Tyne, East (Lab)
Swansea, East (Lab)

Appendix 9 THE FIRST RESULT

Since 1918 when polling in all constituencies at a General Election took place on the same day, there has always been keen competition between Returning Officers to provide the first result declared.

The following constituencies provided the first result of each General Election and from 1950 the actual time of declaration is given.

Election	Constituency	Election	Constituency
1918	Salford, North	1951	Salford, West (10.21 p.m.)
1922	Wallasey	1955	Cheltenham (10.08 p.m.)
1923	Manchester, Exchange		Salford, West (10.08 p.m.)
1924	Salford, South	1959	Billericay (9.57 p.m.)
1929	Oxford	1964	Cheltenham (10.00 p.m.)
1931	Hornsey	1966	Cheltenham (10.04 p.m.)
1935	Cheltenham	1970	Guildford (11.10 p.m.)
1945	Salford, South	1974 (F)	Guildford (11.10 p.m.)
1950	Salford, West (10.45 p.m.)	1974 (O)	Guildford (11.10 p.m.)

Sources: The Press Association, *The Times,* local newspapers.

Appendix 10 THE WEATHER ON POLLING DAY 1945–1974

Election	Weather
1945	Clear and fair.
1950	Sunny and mild until evening then heavy rain.
1951	Light fog and frost in the morning but clearing and remaining generally fair.
1955	Generally fine and sunny but with some showers in the evening.
1959	A dry autumn day.
1964	Rain over much of the country.
1966	Mild day with only a trace of rain anywhere except in the North of Scotland.
1970	Fine everywhere.
1974(F)	Some rain in all parts of the country but especially in the south-west.
1974(O)	Cloudy with showers in some parts but few instances of heavy rain.

Source: Nuffield College studies of British General Elections.

Appendix 11 THE ELECTORAL REGISTER

DATES ON WHICH REGISTERS CAME INTO FORCE

England, Wales and Scotland

1885:	November 8 (Scotland, November 1)
1887-1915:	January 1 (Scotland, November 1, 1886)
1918:	October 15
1919-1920:	May 15 and October 15
1921-1926:	April 15 and October 15
1927-1928:	October 15
1929:	May 1 (special register under the Equal Franchise Act, 1928)
1930-1938:	October 15
1939:	November 15
1945:	May 7 and October 15. Supplementary register of service voters and those who had ceased to be members of H.M. Forces, March 1, 1946.
1946-1949:	October 15
1950-1954:	March 16
1955-	February 16

Ireland (Northern Ireland)

1885:	November 7
1887-1915:	January 1
1918-1921:	October 15
1922-1928:	December 15
1929:	May 1 (special register under the Equal Franchise Act, 1928)
1930-1939:	December 15
1945:	May 7 and October 15. Supplementary register of service voters and those who had ceased to be members of H.M. Forces, March 1, 1946.
1946-1949:	October 15
1950-1954:	April 2
1955-	February 16

PRINCIPAL SOURCES OF PUBLISHED STATISTICS

(Reference to Parliamentary Papers are to the House of Commons Bound Sets of Sessional Papers and indicate the session, the paper number of the session, the bound volume number and the page number within the bound volume.)

England and Wales

1885 :	*Parliamentary Constituencies; (Electors &c) (United Kingdom):* 1886 (47) lii, 641.
1887 :	*Parliamentary Constituencies; (Electors &c) (United Kingdom);* 1887 (124) lxvi, 124.
1888 :	*Parliamentary Constituencies; (Electors &c) (United Kingdom);* 1888 (144) lxxix, 895.
1889 :	*Parliamentary Constituencies; (Electors &c) (United Kingdom);* 1889 (179) lx, 257.
1890 :	*Parliamentary Constituencies; (Electors &c) (United Kingdom);* 1890 (368) lvii, 287.
1891 :	*Parliamentary Constituencies; (Electors &c) (United Kingdom);* 1890-91 (316) lxii, 263.
1892 :	*Parliamentary Constituencies; (Electors &c) (United Kingdom);* 1892 (244) lxiii, 351.
1893 :	*Parliamentary Constituencies; (Electors &c) (United Kingdom);* 1893 (365)lxx, 675.
1894 :	*Parliamentary Constituencies; (Electors &c) (United Kingdom);* 1894 (89) lxviii, 291.
1895 :	*Parliamentary Constituencies; (Electors &c) (United Kingdom);* 1895 (288) lxxix, 287.
1896 :	*Parliamentary Constituencies; (Electors &c) (United Kingdom);* 1896 (76) lxvii, 281.
1897 :	*Parliamentary Constituencies; (Electors &c) (United Kingdom);* 1897 (131) lxxii, 283.
1898 :	*Parliamentary Constituencies; (Electors &c) (United Kingdom);* 1898 (72) lxxii, 283.
1899 :	*Parliamentary Constituencies; (Electors &c) (United Kingdom);* 1899 (78) lxxvii, 263.
1900 :	*Parliamentary Constituencies; (Electors &c) (United Kingdom);* 1900 (116) lxvii, 445.
1901 :	*Parliamentary Constituencies; (Electors &c) (United Kingdom);* 1901 (85) lix, 115.
1902 :	*Parliamentary Constituencies; (Electors &c) (United Kingdom);* 1902 (70) lxxxii, 435.
1903 :	*Parliamentary Constituencies; (Electors &c) (United Kingdom);* 1903 (34) liv, 289.
1904 :	*Parliamentary Constituencies; (Electors &c) (United Kingdom);* 1904 (69) lxxviii, 315.
1905 :	*Parliamentary Constituencies; (Electors &c) (United Kingdom);* 1905 (50) lxii, 333.
1906 :	*Parliamentary Constituencies; (Electors &c) (United Kingdom);* 1906 (Cd. 2807) xciv, 837.
1907 :	*Parliamentary Constituencies; (Electors &c) (United Kingdom);* 1907 (22) lxvi, 469.
1908 :	*Parliamentary Constituencies; (Electors &c) (United Kingdom);* 1908 (44) lxxxvii, 875.
1909 :	*Parliamentary Constituencies;(Electors &c) (United Kingdom);* 1909 (64) lxx, 475.
1910 :	*Parliamentary Constituencies; (Electors &c) (United Kingdom);* 1910 (Cd. 4975) lxxiii, 685.

PRINCIPAL SOURCES OF PUBLISHED STATISTICS (Cont.)

England and Wales

1911:	*Parliamentary Constituencies; (Electors &c) (United Kingdom); 1911 (69) lxii, 679.*
1912:	*Parliamentary Constituencies; (Electors &c) (United Kingdom); 1912-13 (53) lxvii, 483.*
1913:	*Parliamentary Constituencies; (Electors &c) (United Kingdom); 1912-13 (478) lxvii, 503.*
1914:	*Parliamentary Constituencies; (Electors &c) (United Kingdom); 1914 (109) lxv, 453.*
1915:	*Parliamentary Constituencies; (Electors &c) (United Kingdom); 1914-16 (120) lii, 585.*
1918:	*Parliamentary and Local Government Electors (United Kingdom); 1918 (138) xix, 925.*
1919 (autumn):	*Parliamentary and Local Government Electors (United Kingdom); 1919 (242) xl, 797.*
1921 (spring):	*Preliminary Report of the Census of England and Wales, 1921; 1921 (Cmd. 1485) xvi, 257.*
1921-39 (autumn):	*Registrar-General's Statistical Review of England and Wales, Tables, Part 2, Civil.*
1939:	*Parliamentary Constituencies (Electors) (England and Wales); 1943-44 (10) viii, 427.*
1945 (spring):	*Parliamentary Constituencies (Electors) (England and Wales); 1944-45 (107) x, 299.*
1945 (autumn):	*Parliamentary Constituencies (Electors) (England, Wales and Northern Ireland) and Local Government Areas (Electors) (England and Wales); 1945-46 (88) xx, 547.*
1946 (autumn):	*Parliamentary Constituencies (Electors) (England, Wales and Northern Ireland) and Local Government Areas (Electors) (England and Wales); 1946-47 (106) xix, 509.*
1945—	*Registrar-General's Statistical Review of England and Wales, Part 2. Tables, Civil (until 1957), Population (from 1958).*
1974—	*Electoral Statistics (Office of Population Censuses and Surveys).*

Scotland

1918:	as England and Wales, *q.v.*
1919 (autumn):	as England and Wales, *q.v.*
1921 (spring):	*Preliminary Report of the Census of Scotland, 1921; 1921 (Cmd. 1473) xvi, 341.*
1939:	*Parliamentary Constituencies (Electors) (Scotland); 1943-44 (21) viii, 435.*
1945 (spring):	*Parliamentary Constituencies (Electors) (Scotland); 1944-45 (109) x, 313.*
1945 (autumn):	*Parliamentary Constituencies and Local Government Areas (Electors) (Scotland); 1945-46 (91) xx, 597.*
1946:	*Parliamentary Electors and Local Government Areas (Electors) (Scotland); 1946-47 (107) xix, 543.*
1945—	*Registrar-General for Scotland, Annual Report, Part 2. Population and Vital Statistics (from 1968).*

Northern Ireland

1945 (autumn):	as England and Wales, *q.v.*
1946:	as England and Wales, *q.v.*
1949—	*Ulster Year Book* (H.M. Stationery Office, Belfast). Published every three years until 1968 then annually.

Appendix 12 ELECTORATE CALCULATOR[1]

February	March	April	May	June	July	August	September	October	November	December	January	February
16– 0	1–13	1–44	1–74	1–105	1–135	1–166	1–197	1–227	1–258	1–288	1–319	1–350
17– 1	2–14	2–45	2–75	2–106	2–136	2–167	2–198	2–228	2–259	2–289	2–320	2–351
18– 2	3–15	3–46	3–76	3–107	3–137	3–168	3–199	3–229	3–260	3–290	3–321	3–352
19– 3	4–16	4–47	4–77	4–108	4–138	4–169	4–200	4–230	4–261	4–291	4–322	4–353
20– 4	5–17	5–48	5–78	5–109	5–139	5–170	5–201	5–231	5–262	5–292	5–323	4–353
21– 5	6–18	6–49	6–79	6–110	6–140	6–171	6–202	6–232	6–263	6–293	6–324	6–355
22– 6	7–19	7–50	7–80	7–111	7–141	7–172	7–203	7–233	7–264	7–294	7–325	7–356
23– 7	8–20	8–51	8–81	8–112	8–142	8–173	8–204	8–234	8–265	8–295	8–326	8–357
24– 8	9–21	9–52	9–82	9–113	9–143	9–174	9–205	9–235	9–266	9–296	9–327	9–358
25– 9	10–22	10–53	10–83	10–114	10–144	10–175	10–206	10–236	10–267	10–297	10–328	10–359
26–10	11–23	11–54	11–84	11–115	11–145	11–176	11–207	11–237	11–268	11–298	11–329	11–360
27–11	12–24	12–55	12–85	12–116	12–146	12–177	12–208	12–238	12–269	12–299	12–330	12–361
28–12	13–25	13–56	13–86	13–117	13–147	13–178	13–209	13–239	13–270	13–300	13–331	13–362
	14–26	14–57	14–87	14–118	14–148	14–179	14–210	14–240	14–271	14–301	14–332	14–363
	15–27	15–58	15–88	15–119	15–149	15–180	15–211	15–241	15–272	15–302	15–333	15–364
	16–28	16–59	16–89	16–120	16–150	16–181	16–212	16–242	16–273	16–303	16–334	
	17–29	17–60	17–90	17–121	17–151	17–182	17–213	17–243	17–274	17–304	17–335	
	18–30	18–61	18–91	18–122	18–152	18–183	18–214	18–244	18–275	18–305	18–336	
	19–31	19–62	19–92	19–123	19–153	19–184	19–215	19–245	19–276	19–306	19–337	
	20–32	20–63	20–93	20–124	20–154	20–185	20–216	20–246	20–277	20–307	20–338	
	21–33	21–64	21–94	21–125	21–155	21–186	21–217	21–247	21–278	21–308	21–339	
	22–34	22–65	22–95	22–126	22–156	22–187	22–218	22–248	22–279	22–309	22–340	
	23–35	23–66	23–96	23–127	23–157	23–188	23–219	23–249	23–280	23–310	23–341	
	24–36	24–67	24–97	24–128	24–158	24–189	24–220	24–250	24–281	24–311	24–342	
	25–37	25–68	25–98	25–129	25–159	25–190	25–221	25–251	25–282	25–312	25–343	
	26–38	26–69	26–99	26–130	26–160	26–191	26–222	26–252	26–283	26–313	26–344	
	27–39	27–70	27–100	27–131	27–161	27–192	27–223	27–253	27–284	27–314	27–345	
	28–40	28–71	28–101	28–132	28–162	28–193	28–224	28–254	28–285	28–315	28–346	
	29–41	29–72	29–102	29–133	29–163	29–194	29–225	29–255	29–286	29–316	29–347	
	30–42	30–73	30–103	30–134	30–164	30–195	30–226	30–256	30–287	30–317	30–348	
	31–43		31–104		31–165	31–196		31–257		31–318	31–349	

[1]This calendar shows the number of days the Electoral Register has been in force from its publication on February 16 in each year. For Leap Years (1976 and every fourth year therafter) February 29 becomes Day 13 and all following consecutive numbers should be increased by one.

For an explanation of the use of this calendar see the entry under 'Electorate' in the Introductory Notes.

169

Appendix 13 REFERENDUM ON UNITED KINGDOM MEMBERSHIP OF THE EUROPEAN ECONOMIC COMMUNITY — June 5, 1975

	Civilian Electorate	Civilian T'out %[1]	Yes	%	No	%	Service Votes	Spoilt Ballot Papers
ENGLAND	**33,356,208**	**64.6**	**14,918,009**	**68.7**	**6,812,052**	**31.3**	**207,465**	**42,161**
Avon	665,484	68.7	310,145	67.8	147,024	32.2	499	635
Bedfordshire	326,566	67.9	154,338	69.4	67,969	30.6	829	385
Berkshire	443,472	66.4	215,184	72.6	81,221	27.4	2,666	571
Buckinghamshire	346,348	69.5	180,512	74.3	62,578	25.7	2,643	357
Cambridgeshire	375,753	62.9	177,789	74.1	62,143	25.9	3,840	354
Cheshire	633,614	65.5	290,714	70.1	123,839	29.9	128	663
Cleveland	392,672	60.2	158,982	67.3	77,079	32.7	47	308
Cornwall	298,706	66.8	137,828	68.5	63,478	31.5	2,321	572
Cumbria	349,596	64.8	162,545	71.9	63,564	28.1	83	415
Derbyshire	653,005	64.1	286,614	68.6	131,452	31.4	NIL	687
Devon	676,378	68.0	334,244	72.1	129,179	27.9	4,239	991
Dorset	429,752	68.3	217,432	73.5	78,239	26.5	3,200	976
Durham	444,783	61.5	175,284	64.2	97,724	35.8	24	453
East Sussex	511,437	65.8	249,780	74.3	86,198	25.7	104	775
Essex	1,010,317	67.7	463,505	67.6	222,085	32.4	2,648	1,119
Gloucestershire	347,218	68.4	170.931	71.7	67,465	28.3	1,304	504
Greater London	5,250,343	60.8	2,201,031	66.7	1,100,185	33.3	114,900	6,874
Greater Manchester	1,932,717	64.1	797,316	64.5	439,191	35.5	82	2,843
Hampshire	975,440	68.0	484,302	71.0	197,761	29.0	20,142	1,379
Hereford and Worcester	419,866	66.4	203,128	72.8	75,779	27.2	867	642
Hertfordshire	662,177	70.2	326,943	70.4	137,266	29.6	621	1,239
Humberside	607,890	62.4	257,826	67.8	122,199	32.2	1,207	765
Isles of Scilly	1,447	75.0	802	74.5	275	25.5	NIL	8
Isle of Wight	86,381	67.5	40,837	70.2	17,375	27.8	NIL	116
Kent	1,035,313	67.4	493,407	70.4	207,358	29.6	3,653	1,120
Lancashire	1,000,755	66.4	455,170	68.6	208,821	31.4	460	1,302
Leicestershire	590,780	67.2	291,500	73.3	106,004	26.7	1,557	835
Lincolnshire	370,518	63.7	180,603	74.7	61,011	25.3	6,149	445
Merseyside	1,147,920	62.7	465,625	64.8	252,712	35.2	138	1,602
Norfolk	485,229	63.8	218,883	70.1	93,198	29.9	3,016	605
Northamptonshire	351,653	66.7	162,803	69.5	71,322	30.5	166	507
Northumberland	212,846	65.0	95,980	69.2	42,645	30.8	401	231
North Yorkshire	468,998	64.3	234,040	76.3	72,805	23.7	5,853	738
Nottinghamshire	705,183	63.1	297,191	66.8	147,461	33.2	550	1,052
Oxfordshire	355,977	67.7	179,938	73.6	64,643	26.4	4,065	449
Salop	249,463	62.0	113,044	72.3	43,329	27.7	1,860	238
Somerset	293,191	67.7	138,830	69.6	60,631	30.4	1,251	300
South Yorkshire	954,539	62.4	377,916	63.4	217,792	36.6	941	1,060
Staffordshire	706,230	64.3	306,518	67.4	148,252	32.6	973	657
Suffolk	397,626	64.9	187,484	72.2	72,251	27.8	1,993	472
Surrey	720,440	70.1	386,369	76.2	120,578	23.8	2,518	770
Tyne and Wear	872,253	62.7	344,069	62.9	202,511	37.1	110	469
Warwickshire	327,967	68.0	156,303	69.9	67,221	30.1	879	391
West Midlands	1,972,987	62.5	801,913	65.1	429,207	34.9	NIL	2,153
West Sussex	464,396	68.6	242,890	76.2	75,928	23.8	750	719
West Yorkshire	1,485,749	63.6	616,730	65.4	326,993	34.6	65	1,860
Wiltshire	344,833	67.8	172,791	71.7	68,113	28.3	7,723	555

REFERENDUM ON UNITED KINGDOM MEMBERSHIP OF THE EUROPEAN ECONOMIC COMMUNITY (Cont.)

	Civilian Electorate	Civilian T'out %[1]	Yes	%	No	%	Service Votes	Spoilt Ballot Papers
WALES	2,011,136	66.7	869,135	64.8	472,071	35.2	3,855	4,339
Clwyd	272,798	65.8	123,980	69.1	55,424	30.9	554	515
Dyfed	241,415	67.5	109,184	67.6	52,264	32.4	980	491
Gwent	314,369	68.2	132,557	62.1	80,992	37.9	NIL	808
Gwynedd	167,706	64.3	76,421	70.6	31,807	29.4	694	240
Mid Glamorgan	390,175	66.6	147,348	56.9	111,672	43.1	NIL	900
Powys	76,531	67.9	38,724	74.3	13,372	25.7	272	170
South Glamorgan	275,324	66.7	127,932	69.5	56,224	30.5	1,355	705
West Glamorgan	272,818	67.4	112,989	61.6	70,316	38.4	NIL	510
SCOTLAND	3,688,799	61.7	1,332,186	58.4	948,039	41.6	9,295	6,451
Borders	74,834	63.2	34,092	72.3	13,053	27.7	NIL	160
Central	188,613	64.1	71,986	59.7	48,568	40.3	32	331
Dumfries and Galloway	101,703	61.5	42,608	68.2	19,856	31.8	60	179
Fife	235,166	63.3	84,239	56.3	65,260	43.7	1,255	589
Grampian	321,140	57.4	108,520	58.2	78,071	41.8	2,625	507
Highland	127,925	58.7	40,802	54.6	33,979	45.4	NIL	257
Lothian	548,369	63.6	208,133	59.5	141,456	40.5	2,002	960
Orkney	13,157	48.2	3,911	61.8	2,419	38.2	NIL	15
Shetland	13,411	47.1	2,815	43.7	3,631	56.3	163	29
Strathclyde	1,759,889	61.7	625,959	57.7	459,073	42.3	2,191	2,951
Tayside	282,160	63.8	105,728	58.6	74,567	41.4	666	422
Western Isles	22,432	50.1	3,393	29.5	8,106	70.5	301	51
NORTHERN IRELAND	1,028,451	47.5	259,251	52.1	237,911	47.9	10,579	1,589
UNITED KINGDOM	40,084,594	64.0	17,378,581	67.2	8,470,073	32.8	231,194	54,540

[1] In calculating this figure the service votes have been *deducted* from and the spoilt ballot papers *added* to the total valid votes cast.

Special arrangements were made to enable members of the forces and their spouses to vote irrespective of whether or not they were included in the electoral register as service voters.. At the time of the Referendum there were about 119,000 service voters on the register and the Ministry of Defence claimed that their scheme enfranchised 370,200 servicemen and their spouses. Of the 199,000 service voters on the register it would seem that most of them would be eligible to vote under the special arrangements and therefore the actual service electorate must have been in the region of 380,000 to 400,000 giving a turnout figure of between 57% and 60%.

The following explanatory notes were issued by the National Counting Officer in respect of service electors and the counting of their ballot papers:—

The persons who have a service qualification are

(a) members of the forces;
(b) Crown servants serving in a post outside the UK;
(c) staff of the British Council employed in a post outside the UK; and
(d) the wife, or husband, of any person in the three preceding categories if residing outside the UK to be with him, or her.

For the purposes of the referendum (5 June) special arrangements are being made for members of the forces whether stationed in the UK or abroad, and their spouses when residing abroad, to vote in their units, whether or not their homes have been included in the current register as service voters. A corollary of this provision is that, in the case of any member of the forces, or his or her spouse when overseas, who *is* registered as a service voter on the current register and has appointed a proxy, the proxy will not be allowed to vote on his behalf in the referendum. The great majority of servicemen and women, and their spouses overseas, will be voting under the special forces arrangements. Those stationed in the UK, however, who are on the register as service voters, will still be entitled to vote in person or by post, even though their proxies will not be allowed to vote on their behalf. This facility is likely to be taken advantage of by persons who, having left the forces since the current register was compiled, will not benefit from the special forces voting arrangements, and a small number of servicemen in the UK on leave.

REFERENDUM ON UNITED KINGDOM MEMBERSHIP OF THE EUROPEAN ECONOMIC COMMUNITY (Cont.)

The special arrangements will not apply to service voters who are Crown servants, British Council staff or their spouses who will be entitled to vote in person, by post or by proxy at their own polling stations in the ordinary way, and nowhere else.

The votes cast under the special forces arrangements will be counted with the rest of the civilian votes. Votes cast in forces units in the UK will be counted with the votes for the county in which that unit is situated. Votes cast in forces units outside the UK will be counted with the votes for the G.L.C. In announcing the total number of ballot papers he has counted each counting officer will declare what number of these represent ballot papers resulting from the special forces voting arrangements. He will not, however, be able to make a similar breakdown in respect of the totals of valid votes. This is deliberate to prevent separate "Yes" and "No" totals becoming available for the forces alone.

The position regarding service voters will therefore be that some will be voting (in person, by post, or by proxy) in the ordinary way: others will be voting under the special forces voting arrangements. The persons voting under the special forces arrangements will include some who are registered as service voters and many others who are not. In these circumstances it would be misleading to give separate voter totals because there is no way of establishing what proportion of these will have alternative special voting arrangements open to them and how they will exercise their choice.

Sources: The Certificate of the Chief Counting Officer (Cmnd. 6105 of 1974-75).
The Press Association.

Appendix 14 PRINCIPAL CHANGES IN THE ELECTORAL SYSTEM 1832–1975

Date[1]

June 1832	*Representation of the People Act* (known as the "First Reform Act"). Modest reform of electoral law, extension of the franchise and re-distribution of seats.
August 1867	*Representation of the People Act* (sometimes called the "Second Reform Act"). Extension of the franchise and re-distribution of seats.
July 1868	*Parliamentary Elections Act.* Removed the trial of election petitions from a House of Commons committee to the Courts.
July 1872	*Ballot Act.* Introduced voting by secret ballot.
August 1883	*Corrupt and Illegal Practices Prevention Act.* Placed a maximum limit on election expenses incurred by candidates.
December 1884	*Representation of the People Act* (sometimes called the "Third Reform Act"). Extension of the franchise and re-distribution of seats.
February 1918	*Representation of the People Act.* Abolition of property qualification for voting. Women enfranchised at age 30 and over. Charges of Returning Officers no longer to be paid by candidates. All polls at General Elections to be held on the same day. Postal and proxy voting introduced for servicemen. Candidates required to lodge £150 deposit on nomination which was forfeited if they failed to poll more than one-eighth of the total votes cast. Redistribution of seats.
March 1922	*Irish Free State (Agreement) Act.* No further writs to be issued for constituencies in Ireland other than Northern Ireland.
October 1924	First use of radio for broadcasts by the party leaders during a General Election campaign.
July 1926	*Re-Election of Ministers Act (1919) Amendment Act.* Removed the necessity for Ministers of the Crown to seek re-election on accepting office.
July 1928	*Representation of the People (Equal Franchise) Act.* Women enfranchised at age 21 and over. Male and female adult suffrage achieved.
July 1948	*Representation of the People Act.* All plural voting and university constituencies abolished. Extension of postal voting to civilians. Limit on the number of cars which candidates could use on polling day. Re-distribution of seats.
December 1949	*Electoral Registers Act.* Persons coming of age between November and June each year to be included in the electoral register, marked by the symbol 'Y' and eligible to vote at any election from October onwards.
October 1951	First use of television for broadcasts by the party leaders during a General Election campaign.
December 1958	*Representation of the People (Amendment Act).* Removal of the restriction on the number of cars which candidates could use on polling day.
July 1963	*Peerage Act.* Peers allowed to disclaim Peerages for life and thus become eligible for membership of the House of Commons.
April 1969	*Representation of the People Act.* Extension of the franchise to persons at age 18 and over. Close of poll extended from 9.0 pm. to 10.0 pm.

[1] The dates given are those on which the relative Acts came into force but frequently major changes in election law were not effective until the Dissolution of the Parliament then in being.

SELECT BIBLIOGRAPHY

This select bibliography includes all the principal printed sources consulted in the compiling of this volume plus a number of other books which are suggested for the further study of British elections.

Government publications have been omitted due to the profusion of Acts, Bills, Command Papers and House of Commons Papers which have been published since 1885. These publications can, however, be easily traced by reference to the *General Index to Parliamentary Papers, 1900 to 1949* (H.M. Stationery Office, 1961) under the heading Elections — Electors, pages 231-240. Publications since 1950 are listed in the *General Index to Parliamentary Papers, 1950 to 1958-59* (House of Commons Papers, 1962-63 (96) xxxix, 1) and the *General Index to Parliamentary Papers, 1959-60 to 1968-69,* (House of Commons Paper No. 494 of 1974-75), and subsequent Sessional Indexes.

In addition to the sources listed, extensive use was made of the files of the national and local press, leading periodicals and journals. *The British-Union Catalogue of Periodicals* was most useful for tracing periodicals published by the major and minor political parties.

Biographies, autobiographies and the memoirs of leading politicians were also extensively used.

The year of publication is given at the end of each entry and the original place of publication is London except where otherwise stated.

CANDIDATES

For biographical notes on candidates the best source is *The Times Guide to the House of Commons* which published short notes on both successful and unsuccessful candidates from the 1929 edition. For biographies of candidates at the General Election of 1918 see the Special Supplement in *The Times* of December 9, 1918. At each election since 1950, the Labour Party has published a booklet, *Labour's Election Who's Who*, which gave short biographical notes. *The Liberal Year Book* in some editions contained biographical notes on prospective Liberal candidates. At most General Elections since 1918 the major political parties have issued duplicated lists of their candidates with brief biographical details.

Buck (P.W.), *Amateurs and Professionals in British Politics 1918-59.* (Chicago and London, 1963).
Paterson (P.), *The Selectorate.* (1967).
Ranney (A.), *Pathways to Parliament.* (1965).
Rush (M.), *The Selection of Parliamentary Candidates.* (1969).

CENSUS DATA

Census 1966. United Kingdom General and Parliamentary Constituency Tables. (H.M.S.O., 1969).
Census 1971. Parliamentary Constituency Tables. (Office of Population Censuses and Surveys and General Register Office, 1973-74).

ELECTORAL LAW

O'Malley and Hardcastle's Reports of the Decision of the Judges for the Trial of Election Petitions.
Volumes 1-7. (1870-1929).
Rogers on Elections. 1st edition 1820, last editions (3 volumes), 1928, 1929 and 1935.
Schofield (A.N.), *Parliamentary Elections.* 3rd edition and supplement. (1959 and 1964).
Wollaston (H.W.), *Parker's Conduct of Parliamentary Elections.* 1st edition. (1970). (Replacing *Parker's Election Agent and Returning Officer*, 1st edition 1885, 6th edition 1959).

ELECTORAL SYSTEMS

Butler (D.E.), *The Electoral System in Britain since 1918.* 2nd edition. (1963).
Cook (H.K.), *The Free and Independent.* (1949).
Fulford (R.), *Votes for Women.* (1957).
Gash (N.), *Politics in the Age of Peel.* (1953).
Grego (J.), *A History of Parliamentary Elections and Electioneering.* (1892).
Gwyn (W.B.), *Democracy and the Cost of Politics in Britain. (1962).*
Hanham (H.J.), *Elections and Party Management: Politics in the Time of Disraeli and Gladstone.* (1959).
Jennings (Sir Ivor), *Party Politics*, Volume 1. *Appeal to the People.* (Cambridge, 1960).

Lakeman, (Enid), *How Democracies Vote.* (1974). (Fourth and revised edition of *Voting in Democracies* by Enid Lakeman and J.D. Lambert, first published in 1955).
Leonard (R.L.), *Guide to the General Election.* (1964).
Elections in Britain. (1968).
Mackenzie (W.J.M.), *Free Elections.* (1958).
Porritt (E.) assisted by Annie G., *The Unreformed House of Commons (Parliamentary Representation before 1832).*
Volume 1, England and Wales. Volume 2, Scotland and Ireland. (1903 and 1909).
Pulzer (P.G.J.), *Political Representation and Elections in Britain.* 2nd edition. (1972).
Ross (J.F.S.), *Parliamentary Representation.* 2nd edition. (1948). *Elections and Electors.* (1955).
Seymour (C.), *Electoral Reform in England and Wales.* (1915 and reprint with an introduction by Michael Hurst, Newton Abbot, 1970).

GENERAL ELECTION STUDIES

Blewett (N.), *The Peers, The Parties and the People: The General Elections of 1910.* (1972).
Butler (D.E.), *The British General Election of 1951.* (1952).
The British General Election of 1955. (1955).
Butler (D.E.) & Kavanagh (D.), *The British General Election of February 1974.* (1974).
The British General Election of October 1974. (1975).
Butler (D.E.) & King (A.), *The British General Election of 1964.* (1965).
The British General Election of 1966. (1966).
Butler (D.E.) & Pinto-Duschinsky (M.), *The British General Election of 1970.* (1971).
Butler (D.E.) & Rose (R.), *The British General Election of 1959.* (1960).
Chrimes (S.B.) & others, *The General Election in Glasgow, February 1950.* (Glasgow, 1950).
Cook (C.) *The Age of Alignment: Electoral Politics in Britain 1922-1929.* (1975).
McCallum (R.B.) & Readman (Alison), *The British General Election of 1945.* (1947).
Nicholas (H.G.), *The British General Election of 1950.* (1951).
Pollock (J.K.) & others, *British Election Studies, 1950.* (Ann Arbor, Michigan, 1951).
Russell (A.K.), *Liberal Landslide: The General Election of 1906.* (1973).

LOCAL POLITICAL ORGANISATION

Bealey (F.), Blondel (J.) & McCann (W.P.), *Constituency Politics* (Newcastle-under-Lyme study). (1965).
Birch (A.H.), *Small-Town Politics* (Glossop study). (1959).
Dean (K.J.), *Town & Westminster: A Political History of Walsall.* (Walsall, 1972).

Local Political Organisation (Cont.)

Hampton (W.), *Democracy and Community: A Study of Politics in Sheffield.* (1970).

Holt (R.T.) & Turner (J.E.), *Political Parties in Action: The Battle of Barons Court.* (New York and London, 1968).

Janosik (E.J.), *Constituency Labour Parties in Britain.* (1968).

Stacey (Margaret), *Tradition and Change* (Banbury study). (1960).

MEMBERS OF PARLIAMENT

For biographical notes on Members of Parliament the best source is *Who's Who* (annually from 1849) and *Who Was Who* (six volumes containing the biographies removed from *Who's Who* on account of death from 1897-1970). Brief biographical notes are contained in *The Constitutional Year Book, Debrett's Illustrated House of Commons, Dod's Parliamentary Companion, The Liberal Year Book, The Popular Guide to the House of Commons, The Times Guide to the House of Commons.* For biographies of MPs elected in 1922, 1923 and 1924 when *The Times* did not publish a Guide, see the Election Supplements in *The Times* of November 17, 1922; December 8, 1923 and October 31, 1924.

Brookes (Pamela), *Women at Westminster.* (1967).

Bunker (C.), *Who's Who in Parliament.* (1946).

Caunt (G.), *Essex in Parliament.* (Chelmsford, 1969).

Donald (J.), *Past Parliamentary Elections in Greenock.* (Greenock, 1933).

Guttsman (W.L.), *The British Political Elite.* (1963).

Humberstone (T.L.), *University Representation.* (1951).

Jackson (R.J.), *Rebels and Whips.* (1968).

James (C.J.), *M.P. for Dewsbury.* (Brighouse, 1970).

Richards (P.G.), *Honourable Members: A Study of the British Backbencher.* 2nd edition. (1964).

The Backbenchers. (1972).

Shedden (Sir L.), *The Parliamentary History of Kilmarnock.* (Kilmarnock, 1929).

Watson (J.B.), *The Member for Eccles.* (Eccles, 1964).

MISCELLANEOUS

Block (G.D.M.), *A Source Book of Conservatism.* (Conservative Political Centre, 1964).

Booth (A.H.), *British Hustings 1924-1950.* (1956).

Brock (M.), *The Great Reform Act.* (1973).

Central Office of Information, *Parliamentary Elections in Britain.* Pamphlet No. R 5513/74. (1974).

Cook (C.) & Ramsden (J.), *By-Elections in British Politics.* (1973).

Davies (I.R.M.), *Trial by Ballot.* (1950).

Foot (P.), *Immigration and Race in British Politics.* (1965).

Hargreaves (R.) & McKee (P.), *The ITN Election Handbook.* (1974).

Jones (A.), *The Politics of Reform 1884.* (1972).

Labour Party (The), *Labour Party Bibliography.* (1967).

McKie (D.) & Cook (C.), *Election '70: The Guardian/Panther Guide.* (1970).

The Guardian/Quartet Election Guide. (1974).

Madge (C.), *Pilot Guide to the General Election.* (1945).

Morgan (K.O.), *Wales in British Politics 1868-1922* (Cardiff, 1963).

O'Leary (C.), *The Elimination of Corrupt Practices in British Elections 1868-1911.* (1962).

Palmer (J.), *Government and Parliament in Britain: A Bibliography.* 2nd edition. (The Hansard Society, 1964).

Press Association (The), *Final List of General Election Candidates.* Published in book form (previously as Poster) prior to each General Election since 1923. (1923-).

Smith (F.B.), *The Making of the Second Reform Bill.* (1966).

OPINION POLLS

Gallup Election Handbook. (1970).

Hodder-Williams (R.), *Public Opinion Polls and British Politics.* (1970).

Rose (R.), *The Polls and the 1970 Election.* (University of Strathclyde Survey Research Centre, Occasional Paper No. 7). (Glasgow, 1970).

Teer (F.) & Spence (J.D.), *Political Opinion Polls.* (1973).

POLITICAL BEHAVIOUR AND ATTITUDES

Abrams (M.) & Rose (R.), *Must Labour Lose?* (1960).

Allen (A.J.), *The English Voter.* (1964).

Benney (M.), Gray (A.P.) & Pear (R.H.), *How People Vote* (Greenwich study). (1956).

Birch (A.H.) & Campbell (P.), *Voting Behaviour in a Lancashire Constituency* (Stretford, 1950). *The British Journal of Sociology,* Vol. 1, No. 3, September, 1950.

Blondel (J.), *Voters, Parties and Leaders.* (1963).

Bonham (J.), *The Middle Class Vote.* (1954).

Budge (I.) & Urwin (D.E.), *Scottish Political Behaviour* (Glasgow study). (1966).

Butler (D.E.), *The Study of Political Behaviour.* (1958).

Butler (D.E.) & Stokes (D.), *Political Change in Britain.* 2nd edition (1974).

Campbell (P.), Donnison (D.) & Potter (A.), *Voting Behaviour in Droylsden in October 1951. The Manchester School,* Vol. 20, No. 1, January 1952.

Deakin (N.) & others, *Colour and the British Electorate 1964.* (1965).

Drake (M.), *Introduction to Historical Psephology.* (1974).

Jones (G.W.), *Borough Politics: A Study of the Wolverhampton Town Council 1888-1964.* (1969).

Kinnear (M.), *The British Voter.* (1968).

McKenzie (R.T.) & Silver (A.), *Angels in Marble: Working Class Conservatism in Urban England.* (1968).

Milne (R.S.) & Mackenzie (H.C.), *Straight Fight* (Bristol, North-East study). (1964).

Marginal Seat, 1955 (Bristol, North-East study). (1958).

Nordlinger (E.), *The Working Class Tories.* (1967).

Pelling (H.), *Social Geography of British Elections, 1885-1910.* (1967).

Rose (R.), *Class and Party Divisions: Britain as a Test Case* (University of Strathclyde Survey Research Centre, Occasional Paper No. 1). (Glasgow, 1968).

Vincent (J.R.), *Pollbooks: How Victorians Voted.* (1967).

POLITICAL COMMUNICATION AND CAMPAIGN MANAGEMENT

Blumler (J.G.) & McQuail (D.), *Television in Politics: its uses and influence.* (1968).

Howard (A.) & West (R.), *The Making of the Prime Minister.* (1965).

Rose (R.), *Influencing Voters.* (1967).

Trenaman (J.) & McQuail (D.), *Television and the Political Image.* (1961).

Windlesham (Lord), *Communication and Political Power.* (1966).

REFERENCE BOOKS

Butler (D.E.) & Sloman (Anne), *British Political Facts, 1900-1975,* 4th edition. (1975).

Constitutional Year Book (The), Constituency results from 1885-1938, tables, etc. [The 1919 edition (1885-1918), 1930 edition (1918-29) and 1939 edition (1924-38) are required to cover the complete period]. (Annually, National Union of Conservative & Unionist Associations, 1885-1916 & 1919-39; reprint of 54 volumes (all published) with new evaluative introduction by Robert Rhodes James, Brighton, 1970-74).

Cook (C.) & Keith (B.), *British Historical Facts 1830-1900.* (1975).

Craig (F.W.S.), *Scottish Parliamentary Election Manual* (incorporated in *The Year Book for Scotland*). Constituency results from 1918, tables, etc. (Edinburgh, annually, 1954-66).

Boundaries of Parliamentary Constituencies 1885-1972. (Chichester, 1972).

British General Election Manifestos 1900-1974. 2nd edition. (1975).

British Parliamentary Election Results 1832-1885. (Forthcoming).

British Parliamentary Election Results 1885-1918. (1974).

British Parliamentary Election Results 1918-1949. (Glasgow, 1969).

British Parliamentary Election Results 1950-1970. (Chichester, 1971).

Minor Parties at British Parliamentary Elections 1885-1974. (1975).

Reference Books (Cont.)

The Most Gracious Speeches to Parliament: Statements of Government Policy and Achievements. (1975).

Debrett's Illustrated House of Commons and Judicial Bench. Constituency results, tables, etc. (Annually, 1867-1931).

Dod (C.R.), *Electoral Facts.* Constituency results, tables, etc., from 1832-52. 2nd edition. (1853 and reprint, edited with bibliographical guide, by H.J. Hanham, Brighton, 1972).

Dod's Parliamentary Companion (from 1832-64 as *Parliamentary Pocket Companion*). Constituency results, tables, etc. (Annually [occasionally two editions in an election year], 1832-).

Gallup Analysis of the Election '66. (The Daily Telegraph, 1966).

General Election (The): Candidates and Constituencies. (The Daily Telegraph, 1964-70).

Labour Year Book (The), [from 1895-1900 as *The Labour Annual;* 1901-09 as *The Reformers' Year Book and Labour Annual;* 1910-13 as *The Daily News Year Book*]. Lists of candidates, tables etc. (Annually, various publishers, 1895-1913; The Labour Party and the Parliamentary Committee of the Trades Union Congress, 1916, 1919, 1924-28, 1930-32; The Labour Party, 1946/47 & 1947/48; reprint of 32 volumes (all published) with new evaluative introduction by David Marquand, M.P., Brighton, 1970-74).

Liberal Year Book (The), Constituency results from 1885-1938, tables etc. (The 1909 edition (1885-1909), 1918 edition (1892-1918), 1931 edition (1918-31) and 1939 edition (1929-38) are required to cover the complete period). (Annually, National Liberal Printing & Publishing Association, Ltd. (1887-89) and Liberal Publication Department, 1887-89 & 1905-39; reprint of 39 volumes (all published) with new evaluative introduction by Edward David, Brighton, 1970-74).

McCalmont (F.H.), *The Parliamentary Poll Book.* Constituency results, tables, etc., from 1832 to January, 1910. 7th edition. (1910 and reprint, edited, with new material to 1918, by John Vincent, Brighton, 1971).

Mitchell (B.R.) & Boehm (K.), *British Parliamentary Election Results 1950-1964.* (1966).

Parliamentary Gazette [from 1905-06 as *Premier Parliamentary Record (Gazette) and Review*]. List of M.Ps. etc. (Three issues each Parliamentary Session 1905-42).

Political Companion (The), A pocket-size guide to British elections and politics. (Glasgow, now Chichester, quarterly now twice a year, 1969-).

Popular Guide to the House of Commons (The), Constituency results, tables, etc. (*Pall Mall Gazette,* 1885-1911).

Smith (H.S.), *The Parliaments of England.* (3 volumes 1844-50 and reprint, edited by F.W.S. Craig, Chichester, 1973).

Stenton (M.), *Who's Who of British Members of Parliament. Vol. 1, 1832-1885.* (Hassocks, 1976).

Times (Guide to the) House of Commons (The). Constituency results, tables, etc. Published after each General Election since 1880 (except 1906, 1922, 1923 & 1924). Supplements were issued to the following editions: 1945 (January 1948); 1951 (May 1954 and January 1955); 1955 (June 1957). (*The Times* (the issues for 1892, 1895 & 1900 were published jointly with Macmillan) 1880-).

Vacher's Parliamentary Companion. List of M.Ps., etc. Issue following General Election gives constituency results and by-elections are recorded. (Monthly, then bi-monthly, now quarterly, 1832-).

Wilkie (T.), *The Representation of Scotland.* Constituency results, tables, etc. from 1832-95. (Paisley, 1895).

INDEX

This index is intended as a supplement to the Table of Contents and is principally a guide to the information contained in footnotes and in the 'Records and Precedents' section. The names of persons and constituencies are included only in cases where some notable incident is involved.

INDEX (Cont.)

INDEX (Cont.)

INDEX (Cont.)